ON THE WISDOM OF
WORDS

BY GEOFFREY WAGNER

LONDON
GEORGE ALLEN AND UNWIN LTD

PUBLISHED IN GREAT BRITAIN IN 1968

SBN 04 400020 0

PRINTED IN GREAT BRITAIN
BY PHOTOLITHOGRAPHY
BY COMPTON PRINTING LTD
LONDON AND AYLESBURY

CONTENTS

iii

iv

ACKNOWLEDGMENT

Parts of chapters of this book have appeared in
ETC., *Kenyon Review*, *Monocle*, *The Realist*,
Sewanee Review, *Use of English*, *Southern Review* (University of Adelaide), *Village Voice*, and
the Herald Tribune *Book Week*. Editors are
thanked for their permission to reprint.

I incurred a serious debt to Leo Hamalian,
who has been unfailingly generous of his time
and wisdom over many years, and who read the
script of the present book at an early stage. I
also need to thank Estelle Gerard for typing
and Jean Lilly for intelligent and helpful copy
editing.

GEOFFREY WAGNER
City College of New York

If all the good people were clever;
And all clever people were good,
The world would be nicer than ever
We thought that it possibly could.

But somehow 'tis seldom or never
The two hit it off as they should;
The good are so harsh to the clever,
The clever so rude to the good!

ELIZABETH WORDSWORTH *(1840-1932)*

INTRODUCTION

Polonius. "What do you read, my lord?"
Hamlet. "Words, words, words."

WHITE MAGIC: THE SPELL OF WORDS

The World Within a Word

In the seventeenth century learned English divines liked to toy
with the paradox that words were man's world in the sense of his
essential wisdom, the store and substance of his universe. The
world without the word, they proposed, was the world without the
Word—or God, or ultimate knowledge.

This sense of words may be tested, here and now, by the reader's
choice as to whether or not to continue. If the reader chooses to go
on, he or she assumes a formal mechanism by means of which one
experience is related to another; the passage of the eye over marks
on a page stands for, labels or assimilates *something else*. This is
a cardinal rule of language, which Coleridge incidentally defined
as "the embodied and articulated Spirit of the Race." The motive
force in aligning print signs on paper, as I am doing on this page,
has to be an attempt to account for, represent and eventually
transcend the world.

The human being, almost alone, is not himself a word, representative of something else. He has been said purely to exist; the
vocabulary of his being is this magical significance and power of
substitution, of symbols. "Words are magical," observed Aldous
Huxley, "in the way they affect the minds of those who use them."
It was stated once in another way—"For by thy words thou shalt
be condemned." Form, style, conduct, consciousness, conscience
in the true sense, all originate from this harmony with the universe
that we sometimes call symbol-wielding.

The Gospel of St. John defines just this sense of magic, as a
recognition and redemption of reality, and, of course, as a source
of human behavior. Every theory of the genesis of language comes

up against it. Adam named animals, in a metamorphosis on which his God set great store (while declining to be named Himself). The emphasis was echoed, of course, by early English translators of the Bible who were highly affected by their Hebrew studies. "Right speech" is part of the Buddhist's path to perfection, in the Pali scriptures, while Homer or the Homeric poets adulated "articulate-speaking" man.

It is a sort of permanent human poetry that is at stake—let me call it here the wisdom of words, provided that the formulation can be allowed to consort with true magic and miracle. Few students find much *glamour* in *grammar,* but the words come from the same root, via the wizards of the past. Conversely, the village idiot is traditionally one with noticeably defective speech.

The burden of this book is thus neither original nor abstruse; but I hope it can be helpful. It is simply that the world is contained within words. Or, if you wish, that "*In the beginning* was the Word." The French surrealist, Joë Bousquet, once remarked: "After having written to a woman 'I shall take you in my arms,' I have no more than her phantom to embrace." This seems to me a fairly convincing statement of the ultimate nature of language, of what one learns, more elaborately, at the feet of the great linguists and linguistic philosophers, like Sapir and Schlauch, Beardsley and Black. It is a way of saying that there is nothing beyond language. Hamlet's reply to Polonius was doubly evasive. Words, words, words . . . they comprise everything.

Linguists, then, allege that language discovers meaning for us. There may be people in Chicago or New York who have never seen a swan. Yet language—from scientific reports to romantic poems—can show them a swan better than can an icon. Better, even, than were a swan to be set before them. They could inherit knowledge about the swan, its life span, habits, likes and dislikes. They would, in short, have power over it.

Of course, there can be more language about the swan. It is still language. In the beginning was the Word. The swan came after. When the reverse is made to occur, you have language distortions of the kind Coleridge rightly codified as a kind of madness. Those restless jet travelers one meets today, moving from country to country and receiving into their hands pieces of paper or metal with relative values against given commodities, are minor emblems of nonlanguage: take them a stage further and they would become men with minds so infantile or asymbolic that they would have to

2

check their coins against what they could buy every day of their lives.

It is quite obvious that even children can soon learn the practical permutations of a graded vocabulary such as this, and such as is proposed in electronic computing. Out of encyclopedic research, Claude Lévi-Strauss has lately shown us that "the savage mind" might consider the random access memories devised by the Burroughs Corporation, say, or the electrostatic memories of the Brookhaven National Laboratory, or England's Royal Aircraft word generators, or even the linear algebraic equation solvers recently perfected in Israel, somewhat crude and clumsy contraptions. They are all on the level of what I here call "apparent" language.

The terms "apparent" and "transparent" that I use are arbitrary and open to dispute. In general, I mean by "transparent" language that which asks to be translated; "apparent" language does not ask to be translated, it tends to say what it means within itself. Once we agree on the denotational proxy of certain letters and sets of syllables, Wall Street means first and foremost a certain thoroughfare, beginning somewhere and ending somewhere. It could as well be called Law Street, or Minus Tenth Street or whatever. In other uses there is something beyond Wall Street. It has a "transparent" meaning outside itself and enclosed in language, namely, high finance, wicked capitalists (as in *Wall Street hyenas*) and the rest. "Transparent" language is thus full utterance or (would-be) communication; it is what I. A. Richards well chooses to call "dramatic," in the sense that the full use of language alone allows its inherent character to appear.

It is not difficult to discern—indeed any parent knows—that the mental activity involved in dealing with "apparent" communication is different from that pertaining to "transparent" utterance. Were this not so, were the partnership with the world the same in both repertories of language, mankind would—to quote Richards again, formulating the same dilemma—"have to belong to another order of BEING." Another way of putting this is to say that man's reason is limited.[1] If it were not, we could presumably enter into a set piece of constituent symbols with given internal vehicles, such as

[1]"The power of logic and mathematics to surprise us depends, like their usefulness, on the limitations of our reason." Again, "the propositions in which we record the observations that verify these hypotheses are themselves sense-experience. Thus there are no final propositions" (A. J. Ayer, *Language, Truth and Logic*, New York: Dover, n.d., pp. 85, 94).

mathematics or logic, or the arrogant equivalence of chemical formulae, and emerge the next morning with Einstein and Planck. Alphabetic arrangements would yield us Shakespeares as well as Faith Baldwins by the dozen—my friend Marvin Spevack developed his colossal Shakespeare Concordance quite properly with a computer (and equally properly, no doubt, in Germany). If language were all "apparent," and applicable to every case in the manner of a mechanism, a very low order of sociality would prevail. Indeed, the threat of such is the concern of the first part of this book, if not of all of it.

But the psychology of meaning shows repeatedly the legitimacy, the necessity, of verbal magic, of that "knowing together" implicit in a word like *con*-sciousness. This is the property of "transparent" language. The possession of power over the world by word-wisdom is a remarkable mystery, central to our being; it has been the concern of sociologists and ethnographers, of men like Durkheim, Frazer and, more recently, Lévi-Strauss, whose pictographs of obscure Amazonian word-patterns were taken, in a nice language pun, for enemy codes in the war.[2]

> For speculation turns not to itself
> Till it hath travell'd and is married there
> Where it may view itself.

As here, in *Troilus and Cressida*, Shakespeare seems to describe this magic of "transparent" language again and again. When asked how he kept coming up with inventions, a great scientist, we are told, replied, "By keeping on thinking about it." Charles Sanders Peirce believed that the meaning of any linguistic sign was its translation into another, but one "in which it is more fully developed." Freud felt that loving went with naming. We can all surely remember how our affection for flowers grew alongside our gradual mastery of their names. Jean Piaget's Maison des Petits was full of further examples of this activity, this essence of "transparent" language, although in the child you have a communicant talking largely to himself.

This essence goes far beyond the purely functional value of

[2]See the first part of Claude Lévi-Strauss, *Tristes Tropiques*, Paris: Plon, 1955. Lévi-Strauss' difficulties at this time were hardly alleviated by the fact that only three or four scholars in the world could read his scripts.

4

utterance. If it did not, we would simply learn words as an apprentice learns the terms of his trade (or "mystery"). That the apparatus of suggestion is far in excess of the nominal needs of language can quickly be spotted by a glance at the ads for "Word-Power" courses in the press. These programs preach increased vocabulary as a mystique, or panacea: "In community life, the person with a masterful command of language gets attention. You'll find that at club meetings and other gatherings, you're always in the center of the group."[3]

"Apparent" language is a rhetoric of behavior. Here words simply play a part, are there to be used. Rhetoric, or grammar, is a kind of logic, and magical terms conventionally lack grammatical forms. Watching this struggle, then, watching the coefficients of our modern mumbo-jumbo or desire for technological accuracy violate the sacred nature of language, has led to the writing of this book. You cannot pigeonhole language, but in general terms Coleridge can still be appealed to for help in clarifying this interplay, this evidently ineluctable opposition of our days. In common with Hazlitt and other men of letters of his time, Coleridge usually thought of prose as dealing with the ascertainable, with the sort of things that the Socrates of *Euthyphro* considered men *not* to want to fight about—sizes and weights, the number of pigs someone had and so forth. Thus Coleridge thought of prose as *words in their best order*. Poetry was not phenomenal like this, it was noumenal and he phrased its semantic differently—*the best words in the best order* (an echo, no doubt, of Swift's remark that "Proper words in proper places are the true definition of style").

What are the best words? The best words are self-reflexive, they are ourselves, our world, the medium through which we see everything. As Huxley suggests, magic is this mirror activity; his little pamphlet, *Words and Their Meaning*, seems to have been written under the wing of the great ethnographer, Bronislaw Malinowski—"It is the influence of magic on the community practicing it," wrote the latter, "which molds ritual and language." Although his findings must now be considerably qualified, thanks to Lévi-Strauss, Malinowski looked at magic in a new way. Far from being so much "savage" muttering directed at animals, plant agents, the moon and so forth, Trobriand magic was found to be a vital sociological charter. "The magician in uttering his formulas speaks on behalf of each

³The William Morris Self-Enrichment Vocabulary Program.

gardener." Malinowski could not find a single man in Omarakana who was anything but highly familiar with the terms and phrases of this magic.[4]

Language is such a charter. Its binding force is that "the power of words in establishing a permanent human relation, the sacredness of words and their socially sanctioned inviolability, are absolutely necessary to the social order." Technology, the language of ascertainable fact, "apparent" language, cannot turn its back on the language of superstition, sacrament and prayer; and in something like advertising, where there is a considerable consensus of pragmatism and mumbo-jumbo, it does not in fact do so. It is here, I think, that semantics—as in the term "General Semantics"—can have a unifying as well as an alerting tendency.

How Not to Make a Damn Fool of Yourself

The term *semantics* is said to come from the Greek *siemantikos*—the significant, or expressive. But in a short history it has changed a great deal, perhaps more so than almost any other word of its type. To the average man semantics means word study of a limited nature. "It's a matter of semantics," issuing from this senator or that judge, generally implies that some point of terminology is at stake, usually lexical. Testimony that this attitude dies hard was given recently when Mary McCarthy visited Vietnam:

> Almost daily in the press briefing, whenever a newsman raises his hand to ask for clarification of some mealy-mouthed statement: "I am not going to debate semantics with you," the spokesman replies. "Next?"[5]

The average man is further confused by analogous and systematic-sounding terms from the same root, like *semiosis* (Charles Morris' science of signs) or *semasiology*. A lot of these terms seem entirely unnecessary to me; in any event, they certainly show as never before that derivation is not meaning!

Nor can the confused background or heredity of modern seman-

[4]See Part VI ("An Ethnographic Theory of the Magical Word") in Bronislaw Malinowski, *Coral Gardens and Their Magic*, vol. II, London: George Allen & Unwin, 1935 (e.g. "The weirdness consists very largely in artificial form, in the ungrammatical use of certain roots. . . ," p. 230).

[5]Mary McCarthy, "Report from Vietnam III: Intellectuals," *The New York Review*, VIII:9 (May 18, 1967), p. 4.

tic study help us all that much. Early nineteenth-century German philologists began a movement of word study that culminated in a famous work by the incumbent Professor of Comparative Grammar at the Collège de France, Michel Bréal. This aphoristic opus, entitled *Essai de Semantique,* came out in 1897. Historical in orientation, Bréal studied much the sort of thing the average man (and certainly nearly every Frenchman) today understands by the term *semantics.* For instance: The word history of *splendor* (from the color of jaundice), or of *mature* (from the Latin for matutinal), would be advanced to prove how a word could be brought to mean the opposite to that which it first signified—language playback of a kind. Bréal tried to forge other rules, many of which are useful, and in general watched over word-change like a hawk, or French philologist. In *The Meaning of Meaning* Ogden and Richards attack him for being overpoetic, for his tendency "to handle a scientific subject in metaphorical terms," and the attack is understandable, since you cannot make a rhetoric out of the "transparent."

So in the 1880's Bréal was using the term for meaning-changes. At a recent international congress an Austrian linguist, Franz Csokor, defined it as "peaceful intercourse between peoples." At about the same time S. I. Hayakawa, one of the leading practitioners of General Semantics, when asked what it was, replied, "How not to make a damn fool of yourself."

These differences themselves demonstrate that terms used in the study of significance are subject to the laws of the object they are attempting to analyze. This is a fairly rare condition—you don't paint about paintings, unless you are a madman or an abstract expressionist—and the neatest resolution I know of what General Semantics tries to do was I. A. Richards' remark, made in 1964, that it is "a label for the *functional* aspects as opposed to the *phonological* and *morphological* aspects of language." The emphasis is on the use of words—the best words in the best order—on what language does, rather than what language is, if one can talk of such intimately reciprocal activities separately.

Opponents of this approach, mostly interested literary critics, call it the "affective fallacy." In the case of poetry this is, according to W. K. Wimsatt, "a confusion between the poem and its *results* (what it *is* and what it *does*), a special case of epistemological skepticism, though usually advanced as if it had far stronger claims than the over-all forms of skepticism." This horrible state of affairs, then, is seen to be a departure from "the poem itself, as an object of specifically critical judgment," and to derive standards from the effects of the poem. The whole thing ends in "relativism."[6]

As one who has discussed poetry in classrooms over many years, and frequently with groups infected by a naive Freudianism, I tend to agree with the motives for Wimsatt's diagnosis, but I cannot think of a better statement of purpose with which to buttress Richards' view of General Semantics. "Don't ask for the meaning, ask for the use," Wittgenstein used to say. The word is its world. It cannot simply represent itself. Count Korzybski, said to be the impetus of much semantic study in America, wrote, "Whatever one might *say* something '*is*,' *it is not*."

Of course, the determination of what meaning a group of letters or sounds has at a certain period of history is of considerable significance. But it is so in the sense that historicity is a fact of our experience. The word *quisling* (from Major Vidkun Quisling, shot in 1945) would have meant nothing to me in my teens, and I doubt if tomorrow's teeners will recognize the "traitor" label presently given for this word in Webster. The word *descend* has been a feature of the recent "monkey law" trials about teaching evolution. How could man be considered to have *descended* from the animals, in Darwinian phraseology, since you can hardly come down from a lower being? It was even suggested that antagonism to Darwin's theory was created by the very title of his work *The Descent of Man*. Such popular optimists had to be shown that here a second and equally authentic meaning of *descend* was at issue, the sense of originating from (*He is descended from royalty*).

In such cases society ends up getting the "meaning" it wants. It is the use that counts. *Appease* has thus retained the taint accorded it at the time of Neville Chamberlain's Munich visit. At that time *Webster's Collegiate* was defining the word as "to pacify, often by satisfying; quiet; calm; soothe; allay." In 1949 the dictionary added "to conciliate by political, economic, or other considerations;—now usually signifying a sacrifice of moral principle in order to avert aggression." As the new *Fowler*, revised by Sir Ernest Gowers, puts it: "there is no hint in the OED definitions of anything discreditable or humiliating about that word. No one thought any the worse of

[6]W. K. Wimsatt, Jr., *The Verbal Icon*, Lexington, Ky.: University of Kentucky Press, 1954, p. 21. Judging from the "Acknowledgement," it would appear that this definition is shared with Monroe C. Beardsley.

Aeneas for letting Cerberus have his usual sop." No one, indeed, thinks the worse of Jesus Christ for having said, "whosoever shall smite thee on thy right cheek, turn to him the other also" (Matt. 5:39).

These are degradations of magic, and a Bréalian law might be deduced from them, that it is easier to disfigure a word, especially a neutral term, than it is to embellish it. The way in which we have corrupted *controversial* and *radical* and *discourse* (which in Bacon's day meant conversation) says a lot about our society; the shift of *discrimination* from its primary sense of discernment to modern social persecution tells us about ourselves, and casts a slur on the activity of discerning. To know that *to put the kibosh on*[7] probably comes out of Yiddish auction slang tells more about the society that uses such a phrase derogatively than about the nature of word origins. It suggests that British stereotypes of Jewry were more traditional and longer lasting than American.

Semasiology is supposed to specialize in variations of this nature, investigating what happens, for example, to the word *knot* when used in the expression *a knotty problem*. But semasiology seems vague today, and while committed to such interests as those of Bréal, General Semantics ordinarily boasts of Wimsatt's pernicious heresy; it is less interested in word lore than in that miraculous harmony by which one goes through words to the world. In how not to make a damn fool of yourself, in short.

For years semantics of this kind was stigmatized as another modern mystery, an American arcanum whose initiates, emerging into the light of day from Chicago jazz clubs, had found yet another fancy term for something simple. It was a "cult," a "trade name" and so on. A further confusion existed, in the popular mind, between semantics and linguistics (still reflected in the sundry word shows on radio and TV) and, in the scholarly mind, between semantics and freshman chat of the It-depends-what-you-mean-by variety, a kind of philosophical copout.

If by now study of verbal communication has achieved the status of hobby in America, it is still far from a science and is suspect in the academy since it is not amenable to substantive scholarship and is the source of no degrees, and its principles are at variance with normative classroom work. Communication study is Banquo's Ghost at the academic board. Semantics cannot be scheduled under

[7]"Put the kye-bosh on her, Mary" (Dickens, *Sketches by Boz*).

any school, while the pedants of entrenched university departments keep chipping at little bits of it and carrying them off, antlike, in their jaws. Linguistic philosophy takes such a large chunk that it can smile with especial derision at the rest of GS. Psychology claims some more. Logic goes to elementary Philo courses. Principles of definition are tackled in many Law seminars. Aphasia problems are dealt with by Speech Departments, if not in the clinics themselves.

Apart from the imbalance of such special emphases, this fate is not wholly undesirable. You cannot helpfully push the whole of man's human sentience—Coleridge's "all-in-each of all men"—into some single pedagogic discipline. Instead of a chaste exclusivity in the Department of Neology, then, semantics resists the academic anesthetic and might, in fact, be more applicable to a medieval curriculum, properly "catholic," and presupposing the tenet that a teacher must answer any question put to him by his students at any time on any subject.

An entire series of opinion channels exists outside the academy, and, far from being an arcanum, semantics has suffered from the reverse—from being a free-for-all involving worried mothers, angry advertising executives, sex-conscious auto salesmen, baseball coaches, band leaders, cops, robbers, brokers, models[s] and sundry old wives of all ages and both sexes, all hoping to learn how not to make damn fools of themselves. The motto under its exhibits might well read: It Is Forbidden *Not* to Touch. Any good book on semantics soon develops into a medieval Manners treatise, involving a stance, a style. "In speaking one always says more than one intends to," writes Sartre.

Generally speaking, two types of communication will be considered here: that of things and that of ideas, fact-language which shows and idea-language which conceals. But scientifically verifiable data carry no pretension to that rectitude of moral decision. The responsibility of "transparent" language is, however, the "knowing *together*" of consciousness and conscience. This is the harmony of word-wisdom. For language to achieve its potential there must be a listener. The relations of the primitive community to the magician depended very largely on this listening ability.

[s]All categories who have contributed, at some time or another, to *ETC.*, the periodical review of General Semantics. This review has, incidentally, a lively circulation in US penitentiaries. *Verb. sap.!*

One-Way Discourse

Now since you cannot easily teach what you are doing, i.e. communicating, language study is unsuited to the one-way pedagogic approach. When I was at Oxford, attendance at only a few lectures a week was diffidently suggested, and never checked. Such habits have altered, and are inexistent in all American and most European provincial colleges today, where groups of students must listen to lecturers for hour upon hour. Like Thomas Mann's similarly afflicted schoolboys at the end of *Buddenbrooks* "we don't say, for instance, that it is nearly half-past twelve. No, we say, 'It's nearly time for the geography period!'" Physics, Drafting, Math. Psych, Drafting, Physics. As Mann's young Kai was aware, this familiar rote inculcates nonlistening.

Since the trained seal in front of you for the next fifty minutes is going to be talking nonstop, it is unlikely that all he says will be golden. Information is taken down in notes, than which practice even the reading of books tends to be better since the ingestion rate is at least under control. During much lecture time the ear shuts off true intellectual nourishment because the ear has been told to remember rather than to comprehend. Subsequent tests are all too often matters of memory. As Wendell Johnson once put it, "It is as though the instructor were to talk 'into his students' on Mondays and Wednesdays and to 'play them back' in a quiz every Friday."[9]

Thus disposed, questions—the lifeblood of discourse—become highly artificial. A student-listener may not want to ask one that might show ignorance. Jacques Barzun has well remarked that conversation is properly controversy and given impetus by a disagreement our democratic manners veto.[10] We don't meet to agree. "A good listener does not merely remain silent."[11] Yet classroom procedure makes him so. It turns him into a tacit consentant. The "Secret of Socrates" in *How to Win Friends and Influence People* by Dale Carnegie, B.Pd. (biped?) was no less than "*Get the other*

[9]Wendell Johnson, *Your Most Enchanted Listener,* New York: Harper & Brothers, 1956, p. 195.

[10]"Good conversation, like any game, calls for equals in strength. But . . . democratic manners prevent a jousting in which somebody might appear stronger, brighter, quicker, or richer of mind" (Jacques Barzun, *The House of Intellect,* New York: Harper & Brothers, 1959, p. 64).

[11]S. I. Hayakawa, "How to Listen to Other People," *Symbol, Status, and Personality,* New York: Harcourt, Brace & World, 1963, p. 33.

person saying 'yes, yes' immediately." Another chapter of this work, which sold over three and one-third million copies in its first twelve years of publication, was entitled "Never Tell a Man He is Wrong." In his subsequent *How to Stop Worrying and Start Living* the same author was understandably impressed by the "harmony" of the inmates of Sing Sing: doubtless they had followed his Rule 4–"Cooperate with the inevitable."

Fortunately democracy is not a prison society and exists by disagreement and debate. We watch President after President scratching at the irritations of this premise for office. In his great study of Scottish literature Kurt Wittig writes: "One expression of the Scots 'democratic spirit' is the Scottish love of arguing about fundamentals from purely individual points of view. There is truth in the saying that while the English discuss things in order to reach agreement, to find a compromise, the Scots argue in order to disagree, to make their point, to assert their rugged independence and individuality."[12]

Nor is a pedagogic pause a semantic pause at all. It is, rather, a failure or breakdown in the predicated stream of hot air. If a lecturer stops, he is, like an actor, "drying up." The only difference in his case is that the audience dearly hopes that this time he is drying up for keeps. TV, meanwhile, is so terrified of "dead air" that forty million Americans now spend their nights silently watching other Americans talk.

But the failing is far from merely popular. The paradox applies that of all current compartmentalisms within the college the literary may often prove the narrowest, as regards language study. English Departments can constitute the most provincial of classes, and yet, thanks to a certain facility of expression (not to mention a professional pressure to publish), English professors make up a majority of contributors to many opinion-forming magazines. Publish or perish, as the saying goes. One sometimes wishes they would do everyone a favor and accept the alternative.

For this elite is toxic to word-wisdom. It is frequently ignorant of or ignores the essence of symbol-making, and the finest literary critics, like Trilling, Valency, Levin, have been those who have seen literature moving out of society. The difficulty is once more self-reflexive. Criticism or, as it has tended to become, analysis of litera-

[12]Kurt Wittig, *The Scottish Tradition in Literature,* Edinburgh: Oliver and Boyd, 1958, p. 95.

ture is effected in the medium of literary action—words. Northrop Frye summarizes the dilemma in his *Anatomy of Criticism* thus:

> Art, like nature, has to be distinguished from the systematic study of it, which is criticism. It is therefore impossible to "learn literature": one learns about it in a certain way, but what one learns, transitively, is the criticism of literature. Similarly, the difficulty often felt in "teaching literature" arises from the fact that it cannot be done: criticism of literature is all that can be directly taught. Literature is not a subject of study, but an object of study: the fact that it consists of words . . . makes us confuse it with the talking verbal disciplines.

Scholarly nature prefers to place history before action, and literature really seems at times to be advanced to the modern student as a subdivision of criticism; American literary criticism, in particular, bristles with "fallacies" and "rebuttals." But if you send a contemporary science student to, say, the abracadabra of what is known as New Criticism, but is really Old Criticism, he soon gathers what is going on, namely another do-it-yourself cult, with the aid of meaningless entities called "paradox" and "irony" this time round, and a Puritan schoolmaster administering a rap of the rod (or exile to Chicago) if you misconstrue. The fundamentally exoteric character of such exercises seems evinced by, on one hand, the institutional nature of the class concerned—one on which the young have rightly turned their backs—and, on the other, by its vulnerability to *kitsch*. The standards of discrimination in cinema, painting and allied arts (let alone in finance, mathematics, the law) is far from high among these learned illiterates.

In this connection I remember attending a Modern Language Association meeting at the Hotel Statler in New York. In every room, on every floor, it seemed, lecturers were lecturing. Audiences sat in attitudes of respectful attention. Via rosaries of quotations, all indefatigably acknowledged, speakers were moving their muzzles. Nonlistening was high. I recall wandering into something like a nineteenth-century railway waiting room in some Birmingham suburb to catch a Lesbian Thomist from the West, a woman resembling some social worker from the Low Countries, carefully proving plagiarism in T. S. Eliot. In the huge hall adjacent an ex-Lat was indulging in a mouth orgasm over some unpronounceable minor poet of the 1740's, or perhaps it was the 1470's. Finally I filtered through into a gloomy, stockbroker-Tudor ballroom (what balls could have been held there?) to find a Duke authority on early Doric discussing "The Structure of Eyrbyggja Saga." Approximately twenty lonely souls clustered at the foot of this particular dais, and even they, I soon discovered, could have learned little about the subject since the beetle-browed speaker, unused to addressing a mike, was pouring his coruscating oratory into a lamp. It did not seem to matter. His public sat on, "listening."

I have thought it best to push aside this prejudice at the start since the running bibliography of courses in semantics, published in *ETC.*, shows that language study and communication study seem to end up mostly in the hands of English Departments. This is a particular pity within the charmingly fluid American situation. Intent to check and repress, the literary intellectual often despises General Semantics because he fails to understand what it is, and because it militates against his mystery. To him it sounds like another "crap course," something from some General Studies program, to be lumped in value with G.C. 27—*Introduction to Leisure Time Activities* (University of Minnesota), or perhaps *Fundamentals of Camping* (Boston University), or that tempting offering I dug up from one college's ardent Social Science curriculum—*Field Work in Marriage* ("An opportunity for observation and participation in actual field situations for qualified students"). Only the other day someone uncovered a Professor of Packaging.

Language as a Way of Life

"As was said to me once of Welsh," Edmund Wilson reports in *The Bit Between My Teeth*, "by a friend who was born in Wales, 'A language is a way of life.'" Such is what gets distorted in the classroom. One cannot make a course in *un*learning "progress." One cannot turn skepticism into English Two or Speech Six.

One cannot partly because the awareness evoked by self-doubt shows us that the word is the world,[13] that our reality is itself self-reflexive. The practical consequence of a study of awareness is to duplicate; there will, for instance, be numerous observations in this

[13]The ambiguity within the English word *word* can be seen in the wrestling match Wendell Johnson has with defining it in *Psychological Monographs*, vol. 56, no. 2 (1944), pp. 83–86.

book exchangeable with others elsewhere within it. This seems inevitable in discussing word-wisdom, which presents us with constant mirror-images, reversals and the doubles of our experience in one—a physiognomy of things Oscar Wilde borrowed from Baudelaire to call nature following art.

Of course, it does. This is a physiological event. The first person who hears you speaking is yourself. It has been likened to the recoil of a gun, and the mechanics of the explosion are hard to analyze. With its emphasis on the real, or "extensional" as it is sometimes called, General Semantics responds to that romanticism which technology deploys as a smoke-screen against itself. The real-romantic dichotomy of the industrial age is so reciprocal a polarity that scholars never tire of showing that one is essentially the other, the romantic the real and the real romantic, as that admirable semanticist Flaubert acknowledged.[14] The factitious division still haunts our culture, however, and when the two streams are subsumed in some single river, as in the work of Joyce, we find ourselves in the light of such semantic awareness it is literally prescient.[15]

This confidence in the real tends at times, too, to make semantic study seem utilitarian, degenerating into self-help (How not to make a damn fool of yourself), since the major part of our daily verbal production is aimed at immediate use. And it is probably true that prolonged skepticism of this nature, identification of irrational language habits and so on, may militate against the creative. That excellent British periodical *The Use of English* sends criticism of advertising into secondary schools,[16] but overdoses tend to de-

[14] In *Analysis,* XIII, October 1952, for instance, the mathematical philosopher Friedrich Waismann shows how Flaubert exemplified the monotonous flux of bourgeois life by the uniformity of his use of the imperfect tense and the conjunction *and.* Such nuances do not always come over in translation.

[15] Joyce joked about his gift of prophecy, but he knew the predictive power of language. Today his vision looks all too often like hindsight. For example: Bloom's assimilation reverie in "Circe," of becoming that paragon of loyal citizen, Lord Mayor, was turned into reality a few years ago when Dublin elected a Jewish Mayor. Shortly before this I watched Zero Mostel lampooning the idea as a farcical absurdity on stage (*Ulysses in Nighttown*). One Old Testament "prophecy" has been cited of President Johnson—"He that passeth by, and meddleth with strife belonging not to him, is like one that taketh a dog by the ears" (Proverbs 26:17).

[16] These "Looking at Advertising" sheets are available from Messrs. Chatto & Windus. Wallace Hildick has a lively "Close Look" series in the same vein —*A Close Look at Newspapers, A Close Look at Magazines and Comics,* etc. (Faber).

bilitate. Many modern ads are ingenious and full of libido. But if you knock advertising *sui generis* for week after week, you end up hitting at the creative ability itself. "What fools we are to be deluded by ads" soon turns into "What fools we are to be deluded by art."

All the same, language awareness is an esthetic activity. There is an element of criticism, Thomas Mann observed, in all creation. Because it is abundantly creative, America has been notoriously hospitable to self-criticism (the rich love to be loathed, as the latest Ford and Guggenheim grants generally show).[17] The result is often that external criticism, the barbs of a de Beauvoir or Waugh, glance off a reality so tough, since so creative, that it demands to be criticized from within.

To declare General Semantics "obsolete," as has Marshall McLuhan (in the report of Tom Wolfe), is to say no more than that modern man is obsolete. Such will be suggested in my first chapter. Our biological cycles become daily more out of phase with our environment. "BREAK THE ONE-BODY HABIT" cry the Formfit girdle and bra ads, as I write.

In the West the color *white* stands for purity; in the East it stands for sorrow, mourning. Its waves, its bands, are "apparent," they are there to both East and West. The color *white* is intraspecifically ascertainable. But, as the Socrates of *Euthyphro* went on to say, we fight about what is right and what is wrong, rather than about the number of pigs we own. It is the screen of "transparent" language that involves our humanity, our conduct and our honesty. It is when we fake our metaphors that we fight.

Here is the rub. Reading Malinowski on magic, one cannot but be touched by the deep sense of conscience embodied in the Trobriand magician. Before he can utter magic words at all, he must be in the right matrilineal lineage, then he must submit to the rigorous taboos of office, inspire constant hope and confidence in those for whom he works, stimulate them to creative effort, help them to persevere, and eventually he must pass on his word-wisdom to a chosen successor. This act of moral integration is a parable of the function of speech.

Alas, the official magic of our contemporary communities knows no such sense of duty. The engagement with reality, the harmony

[17] I take this up in my article "The Affluent Professor," *The University Bookman*, VI: 3 (Spring 1966), pp. 58–62.

invoked by the Trobriand magician, was not simply to control the environment but to organize a whole sense of enterprise and preparation for the future. For if the words are the world, they contain the future, a function of language A. E. Van Vogt has incidentally exaggerated into a series of successful science-fictions set on a planet called Null-A; similarly, when verbal communication is blocked or distorted, the future is threatened. The argument of the next chapter will be to suggest that our political *argot* or "language pollution" essentially denies a future.

Most magic spells, on the other hand, have an imperative character. They are directive. But, of course, to repeat over and over "COCA-COLA refreshes you best" is inaugurative of no possibility since the proposition is not real, it is synthetic, it is nonsense, and meaning collapses. Anticipation itself is derided and a more and more cynical populace comes to regard language as a medium of deception. Words, we hear on all sides, are "tricky." This kind of misrelation has had its ration of criticism by now, *MAD Magazine* making a Winston ad out of the Gettysburg address to drive home the point:

> Four score and seven years ago, our company brought forth on this continent a new cigarette, conceived in choice tobaccos, and dedicated to the proposition that not all brands are created equal. Now we are engaged in a great advertising war. . . .

The magician's spells were uttered on behalf of each member of the community. Advertising is uttered for the financial benefit of a single company and its relative handful of relatively homogeneous stockholders (all widows and orphans in a pinch, of course). Such jingling has by now become a token of "free enterprise," the French ORTF, virtually a compulsory radio station in France, currently running a song about the delights of preferring ORTF over nothing.[18] The politician's mumbo-jumbo, usually masquerading be-

---

[18]I would hazard the guess that American advertising has very largely thrown off the cloak of "information" some time ago. European advertising still occasionally struggles to evolve some *modus vivendi* between information and persuasion, and the following statement, from a British Advertising Association study published in October 1967, was offered as a change of position: "the distinction between informative and persuading advertising is fundamentally meaningless."

hind the democratic conceit, is equally "apparent," since untranslatable. The legitimacy of verbal magic, Malinowski showed, was the reverse of this. Corn could be seen coming up, rain could be felt falling, and man was involved in that delight in deception which is essential to the esthetic. Today Asian semantic retains, it is said, much belief in this intrinsic nature of esthetic language, in the divine or sublime qualities of the "transparent."

When this covenant is broken, words no more enclose the world. Man becomes a beast making sounds. Aldous Huxley was right to ascribe the rise of mystagogical demagogues, such as Hitler and Mussolini, to voluntary origins in the human psyche.[19] It is becoming easier, it seems, to destroy that anagram of the human which true language makes. For, like a true class, language cannot exist outside itself. The consciousness of the many harmonies of words is continually exciting; the recognition and awareness of word-wisdom today becomes a biological necessity. Semantics can be no less than a technique for survival.

[19]Compare: "Bad art is corruption of feeling. This is a large factor in the irrationalism which dictators and demogagues exploit" (Susanne K. Langer, *Problems of Art*, New York: Charles Scribner's Sons, 1957, p. 74).

PART ONE:
APPARENT LANGUAGE

The world created by words exists neither in space nor time though it has semblances of both, it is eternal and indestructible, and yet its action is no stronger than a flower: it is adamant, yet it is also what one of its practitioners thought it to be, namely, the shadow of a shadow. . . . Imagination is our only guide into the world created by words.

E. M. FORSTER, *Two Cheers For Democracy*

ONE

"I see nobody on the road," said Alice.
"I only wish *I* had such eyes," the King
remarked in a fretful tone. "To be able to
see Nobody! And at that distance too!"
Lewis Carroll, *Through the Looking Glass*[1]

THE DEMEANING OF MEANING:
THE LANGUAGE OF POLITICS

Playing Tug-of-War with Words

Nightmare is compounded of the failure of assumption. A floor
fails to support the walker, clothing comes alive, stones liquefy,
the tongue turns suddenly into a centipede writhing inside the
mouth, an entire city starts throbbing—all these elements are
drawn from the "panic" vision of Antoine Roquentin in Sartre's *La
Nausée*, which, though published as fiction in 1938, described factual conditions in bombed Hiroshima later. Some months before
Ronald Reagan—Sonny & Cher's "Plastic Man"— was elected Governor of California I watched a Bond-style movie in which the
President was replaced by an impersonator (complete with leather-
banded cowboy hat and rancher's jacket)—"An Actor as President!"
exclaimed the indignant hero. Dick Gregory's gauntlet for the 1968
presidential elections in America was, in fact, a comedian against
a cowboy.

The crisis of political discourse in American life, indeed in Western life, pertains to nightmare since it involves a threat, as it were
behind our backs, to habits of spatial and social thinking. So complex in appearance that every refuge seems vain, and menacing all
stability of existence in that it attacks the very duty of language to

[1]Compare:
" 'Someone at the door!' he said, blinking.
" 'Some four, I should say by the sound,' said Fili" (J.R.R. Tolkien, *The
Hobbit*, New York: Ballantine Books, 1965, p. 22).

make us human, this dilemma may still be simply stated. It is this: Political language both asks to be translated and yet, by its nature, cannot be. It is not sign language, it is not "apparent," in that it never says what it means, and George Orwell remarked that "In the case of a word like *democracy*, not only is there no agreed definition, but the attempt to make one is resisted from all sides."

This stretching of language out of true happens all the time. Not long ago the owner of a small factory making cartons found himself in the center of one of these semantic salads. Among his clients was a turkey farm. Having enjoyed a good year, the farmer sent the factory-owner fifty birds at Christmas. The latter distributed these, in the spirit of the season, among his employees.

By the following Christmas the turkey farm had had a hard time of it. Naturally enough the farmer forwarded no excess poultry. But the carton-maker's work force was unionized and after consultation demanded a turkey per operator.

"I tell you it was a *gift*," yelped their boss. "The guy don't have none to spare this year."

In vain. The union regarded the issuance of one turkey per person a *bonus*, and unless and until the owner could demonstrate a decrease in output on the part of any of his hands, he owed each one a turkey. Such he was in fact compelled to purchase and distribute, after the case had been settled in court. That highlander wasn't making any more *gifts* in a hurry.[2]

The reverse of this legend was operating in South Africa, where the labor laws do not recognize a union with colored members. Thus you can work there year in and year out but still not be an *employee,* since that words specifically excludes Cape "coloreds." Although about four out of five workers in most industries are black, they do not exist . . . as laborers. (There is a slight local distinction between blacks and coloreds.) The few all-white unions which make this Alice-in-Wonderland labor situation legally feasible might well be known as "the whites in the woodpile."

The evening I heard of the turkey decision I returned home with half a pound of expensive paté, bought from a French restaurant, under one arm. Before dinner my wife and I ate some of this with relish.

"Tastes as if this paté is based on liver," I innocently remarked.
"Mmn. You're right."

[2]Lest this anecdote sound "anti-union," the writer might add that he is on the Executive Committee of an AFL-CIO affiliate.

"Not unreminiscent of liverwurst, really."

From then on the stuff was mine. If there's one thing my wife can't stand it's liverwurst. Yet she had been happily putting away *paté*. The same is true of jelly, which she will eat when termed *aspic*. In my experience, when a kid asks what's for supper, he usually means dessert.

These verbal acrostics are quite serious. When supermarkets label beef *prime* or *choice,* they are not really using language. The same is true of furniture departments—which is more up-to-date, *modern* or *contemporary?* Is it safer to put your money into an insurance company called *Equitable* than in a bank called *Beneficial?* Certainly a large number of men are ignorant that *prime* beef is better than *choice,* or that *Extra Dry* Californian champagne is sweeter than *Brut.*[3]

In such cases we are scarcely using words. Numbers might be substituted, or even colors. The price virtually suffices. In bookbinding—a trade which should know better—a war went on recently between *perfect* and *superior* bindings. How can you get superior to perfect? (You might as profitably ask, How can you be a partial virgin?) A Christian Scientist refused vitamin pills a few years ago on the ground that they constituted *medicine;* she was persuaded to swallow them when they were rechristened *food.* In 1962 United States Marshals seized 5,400 "giant economy size" jars of coffee, in the first action of its kind taken by the Food and Drug Administration. The *economy* jar was found to cost more per ounce than the regular jar. When I served in the Brigade of Guards in England, the term *a young officer* meant a junior officer (ensign or subaltern); at the beginning of the war I remember *young officers* over fifty. Gilbert Ryle was one of them. Similarly, when revisiting my London club the other day, I found the changing-room attendant still referred to as the locker *boy,* although he had in fact been there forty-six years.[4]

[3] A friend who works for a Bordeaux wine *négociant* told me that a few years ago the industry debated the adoption of a new semantic, partly because the present terms were often misunderstood outside France, and even outside the wine-growing areas. Thus *Premiers Crus* are sometimes thought to be best since they come first. The industry wisely decided against a change of nomenclature as potential of more ambiguity than that they might solve.

[4] The term *boy,* as used of natives by British colonials, is popularly considered to have been condescending, and was so held up by modern racial emancipators. No doubt it was employed in this unpleasant way, but there is evidence that it was originally coined, in India at any rate, in a fraternal spirit.

We are all familiar with such blocks and boffs of daily usage. They form Mr. T. C. Mits'[5] image of semantic problems, though they only impinge peripherally on language. They are the basis of much punning. Are a widow's shares *outstanding* or outstanding? What sort of *interest* is being demonstrated by the loan shark ringing your door bell . . . how *civil* was the Civil War . . . and how much of a *club* is that Christmas Club in your bank? All the same, the passing of such verbal counters in this manner can be a genuine linguistic dishonesty, or perversion. To use words to mean nothing is, as Orwell suggested, a treachery to humanity. Men lose their lives because senior statesmen are not called to the kind of semantic book any college freshman faces in his first English essay.

Now all verbal chicanery is a corruption of word-wisdom and it is hardly new. The wounding is frequently in the nature of euphemism, and will be considered in a later chapter under Taboo. *Slums* or *underprivileged areas? Scabs* or *extra help? Relief* or *unemployment insurance?*[6] *Minimum price* or *fair trade practices? Arbitration* or *third-party determination? Desegregation* or *integration?*[7] Everyone can make up his own list from the day's papers, much

[5]In T. C. Mits I refer to "*the* celebrated *man in the* street," as defined by Hugh and Lillian Lieber in their popular *The Education of T. C. Mits* (New York: Norton, 1944).

[6]I am aware that there is a technical distinction between the terms. Unemployment itself has recently been euphemized in England under the rubric of *redeployment.* But such terms show, I think, a conscious retreat from the old British *dole,* with its lugubriously nineteenth-century connotations that the poor are poor because they're wicked, and that consequently you *dole out* a pittance to them.

Still, this old term has left its legacy—"Opposition by half of the powerful House Rules Committee has stalled plans for House action early next week on a Democratic-sponsored plan for special unemployment benefits. Committee Chairman Smith (D-Va.), Rep. Colmer (D-Miss.) and the four Republican members of the 12-man group yesterday attacked the measure as a 'dole' which they contended might threaten the present federal-state jobless insurance program" (New York *Post*).

[7]"In a small town that was borderland South, three youngsters—two of them white and the third a Negro—burst into the soda fountain, clambered onto the stools, and ordered chocolate milkshakes. The owner, who was behind the counter, took in the situation at a glance. With baseball gloves hanging out of their jeans, the boys had obviously come from the community's newly integrated play program.

" 'I'm sorry, boys,' the man began in a not unkind but firm tone of voice, 'don't you know we have segregation here?'

" 'Sure,' answered one of the white boys, 'but we've segregated him—he's sitting between us!' "(*Reader's Digest*).

in the spirit of the character in *The Merchant of Venice* (I, i, lines 46–49):

> "Then let us say you are sad,
> Because you are not merry; and 'twere as easy
> For you to laugh, and leap, and say you are merry,
> Because you are not sad."

The technique and degree of dilution vary—a *moderate* drinker can be found *moderately* drunk—as does the gravity of the subject matter; but in general, when we call a *blockade* of Cuba a *quarantine,* or a *recession* a *rolling adjustment* (Eisenhower), we are pretending that all language is "apparent," so many tags stuck on the extensional in the manner of that store which, occupying an entire block, found it could call all its four entrances *front doors.* Something like *agricultural parity,* as presently employed, has very little to do with parity in the normally conceived sense, but users are often asking that it be taken that way. Though words like these are issued in a transitive stream, nothing is being said, and to use lanluage to mean nothing is indicative of contempt. One recalls the old Buick ad promising to "make you feel like the man you really are,"[8] an insult of semantic proportions.

Political language is thus at the base of our study since it is, in this sense, a primary language damage and, as such, threatens our survival. When government spokesmen elected to "speak" for us use a symbol today to stand for x ("advisers . . . technicians") and use that same symbol tomorrow to stand for y (Thunderchief bombers), they are spitting on language itself and performing that shiftiness we call crime when performed in our friendly neighborhood grocery store. "To say a word 'means' something," writes the British solicitor, Arthur Owen Barfield, "implies that it means that same something more than once." If it were not to make like Bertrand Russell *après le jour,* I would dub this the meaning of meaning of meaning.

The cynicism toward communication as a whole, latent in such chicanery, becomes stifling, and causes the electorate to become

[8] "A cigar brings out the Matador in you" (Cigar Institute of America, Inc.); "Every dog is more dog when he's fed the DIET OF CHAMPIONS" (Ken-L Biskit).

verbally calloused. And why not? The same extensionally verifiable rocket is called on the same day *a factor of peace* and *an instrument of aggression.* A treaty is broken because arms *limitation* is construed differently from arms *reduction.* A Berlin tunnel is an *escape route* for beleaguered East Berliners at the same time that it is a *hole for smuggling* Western agents into clean Communist territory. But verbal tugs-of-war of this kind arise from hostile camps, and indicate that lack of agreement between rivals Orwell was thinking of in *democracy.* The years of fighting in Vietnam have been a tragic history of language damage (the so-called credibility gap) within a single camp.

Years ago, before our *advisers* started bombing their *technicians* in Vietnam, and Robert Kennedy was Attorney General, he was asked the nature of the *war* in South East Asia. He answered guardedly, "We are involved in a struggle." Pressed as to the distinction, one the participants doubtless found hard to discern, he went on, "It is a legal difference. . . . It is a struggle short of war." A *struggle,* it could be added today, against a population 54 percent of whom are currently under sixteen years of age.[9]

In a sense he was right. The Korean "police action" (the phrase was Harry Truman's), in which there were 33,629 battle deaths and 157,530 casualties, was subsequently redefined a *war* by an Appellate Court, to the undisguised joy of insurance companies, who exclude losses resulting from war or insurrection; the latter term was used to cover the Watts racial riots in Los Angeles, while the 1967 Newark disturbances (euphemism! euphemism!) were termed by Stokely Carmichael *rebellions* rather than *riots.* Listening to this grim comedy of words daily, who can lightly dismiss the comment of folk singer Joan Baez—"Everyone says I'm politically naive, and so I am. So are the people running politics, or we wouldn't be in wars, would we?"

Here the word no longer contains its world. "Our purpose is not war but peace,"[10] says the President of the United States. We trust

[9]See William F. Pepper, "The Following Acts . . . Are Crimes," *Columbia University Forum,* IX:4 (Fall 1966), pp. 46–48. The figure given stems from a UNESCO study.

[10]Des Moines, Iowa, July 1, 1966. "I want to be very cautious and careful, and use force only as a last resort when I start dropping bombs that are likely to involve American boys in war in Asia with 700 million Chinese . . . so we are not going North . . . and we are not going South . . ." (as presidential candidate, Manchester, N. H., September 28, 1964).

he says this in sincerity, but as he does so his bombers are raiding Haiphong and Hanoi and we learn that a smaller proportion of the Gross National Product will be expended on nonmilitary programs in fiscal 1968 than was spent, by Truman, in 1948. The language system is wrenched off its rails when we can calmly use an oxymoron like the *war for peace;* for the word *peace* is itself fractured when forced to contain visibly within itself children and old people, horribly burnt and mutilated, and when, according to one calculation, 80 percent of an American's income tax goes to military spending. Indeed, the destruction of the word is seen in the kind of embarrassed caution with which it has come to be used in America today. President Johnson has spoken with derision of *peaceniks* (a Semitic coining).

Lou LaBrant tells the story of a child playing with his grandfather's shirt, and learning language thereby. As he sits on the old man's knee he repeatedly exclaims, "Buppon . . . buppon." Granddad smiles assent. Finally, the kid toys with the scarf pin. "Buppon," he declares. "Well," comes his grandfather's reply, "it is like a button. Only I *call* it a pin. . . ." War? Well, these days we *call* it peace. It is all rather like the preacher at the drive-in church who is said to have said, "Your prayers are answered, folks. Because whatever happens, that's the answer."[11]

It is, then, this contempt for the dramatic and inherent nature of language that is today playing Russian roulette with the human race. Speaking at the P.E.N. Congress in Oslo of June 1964, R. F. Thanh Lang (Vietnam) described this rape of language by politics as a principally occidental phenomenon:

> In Vietnam, for instance, those beautiful terms—peace, liberty, democracy, equality—were imported into our country by Westerners at the end of the nineteenth century . . . in fact, we were much freer, and more democratic, before we had the good fortune to be able to pronounce these words with our mouths; and today if you utter such words in front of any

[11]Semantic tail-chasing reached some sort of peak not long ago when an unidentified Indonesian newspaper was quoted by the Chinese *Hsinhua* as follows: "Imperialism tried to spread through the Indian Prime Minister a tune of peace at the conference in an attempt to make people forget the ferocity of colonialism and imperialism." The new *Fowler* notes that by the middle of the twentieth century *imperialism* was "a word so charged with hostile meaning as to be almost useless."

Vietnamese, he will simply give you a good-natured smile. For a Vietnamese liberty means: Liberty to go to prison. . . .[12]

One could put beside this the exposition of the Oriental concept of *freedom* recently made by the Japanese Professor Kenji Takahashi, who shows that throughout Japanese literature this word has usually been synonymous with "unruliness and wickedness." Takahashi gives the usual explanation for this, namely that human relationships in Japan have normally been vertical, and thus occidental *freedom* has been seen as arbitrary, willful and disruptive, but it is unlikely that our political leaders are familiar with it.

To say that this development, or attrition, of language endangers our survival may well turn out to be the understatement of the atomic century, and our task must be resolutely to identify the anti-human symptoms steering our language systems off course. For meaning is dependent on an organization of various elements, including, as we shall see, what is *not* said. The meaning of a word, in I. A. Richards' well-known formulation, is the missing part of its context. "When you think of a concrete object," Orwell wrote, "you think wordlessly."

In a society without true liberty (i.e. of objects) man submits to this situation, rather in the manner of a neurotic, whose neurosis *is* its own symptoms. He learns to "live with" himself. (We hear of the German Max Bense writing computer poems and being specifically irritated by the concept of any meaning at all—he boasts of dealing entirely in quantifiables, like some man-mechanism out of La Mettrie.) Our sensibilities become benumbed as we allow our official Humpty Dumpties, of whatever faction, to defile words, dragging them to and fro and stretching them to cover contradictory meanings. It is for this reason—that political utterances, about *democracy* and so forth, are pretentiously "transparent" and demand to be translated—that politicians choose woolly language, on a high level of abstraction, behind which to maneuver. The American Constitution would appear to be a masterpiece of applicable abstraction, created out of direct images. Clear thinking calls for

[12]R. F. Thanh Lang, Session Four, reprinted in *Arena,* no. 24 (October 1965), pp. 58–59 (my trans. from the French). Compare Orwell's Appendix to *1984*: "The word *free* still existed in Newspeak, but it could only be used in such statements as 'This dog is free from lice' or 'This field is free from weeds.' "

images and, as Orwell suggested, it is much easier to obfuscate meaning and to use *democracy* as a vague term of approval than as a specific way of acting. Here we collide with the question of jargon.

Jargon: The Afflatus of Office

Political jargon in particular is a bogus incantation of the false magicians. I well remember listening to the Eisenhower-Macmillan "debate" of September 1, 1959 ("Issues Confronting the West"). After about a quarter of an hour my wife remarked with a frown, "They must say something soon." But they didn't. A subsequent inspection of the transcript revealed that no real context could define the verbal situations created. (I have had much the same sensation listening to the rhetoric of Ayn Rand.) To set individual words in a unitary mold at odds with the parts of speech of which it is composed is the characteristic afflatus of technological office today, and represents a serious breach of personality. By its construction alone it cannot convey meaning, and typically serves a technocracy whose relationship to reality is ahuman. Such led Orwell to write that in most political discourse today "one is not watching a live human being but some kind of dummy." Nontalk presupposes nonlisteners, or automata.

It is important to follow this through, as Orwell perhaps did not quite do, or try to do, in his essay on "Politics and the English Language" from which I have been drawing. Written at the end of the last war, it shows Orwell's recognition of the danger of reduced consciousness implicit in modern political utterance. He well suggested—what Thanh Lang reinforces for us twenty years later—that such utterance is a rupture of the symbiotic bond, in which sign and signified are made to betray each other. What demands to be translated cannot be translated and language poisons itself off its own vomit.

Once more, the word is its world and the entire breakdown of the English Groundnuts operation in Africa some years ago was forecast in official language about it, of which the following is a characteristically nutty example:

In the Nuts (Unground) (Other than Groundnuts) Order, the expression Nuts shall have reference to such nuts, other than groundnuts, as would, but for this amending Order, not qualify as Nuts (Unground) (Other than Groundnuts) by reason of their being Nuts (Unground).

Any editor, finding this passage in a parody, would ask the author to modify it, to exaggerate less; but as an order-in-council it passed muster.

Ever since a notable essay on the subject by Sir Arthur Quiller-Couch, and no doubt before it too, jargon has been served up in handbooks as Something to Avoid. The suggestion follows that everyone else is guilty of this vice but you. Yet today everyone—doctor, lawyer, social scientist—suffers from what a young friend of mine calls the botanical speech impediment: he talks flowery. Expedition, deactivation, escalation, defoliation—such is the core curriculum of seatwork essential for all true testees of jargon, keen to rezone their verbal relatedness.

Indeed, the last place one should find jargon is often where one finds it first, in literary criticism and discourse.[13] Perhaps the very last place of all might be in semantics itself, but I am sorry to have to say that GS is far from free of jargon.[14] Every art seems beset with its own jargon, even the dance ("Taking it or not," writes Jill Johnston of a modern dance well called *The Mind Is a Muscle,* "is one good pressure point of a stance not bent on captivity"). But when a painter is described by *Art News* as depicting "the stultified intricacy of tension at the plasmic level; his prototypical zygotes and somnolent somatomes inhabit a primordial lagoon where impulse is an omnidirectional drift and isolation is the consequence of an inexplicable exogamy," then we long with a yawn that makes ignorance seem bliss for some literary Lysistrata. We reach for our Pasternak, whose Doctor Zhivago reflects:

[13]Sir Herbert Read refers to Susanne Langer's straightforward *Philosophy in a New Key* as a "synoptic" work. McLuhan's *The Gutenberg Galaxy,* an anthological book, is praised by John Wain in similar academic jargon— "This is one of the great panoptic books of our time." One wonders if Wain knows what he means at all.

[14]The bulletins of the New York Society for General Semantics specialize in GS jargon. Thus a book by McLuhan is, for them, "written in the form of what General Semanticists call an 'is of identity' statement, it implies 'allness' attitudes," etc. To the same bulletin Abraham Maslow contributes the definition of "self-actualization" as "ongoing actualization of potential capacities and talents . . . as an unceasing trend toward unity, integration or synergy within the person."

"Oh, how one wishes sometimes to escape from the meaningless dullness of human eloquence, from all those sublime phrases, to take refuge in nature, apparently so inarticulate, or in the wordlessness of long, grinding labor, of sound sleep, of true music, or of a human understanding rendered speechless by emotion."[15]

In criticism of the arts jargon insults us peculiarly. The purpose of criticism is to get at meaning, not to complicate it. In an ideally constituted society it would be unnecessary, and today its polysyllables can be seen proliferating in measure as man gets distanced from true magic, and the human. Pedaguese, as James LeSure called it in a recent diatribe,[16] tries to turn the arts into rival technologies, and intervenes impertinently between us and them. It has become, for instance, far harder to understand writing about *Finnegans Wake* than the book itself.

To some extent this must presumably be seen as another defense mechanism, an incantation of office, and, in the case of the literary intellectual, another demonstration of insecurity. A *hybris* of rationalism has its own insanity. The methodology that much literary criticism has become does not seem to be sustaining much—except young professors in office—and its pretensions to be an art, of a kind scholarship does not make, all too often end in a vulgarization of Nietzsche's Apollonian instinct as a sort of MLA policeman.[17]

Before returning to the pitfalls of our political business, one might add that many special slangs, like jazz or hipster language, often adduced as jargons, really are not such. These forms are merely hiding from translation; but they are lexically translatable,

[15]Boris Pasternak, *Doctor Zhivago*, New York: Pantheon Books, 1958, p. 139.
[16]James S. LeSure, *Guide to Pedaguese*, New York: Harper & Row, 1966. Actually Donald J. Lloyd featured this word in his article "Our National Mania for Correctness," in *The American Scholar* for Summer 1952. Also amusing is Robert Escarpit's *The Novel Computer* (London: Secker & Warburg, 1966), a fictional satire of technological jargon—"of all the suffixes going, my friend, the best bar none is *tron*."
[17]For an admirable criticism of the tendencies I so briefly arraign here, see William Arrowsmith, "Turbulence in the Humanities," *The KEY Reporter*, vol. xxxi, no. 3 (Spring 1966), pp. 2–4, 8. This article seems to have been the seed of a fuller attack, on graduate academies in general, made by Arrowsmith, Chairman of the Department of Classics at the University of Texas, in *Harper's Magazine* later. As E. M. Forster has remarked, "There are no questions to be asked about literature while we read it."

though most of them soon die of self-suffocation. Lincoln was reduced by *MAD Magazine* to the following:

> Fourscore and like seven years ago our old daddies came on
> in this scene with a new group, grooved in free kicks, and hip
> to the jazz that all cats make it the same. Now we're real hung
> up in a crazy big hassle. . . .

Here we have a mere matter of transliteration, though I confess
that this itself can become rather rare, as when we read that The
Fugs will present "the hydrogen foot fetish, meat cackles, round
pounds, spurt salutes, juke box sex flashes, & pandemic lip-lob
frenzy shimmers!!!" As Horatio put it, when Hamlet slipped into
Osric's jargon, "Is't not possible to understand in another tongue?"

New vocabularies of this sort are frequently a response on the
part of the young to the betrayal of word-wisdom by their elders.
A common speech confers solidarity. Bop and jive talk craved quick
new verbal counters with which to escape the chicanery of the old.
Already the Glossary of hipster slang, appended to as recent a work
as Lawrence Lipton's 1959 *The Holy Barbarians*, looks meaning-
lessly dated. The yearning is for "apparent" language, Faust's longing *Vor dem Tor,* and a convenient summary of our civilization is
that Faust felt it all first. As the philosopher's epigram had it of
Plato, wherever we go in our minds these days we always meet
Faust—coming back.

The escape hatch is often a high degree of rhyme and rhythm,
nearly always a feature of concealment vocabularies. *See you later,
alligator* is hopelessly dated, but the resort to a cyclical body rhythm is perennial. (To one such teener, who asked a few years back
if she could "hit the flick," a semanticist mother replied, "Only after
you've rubbed the tub, scoured the shower, spread your bed and
swished the dishes.") The technique of rebel rhythm is also evidenced in prison slangs, and in the now almost forgotten Cockney
rhyming slang.

Originating, it is said, around the London theater, this colorful
argot consisted for the most part of an assonantal shorthand; thus
a shirt was a *dicky* (Dick Dirt = shirt), a hat a *titfer* (Tit for
Tat = hat), shoes were *me-and-you*'s, and so forth. Wife disguises
were endless, of course—Carving Knife, Storm and Strife, Joy (Joy
of Your Life). Amenable to rapid improvisation, and rich in ob-

scenities, the "conjugations" of Cockney rhyming slang could get respectably rococo. But I had not realized how dead it was until a year ago in London I watched an American girl moderating a British TV quiz program and imitating it for the benefit of her participant, a youth from Putney. These vocabularies of evasion are likely to continue high in physiological stimuli and, in America, a country of quickly changing sense ratios, are to be treasured for such. But they are not what Orwell was indicting. They are semantic funkholes, shelters from language pollution. A recent ad puts it for me best: "THE BIG BEAT speaks a nonverbal language to very young ears and feet. It says, 'You belong!' Best of all, adults don't get the message."[18]

The Incredibility Crap

As "Q" saw, political language is composed of roundabout or inflated phraseology for simple expressions, of a plethora of suffixes, of the overuse of copulative verbs, of the telltale substitution of the passive for the active. In active forms you are responsible, not someone else; the Gettysburg Address is almost wholly active, even in Higher Hipster. Jargon flourishes when the behavior of a society is of the same order of motive as that which generates a divorce from reality (Orwell's "When the general atmosphere is bad, language must suffer"). In every way this linguistically fictitious entity is proper to robots rather than to me.

F. D. Roosevelt was apparently forever unscrambling governmental jargon. A Public Administration order of 1942 ran:

> Such preparations shall be made as will completely obscure all Federal buildings and non-federal buildings occupied by the Federal Government during an air-raid for any period of time from visibility by reason of internal or external illumination.

Roosevelt derobotized this to: "Tell them that in buildings where they have to keep the work going, to put something across the windows," a particularly enheartening revision of official gobbledegook since it is nongrammatical, containing an "open" noun clause

[18]In a British equivalent an English teener is given the same aspiration in a recent ad: "OUT are striped watch straps. I saw a friend's mum wearing one and that was enough for me."

of the kind an English instructor sees it his mission to massacre. The meaning still comes briskly across.[19]

While Roosevelt's crisply active rephrasing has the ring of democratic commitment, avoiding the anonymous passive, the matter cannot be written off as one of substituting simple words for circuitous expressions. This is Orwell's recipe for jargon, and it would assist the immigrant plumber mentioned in my footnote, or Mark Twain's Buck Fanshaw, who so superbly misunderstood all obfuscations. Yet it would hardly apply to the later Henry James. The problem must be seen within the language system itself. Although French is becoming more and more prone (*facturation, viabiliser*), English and German seem to lend themselves to the camouflage of thought by jargon especially readily.

German admits as much by being a language of compound and multiple nouns, and of a pronounced verbal interval (one UN translator, after a particularly long pause in giving us a German's peroration, apologized, "I am waiting for the verb"). This was the basis of Johann Fischart's sixteenth-century *Geschichtsklitterung*, which parodied humanist word formation as hilariously as did Rabelais' grotesque word-families. In short, since the pedants were delighting themselves with the wealth of synonyms in German, Fischart inflated these into monstrosities of incestuously copulating nouns, all showing phonetic relationship alongside lexical incompatibility, or sheer nonsense.

Simplification is the cure for verbal redundancy, or pleonasm—*(exact) replica, (added) bonus, (perfect) stranger, (general) consensus of opinion,* even the widely used *revert (back).* But the English language has since an early period depended on clusters of consonants, and it is dangerous when language is not allowed to accommodate neologism. *Television* may be a bastard word, but how else

[19]Another transliteration of the sort involved an immigrant plumber who wrote to the Federal Bureau of Standards about the excellence of hydrochloric acid in clearing drains. The Bureau's turgid replies ("The efficacy of hydrochloric acid is indisputable, but the corrosive residue is incompatible with metallic permanence") had eventually to be modified to "DON'T USE HYDROCHLORIC ACID. IT EATS HELL OUT OF THE PIPES." Richard Altick attributes this anecdote to a Dean of M.I.T. (*Preface to Critical Reading,* New York: Henry Holt, 1951, p. 87), but I must say I heard it years before when working as Press Officer for Imperial Chemical Industries in London. In 1935 a London Transport notice read, "No vehicle may use this forecourt without special authority, except private cars and taxicabs conveying or calling for passengers." In 1958 this was changed to "NO PARKING." *Eheu fugaces. . . .*

do you express the phenomenon today? A recent article in *Physical Review Letters* on "antimatter particles" pinpoints this problem. Brookhaven National Laboratory tests suggest that there may be an entire universe made up of . . . well, antimatter. Such is the best that can be done to define it verbally. Thus, antimatter civilizations might exist complete with . . . antipeople. To whom, of course, we ourselves would be antipeople. This may seem nontalking, but in fact communication between the two antiuniverses (or antiverses?) might be possible since light and radio waves appear the same in both matter and antimatter.[20]

Simplicity is a side issue. What is important is to identify the movement of words within an established jargon. This is nearly always away from meaning and toward anonymity, and the ahuman; it gets its head, of course, in social conflations, or redundancies, like marriage counseling ("Do you promise, to love, honor, and relate to one another?") or schools of education ("Hands up, all over-achievers"). Military directives may be conventionally of this nature, but when the same serial relationship is imported into political directives, then what Forster calls the imaginative function is usurped; it is usurped on behalf of nothing at all, or several things at once (which comes to the same).

"Apparent" language is typically verifiable by performance. Wall Street leads to Wall Street, else the sign is taken down. To look at an example of particularly active prose, imbued with a direct social predicament:

> Fourscore and seven years ago our fathers brought forth on this continent a new nation, conceived in liberty, and dedicated to the proposition that all men are created equal. Now we are engaged in a great civil war, testing whether that nation, or any nation so conceived and so dedicated can long endure. We are met on a great battlefield of that war.

An enterprising advertising executive turned this into Eisenhowerese:

[20]In the 1950's "Harriet Daimler" wrote two pornographies for the Olympia Press entitled *The New Organization* and *The Woman Thing* (reissued as *Woman*); both, but particularly the former, played cleverly with coinings of this type and the poverty of vocabulary to describe new situations at the same time.

I haven't checked these figures but eighty-seven years ago I think it was, a number of individuals organized a governmental set-up here in this country, I believe it covered certain eastern areas, with this idea they were following up based on a sort of national-independence arrangement and the program that every individual is just as good as every other individual. Well, now, of course, we are dealing with this big difference of opinion. . . .[21]

The flaccid hesitancies and bumbling tergiversations of Eisenhower oratory (or its close parallel rather than parody, above, by Oliver Jensen) were evidence of an unsure mind, the opposite of Lincoln's moral certainty. It is a way of hiding from thought, in the hope that if you utter words in a stream they must eventually qualify something. They must be translatable, but in fact are not. The point about political jargon is to identify the source of why they are not.

Whether words should be something they are not, whether we should write or speak an adjective for an adverb or vice versa, must be concerns outside my study; the fact remains that these parts have been pushed into certain situations in a given sentence: such is an aggregate of social pressures. As far as I am concerned, the overuse of nouns—notably of compound nouns and nouns in apposition—is first and foremost a guide to the extent of reflection going on within the sentence. Matters of "decay" must remain opinionative, as when, in *Plain Words* (London: H.M.S.O., 1948), Sir Ernest Gowers quotes Lord Dunsany to the effect that one can virtually date a passage by the frequency of multiple nouns, and so record "language decay progress." Reluctant as I am to leave the main line of my argument, I must pause here to make this emphasis clear.

English English

Social conventions can be powerful magic. Systematizing sounds or even stresses as parts of speech is lent authority by social strati-

[21]In "Politics and the English Language," collected in *Shooting an Elephant and Other Essays* (New York: Harcourt, Brace, 1945), Orwell did much the same with *Ecclesiastes:* He converted "I returned and saw under the sun . . ." into "Objective consideration of contemporary phenomena compels the conclusion. . . ."

fication, extremely active at one time in England. So one part of speech would be considered conventionally "correct," another "incorrect." "WINSTON TASTES GOOD LIKE A CIGARETTE SHOULD" was deliberately "incorrect," and made enduring appeal by underlining the majority use of *like* as a conjunction—Margaret M. Bryant's *Current American Usage* finding *like* two and a half times more frequent in this form than *as* throughout spoken American. It is always healthy when T. C. Mits is freed from another language inhibition. In fact, *like* was used as a conjunction by both Shakespeare and Keats, it appears so through the *Psalms*, and *like* and *as though* are used with equal frequency in the upper Midwest. As Jacques Barzun points out in his admirable revision of *Follett*, the primary meaning of *like* in 1400 was *as if*. We are simply caught up in a social convention.

When I first came to America, my education, including daily Latin from seven to seventeen, made such uses to which I was not accustomed sound unpleasant. Adverbial *real* (as in *real good*) sounded semiliterate or "vulgate," in the social sense—though any other sense of this term fails to make sense, and *The Times Literary Supplement* reviewer who deplored the "rather vulgar popularity" of Evelyn Waugh's *Brideshead Revisited* was writing rubbish, or at least a pleonasm.

To remind the reader of Richards' definition again, semantic study of the kind I am attempting is functional rather than morphological. To go away satisfied that adverbial *real* is merely a corruption which should always be written *really* is to miss the nuance of American idiom. "I want to get there real fast" is simply not translated by "I want to get there really fast." The group noun which Gowers ridicules is subject to the same shades of transmission, a point important to remember in political utterance.

The operation of conversion, from one part of speech to another, is subject to much technical debate.[22] "The philologist," Bréal points out, "notes that in all languages the adjective has a tendency to replace the substantive." (Thus we take the *express* or the *local*.) But the resultant piece of language—whether homonym for noun, eliminated relative clause, unidentified adjective, and/or slipped past participle (the most current theories)—is a new en-

[22]For a typical exchange see the Merriam *Word Study* issues for February and December 1955. These controversies get decidedly acerb.

tity. "The form of the word is not fixed," as E. Kruisinga put it, "but depends on its service in the sentence."[23] Look how Swift handled "the form of the word" in his letters to Stella. Then enter the *supermarket* (itself such a coining, of course) and admire the *bottle beer, dice carrots, ice cream* and *slice melon*. All I can say is that these are not the same as, they are other kinds of objects from, *bottled beer, diced carrots, iced cream,* or *sliced melon.*

The dropped *d* in each case, like the omitted *s* common in America (*barber shop, sport shirt, math*), may simply come down to a matter of speed. But the avoidance is being passed back to England, in typical language infection. So H. W. Fowler's books on usage, and misusage, seem to me those of a literary satirist, or at least of an esthete. A man of his time, Fowler was concerned with elegance, the look of words, and other subjective matters such as "ugliness" of phraseology. His emphasis, intensified if anything by Gowers' revisions, is reduced to final triviality by someone like Theodore M. Bernstein, a former *New York Times* rewrite man, and now Managing Editor, who trots out tomes on standards of usage without, so far as I can see, knowing much about language. The Fowler (Gowers)-Bernstein axis is keyed to standardization and gentility. One idiom is "offensive"—whatever that may mean—another is not. "These are but wild and whirling words, my lord." The Beatles did a great deal to lampoon this frame of mind. "Every good literary craftsman," said Shaw, "splits his infinitives when the sense demands it."

Posting up passages of English to show the errors of others (as Bernstein is reputed to do in the *New York Times* office) is so much misplaced self-congratulation. Language cannot be approached as a set of exhibits. Some of Eric Partridge's books smack of collections of howlers by an industrious don.[24] Norton Mockridge, author of the popular *Fractured English,* appears to make a profession out of this practice, holding folk etymology up to daily derision on the basis that to be verbally irregular or eccentric is to be funny, like the stage Scotsman of the old London music hall. For instance, Mockridge imagines it will break us up to hear about someone who referred to the *Adam bomb* on Hiroshima. But if we smile, we do

[23]E. Kruisinga, *The Phonetic Structure of English Words,* Berne: A. Francke, 1943, p. 1.
[24]See, in particular, Eric Partridge, *A Dictionary of Clichés,* New York: Macmillan, 1940.

so at sound. The term is instantly understood as a meaningful unit—after all, the bomb was the first of its kind. Moreover, a linguist might well object that the closure of sounds by "words" is artificial and that here the meaning unit consists (according to the Trager-Smith system) of three morphemes. Seventh Day Adventists stamp out their directives in just such sensory illisions rather than in strictly closed words. "The word Papa, besides," says Mrs. General in *Little Dorrit,* "gives such a pretty form to the lips." If it does, it is not a word. A Russian calls his Uncle Igor *dyàdya.*

Revisiting London some years ago I found *minicabs* in existence. The word was new to me at the time, but I realized what it meant at once—without having to be told, by Fowler, Partridge, or Logan Pearsall Smith, that it was an "ugly" contraction of miniature cabriolet. A year later I met *miniskirts* and needed no Bernsteins to guide me. The semanticist's interest in miniskirts is not their morphology (their erotic stimulus, and so on), but their symbology, the fact that they anticipated a certain financial climate. The French Finance Minister, Michel Debré, developed the connection between stock statistics and miniskirts in a notable speech in late 1967.

Foreign languages are learnt this way. I remember the blunders I made when I arrived in America and found a waistcoat called a vest, a vest an undershirt, and trousers pants. The automotive vocabulary teemed with potential pratfalls—a UK bonnet becoming a US hood (inanimate variety), a wing a fender, a boot a trunk, a windscreen a windshield, a headlamp a headlight, and so forth. A British shooting brake is an American station wagon, a puncture is a flat—which both French and German subsume under the inclusive breakdown term, *panne.*

Again, semantics is scarcely at issue here. The exchanges are purely "apparent," like *prime* and *choice* for beef. In England a screw may be your salary, but even today Dickens' story "Sunday Screw" might have to be retitled for certain American magazines. The English girl who came to New York and called down to Room Service, "Knock me up in the morning, any time will do" can scarcely have expected the (respectful?) gasp her remark received. (Of Llandudno's gastronomic facilities *The Observer* for July 23, 1967, admonished, "it's not everywhere that a waitress can knock you up a delicious French dressing on the spot.") Similarly, the no doubt equally apocryphal American, buying writing paper in a Yorkshire village and asking the saleslady "Do you keep stationery?" must have been just as nonplussed by her reply: "No. I always wriggle a little." The small print of *Playboy* thrives off such semantic banana-slippings. They are purely lexical and can just as well occur within America. At the City College of New York, where I teach, coeds sometimes wear sweaters sporting the college mascot, a beaver. When they go to the West Coast, they can find that a beaver is a term for a promiscuous girl, and that the sweater's symbolism (so we hope) alters.

Anglo-American usage is always full of true semantic interest. The American dialect of English was itself an aspect of political independence, and studies of specifically American English date back at least to the early nineteenth century, owing a particular debt to John Pickering's celebrated *Vocabulary or Collection of Words and Phrases Which Have Been Supposed to Be Peculiar to the United States of America,* of 1816. Since when dozens of word lists and studies of Americanisms have appeared, there are historical dictionaries devoted to American English (such as those edited by Mitford Mathews or Craigie/Hulbert), and authorities on early American speech, like Professor Thomas Pyles of the University of Florida, have thoroughly covered adoptions from foreign tongues.

To have lived the change in one's lifetime, however, is a curiously intimate way of learning language as a social system. Indeed, since the American and British tongues are—*pace* G. B. Shaw—the same, the paradox exists that for a limey the transition to "the States" is more difficult than, say, for a Greek or Italian: less psychological capital tends to be invested in the new land.[25] Thus when I arrived in America *compromise* was a meliorative term in Britain, pejorative in America. This tells you quite a bit about the social history of the countries concerned.

What the Bernsteins of this world call "standard" English is often its own jargon. When recently I published a novel in both England and America, I learnt that Americans spell British *bale out* as *bail out*. Both spellings have logical antecedents, so which is "right" and which is "wrong?" In answer we might be given some gratuitous opinion, as that *bail out* is "uglier." But to call variation incorrect, or unesthetic, is to set up as a supererogatory language

---

[25]In Wilbur S. Shepperson's *Emigration and Disenchantment: Portraits of Englishmen Repatriated from the United States* (Norman, Okla.: University of Oklahoma Press, 1965) the suggestion that the British assimilated *less* easily than those who could *not* speak the common language seems well substantiated.

constable; it is to assume that the standard is the beautiful. The corollary then follows that what you assume to be good-looking is "standard," as in the selection of airline hostesses. At which point one hears the words of the Sonny & Cher ballad *Love Don't Come*, "I can't play because I don't know how to win."

The Semantics of Extermination

The gravity of Orwell's insight into our political language system has now become a matter of life and death. "Apparent" and "transparent" language are made to betray each other. He condensed this well—"In our time, political speech and writing are largely the defense of the indefensible." He cited British rule in India, the Russian purges, the atom bomb.

In short, you cannot tell your constituency or bailiwick that you are dropping burning petroleum jelly on a group of Asiatics beside whose flag you were raising your own a few years back. You cannot say aloud, in public, that you are deporting Asiatic peasantry en masse and at gunpoint, eradicating their houses and crops, and herding them into insanitary camps; instead, you say that you are resettling a number of *refugees*. (It became so obvious to observers that such indigenes were not seeking refuge that they were subsequently rechristened *returnees*.) When I heard General Westmoreland's address to the Congress in 1967 I saw the force of Orwell's point about the modern political dummy. Indeed, a good exercise in verbal sincerity is to give a group the task of writing one of President Johnson's speeches, on a given subject, before he delivers it. The language will be bound to be bafflingly question-begging and soporifically vague, so that an intelligent student can sometimes provide whole paragraphs in advance.

In a strange way this exercise, far from being one in parody, is advanced as a sort of policy in contemporary classrooms. Political newspeak is—if not taught—at least regularly conveyed. A recent national Commission of English, established by the College Entrance Board, reported: "*Macbeth* vies with the writing of thank-you notes for time in the curriculum, and lessons on telephoning with instruction in the processes of argument."[26]

[26]*Quis custodiet custodies?* Compare the following jargon: "The director of a modern math program in one large school system says that while his advanced students' mathematical reasoning ability soars as they become seduced by the system's computer facilities, their verbal and socio-emotional development often suffers as more and more energy is poured into a limited area" (Douglas H. Heath, "Do 'Modern' School Curriculums Help Students Mature?" *College Board Review*, no. 58 [Winter 1965–66], p. 23).

And why not? To paraphrase the classics in the manner of the Everyday English series put out by the Coles Publishing Co., of Toronto, is usefully to introduce the student to . . . everyday English. To turn Hamlet's summary of the supernatural into "The universe, Horatio, contains many wonders that the science you are addicted to has never even imagined as yet" is to prepare a pupil well for political prevarication. He will be able to behave in a bank. Or a Congress, a House of Commons. How recognizable today is Hamlet's ejaculation during the play within the play, "And for whose sake? Hecuba's! What special relationship do they bear to each other that her sorrows move him to tears?" Everywhere the tedious original has been conflated into useful Eisenhowerese,[27] Hamlet's famous reflection on suicide becoming "Shall I continue to live or not? This is the momentous question I am called upon to make." Here Hamlet remains faithful to officialese to the end, "The rest is silence" being turned into "Death now closes my utterance."[28] *Tradutto o tradotto?* So long, sweet elected official.

It has been said that it is this assault on the charter of language itself that is sickening our young, and inducing cynicism toward verbal communication altogether. The *war for peace,* headlines like "PEACE SCARE SHAKES WALL STREET!" and "PEACE RUMOR SENDS STOCKS INTO TAILSPIN!"[29]—these are the verbal symptoms of a sick, or very tired, civilization, one that can boast the coinage *overkill* (or McNamara's *overdestroy*).

The speech figure represented by such terms is an oxymoron, combining contradictory referents, e.g. *darkness visible* (Milton), *noiseless noise* (Keats), *colossal wreck* (Shelley). Something like

[27]The Ghost's speech in *Hamlet,* I, v, is Eisenhowered to the following: "Were it not that I am compelled to remain silent concerning the nature of my place of correction, I could give an account, the most trifling detail of which would acutely distress your mind, congeal your youthful blood, cause your organs of vision to shoot wildly from their orbits, and each individual hair of your matted and tangled ringlets to spring up and remain erect, as the spikes of the porcupine do when that animal is irritated."

[28]This is arguably further from the sense of the original than translations in other tongues, e.g. the German *"es ist vorbei"* (Wieland), *"das übrige ist Stillschweigen"* (Eschenburg), *"der Rest ist Schweigen"* (Schlegel). In the classic-comic *Hamlet* the prince meets his death as follows:
"Alas! I have been poisoned
And now I, too, go
To join my deceased father!
I, too—I . . . AGGGRRRAA!"

[29]Both headlines appeared in recent New York newspapers. An April 1962 *New York Times* headline ran: "WELFARE STATE TERMED A

pianoforte is a single-word oxymoron. So we have had the *clean bomb,* or *light casualties,* or *safe accidents* (in an investigation into auto safety). *A Book for the Few—New Large Printing* was similarly oxymoronic, as was the ad *Assemble Your Own Antiques,* and the Welcome Bureau at Orly was taken to task for just such self-canceling nomenclature. Sartre's *Bouville* (mud city) in *La Nausée* was an apt oxymoron for his purposes in that book, and a recent article in *The New Leader* (where else?) by Michigan State Professor Wesley Fishel startled some with its ringing title—"Vietnam's Democratic One-Man Rule."

But the habit is truly semantic, and not confined to short groups of words. It is a matter of mind. If you spell it backwards, it spells Nature's. LBJ's tail-clutching announcement "We will continue fighting in Vietnam until the violence stops" is a thoroughgoing oxymoron, and makes about as much sense as the Greek Prime Minister's remark in July 1967—"With a free Press," said Mr. C. Kollias, "newspapers which printed the truth would not be interfered with, while those who printed lies would be put in prison." It is interesting that when Shakespeare used a hyperbolic oxymoron like *overkill* it was usually in the technique of Longinus, and given to characters who, if not actually insane, were at least pushed to the stage of neurotics by emotional situations—Hamlet's speech in Ophelia's grave, or Othello's longing to have Cassio "nine years a-killing" (*overkill*). In a 1966 New York City ballot *yes* was deformed to mean its opposite *no,* when voters had to vote *yes* if they were against civilian review boards for the police, and *no* if they wanted to express, "Yes, we'd like them."

Paul Goodman has called the student generation the new power elite. Students in college certainly form the most critical subculture in America today. The median age of an American as I write is 27.7, and growing younger; it is said that half of all speakers of American English are now adolescents (thus fulfilling the Sonny & Cher prophecy in *The Beat Goes On,* "Teenybopper is our

---

THREAT / N.A.M. Head Calls for Action to Halt Bit-by-Bit Gains." Early in 1966 a leading stock analyst was quoted by the New York *Herald Tribune* as saying: "Of course, if there were a sudden surprise settlement in Asia, we could have a pretty sharp shakeout. I think it would be a very short one, but it could hurt." I am personally well aware that peace or peace moves can also send the stock market *up,* but the fact that such headlines can be so complacently written, and such analyses made, at all, seems an undeniable indictment of our times.

new-born king, uh-huh"). However shaky, Margaret Schlauch's theory of the growth of language paralleling the psychic development of the individual suggests that the adolescent and postadolescent are particularly percipient of irrational verbal habits.

This group would seem undeceived by the policing of words that proceeds in public to assure Mr. Mits his elected leaders are acting as language watchdogs. I refer to rulings by the FTC, SEC, CAB and so forth, to the so-called consent decrees against various companies (who can do little but "consent" in such cases), as well as to numerous nongovernmental organizations protecting consumers from being bilked in general. But the selection and purchase of goods, or their symbols (share certificates, trading stamps), is of another order of abstraction from the choice of a political "platform." It is a convenient safety valve for the technocracy to let its public think they are enjoying verbal hygiene via a monthly dose of *Consumer Bulletin* or, in England, *Which?* You are allowed, in short, to detect semantic legerdemain in the supermarket, in mislabeled cereal cartons and the like, but it would be an error to imagine the same level of misuse in a manufacturer's advertisement of "dynamic obsolescence" in his latest auto, and a politician's offer of the oxymoron *a peace offensive*. The disenchantment on the part of the young resulted in President Johnson's hand-wringing realization that less than half the eligible electorate under twenty-five exercise their right to vote.[30]

Writing these words, I realize I have been in America about as long as today's average student. Since I came to the country not long after doffing uniform in a world war, I tend to think of young Americans as having known only peace. Most of them have not, after all, seen bullets fired in anger. But the orientation is quite likely erroneous; the average student I am thinking of was born during the Korean *police action*, has known *cold war* all his life, plus a *selective service* (a "selection" he declines at his peril). Unlike most Europeans of his age he has heard air-raid sirens tested all his life, those banshee wailings that flash through the sensory systems of children and misalert their biochemical body timings. Indeed, so susceptible are children to such alarms that a neighborhood could recently advance in court the interruption of children's

[30]Bob Dylan had told us as much before the polls. In a particularly gravel-voiced ballad, *The Times They Are A-Changin'*, this latter-day Ezekiel warned, "O mothers and fathers throughout the land . . . your sons and your daughters are beyond your command."

44

dreams by the roar of jet liners (for linguistic mechanisms are at work asleep) in its attempt to forestall a local airport. Finally, the average student, watching a huge bomb-shelter program abused by greedy building contractors, and finding complacent ads for bomb-shelter comforts in his glossy magazines,[31] is invited to consider that an illegal war, in support (until recently) of a Premier who openly abused democratic procedures and admired Hitler, is a patriotic duty. If he fails to do so he may well find his carefully considered reluctance dubbed *draft-dodging,* and end up in the penitentiary pondering over the apparently criminal nature of critical activity itself.[32]

It means little to object that the average youth concerned was in a cradle when Senator Joseph McCarthy was orating. The semantic background in which first attempts at communication would have been made was qualified by this world, and the semantic spawning has proceeded apace, from the tactfully inconspicuous racial alteration of the disemboweled comic-book villain to the relabeling of *Jap crap* (goods made in Japan) as the prestigiously *imported.* Buz Sawyer's enemies have been conveniently "Asiatic" for many years now, and Defense Department assistance is promised to a Hollywood producer making a movie about what he calls "those dirty sons-of-bitches" in Vietnam. *Power politics* are now inevitably synonymous with dirty politics. The credibility gap widens as the incredibility crap pours in. Today's student has noted a respected historian, and ex-presidential adviser, declaring to a reporter who confronted him with an objective lie (concerning the Bay of Pigs' invasion), "Did I say that? Oh, that was the cover story." In May 1965 the same student learnt that the New York State Assembly had triumphantly defeated *ethics legislation* and was no doubt reminded in this month that he must not cheat on examinations. The semantic sophistry is such that he must wonder why, as they say, people tell lies when the truth is so misleading.

A plural society puts high premium on words. Margaret Mead has told us that we Americans have substituted anthropology for

[31]"BOMB SHELTER CANDLE—Burns 4 Days—Contains Air Freshener—Deodorant—$2.50 each, 2 for $4.90 ppd. SHELTER SPECIFICATIONS REQUIRE CANDLES—Satisfaction guaranteed" (advertisement from Jack and Jane Hicks, Southern Pines, N.C.). One wonders whether Jack 'n' Jane will be around to make good the guarantee, should the deodorant fail.

[32]In 1966—not 1866—a nine-man Iowa Supreme Court refused to award custody of a son to a father on the grounds that the latter was "unconventional, arty, Bohemian."

history.[33] Lacking a "depth" relationship to culture, the legality of our existence in America is often heavily verbal. Particularly is this true of recent immigrants like myself. Art, which is symbolic, seems to serve the semantic consciousness less in what Mead terms "the most crucial period since, perhaps, the discovery of fire," while religion often fails to function against a plural attitude that includes tolerance as a social specific.[34] The pressure is then strong, when reality becomes unbearable ("indefensible"), to try to change reality by changing words.

Euphemism, as I shall suggest in a later chapter, has its place in hospital procedures and suchlike, where meliorative terms (e.g. *tumor*) have been found actually to assist someone afflicted with *cancer*. A *fix* is said sometimes to be rephrased as an *inoculation*. Today we have become the patients in the hospital. When the word *napalm* was first coined, it was a technological neologism drawn from naphthenic and palmitic acids. But it soon became so closely attached to the dreadful reality it was that a new word was introduced, to anesthetize the reality or, as Orwell had it, to defend the indefensible—*incendigel;* South Vietnamese newspapers were instructed to use this word. To the Asiatic peasant anointed with one or the other such subtleties must seem the luxuries of a very rich and a very callous society indeed—he has still been burnt raw by gelled gasoline fluid. When Morihiro Matsuda, a Japanese businessman leading a one-man peace campaign, placed an ad in *The Times* (London) we were told: "Some of the language was also delicately altered to suit the style of *The Times*. There were some refinements in translation too: 'poison gas' became 'herbicide'. . . ." Just as white phosphorus incendiaries are now cosily rechristened Willie Peters. In such cases, as Humpty Dumpty told Alice, it is not a matter of language; it is a matter of who is to be master, that's all.

Bad words break no bones. We may not be hurt physically but we are hurt mentally when language is defiled to the point of having to say the unsayable. "New experiments in escalation are first denied," writes Arthur Schlesinger, Jr., "then disowned, then discounted and finally undertaken."[35] Art Buchwald's parodies of such

[33]Henry Brandon, "Who Are The Americans? A Conversation with Margaret Mead," *The Sunday Times,* May 18, 1958, p. 23.

[34]See my article "The Classroom as Pulpit," *ETC.,* xx:2 (July 1963), pp. 171–180.

[35]Arthur Schlesinger, Jr., "A Middle Way Out of Vietnam," *New York Times Magazine,* September 18, 1966, p. 47.

doubletalk are enacted before they are written.[36] We bomb for peace because "Our honor is at stake." Inevitably one is reminded of Dickens' Hannibal Chollop, killing for freedom.

Closer home, the observation is made in a book on the Hiss-Chambers confrontation that the more the latter admitted perjury the more credence was given to his evidence (the Nixon and Charles Van Doren confessions in public come equally to mind). Thanh Lang tells us that the Vietnamese word for propaganda, *puin jen,* is now wholly equivalent with the word for a *lie.* Of course, *propaganda* is similarly poisoned in our own tongue, but it is hard to resist Thanh Lang's contention that the symbolic bond is ridiculed to the point of destruction when used to deceive in the manner of modern advertising, rather than to assist man to survive. "Twenty years worth of Americans were taught that to lie was the highest morality," wrote Andrew Kopkind in *The New Statesman* for February 24, 1967. It may be a histrionic exaggeration to say that they were *taught* to lie, but it is almost certainly the case that they have been made suspicious of all words altogether, turning with a shrug to drugs or Zen or the vogue for McLuhan or even the center spread of *Playboy;* sex as bait, license as lure, have been traditional come-ons of dictatorial societies, Thomas Mann's "magician" parody of Fascist Italy holding the liqueur glass in one hand as well as the whip in the other. You are not going to defeat the Great Society by indulgence; you are far more likely to do so by abstinence. Student groups of opposing persuasions concerning the war in Vietnam have *fasted* for peace but (we note) *feasted* for victory. Toward the end of 1967 a Senator remarked that the reputation of the Congress had never stood so low. "Most of us are under suspicion," was how he put it. For today's youth our politicians have turned into what Twain called them, "a distinctly native American criminal class."

[36]"Every time we fire our flamethrowers," says a mythical Art Buchwald Sergeant, "we are renewing our pledge to fight oppression, poverty, and disease in Southeast Asia" (New York *Herald Tribune,* February 22, 1966). Less moderate remarks were made on the Senate floor at the same time. Compare the following, from an "open letter" to President Johnson from US author Richard Tregaskis: "There is a problem of demonstrating the reality of our power to all of Asia. My view is that one or two hydrogen bombs can do the job with the least risk of life to our forces and the maximum effect on our future in Asia. . . . I propose it as establishing maximum effect and gaining great respect for the United States, to end the war and demonstrate not only our great strength but our respect for human rights" (New York *Herald Tribune,* August 31, 1966).

Yet this is not the worst. The way in which we have allowed ourselves to handle the terminology of extermination, to put the indefensible into images, is possibly the most telling temperature chart of our times. After all, this average student I am positing grew up alongside a book called *On Thermonuclear War,* by Herman Kahn, in which occurs the now celebrated assertion—so celebrated we seem to have lost all shock of it—that to cede sixty million American lives in an initial thermonuclear attack would be a perfectly assimilable figure. "Radioactivity would damage American genes, and genetic damage might continue for up to forty generations," the author confesses, but he assures us in the same breath that this would still be a long cry from *annihilation.*

This whole book seemed pure self-parody, as if written on the side by Terry Southern or Joseph Heller. It made Bob Dylan's jeremiads (as in *On the Eve of Destruction*) sound mild by comparison, and it stretched a word like *defense* to denote the destruction of a third of the national soul. Yet the author of this work not only pretends to sanity, he has advised Air Force Generals and the top brass of the Pentagon (though lately General Ridgway has mildly protested that ownership of an Asiatic cemetery might not quite constitute *victory*). So language is wrenched off reality, in the way some cruel parent might prize off the grasping fingers of a child, and insult is added to injury when this is done in the interests of "looking facts in the face."

The coining of new terms, new words, does not mean increased understanding. The increase of literacy meant a reduction of literature, as Mrs. Leavis has shown us, and the spurious "enlarging" of our vocabulary goes hand in hand with a decline in communicative ability.[37] The word-store is said to be rising—the tongue is the most mobile structure in the human body—and the dictionaries duly fatten. But the daily logorrhea which perplexes Mr. Mits shows a depressingly low level of individuation. There are about 600,000 words in the English language, yet the perennial word-counts, by Thorndike, Lorge, Fairbanks, Mann, Witty/Fry and other expert testers, show that we use fewer and fewer of them. In a study of telephone conversations, published in the *Bell System Technical*

[37]Such was the subject of the Fourth Visual Communications Conference of the Art Directors Club of New York (see "Symbology," in *The Use of Symbols in Visual Communications,* ed. Elwood Whitney, New York: Hastings House, 1960).

Journal, the 100 most frequently employed words comprised 75 percent of the whole sample. And in case this instance might be thought artificial, another test, not concerned with telephone usage, showed as few as ten different words comprising 25 percent of a total of 67,200 words employed.

The thickening of Webster is made up largely of graftings from specialist vocabularies. It is technology admiring itself in a mirror. Language communication is always hurt when words multiply at the same time that connotations retract. We now have *napalm* and *incendigel*—there is even a further coining that may or may not last —and will soon lose our semantic index. But language is a Janus and will revenge itself on those who abuse it. The way a society tells its lies is highly indicative. In the spirit of semantic despair the layman exceeds the scientist. The contemporary intellectual ends up like a child watching a Punch and Judy show; he has seen it all before but is condemned to go on shouting his warnings to whoever is next to be hit on the head. Writers (like Norman Mailer and Arthur Miller) figured among the first critics of the Johnson Administration perhaps because the artist quickly sniffs out chaos behind apparent order.

Nature follows art. We live *Dr. Strangelove* a few years after it has tumbled us in the aisles as a preposterous parody. The most grotesque caricatures of technology, imagined as a libertarian warning by H. G. Wells in the nineties, have long since come to pass (while Evelyn Waugh's *Black Mischief* was pale "black humor" beside the facts of Tschombe's kidnap in 1967). The Trobriand magician's spells contained the future. Pentagonese redesignates an *atomic bomb* a *nuclear device* not in our interest, but against it. In 1962 the New York University semanticist Neil Postman invented a parodistic list of this semantics of extermination, suggesting that to make things more painless all round we use words like *anthromeg* for every million killed by nuclear blast, *filteration* for radiation, *thermalicide* for death by nuclear weapon, and so forth. But by now Washington has improved on Postman's dreadful glossary, and in 1966 an Oakland student paraded with a placard demanding the outlawing of such terms as *defoliation* and *megadeaths*.[38]

It was, of course, against semantic insanity itself that the student

[38]See Lieutenant-General E.L.M. Burns, D.S.O., *Mega-Murder*, London: Harrap, 1966.

was protesting, against language forced to say the unsayable, and a human bond distorted to the nausea of an Antoine Roquentin. For Sartre's book anticipated the inverted symbolic relationships toward which urban man is moving ever faster ("All they have ever seen is trained water running from taps, light which fills bulbs when you turn on the switch . . . lead melts at 335 degrees centigrade"). Hiroshima disproved the reliability of these laws and thus was nightmare incarnate.

There is a parable of this playback effect in Hollywood at night: here, along the segment of Sunset Boulevard known as Sunset Strip, there is so much light at night, from floodlit façades and driveways, not to mention swimming pools and patios, with the further illumination of cars with serial-flashing rear lights and trucks lit as for some Christmas on the freeways, that it is night itself which seems artificial. (In fact, the new "Vita-Lite" lamp, introduced by the Duro-Test Corporation, offers us permanent daylight in our cities.) At the last New York World's Fair I saw a frontage that lit up each time an American was born (Equitable Life Assurance). It too appeared self-parody—you could as well claim that the bulb was lit and the next American born thereafter. "KILL A COMMIE FOR CHRIST" was originally the injunction of a parody button, presumably worn by readers of *The Realist* and the like; it backfired into reality when groups of superpatriots carried just such placards in all solemnity behind effigies of the Virgin in a New York march to support the war in Vietnam in 1967. One wonders if the same fate may be reserved for *Kill for Peace*, the parodistic national anthem of The Fugs ("Strafe them creeps in the rice paddy, daddy").

It is a matter of sanity. Orwell was right. The language of contemporary politics is that of robots. (Reciprocally, Lévi-Strauss shows us the astonishing sophistication of the "savage" mind which particularizes constantly.) Used as they have been recently, words like *democracy* and *freedom* end up as no more or less significant than so many street cries—it was Joyce's Dedalus who called God "A shout in the street." Man then has no being beyond that of phenomenon. We shall see Heidegger's First Law demonstrated by the French New Novel, which derives considerably from *La Nausée*. Lest we dismiss such madness of method in our technology as another artistic exaggeration, we should remember that official report, cited in Robert and Leona Train Rienow's *Moment in the Sun*, recently discarding the calculation of population density based on people per square mile in favor of automobiles ("The crucial figure for United States planning is now density of cars"). Two out of three persons now live in the 219 metropolitan areas in the United States. If people are reduced to things, things become people: "My rifle without me is useless. Without my rifle I am useless. . . . My rifle is human, even as I. . ."[39] Such is not drawn from a parody by Robbe-Grillet, but from a current Marine handbook. MANIAC is an acronym for a weather-computing device—Mathematical Analyzer, Numerical Integrator And Computer—perfected by Dr. John von Neumann. Since official obfuscation by acronym is another prevalent form of nontalk, we might pause briefly to consider it here.

Initially Speaking

Abbreviation appears to simplify meaning. There has surely never been such a sprouting of initials in officialese shorthand as recently. It is another symptomatic distortion, or retreat into nowords.

An acronym is a language playback. You abbreviate to RADAR, find the letter sequence pronounceable, and give *radar* back to the language as a word. Few who use it today could recover the series for which it stood—*radio detecting and ranging*. In *The Making of English* Henry Bradley tells us this appears most frequently with Latin phrases, and certainly a Latinate or Greek shadow is popular in political coverups. There are today, of course, fake acronyms, like the pseudoinitials of a militant Negro movement, ACT, which looks like an abbreviation but is no more than a word (except when used by a British union—Associated Cine Technicians).

Originally, official abbreviations of this nature appear to have been intended to conceal (SMERSH). The CID and CIA alike shortened Central Intelligences in this manner, while the French *sigle* DST hid the Direction et Surveillance du Territoire, a counterespionage agency.[40] But mystery is drained out of such robotese when acronyms are stretched to cover several, and even rival, elements or institutions. A recent Navy mailing marked MOM was interpreted by one agency as Military Ordinary Mail and by another as Military Official Mail. There are, for instance, at present eight

[39]Parris Island (USMC) Yearbook, 1966.
[40]Formerly SDECE, and before that, as founded by the famous Colonel Passy, BCRA.

other official NASA's beyond the original (National Aeronautics and Space Administration) in America. There are five or six CIA's (including the Cotton Importers Association, the Council of Islamic Affairs, and the Culinary Institute of America), while the Department of Defense's DOD can mean both *died of disease* and *direct outward dialing.*

Though de Gaulle sneers at NATO, SHAPE and UNO alike as "bodies known to the world by a collection of letters," the French adore acronyms and pour out baffling combinations, like BIEM, ONERA, and SMIG (Salaire Minimum Interprofessional Garanti). In France PC (pay-say) can indicate *Parti Communiste, Poste de Commandement,* or *Permis de Conduire* (driving license). International exchange of acronyms thus fogs things up even more: the sturdy German MAN (Maschinenfabrik Augsburg-Nürnberg AG) sounds well in England, but would misfire in France. Russia is the USSR in England and America, the URSS in France, where ONU stands for our UN and our NATO is, or was, their OTAN. The USA becomes the EU which until 1968 could be used on or near the plates of certain cars in France to designate *Europe.* England's FBI was for long the Federation of British Industries.

As I write, UNITAR (United Nations Training and Research Institute), in co-operation with UNESCO (United Nations Educational, Scientific and Cultural Organization) and ECOSOC (Economic and Social Council), is preparing an international dictionary of acronyms. What wasted effort. For, once again, derivation is an untrustworthy source of understanding. A new word can be illuminated by knowing how it came into being. *Jeep* is a free morpheme taken off the instrument panel of that vehicle, designating it as GP, or general purpose. But a jeep is not a general purpose. *Seabees* were originally CB's, members of Construction Battalions in the Pacific War; in the British Army "He is seabee for two weeks" meant Confined to Barracks for two weeks. On the old P & O (acronym! acronym!) liners, plying from England to the East, the most desired cabin space was Port Out Starboard Home; one theory has it that this gave rise to the British non-U[41] term *posh.* Dozens of ori-

---

[41]"Throughout, I should like to borrow the abbreviations *U* and *non-U* for British *upper-class* and *non-upper-class* speakers from Alan S. C. Ross, whose essay "Linguistic Class-Indicators in Present-day English" first appeared in the Finnish philological journal *Neuphilologische Mitteilungen* (Helsinki, 1954). That Professor Ross' deftly satirical essay in sociological linguistics gave rise to some inconsequential journalism by Nancy Mitford, and others, does not

gins are given for O.K., or *okay*, ranging from Choctaw *hoke* (It is so) to *Old Kinderhook* (headquarter town of the party of the eighth President of the United States, Martin Van Buren).[42]

I sense that officialdom finds a nice solid acronym confidence-inspiring. As the abbreviation forms another word, you get a *calembour* of a new kind, an ambiguity beyond William Empson's many types, and thus turn into a Pentagon poet. It is, in fact, a sort of lipogram you are constructing, a poem written without certain letters. The World Health Organization simplifies to WHO, the Institute of Radio Engineers to IRE, the Federated Associations for Impartial Review to FAIR. We see also SANE, and HOPE, and AID, and MANA, and TEAM (a computerized dating service). One particularly successful example was, perhaps, SCUM—to represent the feminist Society for Cutting Up Men ("to eliminate through sabotage all aspects of society that are not relevant to women"). One Argentine rugby team decided, in 1967, to cease identifying itself by its club's initials—CUBA (Club Universitario Buenos Aires), while it could be argued that special numberplates are of this order, Elizabeth Taylor using, as Mrs. Mike Todd, ETT 1 and British sex-kitten Sabrina using S41 (her bust measurement at the time). One brassiere manufacturer employed BRA (which only means good in Swedish) and a Blackpool tycoon devised XTC for Ecstasy.

During the last war English servicewomen entering a branch of the Army were known as ATS (Auxiliary Territorial Service—now Women's Royal Army Corps, or WRACS). It seemed that there was always something more appealing, however, in being a WREN, as a member of the Women's Royal Naval Service was known, since this formed another word. One of my sisters served in the so-called Fannies, from FANY (First Aid Nursing Yeomanry); it was not until Americans came over that this acronym be-

---

matter; as the philosopher Max Black puts it, "He can claim to have added the expression 'non-U' to the English language as now spoken." In actual fact, *posh* is one of those originally non-U euphemisms which get used in a kind of U slang.

[42]H. L. Mencken, in *The American Language,* and Thomas Pyles, in *Words and Ways of American English,* both summarize the numerous theories for the origin of O.K., and the latter its ready exportation; that indefatigable lexicographer Allen Walker Read, of Columbia, would seem to have competently established the *Old Kinderhook* origin—Van Buren was called the Kinderhook Fox by his enemies—in an article contributed to the *Saturday Review of Literature* of July 19, 1941.

came a pun, but the one it then produced was fairly catastrophic since US fanny is the derriere and GI Joe could watch her beam with delight, the cut of the uniform distinctly emphasizing what a Shakespearean character forever euphemized as the "afternoon" of the body.

"Look Out, Kid!"

It's time you did, as the folk poet tells us. "You're going to get hit." For the crime of political language today is its dissociation of personality, and it is one repeatedly forgiven by technology. The Donald Duck stories have continued from generation to generation, but today technology replaces the "real" magic of old. No longer do the Ducks fly round the world on their magic carpets but (like us) they travel on Uncle Scrooge's airline—to titanium mines. The incredible machines are found to be invented by Gyro Gearloose; logic shuts off fantasy.

The parable is what the French might call *exact*. Wonders must be the wonders of technology, and one had but to stand in the shuffling lines of nuns and teen-agers outside the Dupont or Johnson Wax pavilions at the last World's Fair to know just how "scientific" everyone is, how free will has been intimidated by our inexorable partiality for disillusion. We are all scientific, of course, as we are all contemporary. Literature is being rewritten as pseudoscience; and, as a Spanish critic put it, you could write *Don Quixote* word for word today, but it would be a very different work from the original.

As the semantics of extermination proceeds, a voice from above asks, "Why bother with words at all?" All that is needed for our purposes is the "apparent," the verifiable. Or what Orwell proposed as the language of dummies—the untranslatable because indefensible. A world of things exculpates man from being human, and we shall soon all be able to talk like Herman Kahn. As in Faulkner's *The Sound and the Fury,* as in Sartre's *La Nausée,* as in Robbe-Grillet's "fiction," time is dislocated only by space, and shapes assume their own meanings, and identities.

Yet we can still observe that the deuteragonists of these tragedies set in some permanent present are all psychotic, or—at best—deeply disturbed. Sartre's Roquentin, so often misunderstood, may reject history but he pleads at the end for a universe with meaning, i.e. *with a future.*

Language offers this future. Without language man is *de trop* at last. Such is the nature of our nightmare. In a sense it is to be destroyed by language, like Cocteau's hero, Orphée. Teachers like Socrates and Gotama and Jesus preached a proper use of words because they respected the harmony resident within language itself. This harmony predicates a faith in the human and was described many years ago by an authority on American-Indian languages, Edward Sapir, who stated categorically, "No tribe has ever been found which is without language, and all statements to the contrary may be dismissed as mere folklore." It insists that language uncovers meaning for us.[43]

This ability is denied by the political language system, in which Peirce's idea of the expansive power of translation is quite negated. According to recent tests on the interpretation of expository language, the power of this babble appears to be powerful magic indeed. Those who do best on such tests are mostly the young and the very old, and occasional special classes like lawyers. One of E. M. Forster's wisest old ladies, Miss Raby of "The Eternal Moment," speaks "what was true rather than what was intelligible." Miss

[43]"If a man who has never seen more than a single elephant in the course of his life, nevertheless speaks without the slightest hesitation of ten elephants or a million elephants or a herd of elephants or of elephants walking two by two or three by three or of generations of elephants, it is obvious that language has the power to analyze experience into theoretically dissociable elements and to create that world of the potential intergrading with the actual which enables human beings to transcend the immediately given in their individual experiences and to join in a larger common understanding."
This whale (or elephant) of a sentence is, like my other quotation from Edward Sapir in this paragraph, drawn from his *Culture, Language and Personality* (Berkeley and Los Angeles: University of California Press, 1961). Identical principles can be found in his *Language: An Introduction to the Study of Speech* (New York: Harcourt, Brace, 1921, renewed 1949). In the sentence I have footnoted here Sapir supports the principle mentioned in my Introduction: words, or art forms, can give us a more real reality than "reality." I have only seen about one nightingale in my life, so that "my" nightingale is really something for which Keats is responsible, not me. A young person can sometimes test this by asking himself how well he "knows" a favorite sports player: is it not often through reading and hearing about him, rather than through seeing him a couple of times from a badly placed stadium seat? We are back here at Bousquet's kiss. The same young person might ask himself what semantic refraction exists between seeing the favorite ball player in the flesh and seeing him on the TV screen. As regards plastic art, the theory of *"virtual* space" which Susanne Langer drives through her *Problems of Art* could be set in sympathetic opposition to many of Sapir's principles of language. "The arts objectify subjective reality," writes Miss Langer here, "and subjectify outward experience of nature."

Raby's *rather than* gives hope, as do, perhaps, certain student attitudes today. In his famous *Subterranean Homesick Blues* Bob Dylan exhorts the contemporary teener everywhere to beware—"Look out, kid!" This being on guard is being a semanticist ("You don't need a Weather Man to know the way the wind blows"). Without such repudiations of the treachery done our tongue in recent times we might well be on the way to refuting Sapir and becoming the first wordless tribe.

TWO

There was speech in their dumbness, language in their very gesture.

Shakespeare, *Winter's Tale*

INSTEAD OF A SONATA:
THE SOUNDS OF SILENCE

Words Don't Fail Me

When I was a small boy, a man with a beard used to give me sixpence if I could sit still without saying a word for five minutes. I fear that my grandfather knew he was not buying silence so much as suspended sound. Such is what silence is for the human being, a moment of inarticulation before language through which conceptual activity flows. As such, it should be considered here since it generates problems of "apparent" language. To borrow from Susanne Langer: To a dog a wet street is a street with water on it. To a human being it may be one of many things, a street on which rain has fallen, over which a sprinkler van has passed, onto which a water main has burst.

For us silence must be discursive. When John Cage first sat at a piano and "produced" several minutes of silence instead of a sonata, he can scarcely have surprised semanticists. "For each correct pause has in it the power to stimulate the spectator's attention and compel him to be more alert than he already is."[1] Such a pause prepares an audience for action, and ensuing verbalization. "What's this sudden silence," asks an early Musil character, "that's like a language we can't hear?"[2]

[1]Michael Chekhov, *To the Actor: On the Technique of Acting,* New York: Harper & Row, 1953, p. 97. Cage's "revolt" was paralleled in painting by the revolting Yves Klein, who staged an exhibition with no pictures hung. When forbidden to disseminate "literature" by the police, the Amsterdam *Provos* handed out blank sheets of paper. "Despairing literature," wrote Albert Camus, "is a contradiction in terms."

[2]Robert Musil, *Young Törless,* trans. Eithne Wilkins and Ernst Kaiser, New York: Noonday Press, 1958, p. 26.

In the text of most plays, then, silence is indicated in this way—
Pause. Today the dramatic situation for most of us is that of the
contemporary city, in which sounds are insistently continuous;
within this drama a pause is a communication with the future. It
would be tempting to link with this principle that of Western theol-
ogy, which makes life without death meaningless and asks us to
consider our passage on earth as a little pause, before eternity. It
would be equally tempting to discuss related problems of language
philosophy, examined by Russell and Whitehead. Is a poem that
exists only in your head a poem? Is an unobserved and unobservable underwater color scheme in permanent darkness a great work
of art?[3] Suffice it to say here that in the area of prelanguage which
I am considering at this point silence plays its part. As far as language can be "opaque," this area is so; if not understood for what
it is, it is misunderstood.

Today the study of silence is made under the term *nonverbal
communication*. Therapists find they need a third ear for silence.
Books on nonverbal communication, in truth a form of pointing, do
much of their work by photographs.[4] In the telephone we can see
some elements of what is meant by silence as prespeech.

The telephone exists by virtue of its action as a means of communication. That its silences are artificial, or pseudospeech, can be
seen in Browning's monodramas, which may be read as one-ended
telephone conversations in advance. In such poems Browning liked
to involve a speaker with a listener, and sometimes with listeners
(the party line, perhaps?): a Duke addresses an emissary, a painter
his wife, a Bishop his sons ("nephews"); and a homicidal maniac,

[3]For a convincing challenge to the well-known Crocean position in this
regard, see "Form and Being," Section 3 of Chapter iv of Etienne Gilson's
Painting and Reality (Cleveland and New York: Meridian Books, 1961); e.g.
the discussion of Delacroix's esthetics—"There is no other criterion of success
or failure in the art of painting than this golden rule: a painting is good when
it actually exists as the fully constituted being that art can make it; inversely,
a painting is bad when it fails to achieve actual existence as a fully constituted
being" (pp. 134–135).

[4]E.g. Weldon Kees and Jurgen Ruesch, *Nonverbal Communication,* Berkeley: University of California Press, 1956.

Experts in speech disturbances (one to commit that ultimate summary of
his subject, namely suicide), Kees and Ruesch suggested three categories of
the nonverbal: *object language* (including the display of material goods, etc.,
which I develop in this chapter); *action language* (all movements not used
exclusively as signals); and *sign language* (the supplanting of numbers, punctuation and so forth by gestures). Their system can be tried on tomorrow's
fellow bus or subway rider. It can even be tried on oneself.

the killer of an oversexed girl, talks to his most enchanted listener, himself. The word creates its world since all speakers show the intensity which exists directly you remove yourself from the harmony of reciprocal or social discourse.

You cannot speak "freely" on the telephone since, for one thing, you cannot count on silence being assent (this very semantic brings into being overhearing devices). As a matter of fact, for Browning's famous Bishop silence was evidently dissent. Moreover, like a Browning soliloquist, you tend to use the telephone when you think you have something to gain by speaking. Bell Telephone's Communication Consultants trade on this artificiality by suggesting that if you buy a better telephone, or telephonic system, you will communicate better.[5] A glance at teeners crawling up the sides of pay phones belies this belief: the glued sightless eyes, and twisted body, and shoved-off sneakers as they aim down the mouthpiece show how dissatisfied with one-ended speech such communicants can be.

It follows that a great deal of instruction in nonverbal techniques turns out to be little more than guidance in etiquette. A number of brochures annually cross my overburdened desk, touting the magic of this or that course in prelanguage.[6] A lot of these relate to "group dynamics," the study of "unstructured situations" in which a number of bodies gather to form a group, with the handling of cigarettes and so forth indicating feelings.[7] A cocktail party is a typical "unstructured situation." A classroom is strongly "structured."

A visit to one or another of these courses proves disappointing, if not actually preposterous, and often reminiscent of the kind of practical guidance (about posture and such like) for secretaries that sent Helen Gurley Brown laughing to the bank. Hawaiian girls

[5]"MR. NO is frustrated. Sales are down. Profits are suffering. 'New Business is tough to get these days,' says he. 'So we'll have to cut costs to the bone—even things that have been a necessary part of the business for years.'

"MR. GO has profit problems, too. But says he: 'We have to *go after* new business. We must use more Long Distance calls between sales visits. That way, we'll make more contacts, be Johnny-on-the-spot, keep ahead of competition!' " (Bell Telephone System ad).

The medium is the message?

[6]Thus a "ten-week course" in "DEVELOPING NON-VERBAL AWARE-NESS" with Charlotte Read promises: "We will endeavor to become more aware of non-verbal, 'physical,' organismic . . ." etc.

[7]See the description of "T" or "D" groups in the manuals for dynamics of participation groups put out by the National Training Laboratory of Group Research.

did not originally have to be taught the hula, any more than a Victorian miss had to be informed that the flutter of an eyelash carried a narrative to the other sex. Painstaking manuals informing the office force of America that a tight skirt is a come-on, or exposure of erogenous areas titillative, obviously miss the point by being obvious. (None I have seen, incidentally, mentions that a split skirt invites a ripping-off fantasy.) The saddest story is that such schools have now started in France, home of woman's *je ne sais quoi*. In 1966 Tessa Beaumont, a former Opéra dancer, decided that the French woman had had all her celebrated mystery citified out of her and opened a seminary for gesture instruction, and general femininity, in Paris.

Converted into a pedantry, this sort of thing can become silly enough. It has been claimed by a practicing psychiatrist, allegedly in his senses, that when a woman squirms on a seat (except, presumably, when sliding into a sun-baked sports car) she is showing her "availability" and *at the same time* "anal regression." Wow! This is as bad as Chinese propaganda pictures showing tiny tots all "bursting with health and testifying to a new young life which, with clenched fists, affirms itself. . . ." All babies clench their fists at a certain age, whether anticipating a glorious socialist future or being ground under by capitalist exploitation. Too, there is an entire vocabulary of conventionalized gesture in dance to take into account.[8] By giving Mary Quant the OBE, the Queen of England decorated the miniskirt and its implications.

All this is to say no more than that it is at times ecologically necessary to communicate without words. Biotelemetry is telling us more and more about our bodily meshing with diurnal and lunar rhythms, and of our resultant phases of effort and moods. A slap on the back in congratulation, a mother's frown of disapproval, the shake of a hand,[9] such are often the most genuine coin of our emotions in symbol-ridden cities. A squeeze of commiseration to one bereaved says far more than a spoken "I'm sorry." A man describing his prize catch of fish needs his arms.

The grammar of this kind of "apparent" language can be observed in dozens of different forms daily. It is not a failure of "trans-

[8]For the esthetics of dance as an encounter, see Maxine Sheets, *The Phenomenology of Dance,* Madison, Wisc.: University of Wisconsin Press, 1966.

[9]A 1967 poll showed that 23 percent of all German adults are against handshaking as a form of greeting.

parent" language. To look on it as such seems to me an inexcusable clerkly treason; it is to confuse disparate mental functions and, in doing so, ultimately to deny the poetry of our human structure, ultimately to consort with that curious preference for the mechanical, statistical, and material which is the most favorably regarded egoism of our days. Better to keep one's mouth shut and appear a fool, as the saying goes, than open it and remove all doubt. At which point one can appropriately consider the hypomania of Herbert Marshall McLuhan and his followers, whose huge elation is but the pathological inverse of man's distress at being made into a mechanism.

On Misunderstanding Media: Obscurity as Authority

To attach significance to the clarion call from Canada that "the medium is the message" we must surely be given something more than this worn cliché. It is, at first glance, simply to restate that style is vision, that man evolves new forms in answer to the non-animal stresses of his environment. The so-called problems introduced by new media are almost wholly contained in word-wisdom, as is annually testified by those pointless meetings during which writers discuss the implications of TV or radio (nearly all ending up in matters of marketing). If we have evolved color and closed-circuit TV, and visual telephones, our recognition of reality was such as to demand them, not vice versa. They are an answer to some disrupted cycle. The film emerges in literature before it does so on the screen, as shown by the early work of Willy Busch or "Bonaventura" 's Nachtwachen in Germany. "Even in the most explicit verbal narrative," writes Louis Salomon, "what is said is as much a function of its tone as of the incidents depicted."[10] Language is for listeners; it is an awareness from which media result.

At second glance, however, we realize with Kenneth Burke that as we follow the Toronto sage we are barely dealing with words at all, rather with matters of "terministic policy." The medium is the message or the massage, it does not matter which since the contempt for words is total; in fact, writing at what would appear to be the height of McLuhan's popularity (his theories even seeping into the Beetle Bailey comic strip), I have a feeling that the medium is also the money. As far as can be defined, all new "media"

[10]Louis B. Salomon, Semantics and Common Sense, New York: Holt, Rinehart and Winston; 1966, p. 124.

here seem axiomatically good, although, as stated by a manufacturer at Senator Long's hearings on snooping devices, human "needs" also developed wall listeners, and phone monitors, and the repulsive repertoire of bugging so dear to the FBI.

Needless to say, the world does change. Everything is not always the same. Jet travel, electric daylight, blind discourse on the telephone, all interfere with biological rhythms. We include our perceptions of such disturbances in the truth of understanding them. In general, McLuhan's work seems a largely unacknowledged application of Benjamin Lee Whorf's "metalinguistics," his contention of the need for a synthetic "grasp" echoing Whorf's theories about ideograms. In his comments on the phonetic alphabet Whorf phrased a similar dislike for any dissociation of sense and function such as we find popularized by the Canadian thinker.

There is, moreover, the matter of how much thinking is proceeding in this instance. The intrinsic contradictions of McLuhan's reasoning, or prose, have been pointed out often enough by now.[11] The reply is invariably the same: the conclusions are not meant to be such. They are, rather, so many stimulating insights. McLuhan is "probing," not "packaging." The loading of the terms is itself symptomatic: the contrary of the meliorative *probing* is not the pejorative *packaging*, and to renounce the effort of drawing conclusions is to shirk the duty of the true intellectual.

Thus McLuhan can mistake an effect for the cause of that effect, without incurring challenge—he has provoked the liaison, and is simply asking questions. It is all very convenient, and one wishes one could cop out as easily in the classroom. While it seems certain he does not, from his writings to date, understand the difference between electric and electronic (the first the grosser, power-carrying aspect of electricity, the second the finer, sensory or switching aspects involved), it is to be debated whether he, or any of his fellow Druids, knows what a medium is at all.[12]

[11]E.g. Ross Wetzsteon, "The Doubtful Necessity of Understanding McLuhan," *Village Voice,* May 12, 1966, pp. 19–21; Hugh Kenner, "Understanding McLuhan," *National Review,* XVIII:48 (November 29, 1966), pp. 1224–1225. As Kenner puts it, "everything, alas, is something else; and if content is negligible so are facts."

[12]The medium is the message—"Give your child better grades by Christmas. Start his school year off right with a Royal Galaxy portable typewriter. For typing improves grades . . . and report cards prove it. When students start typing assignments, school work (and grades) start to improve almost immediately. Educators acknowledge it. Classroom tests have proved it. But

The medium of a radio program is its "carrier" frequency, ten twenty megacycles on your friendly dial. The message is the music that is "modulated" or superimposed on the carrier. Radio theory has long stressed the distinction between medium and message, and any licensed radio operator will rhapsodize on it for hours. Mc-Luhan is here hardly revising communication theory. Similarly, if I receive a letter from my Auntie Loo, the medium is not the post-man, it is the written word. Yet it is for McLuhan, whenever it suits his purpose ("with the telegraph came the integral insistence and wholeness of Dickens," and again, "print created individualism and nationalism in the 16th. century"). If you make no difference be-tween nervous and physical functioning, you can get as glib as *Time* in no time.

Indeed, the ease with which these lucubrations about participa-tional culture were assimilated by popular journalism showed how Mr. Mits loves a pundit: also that there is nothing as infectious as lyrical enthusiasm about defeat. It was all so gloriously easy. Tech-nology was given a heart. This time the radiation was emotional: the whole "psychedelic" craze—from "psychedelic knits" to "psy-chedelic yoghourt"—was enough to alert the serious-minded to the fundamentally frivolous nature of the trend. That the world is watching television hardly means the world is right. But according to that arch-apostle of conformity, Marshall McLuhan, almost any-thing that happens *should* happen. The vices of our times were suddenly converted into virtues, our contemporary cretinism rein-terpreted and transposed into intellectual terms. Idiocy was made over into ecstasy, everything was forgiven. It was all a slap-happy ad-man's dream come true, and the Ballet Luce cheered lustily as the parade roared down Madison Avenue.

The total confusion—or, rather, that sleight-of-hand always con-sidered "scientific" in the popular mind—between chicken and egg made it possible for McLuhan to point to TV as a medium stirring participational desires in the young. In fact, any concern for in-volvement aroused by this new medium—which is not as new as all that, and was kidded in advance by Joyce—is likely to have caused a disgust with TV as yet another semantic treachery. Of course, a cause can be a previous effect. Orwell cites a man who boozes be-

for truly first-class work, a student needs a portable that's easy to type on, easy to learn on . . . a Royal Galaxy" (advertisement in the *New York Times,* April 10, 1960).

cause he thinks he is a washout, and promptly becomes a washout because he boozes. This is the familiar *post hoc* fallacy; my income goes up, I buy more stock, my income goes up. Loss of appetite increases anemia, anemia increases loss of appetite. With McLuhan the point of departure suddenly becomes the thesis proved ("With the arrival of electric technology man extended, or set outside himself, a live model of the central nervous system itself"). In this way we learn that it was really the fishes that discovered water. In truth, medium and message are here terms which can be used coterminously, interchangeably, as can McLuhan's convenient categories of "hot" and "cool." We end with another thick jeer at the compact of language, since an inherent characteristic of language is to form classes.[13]

For instance: McLuhan typically misunderstands for us the audiac, a device that allegedly deadens the pain sensors by "superstimulation" of the aural. He cites the "autoamputation" of Jonas and Selye as that device whereby, when the source of irritation cannot be located or avoided, the sensory apparatus is deadened, "amputated" so far as the central nervous system is concerned. McLuhan extends this: Under the stress of "superstimulation" the nervous system protects itself by "amputating or isolating the offending organ, sense, or function." According to this argument, then, the dentist's drill should be more, not less, painful under audiac, since the other senses are said to become more receptive after "amputation." The tautology is anticipated in McLuhan's *The Gutenberg Galaxy* (Toronto: University of Toronto Press, 1962), where we read that "no sense can function in isolation" (p. 53), but that a kind of audiac hypnosis may be produced by "the filling of the field of attention by one sense only" (p. 17). Interestingly enough, McLuhan here adduces a quotation from Edgar in *King Lear* that should tell him *the opposite* of what he gets out of it ("Why then, your other senses grow imperfect / By your eyes' anguish . . ."). There are more examples of the same confusion, but to chase a lie only gives it legs.

Perceptions must remain poor assumptions with as low a level

[13]"The tremendous practical value of language lies largely in its power of generalization, whereby the naming of any object immediately establishes the *class* of such objects. This is a very rudimentary abstractive function inherent in language as such, as Ribot observed more than fifty years ago, and as Cassirer has demonstrated in *The Philosophy of Symbolic Forms*" (Langer, *Problems of Art*, pp. 169–170).

of rationality as this, without some sense of reality, or what is plainly going on. What McLuhan is here referring to, in his characteristically cavalier fashion, is audioanalgesia, in which the sense of hearing is insulted, chiefly by "white sound" (cascading water, and the like), in order to anesthetize another sense. Audioanalgesia has, after some initial enthusiasm, largely fallen by the wayside as unworkable since, like hypnosis, it requires unusual co-operation from the patient, and since it introduces more problems than factors of advantage over routine anesthesia.

In *King Lear* Edgar feigned mad. Playing conjuring tricks with reality is, according to Lévi-Strauss, the chief vice of our intelligentsia. It is a kind of bankruptcy. Surely there is something nearly deranged about this excess of ecstasy. McLuhan emerges as a man of the study substituting metaphor for equality and mistaking abstraction for universal truth whenever he wishes, not to mention misreading literature right, left and center. He takes Buckminster Fuller's simile of tool as extension of man, with no reference I can find to the originator, and restates it as equality. Intellectual balloonism of this order funks that confrontation with reality demanded by intelligence. I have suggested that this may be the convex of despair. Unable to look the Gorgon's head of technology in the eye, such false mages hold up their distorting mirrors, reversing truth and keeping sybaritic court among the monotremata of our times. As fellow-Canadian A.J.M. Smith has it:

> McLuhan put his telescope to his ear;
> What a lovely smell, he said, we have here.[14]

Language Mix

The lure of unified perception in modern media is nothing new to semanticists. On the popular level to which it has been referred, it is another belated recognition of nonverbal needs, responses to new tempos and artificial situations, a hunger dramatized by the manner in which our arts appear temporarily to be moving back to a stage Northrop Frye has categorized as the *auto*. Whether we like it or not, we are still animal, and a number of utterances are admitted into discourse from the earliest, or most undifferentiated, stages of man. What are public holidays and manifestations like

[14]A.J.M. Smith, "The Taste of Space," in *Poems New and Collected*, New York: Oxford University Press, 1967, p. 100.

Guy Fawkes' Day, Bastille or Thanksgiving Day, but collective nonverbal exclamations? "A riot," said Dr. Martin Luther King after the Detroit violence of summer 1967, "is the language of the unheard."

Language itself testifies to these "apparent" needs. Coinings of a concertina kind pay court to such, from Lena Horne's recent *sinerama* to Peanuts' (1967) *grassture* for cows or the nicely telescopic *remiknits*—Sonny & Cher's term for Grandma's activity in the rocking chair. The Babeling of language in general, or what Germans call *Sprachverwirrung*, evidences these social strains. The fuss about *franglais* makes a case in point. I refer to Professor René Etiemble's much-discussed *Parlez-Vous Franglais?*

This was a protest against the infiltration of "classical" French by the barbarisms of *anglais*. But the originator of a criticism often fails to understand it himself. Incorporations of the type Professor Etiemble finds especially heinous, like *le babysitter, le bluejeans,*[15] *le checkup, le playboy, le mixer, le surprise party, le bulldozer, le self service, le drugstore,* are no more than admissions by the civilization involved that it was vulnerable to, or desirous of, what such words represented extensionally. They are cases of natural symbolism. To any American living in France at the time, as I was myself, it was apparent that not only was US usage almost alone being indicted—no one was coining, for instance, *ce n'est pas cricket*—but US usage of a particular type.

In a work that came out in 1929 Salvador de Madariaga suggested that international importations of this nature were keys to culture. Thus French gives Europe *cuisine* because this event seems particularly theirs. German lends us *Sehnsucht* because this quality is somehow considered native to them, and therefore untranslatable. England exports its emphasis on *gentleman, fair play* (one irony here being that *sport* is a French reborrowing, like *budget*). The explanation is satisfactory to a point; but the ease of absorption of new terms like these is usually due to an imitative venue in the culture itself. Emporia like the famous Drug West at Saint-Cloud are language surrenders, testimony to America's ability to throw up a faster-moving symbolism as self-protection for the human in an age of communication by satellite. In 1967 France had 9,957 *drug-*

---

[15]Actually, *jeans* derives from a material made in Genoa, while French complaints about *le budget* are self-reflexive; this word was given to English, out of the little wallet of money once worn, *bougette*.

stores or *libres-services* (the retranslation of *self services*) as against two in 1948. But the words came to them first, before their enactment.

Obviously words or phrases singled out for opprobrium by a verbal Customs Officer like Professor Etiemble are those indicating a new way of life, and dislocating old forms. His objections are paralleled in England. Writing on "The Americanisation of the English Language" in a recent issue of the London *Sunday Times*, Wallace Reyburn chose just such representatives of social relationships, *commuter, bobby-soxer, middlebrow* (this as British in origin as *fall* for autumn). A little research showed me that Reyburn's dislike gets phrased at least every generation in England, probably going back to Sir John Cheke, who initiated a translation of the New Testament in which only native words were to be used. A 1933 version objected to *rubberneck, lounge-lizard, stop over, racketeer.* More recently in the French press I have seen *boycottage* and *les hippies.*

Both babysitters and blue jeans filled needs in France, and *hippies* helps to express a new social relationship. New buildings at ancient universities, like Caen, Grenoble, Toulouse, now face stretches of lawn called *le campus.* As in British universities, the true tribute is to the nature of American general education taking place there. The previous vocabulary, that is, could not both express the new needs and show affection for them at the same time. The verbal Customs Inspector will no doubt go on sneering at *le campus,* but what the campus represents will go on winning.

The criticism, then, is of the importing rather than the exporting culture. *Sprachverwirrung* is naturally self-reflexive in that it is an imitation of an imitation. French incorporates *bulldozer* and *drugstore* because Frenchmen saw bulldozers flattening tracts of land for drugstores. (Someone also told them at this time that they might prevent disease by an annual *checkup.*) Yet neither Sweden nor Japan has yet brought in these terms, though much the same phenomena have been proceeding there. The difference between Holland and Belgium is acute in this case; the former linguistically declines to be a sub-America, while the latter is ecstatically becoming one. What should have worried Professor Etiemble was *franglais* for already existing phenomena (e.g. *le bestseller*); similarly, I have observed that *le bitnique* has lasted far longer in France than in America, although France knew proportionately fewer beatniks.

The situation is summarized in a survey by *L'Express:* "We are not becoming Americans. We are not remaining French. We are turning into what the French think Americans are."[16]

Lexicographic chauvinism is a symptom of decline. Who objects to *kowtow* (from China), *buckshee* (Egypt), *kiosk* (Turkey)? There is, as yet, no threat to a way of life here. What, incidentally, about the dangers of *Englitsch?* Our tongue can be seen reverting, or modifying, to German in instance after instance. Thus German has only one pronoun for English *this* and *that.* Their cognate of our *that* is *dass,* and *dass* is used relatively or conjunctively, not demonstratively. So, to say *This I like* is really substituting *this* for *that,* as well as Germanically inverting. *This I won't do.* In the same way, English *hopefully* seems used more and more as a transliteration of German *hoffentlich.* The influence on American, at least, may well be through Yiddish here, but to say *Hopefully he'll come* is for Fowler and Gowers to mean *He will come full of hope.* It is, rather, a transcription of *Hoffentlich wird er komnen.*[17]

It will be interesting to see if this conversion, from what is an adverb in German to what is a verb in English, will expand: German has *vermutlich* for *I suppose* and *bekanntlich* for *as you know.* So German here possesses a refraction between two parts of speech which cannot be followed literally in English. No good German translator would translate every *I hope* or *I suppose* or *I am afraid* by a parallel verb construction. One of these eminently useful German adverbs, like *vermutlich* or *wohl* or *gern* or *zwar* or *leider,* would be pressed into service; and the resultant sentence would be shorter and tidier than the English as a consequence. But when all is said and done I have not seen German objections to *gekidnapt, gehandicapt;* these imports should be seen on a fraternal basis.

When they are not seen as colleagues, language mix is often simply so much social pretension. This is like bringing back something that shows foreign travel, or choosing an aperitif known only in some obscure Balkan cellar. I recently amused myself by noting examples of the French *expertise* in recent literary criticism on

[16]Georges Suffert, "Devenons-Nous Américains?" *L'Express,* no. 840 (July 24–30, 1967), p. 18 (my trans.).

[17]"I am thinking of such books as Norman Mailer's *An American Dream,* Nat Hentoff's *Call the Keeper,* and Jay Neugeboren's *Big Man,* as well as (hopefully) my own *The Last Jew in America*" (Leslie Fiedler, in *Midstream,* XII:10 [December 1966], p. 22).

both sides of the Atlantic. It seemed wholly misused. In the country of its origin an *expertise* is an appraisal, or inventory—if a French insurance agent comes to assess damages, he comes *pour expertiser les dégâts*. As was shown by some particularly futile correspondence in *The Times Literary Supplement,* however, supposedly cosmopolitan literary intellectuals wanted it to mean *expertness.* Adopted journalistically at a moment of evident transition, this usage can lead to serious ambiguity, as when a *New York Times* headline referred to an overseas bridge-building project, "HIGHER OVERHEAD CANCELS ADVANTAGE IN EXPERTISE."

Here the lexical lesson is that a literary intelligentsia considers expertness especially French. The neologism will be conserved if it is useful to society at large in this sense, but neologisms of such nature seldom spring from outright misunderstanding. German *Weltschmerz* is thrown around a lot of our criticism, but it is not met by the same word in an English context. To a German reader this word has archaic and literary associations which are frequently not intended by the English user, and the well-known Melville translator, Dr. Fritz Güttinger, used *Weltschmerz* to translate *spleen.*[18] French *anticiper* is to do something ahead of time. ("Do you prevent his coming" was the rather pompous instruction of a churchwarden of my youth to a rather stupid acolyte concerning a Bishop's visit to the parish; based on the Latin *prevenire* it meant, Get there first. The choirboy thought it was an injunction to stop the dignitary's arrival by some act of sabotage, and so complained to their senior.) French *récupérer* means to retrieve, or even fetch, rather than to recuperate. There have been dictionaries of such "false friends."

Pseudointellectual attempts to appear sophisticated by use of foreign words are, of course, barely deserving of comment, except that they show some half-baked desire to expand language. Higher journalism is the abode, and often permanent left-luggage room, of such importations. What on earth Cyril Connolly meant I do not know when he wrote of William Carlos Williams' *Paterson,* "It is something one does not understand and does not get tired of because the general *matière* is so pleasing, like the brush-work of

---

[18]Dr. Güttinger justifies his choice in *Zielsprache: Theorie und Technik des Übersetzens,* Zürich: Manesse Verlag, 1963: e.g. *"Der Ausdruck 'Weltschmerz' dagegen hat für den deutschen Leser einen ähnlichen Gefühlswert wie 'spleen' für den englischen"* (p. 66).

Bonnard." In his delightful study of the technique of translation Dr. Güttinger cites a host of German words used in a few issues of *The Observer,* and all needlessly so since they are all conventionally translatable (*Hinterland, Anschauung, Anlage, Strandbad, Kulturgeschichte, Geschicklichkeit, Leitfaden*).[19] The common use of *Angst* makes a complementary case. Recent British fashion columns sometimes seem to me to have been written out of the latest issue of *East Village Other.* The short "Hers" feature of *The Observer* for July 24, 1967, for instance, contained so much US slang it was virtually incomprehensible (in a couple of columns I culled *drag, the scene, in-in people, pot, freak-out,* and *psychedelic).* As "Harry Stotle" put it in his *Rhetoric,* "People grow suspicious of an artificial speaker, and think he has designs upon them."

The Sense of Senses

The more man is seen as analog to the machine, the more he will yearn to express his undifferentiated potential. Synesthesia is a means of doing this, via a short circuit from one sense zone to another. "Oh, if you could only taste words!" rhapsodizes the J&B ad; another leading Scotch is described as "smooth as a kiss."[20] A 1967 *New York Times* editorial was entitled "Supersonic Noise Pollution." Presumably someone like McLuhan might point out that such popular poetry was anticipated by the Romantics. "Oh that my words were colours!" wrote Byron in *Don Juan* (VI, cix); in Baudelaire's 1846 *salon* Delacroix's paintings are at one moment poems, at another melodies reminiscent of Weber.

But to point this out is only going halfway. The desire for increased or multiple perception must tax words heavily, yet their stretching to this end can equally be said to have warned us in advance of the lost sensory harmony intrinsic in language, and now cauterized by the new egoisms of technology to which we daily pay homage, from electronic satellites to underwater scooters, sunpowered transistors, "instant" wine and "feelie" cinemas and multi-image discothèques and dresses that change color at the blast of a supersonic whistle. It was the orphic visionaries of the French

[19]Güttinger, *Zielsprache,* p. 19.
[20]Compare the recent Sprite ad: "SPRITE. The soft drink with a message: tingling tartness. The sound of Sprite is a real taste quake. Switched on. Exuberant. Noisy. . . ." American parents will doubtless be aware that there are now several reading systems for children which follow Rimbaud's poem on vowels, and equate sounds with colors.

nineteenth century who sensed in synesthesia a rupture of accepted modes of reasoning, and thus a getaway into, a gateway into, a lost paradise of the whole human being.

Examples of synesthesia are generally given, without comment, from the poetry of Keats ("sunburnt mirth," "the touch of scent," "embalmèd darkness"). Proust will describe a peal as "gilded," and the multiperceptual nature of certain modern "cultural" manifestations was parodied in advance by J.-K. Huysmans, whose Des Esseintes found that liqueurs corresponded to the sounds of various instruments, or that a man's sensory makeup evoked color reactions. The repetitive nature of contemporary claims of this order must class such efforts as, at best, Coleridge's "secondary" imagination; the "primary" use of the word contained its world. To twist Irving Babbitt's saying somewhat, nothing is so conservative as stale eccentricity. The children dancing nightly at New York's Cheetah are reminiscent of some quaint Victorian parlor sing ("Drink to me only with thine eyes . . .").

The first beatniks of the French 1830's sought out their harmony in the teeth of the awful logic of predicative progress that is upon us all today; they did so in a variety of methods—via number mysticism, the Kabbala, hashish, Isis cults. What chiefly divorces them from their contemporary imitators was their knowing marriage of nineteenth-century illuminism with socialist aspiration. Thus Gérard de Nerval could title his book on mages of the past *Les Illuminés ou les précurseurs du socialisme*. Rimbaud wrote a projected Communist Constitution. Reciprocally, the Romantic physicists (like Passavant, von Schubert) gave considerable credit to the power of the oneiric and irrational, as did the doctor, one of the first great psychiatrists, who finally tended Nerval.

Nerval's *Aurélia*,[21] the last pages of which were in his pockets when he hung himself, concludes with a moving picture, a parable of language, as the poet humbly attempts to assist a fellow patient in his mental home, a man who has lost the gift of speech. Today speech clinics have found this loss to be the commonest symptom of psychoneurosis, close followed by its twin, stuttering, and allied impairments like loss of hearing. There are nearly sixteen million with speech problems and defects in the United States, excluding the present President. It is hardly the size of language that matters

[21]A translation of this document is available in my *Selected Writings of Gérard de Nerval*, New York: Grove Press, 1957.

(Basic English has but six hundred nouns), it is its health as a system of transmission.

The French symbolist poets, and impressionist painters, to say nothing of a multiperceptual genius like Wagner, knew that this system lay under the ban of a technology which would see all language as purely "apparent." With their backs to the industrial wall, poets like Baudelaire (and, in Germany, Hoffmann) wrote about the music of colors, the sounds of smells, since not only did such "establish" the poet as seer, but this cosmogony of correspondences was also man on earth. Baudelaire and Wordsworth were alike interested in children, who are high in synesthesic vision; and when the latter wrote a poem on a reaper he was inspired by a prose passage that suggested the tactile value of sound—"Her strains were tenderly melancholy, and *felt* delicious long after they were heard no more" (my italics). Dyslexia is the current clinical term for word blindness, commoner in boys than girls.

Mendelssohn, who made a German translation of the Psalms in Hebrew characters, and one of whose favorite cadence formulae was derived from Jewish service music, echoed this desire to get to some organic human harmony beyond words:

> The thoughts which are expressed to me by music that I love are not too indefinite to be put into words, but on the contrary, too *definite*. And so I find in every effort to express such thoughts, that something is right but at the same time, that something is lacking in all of them; and so I feel, too, with yours. This, however, is not your fault, but the fault of the words which are incapable of anything better.

Cage has claimed the same—"New music: new listening. Not an attempt to understand something that is being said for, if something were being said, the sounds would be given the shape of words." It has been observed of the followers of Schoenberg that they behave as if music should be seen and not heard. In a similar spirit Pavlova remarked after a performance, "If I could have said it in words I would not have danced it." When asked to define New Orleans jazz, Louis Armstrong retorted, "Man, when you got to ask what it is, you'll never get to know."

This may be familiar enough. But there is a distinction to be made. The Romantics saw the ogre of totalitarian technocracy advancing, sensed how it would lay its hand on language, and reminded man of magic. Today we live under the ogre, and the use of synesthesia in advertising I have instanced simply runs parallel to the craze for mixed media puffed out by McLuhan. This is a safety valve, confirming us as happy in our civilization. "How do you spell a whistle?" asks a recent Delightform foundation ad. I have noticed that acknowledgments under the photograph of a model in *Vogue* or *Harper's Bazaar* now frequently include one for perfume. The distinction I am making could perhaps be summarized as that between the native of a West Indian island I frequent who offers one *a smile of whiskey* (who can refuse?), and is thus using full language, and the advertisement for a *cocktail which purrs,* which is faking metaphor.

I have mentioned the theory of dramatic forms made by that astute generic critic, Northrop Frye. Frye finds realism (or "mime") declining in our culture; the movement he traces is through comedy ("dianoia") back to the old processional or episodic forms. Comedy contains within it an emphasis on conduct, on "the establishing of a desirable society," and, Frye thinks, still exerts a teleological role in literary forms. Surely most observers would agree that our arts have been moving away from absolute representation (what Frye nicely terms an "idolatrous form of mimesis") into areas of multiple expression.

A feature of this phase is the exaltation of the audience, as it advances to community on the stage. This concurs with Wyndham Lewis' theory of the "dithyrambic spectator," when everyone is allowed to join in the dance, or dithyramb, and everyone can become an artist. Today almost everyone is. The mage is dead, and the horizontal society invites the public to flood the stage, as is nightly attested by TV, and not least by those who write in to TV heroes and heroines as real people, a symbolic confusion McLuhan claims has increased since TV took over the movies,[22] though the bells of England tolled when Richardson's Clarissa Harlowe "died."

This is the phase of "apparent" culture, and in it, we note, music and dancing are utilized to enhance the idea of a supremely happy society, with stock plots and characters as archetypes. The TV commercial seems closely to parallel the Jacobean masque, with the consumer product (or its humanized alias) replacing the seven-

[22]Marshall McLuhan, *Understanding Media: The Extensions of Man,* New York: McGraw-Hill, 1965, p. 318.

teenth-century Duchess; and when Milton set his seal on the masque tradition in *Comus* he gave us a little allegory of semantic silence, of the human element struck dumb among beasts. Our advertisements heap up a thesaurus of archetypal (or would-be archetypal) images, Esso's tiger in the gas tank suddenly transported to the back seat of the new Pontiac, and so forth. The errand of this culture is to convince all concerned that they are living in paradise, and its principal ingredient is self-admiration. I do not by now have to stress how dangerous it is when the exchange between word and world is blocked like this and, with the dancers in our discothèques, man simply admires himself in mirrors. The playback effect, first commented on, so far as I know, by the British anatomist, J. Z. Young, can become fatal when intercepted. Mussolini, it was said, was his own most enchanted listener and came to take his own words for reality; de Gaulle has observed, *"Quand je veux savoir ce que pense la France, je m'interroge."*

The "elimination" of silence, from the gabby cabbie to the compulsive neighbor at the automat, is a symptom of an unhealthy language situation. Silence is a sound. That it is today regarded as an enemy, a refusal to participate, a kind of subversive "taking the Fifth," can be tested daily in any large American city. "ARE YOU EVER TONGUE-TIED AT A PARTY?" was cited as one of the most successful advertising headlines of recent years.[23] Instruction on how to use words lightly, on how to debase the golden coin of silence, streams out: one market for such books appears to be that of girl teeners, who are advised to get the chitchat onto baseball at an early stage of dates, and keep it there.[24] But to presume someone guilty because he stands mute is a first step down the road to torture and coercion. When properly employed, language contains the sense of senses. As Friedrich Waismann put it:

> language, far from serving merely to report facts, is a collective instrument of thought that enters experience itself, shap-

---

[23]Analyzed by Schwab and Beatty Inc. as follows: " 'That's me! I want to read this ad; maybe it tells me exactly what to do about it.' " The analyst accepts the distortion.

[24]"LESSON NO. 2—*Getting Acquainted* . . . Are you at a loss for words when you meet strangers? How to be at ease with anyone, anywhere, is the theme of this Lesson: Entertaining conversation in mixed company. . . .

"LESSON NO. 11—*Long Conversations* . . ." (from the advertising material of Conversation Studies, 835 Diversey Parkway, Chicago 14, Ill.).

ing and molding the whole apprehension of phenomena (such as color and luster, e.g.) in a certain definite way, and, who knows, giving to them just that subtle bias which makes all the difference.

The Many Tongues of Gesture

After silence the next moment before language is gesture. Animal language—of the kind examined by Max Müller in the last century —shows differences of instinct, and degree, from human discourse. It is undeniable that reflex actions, such as those of pain or alarm, can be perfectly communicatory. But they are perfectly "apparent." They must be what they are. Jackdaws are said to have a fairly elaborate system of calls, and bees, as described by Karl von Frisch, use a dance routine to indicate the source of food.

Sapir was clear on this in his *Language: An Introduction to the Study of Speech* of 1921: an animal cry of an instinctive nature cannot be allowed to constitute communication. We conventionalize a cry of pain, or of warning, in a set of sounds, but these are scarcely symbolic. Take the cry of pain.

This, Sapir says, is "a more or less automatic overflow of the emotional energy; in a sense, it is part and parcel of the emotion itself." It simply informs us that an emotion is being felt; printing it as "Oh!" is thus a falsification. I would exemplify Sapir's point out of Frederick Olmsted's travels through the South in the last century; riding through the fields with the overseer of a large estate, Olmsted watched a malingering worker, a Negress slave, apprehended and thrashed. At each cut of the lash, he reported, the girl gasped out a verbalized "Yes sir!" But this pant of pain was not a communication; it was not really addressed to the overseer, it was not a true creation of the human mind. It was instinctive and asymbolic, indicative of pain. Similarly, a cry of warning as one crosses the street in front of a speeding car would "come across" whether uttered in English or Latvian. You could call it close to the motor process in all senses.

The warning shout is an animal cry, and language best duplicates it when tinged with bodily rhythms. (Try saying "You sonofabitch!" without any rhythmic overtones at all.) Sapir summarizes the matter: "If the involuntary cry of pain which is conventionally represented by 'Oh!' be looked upon as a true speech symbol equivalent to some such idea as 'I am in great pain,' it is just as allowable to interpret the appearance of clouds as an equivalent symbol that carries the definite message, 'It is likely to rain.'"

It is for this reason that, although certain nonverbal codes—Morse, semaphores, deaf-and-dumb signs, Braille, dance notation, railroad and umpire's signals and so on—have been evolved to complex stages, presymbolic communication in everyday affairs can often be more of a hindrance than a help. Transfer systems of this kind work from the rigidity of logic.[25] When Arabs poured out of Jerusalem's Old City into the New in 1967, Arab children watched the traffic lights with delight for hours on end, imagining the movement of cars and pedestrians each time the lights flashed green to be some sort of display, and bursting into applause as a result.

That such codes can be more effective than words in certain situations, like a Trappist monastery or a barrack square, proves only the imperfect and artificial nature of those special situations. Possibly the ring of an alarm clock awoke you this morning, there was later a knock on your door, and after that you drove to work using a car horn. These sounds represent transfer systems, but a one-for-one equivalence is poor language. The car horn provides an easy instance here. Assuming your klaxon contains but a single note, the beep it emits cannot differentiate between the intention to convey "Hey, you living doll" as you pass a pretty girl, and the blast designed to bray "Move it, you moron." Such sounds are indeed so unireferentially fixed that one *Saturday Review* cartoon carried the picture of an infuriated housewife rapping on a bus door in busy mid-Manhattan with a hard-nosed driver replying from within, "Who is it?"

There are dozens of examples of these transfer systems, designed for special situations, ranging from the gesture language of the North American Plains Indians to that of South African Bushmen. On one of the Canary Islands, where deep gorges make close communication difficult, whistling has been developed to a high art; and the *silbadors* (from *silbo,* Spanish whistle) can carry on conversations at a distance in this way.[26] Yet such is only substitute

[25]One instance of such rigidity was furnished me by a parachute jumper. His "stick" of nine enlisted men had been trained, and trained again, to jump from their plane at the slap of the Jumpmaster's hand on the rear. One day the Jumpmaster could hardly stand on his feet owing to turbulence outside, and so orally signaled the "tap." A Staff Sergeant, standing in front of my friend, was so conditioned to expect the slap that he froze without it. "Hit my ass, for God's sake," he finally begged. "Hit it." My friend complied and the Sergeant jumped. Tactile communication, indeed.

Spanish. They could do better with language, given walkie-talkie sets. A shepherd passes my house in Corsica at 5 o'clock every morning, emitting whistles, grunts and shouts at his flock. They understand perfectly, of course, but not all human beings are sheep, and in fact most Corsican shepherds tend to find protracted conversations, involving linguistic transfer, extremely fatiguing.[27]

The acceptance of a presymbolic transfer system on the same terms as language, as verbal symbolism, causes trouble. However rich the terminology of such systems, they are not "transparent." In Turkey head-shaking means assent. When GI's arrived in Italy in the last war, the wolf-whistle at sight of a girl was shown to be of local currency, like a jackdaw's cry; itinerant Italian womanhood simply did not at first know what was going on. A Portuguese might pinch his ear to show the same appreciation, in his case indulging in a surrogate physical activity. But Mr. Mits can frequently find himself in such instances frantically flag-signaling to someone untrained in the mathematics of such signals.

Interjections like "oh!" are thus a stage on from silence, but they are not language. Writing before the grosser development of comic books, Sapir called such "merely conventional fixations of the natural sounds." With "AAARGH!" and "POW!" and "AWKK!" comic books have tried to transcend these conventional fixations, and report the involuntary nature of emotional overflows. Kellogg's Rice Krispies transliterate their "SNAP! CRACKLE! POP!" to "POKS! RIKS! RAKS!" in Finland, to "PIM! PUM! PAM!" in Mexico, and to the Afrikaans-like "KNAP! KNAETTER! KNAK!" in South Africa. One should applaud such efforts, rather than carp at them. The *Spider-Man* comic, a sophisticated Superman story containing its own self-parody, had a short fight sequence in no. 38 (July 1966) represented by the following—"KAK . . . BTAK . . . FTAK . . . BUTOOP . . . YAGGHHHH . . . KAPOWK . . . FOOM . . . SZAK . . . BOK . . . THWIK . . . THAK . . . BRUP . . . KLIP!"[28]

These individuals must either be dying or having an orgasm (or

[26]André Classe, "The Whistled Language of La Gomera," *Scientific American,* 196:4 (April 1957), pp. 111–120. The article carries charts of pitch contours, musical staves and X-ray photographs.

[27]See my article "The Corsican Berger," *The Countryman,* 58:3 (Autumn 1961), pp. 456–467.

[28]"Amazing Spider-Man," Marvel Comics Group, Non-Pareil Publishing Corp., 625 Madison Avenue, New York, N.Y. 10022. For the effect of noises on opinions see "The Operant from Rat to Man," in Eugene Leonard and R. E. Hartley, *Outside Readings in Psychology,* New York: Crowell, 1957; also Kingsley Davis, *Human Society,* New York: Macmillan, 1959.

possibly both at once, as in William Burroughs' "Orgasm Death"). For, in sexual intercourse, writes the Danish drama critic Jan Kott, "Language goes back to its roots, to the moment of its birth. It is either nonarticulated, a cry and onomatopoeic sound . . . or it is articulated and then its function is magic." If gesture can be wordless symbolism, it is still not language. As Susanne Langer put it, "poetry means more than a cry."[29]

Unsayings

In cricket an umpire will sometimes stretch wide his arms after the bowler has delivered the ball. This conveys a "wide," or ball a yard either side of the wicket. The bowler returns for his run with a curse, shaking his head at the limited vision of umpires in general. On the other hand, a Plains Indian, or American professor, might imagine the umpire opening his arms for a sudden, unexpected greeting. The gesture is the same, and Joyce's cricket jokes in *Ulysses* have, as a result, caused some glorious howlers among literary critics. This happens when a presymbolic or purely "apparent" transfer system is taken as symbolic or "transparent."

In cultures which still accommodate expressive gesture, an inverse ratio may be discerned between the message and the terminology of its transmission. In relatively tactile communities, such as Spain or Japan, the more flowery a salutation is, the less it is intended to be translated literally: cf. the close of a Spanish letter with *Póngame Vd. a los pies que beso de su señora* or the use of the Japanese suffix -*kun*. Polysyllabic interpretations of Conrad's *Lord Jim* often dwell on the subtleties of *tuan* for English *Lord*. But *tuan* is not English *Lord:* I must have heard it a hundred times a day in my youth in Malaya, a typical courtly salutation common in shops and on the street. Viennese butcher boys used to deliver your steak with the equivalent of "I kiss the hand of the noble lady."

Although industrialism has ironed out such kinks, relics remain here and there. In England *Yours very sincerely* at the end of a letter is *less* cordial than *Yours sincerely*. This unsaying is a remnant of leisure-class habits requiring some show of archaism or obsolescence in writing and speech. You waste more time writing *Yours very sincerely*. It is therefore paradoxically more formal. Re-

[29]Susanne K. Langer, *Philosophy in a New Key*, New York: New American Library, 1951, p. 81. Langer carefully sifts and resumes the literature of this subject, especially the positions taken by Russell and Rudolph Carnap.

ciprocally, the verbal greeting "Pleased to meet you" is non-U in Britain because it argues a lack of obsolescence, and it is usually met with silence, or its equivalent (after all, to repeat, as do the British, "How d'you do" when someone says to you "How d'you do" is not saying very much). In a Brigade of Guards mess someone who asked for a copy of *"The Times"* would be frowned on; *"The Times* newspaper" would be better and, best, *"The Times* daily newspaper."

If anachronistic redundancy of this nature sounds strange, perhaps farcical, to American ears, it is that American speech standards have been mainly regional. In England it used to be a social disadvantage—one the Beatles mocked—to have a Liverpudlian accent. You couldn't argue that a southern or western accent would penalize you in the same way in America. The redundant *Yours* (faithfully, truly) has largely vanished from the close of most American letters, though it is retained in England. The British habit of writing about contemporaries as *Mr.* is a courtesy which, when translated to German *Herr,* can come over as a definite discourtesy. The French can still sometimes be heard saying "Enchanted!" when introduced to a total stranger, and it is notable that the French are constantly touching each other. You shake hands all the time in France. Even the grease-monkey who has just lubed your car will proffer an elbow if his hands are too oily, but you must touch something in farewell. It is the contention of my colleague, Leo Hamalian, that Arabs are more gesture-conscious than most groups. From what he writes it would seem logical to assume that overdependence on gesture can be the index of an infantile culture pattern.[30]

Gesture supplements symbolic language. The fact that there are numbers of transnational gestures (from a military salute to the touching of glasses in a toast) should not blind us to the properly assigned value of the transfer system. Since human beings are human, everything around them is going to claim symbolic rights. The empty chair "signifies" absence, the barred window "means" confinement. The fact that we have agreed on the umpire's signals, in the way a madman has not, will interest a semanticist as so much social definition.

[30]Leo Hamalian, "Communication by Gesture in the Middle East," *ETC.,* XXII:1 (March 1965), pp. 43–49.

The human head is vulnerable, and its exposure in the presence of a woman is said to derive from the raising of the helmet visor when among weaker people or friends. The University of California anthropologists, Washburn and DeVore, tell us that monkeys exhibit similar pacific intentions by showing their backsides. Anyone can observe that, unlike Americans, or some Americans, the British tend not to remove their hats in lifts.[31] I suspect such to be partly climatic, but the prevalent desire not to talk, not to mix, visible in any English railway carriage, no doubt played its part in the custom. It is not for nothing that the emergency cord on a British railway is called the *communication cord.* As if to suggest that you communicate only in an emergency. In any case, the wearing of headgear out of doors was obligatory for males until very recently, as any street photograph more than half a century old will show. In one of Joyce's stories a Dublin clerk tells if any of his work force has left for a nip by a glance at the hatrack. One character manages to slip out to a pub with a plaid cap stuffed in one pocket. But we note that he has to have something on his head.

Doubtless the truly evocative gesture is irreducible, and cannot be assessed in words without loss (Aquinas believed that all great teachers, like Socrates and Christ, were necessarily oral). Yet the assigned sign is a compulsion of the word into an absolute equivalence which, as mechanical translators show, deprives language of its intrinsic character. Masonic ritual, the sign of the Cross (parodied as the sign of the T, or model-T Ford, in Huxley's *Brave New World*, and as a dollar sign in Ayn Rand's *Atlas Shrugged*), or the act of rising when a woman—in Germany still, a teacher—enters the room, these are substitute words. If it were more polite to sit when a woman came in, we should sit; women rise when a King comes in. The physiology of gesture has a genuine role in life and is often better understood by those on the threshold of life, children, than by adults.[32]

---

[31]A British *lift* is an American *elevator;* it is also a *ride* ("Could you give me a lift home?"). But there is another *elevator* in America. A third-grade multiple-choice test recently offered, among wrong definitions, "a machine for raising people inside a tall building." There was no inclusion of the grain-storage denotation. This says a lot about those who think up such tests.

[32]Its application in pathological conditions is of the greatest importance, of course. See Laura L. Lee, "Some Semantic Goals for Aphasia Therapy," *ETC.,* xviii:3 (October 1961), and Wendell Johnson, "The Six Men and the Stuttering," *ETC.,* xvi:4 (Summer 1958).

Apart from his head, the human being is notably sensitive about the hand since it is his organ of spatial sensibility, the cat's whiskers. It can be a sturdy vehicle in the transmission of thought. Vibratory signals through the skin cannot be shut off, unlike those to eye or ear, and it is for this reason that in landing an aircraft "rates" can be most safely transmitted through the skin.[33] There are the well-known lie-detector tests, and the "vibratory barographs" of frogmen. Next time you catch a plane, watch the airline hostess at takeoff: if she is doing her job, she won't simply check the bolts on exit doors with her eyes but will go over them with her fingertips.

The hand-clap is thus a common transfer signal which shows up as less than a word, since its discourse usually relies on a previously agreed code. Russian actors clap an audience, while clapping hands for a waiter in a French café has such a purely assigned, and nonemotional, significance that American tourists, uneasy at its authoritarian nature (the emotional translation), find it hard to perform naturally at first. One thinks, too, of the cracking of fingers or "skinning" of palms prevalent among US Negro teeners. Again, the Japanese bow is a shade servile for the comfort of the same tourists, as might well be the rubbing of noses, popularly held to be Eskimo greeting drill (and definitely in use between Tamils).

Most children have a high sensory esthetic in this regard, and it is partly for this reason that skin color means nothing to a kid. Bias about skin pigmentation is conveyed by thought, not feel. It has to be implanted and, alas, it all too often is. The playgrounds of any big American city in the North should show this point in action, but any reader can check his sensitivity to kinesic effects daily: you can, for instance, judge just how much warmth was in that verbally effusive welcome Mrs. Mits gave you by the temperature of her handshake accompanying it, or by its manner. On the other hand, if she tickled your palm with one finger she might have been suggesting an assignation. Then again, how close was she to you physically? It has been computed that the average American male, talking to a man he doesn't know well, stands 18 to 20 inches away; in Latin America the same distance is only 8 to 13 inches.

[33]B. Von Haller Gilmer and Lee W. Gregg, "The Skin as a Channel of Communication," *ETC.*, xviii·2. (July 1961), pp. 199–209. Receptor response is under study in the biocybernetics labs of Rockland State Hospital (Orangeburg, N.Y.). "Smell receptors," claims the director of this research, Dr. Manfred Clynes, "respond only to smells and not to the absence of smells." This principle, of unidirectional "rate," explains why you might become accustomed to, say, a smell of gas in a room, and seems to me again to refute McLuhan's audiac theory.

Flaubert contrived to condense a whole cultural critique into such exchanges. When his Léon leaves Emma Bovary for the first time, he advances to say good-bye with hand outstretched. "*A l'anglaise donc,*" Emma says, accepting it.[34] Here the more natural kiss on the back of the hand is shown under the emotional circumstances as *less* intimate than a handshake. By infringing custom, that is, the handshake is warmer, and is so out of the gesture repertoire of a supposedly more frigid people. Flaubert understood the society he was depicting so well he could toy with many such paradoxes of assigned custom.

Later in the same book Emma folds her glove in a glass at the Vaubyessard dinner. This became a celebrated teaser for Anglo-American critics until local lore revealed it as a push-button signal of its day and place. By means of it Emma informed the wine waiters that she did not want champagne; and by means of it, too, she once again demonstrated, to the more sophisticated about her, her provincial upbringing. Here Emma was using object-language. She could have told the wine waiters she did not want champagne, but social custom impeded her from doing so. A transfer technique of this sort is nearly always provoked by an artificial social situation or need.

Object-Language

Communication via things is auxiliary to language, in that such signals are the results of previous knowledge or agreement. Take the following memento to the Academy of Lagado:

> Samuel Butler goes further still. He maintains that we may have a sentence without words at all. In support of this view he tells a story of Mrs. Bentley, wife of the famous Dr. Bentley of Trinity College, Cambridge. When she wanted beer, instead of sending a written or an oral message to the college buttery, she sent her snuff-box. That brought the beer. For it had been agreed between Mrs. Bentley and the butler that the snuff-box should mean *Beer, please.* There were here the con-

[34]*Oeuvres Complètes de Flaubert,* tome 1, Paris: Société des Belles Lettres, 1945, p. 137 ("*la substance même de tout son être lui semblait descendre dans cette paume humide*"). Compare the moment that replies to this a little further on, when Rodolphe takes Emma's hand during the agricultural show.

ditions necessary and sufficient for authentic language—a
sayer, a sayee, and a covenant.[35]

Everyone can identify dozens of these oral snuffboxes daily from
the barber's colored pole or sign (its red a reminder of bleeding) to
wayside waiters made of plasterboard to signify the proximity of a
restaurant. One pull-in I know off the road out of Rome simply sets
a table with a wine bottle at the turnoff. It is still the custom in the
remoter villages of Mexico and Guatemala to affix something green
to pulquerías to indicate that fresh pulque has been brewed. In
the villages outside Vienna the Heurige wine houses continue to
display a green bush to say that the new wine is ready—and by law
this must be their own. Crepe hung in mourning constitutes another
such sign. Trees carry varying "apparent" associations. In Las Vegas, it is said, you don't even need a snuffbox to produce beer; a
chip from any major casino will do the job, there being a collective
agreement in local stores and bars that such may act as tender. The
1967 small-coin shortage in Italy saw all sorts of objects pressed
into service as barter or, rather, guarantees in this manner.

Gaston Bachelard has suggested that an object can reveal more
to us than we about it. Mrs. Bentley's snuffbox will always be a
snuffbox; we can only go on describing it as such. On the other
hand, we can interpret ourselves through it. We can short-circuit
the predication of a normal sentence and set up the ideogram:
Snuffbox equals beer. Here we are not taking into account a true
listener; we are interpreting ourselves, or putting a penny in the
slot. The snuffbox only produced beer at the Trinity buttery.

One could compare the trials of the so-called dysphasias (impairment of communication by cleft palate, stuttering, cerebral
palsy and the like). After surgical removal of your vocal chords,
you are sometimes provided with an artificial larynx. By means of
this device you utter certain sounds which ask to be interpreted as
whole sentences, like Mrs. Bentley's snuffbox. In fact, Butler went

[35]Philip Boswood Ballard, *Thought and Language,* London: University of
London Press, 1934, p. 67. Ballard, an enlightened traditionalist in the field
of grammar, here refers to a lecture of the same title as his own book, which
Butler gave in 1890; in the lecture itself Butler commented on the snuffbox
syndrome as follows: "It sounds strange to say that one might take a pinch
of snuff out of a sentence, but if the servant had helped him or herself to a
pinch while carrying it to the buttery this is what would have been done."

on to instance the Earl of Essex's ring sent in ultimate appeal to Queen Elizabeth. Supposedly the ring did not reach her, and since there was no listener there was no message. Essex might as well have talked to a stone.

If it fills a need, the auxiliary system still remains such, and is inferior to words. An empirical structure will not allow what Richards calls the "dramatic" character of language to eventuate itself. The traffic light substitutes for a cop. Unlike the Arab children in Jerusalem, we agree to respond to the light as a verbal directive. The old systems of beacons and smoke signals set up similarly artificial congruents. This is not to deny, however, that the ideogramic transfer of such codes can provide a high-voltage method of transmission in particular situations.

Band leaders, longshoremen, theater usherettes, short-order cooks, all have their private snuffboxes. The Fascist salute was originally an attempt to fix up a sort of psychological hot line with Old Rome. Recently, the *Saturday Evening Post* ran an article alleging that in one city high school the girls had rigged up an elaborate communication system based on the color of their clothes, green equaling pregnancy, red a desire to incur such, and so forth. The raised-skirts attitude of this article must have made big-city high-school kids smile. Any one who has taught in a high school like Roosevelt in the Bronx could trade dozens of such exempla—ankle bracelets worn left or right to indicate availability, or lack of same, one fold in bobby-sox implying unavailability, down (or up) to the celebrated "virgin pins." Clients in a Greenwich Village bar used to wear a glove in the epaulette of their leather jackets, on the left if they were masochists (*macaroni*), on the right if they were sadists (*spaghetti*). Society forbids you, or inhibits you, from going around saying you are a sadist, as it inhibited Emma in the matter of the champagne. But if it did not do so, those inclined might have been saved the purchase of a pair of gloves, and the bars sequestering such devotees of Thanatos would not have to advertise their "Spaghetti" so insistently. Peruvian Incas had a system of knots, and there are Latin-American courtship curls used in just Mrs. Bentley's manner. Boy Scouts have established international object signals. Rosary beads make an interesting case in point; the designated function of the bead was to transmit a message, or prayer, but in practice this function became so artificial in most circumstances that it was taken over by the physical, the beads—like Greek *kombolai*—being used simply to keep the fingers employed.

Pasimology

In *The Story of Language* Mario Pei refers to gesticulation and/ or object-language as pasimology, citing Darwin's "fairly satisfactory, though somewhat mechanistic" belief that gesture-language tied up the hands or arms and was dropped when the exchange of words first liberated our forebears. Verbalization could communicate in the dark, or round corners, and so on. We therefore deduce that when gesture has to substitute for language, it is the world (a rocky island, a Trappist monastery), rather than the word, that is askew.

Still, if gestural language preceded oral utterance, as seems generally agreed (just as our physiological "precedes" our mental life), and only differs from its offspring in degree rather than in kind, it remains incumbent on us to respond to gesticulation by apparati other than, or as well as, the ear. Take the thumbs-down sign, or some of the ruder Italian finger signals. Russell instances the Frenchman's shrug—"any kind of externally perceptible bodily movement may become a word, *if social usage so ordains*" (my italics). Pei's point is illustrated by the old British pub signs. In common with the pulquería, an English inn originally identified itself by an icon—the Pig and Whistle, the Bull and Bush. You could send an illiterate to either for beer without worry. It was only later, with increased literacy, that the swinging signboards were substituted.

Thus today pictorial or iconic juxtapositions affect us unnaturally, more than we might care to admit. Churchill is associated with the bulldog, Johnson with the eagle. The more incongruous the items, the more rapidly does the resultant zeugma, or bringing together, flash its message across and do its work. A baby's behind is "attached" by advertising to insurance ("Are You Sure You're Covered?"); a dancing girl reinforces the appeal of a bank ("Why Do Our Savers Swing?"). The short circuit finds us semantically vulnerable since in urban centers we have lost hold of one side of the disparates.

By means of a disjunctive grammar advertising ducks out of symbolic communication in this manner, in common here with political language. The contention of McLuhan that speechlessness would "confer a perpetuity of collective harmony and peace" seems to me halfwitted, a childlike smashing of the authority of the mind. Words do not dim our vision, block our ears, or dull our touch. Life, the social complex, can do this in the form of some artificial ratio, like that imposed on a Trappist monk or throat-cancer victim. An argument against capital punishment might be accompanied by a model or maquette against hanging, but the symbolic wisdom of the argument could not be replaced in this way. Accompanying political rhetoric with short-skirted cheerleaders, as in that celebrated circus, the American political convention, is all too obviously to block discursive communication. The antirational becomes the antidemocratic.

Ishkabibbles

Possibly the Indian past lies behind the fact that America is the land of the cheerleader. In any event, cheerleading is an emotional spill-over of exactly the kind Sapir mentions in his description of interjections, the opposite perhaps of keening (tear-leading), an extension of the nervous system culminating in a crescendic bang—the jump called a *reindeer* accompanied by the cheer known as the *Ishkabibble*.[36]

This is a rite about a rite, a mirror activity that reinforces the thud of bodies on the field in a most satisfactory rhetoric, one that can only be the envy of Europeans. Indeed, there seems something devout about these clean-limbed *dramatis personae*, with their loose sweaters, cheekily swinging skirts, and springy sneaks. (There is the same touching vulnerability about Spanky and Her Gang.) This is Malinowski's "phatic communication," or "pure persuasion." We are close to magic.

The rupture of discursive units in advertising, particularly for products high in sensory appeal (olfactory or gustatory), can tell us much about our loss of such magic today. The Ishkabibble of advertising is a false certainty (negators like *no* and *never* have been found to be half as frequent as *all* and *every* in the body copy of contemporary advertising); it is the exorcism of doubt. As such it bears pathetic testimony to a sane desire for some last consensus of our faculties before we are fried alive. The Kees/Ruesch study of object-language shows us this invariably moving desire. Ads for

[36]"With much shouting and stamping and leaping into the air, cheer leading came into its own as a pure spectator sport yesterday afternoon in the Bronx. A highly partisan crowd of 4,000 screaming aficionados added to the tumult as 1,400 girls went through their noisy paces in the Fordham University gym. At stake were the high school, parish and elementary school crowns in the Catholic Youth Organization's seventh annual archdiocesan cheer leading contest. The absence of any athletes did not detract from the occasion" (New York *Herald Tribune*).

perfume, an explicit aphrodisiac, virtually have to be irrational to "mean."

Yet our cultural need for the nonverbal is itself an exaggeration. By the canons of some semanticists we should "understand" a political orator better when listening to him with an ice-cream cone streaked red, white and blue between our lips. (McLuhan should have been called in to write the copy for Stripe, and by this time probably has.) You might as well allege that sitting in a girdle with the Stars and Stripes imprinted across it, in the formulation successfully objected to by the DAR, would give you a more "rounded" political vision. The entire flag sensitivity in America today, culminating in the recent flag desecration bill (H.R. 1207 by Congressman Richard L. Roudebush, Indiana), can be seen as an inarticulate expression of this general need to make a symbol.[37] Alas, the vitality is so exaggerated, because blocked (or "cathected"), that it has virtually run amok, and if today you defaced a piece of plain white cardboard on which you had written the words *American Flag* you would be quite likely to get one year in jail and a $1,000 fine. Anyone who travels on US Line ships may notice how the flag is used conspicuously, almost as a trademark; on the mats on which you walk, however, the screaming eagle has been tactfully substituted.

Our urban environments are going to push us into more and more of these artificialities, as the word-world harmony gets broken. Roll a radio knob from station to station: the result will be a collage or kaleidoscope of fragments worthy of Ezra Pound in his worst moments, and which might be dismissed as surreal, were they not representative of the crazy quilt of contemporary language "happenings":

> It's the candy that melts in your mouth, not in your . . .
> —post-nasal drip or clogged sinuses? Dristan will protect you from . . .
> —income tax. This week, Congressman Paul A. Fino promised to rid the White House of all . . .
> —black, seedy roaches or ants. Bugsy's roach killer will help you . . .

[37]Rep. Roudebush, a past Commander-in-Chief of the Veterans of Foreign Wars, has an article, or diatribe, on flag desecration at Purdue University in *VFW: Veterans of Foreign Wars Magazine*, vol. 54, no. 10 (June 1967), pp. 8, 41. It makes salutory reading.

—drive your own car. Let Hertz put *you* in . . .

—Rockland State. He is dangerous. I repeat, DANGER-OUS! Be on the lookout for . . .

—junior high, high school, and elementary school teachers. . . .[38]

Primitive societies were, of course, held together by a proper zaniness in their semantic. But this owed to their respect for the separate operations of "apparent" and "transparent" language. When life is no longer meaningfully organic, the vital reciprocity between the modes is lost. There is one way of making my point about "apparent" language and that is by asking someone to translate Christian Morgenstern's poem *Fisches Nachtgesang (Night Song of Fish)*. He will find he can hardly go wrong since the entire poem is composed of punctuation marks.

Flabbergasterisks and Stupendapoints

Punctuation is a written extension of gesture and, as such, almost totally "apparent." If speech grew out of gesture, punctuation grew out of speech, and today press copy tends to imitate speech rhythms to such an extent that it "expounds a kind of grammatical patterning far removed from that which punctuation normally has to deal with."[39] Furthermore, punctuation betrays national exigencies—the Spanish double exclamation point, the German lower opening quote, or inverted comma, the French cedilla.

But the association of such marks on the printed page with grammatical meaning is by now worn thin, and the system by which the book you are reading was punctuated is extremely limited. Someone like e. e. cummings, who played with typographical arrangements, could have gone much further than he did had he known as much about printing as Joyce.

Far from being a gestural extension of the nervous system, modern punctuation has declined to a set of rules. This standardization

[38]From a Monroe High School, N.Y., *Yearbook*. It was significant that when *MAD* (September 1959) ran a similar scramble of half-finished billboard ads, via an errant or crazy paster, the resultant jumble backfired: "DOGS LOVE / Calvert Reserve" or "Know the joy of good living / . . . Fill up with Mobilgas Special." Such was too like reality to be funny. No one wants to die laughing.

[39]Geoffrey N. Leech, *English in Advertising: A Linguistic Study of Advertising in Great Britain,* London: Longmans, Green, 1966, p. 63.

was accelerated in the eighteenth century when grammarians taught that the comma equaled a time count of one, a semicolon two, a colon three, and a period (or fullstop) four. Punctuation lost its configuration features, and degenerated into rules taught in classrooms; commas are "restrictive," "nonrestrictive," "serial," and so on. Even the more imaginative systems of punctuation cannot, in the manner of a juncture signal, contain the gestures of our tongue. With the development of the novel it became conventional for authors to set up the narrative and reflective passages in "standard" English, allowing irregularities in the representation of speech. This is how Dickens effected much humor. *Great Expectations* contrasts representational dialog (of the young Pip, of the Gargery entourage and so on) with the staid, rather circumlocutory reflections of the matured man who is giving the story. Dickens' convict Magwitch is thus made to talk about *wittles*, which is his pronunciation of the written *victuals;* in fact, it would have been equally incorrect to pronounce *victuals* as spelt.

Today we do not expect a novel to make any strong division between spoken and written language. There is but the mildest of refractions between the two in most of our commercial novelists, like O'Hara, Wouk, Auchincloss, Snow. The passage of such fiction to other media, such as the theater or screen, is then so painless as to suggest that for such writers the novel is really felt as ancillary to other forms.

That punctuation has grown arid of gesture is evident in the various break-out attempts that occur from time to time, like Wyndham Lewis' periodical *Blast*. Actually *Blast* was *BLAST*, a strident shriek or sprawl of print across a puce-colored page that occurred in synchrony with the outbreak of actual blast, World War I. In the same way, since there is no real correlation of certain physical and mental states possible within our present sentence structure, Joyce blasted open the sentence at the end of *Ulysses*, and later in *Finnegans Wake*. Normal sentences would have been totally artificial units for Molly Bloom's 25,000-word soliloquy, whose lack of punctuation so angered early reviewers but which, appropriately for a pseudo-Greek epic, harks back to the method of Greek manuscripts. (In the light of ancient manuscript practice a space between words is also punctuation.) In *The Bear* Faulkner follows suit with a reflective sentence that goes to six pages in most editions, and years ago the *New Yorker* used to run a "Non-Stop

Sentence Derby" over heinous examples collected by their staff. It was pointless . . . to the point of being unhealthy. Even the readers of the "Non-Stop Sentence Derby," encouraged to such language condescension, must have tuned in to a disc jockey now and again. Disc-jockey parlance cannot be contained within a sentence.

This inadequacy of modern English punctuation is known to those of us who still use a pen and write letters by hand, inventing private signs and countersigns as we go along to convey nuances of meaning. Even those who type their personal correspondence do the same, and the facetious ?! sign, supposedly nonstandard (?!), has become current enough to achieve recognition in several grammar guides.

Today advertising copy everywhere butts into the dead end of system in punctuation, and at least one pair of ingenious critics has tried to evolve a method to accommodate greater physiological representation in the field. The exclamation point being clearly too feeble to carry the stress laid on it by our more slap-happy visual ads, to say nothing of our daily discourse, these writers propose an intensified form called a *flabbergasterisk*. One stronger than that would be a *stupendapoint*. Their system further includes wavy underlinings *(fluctustresses)* for our unvarying italic type (which, after all, has to do equal duty under names of magazines, ships and foreign words as for speech emphases). It also sports *demi-semi colons* (⁏), *summa colons* (.;.), *misquotes* (❞), and the like.[40] Comic books have in fact broken the young out of the punctuation straitjacket. The harness is then wearily restored by the English teacher. Eventually it is the latter who will lose out in the tug-of-war.

About the closest left to gesture in such systematologies are quasi-runic signs attached to letters, such as the diaeresis, German umlaut, French circumflex or cedilla. Omission signs like the circumflex (*maître* for the old *maistre,* still retained in some uses) are pregnant with a suppression close to the physical. The couple whose restaurant I pass in France every so often showed a healthy impatience with punctuation rules when they called their place *Ranch Hô*. The circumflex is gratuitous on their signboard since *Ho* omits nothing; they simply wanted to intensify the word, or exclamation.

[40]Fred Flanagan and Stan Merritt, "Simplify Your Punctuation Problem," *Printers' Ink,* CCXVIII (February 7, 1947), p. 160.

Shaw showed Eliza Doolittle's dropped haitch as a satire of a habit of mind—aptly enough, since the speech liability in this case becomes an asset in "county" English. In an ad for a woman's shaver before me a leggy and exotically lovely lady, dressed in a tight red sheath, is shown lounging on the floor. She reclines in a voluptuous spread across two full pages. The caption occupies less than 8 percent of the total space and reads simply: "Gimme . . . gimme . . . gimme. . . ." This ad is participational in the sense that it invites you to complete the ellipsis, and therefore into the picture. The imagination goes to work. Perhaps the lady is a lush, and the words *another drink* should be supplied. But clad as she is, and looking as she does, the most compelling interpretation of her role is that of a hooker, for she has sold her services to the ad, and her financial ambitions are identical with those of the shaver-maker. *The money first, honey* is what she seems to want. And this is again to say that you can't fool around with language. The word reveals your world. The lady in the picture is not saying "Gimme" to a shaver. No one would. The word is, rather, the manufacturer's demand of his economy.

Suspension points of this nature carry a mood into the physical, simply by ceasing to be verbal. There was the case of the author who sued her publisher for splashing "Take me . . . take me . . ." across the paperback cover of her novel, on which a Formosan version of the Red Dean of Canterbury was shown working like a rescue team over the voluptuous shapes of a blonde. Evidently the only time the girl in the story said "Take me" was when those words were completed by "to Philadelphia." Similarly, Noxzema Shaving Cream's temptress advocated on TV, "Take it off. Take it all off."

Indeed, a run of sexy ellipses in American advertising in 1966 fortified this point. These were founded on the highly successful "Does she . . . or doesn't she?" Miss Clairol ads, basically rather a crib of those two famous titles of 1895 *The Woman Who Did* by Grant Allen and its close-followed successor *The Woman Who Didn't* by Victoria Crosse (pseud. Vivian Cory). That the Clairol ellipsis was an obvious *double entendre* became clear when the caption started spreading its verbal implications back into the icon. For originally—as refused by *Life*—the photo simply showed a pretty girl ("the freshest and loveliest kind of gal," in the words of the agency involved). Through some accident in the studio a baby got into the picture. The age of the kid then increased progres-

sively—up to a point at which *MAD* parodied the whole performance by calling for a Miss Clairol "Date-Age Kit" ("grays his
temples . . . bags his eyes . . . doubles his chin . . . blows his
nose"). Marchand Golden Hair Wash, starting in the July 1966
Good Housekeeping, showed a sexy blonde gazing at the reader
over the rubric, "Why not tonight?"

Early in 1966 Chateau Martin wines ran the by-line "Had any
lately?" under the inviting picture of a blonde. Subway scrawlers
soon knew what to do with that one. But this formed a completed
utterance and, on the whole, belongs with puns. However, the New
York-New Jersey-Connecticut Chrysler Dealer Association ads that
followed depended on the ellipsis for effect, and were suggestive
enough to be refused by the stuffier newspapers. It could be said
that Ralph Ginzburg was convicted by standards applicable to the
New York Times for its lingerie ads.

A beautiful girl, her face expressive of sexual ecstasy, was shown
over such elliptical captions as: "Don, I might . . . if you drove a
Chrysler," "Perhaps we could, Paul . . . if you owned a Chrysler,"
and "Marty . . . Marty, if you drove a Chrysler." A slew of similar
appeals succeeded these, partially because this particular word-
world is listening to itself, and so gets caught up in an incest semantic; as the original copywriter who thought up the Clairol
double meaning put it, "it's part of the cult of showing off to the
other copywriters." The Chrysler innuendos were soon matched by
those counseling the acquisition of men's lotions and colognes.
"Was it him . . . or his Piping Rock?" was the Freudian pun, or
lapsus, under the picture of a very done-looking girl indeed. "Look
at what Mr. John made" was the copy accompanying another, to
advertise wigs. *Seventeen* magazine's representative girl was able
to "turn eggs into omelets and boys into men."[41]

The attention-getting aspect of such "apparent" ads, calling for
physical processes to complete verbal suspensions, is beyond question. "The ads accomplished what we wanted them to do," primly

---

[41]Cf. photographs of nude girls accompanied by: "It's a long way from a dab
behind the ears" (Lanvin's Arpege); "Don't do it with just anybody . . ."
(Strega); "What makes a shy girl get Intimate?" (Revlon's Intimate); "Come
in . . . and see our TOPLESS MODELS" (King Ford, Bronx, N.Y.) The
"Sheer Pleasure" of Topaz's Comfy Tops stockings is shown as a lead to
sexual pleasure by photography ("How bare do you dare?"). "Shiver her tim-
bers" suggested the Seven Seas men's cologne ad, while the Howard clothing
chain claimed to make clothes "for men who make love."

declared the agency for the Chateau Martin campaign, which lifted the sales 60 percent after station WINS accepted it. As gesture language, punctuation is substitute word-wisdom. A spokesman for Young & Rubicam, who handled the Chrysler ads, expressed surprise at the provocation stirred up by such captions. "The ads were not meant to be sexy," he said. He forgot that he was dealing with words.

Rhyme as Gesture—the Tom-Toms of Our Time

Penalty is exacted by language from all who monkey around in the magician's chamber of words. All Faust did was to change one word in the opening sentence of the Gospel of St. John already cited. He altered *das Wort* to *die Tat* and a world of deception opened at his feet.

The study of rhyme tends to get lost between two approaches. On one hand, it is taught by literary critics as an element of poetry. This is, of course, just how it should not be taught, viz. as a sound effect employed in building up some literary masterpiece. The student learns that there are masculine rhymes, and feminine rhymes, and catechreses,[42] and what-have-you. At the end of the term the teacher is then served back a batch of papers which duly point out masculine and feminine rhymes, obediently observing rhyme patterns like abba/cdcd/efef/gg and the rest. The student usually departs ignorant of the purpose of rhyme, of its proximity to human experience and its resultant ability to transmit meaning.

On the other hand, essays and books on sound systems tend to subordinate rhyme to the physiological—to labials, nasals, allophones, velars, affricates, fricatives, glides and whatnot. One such study, by a celebrated palate-and-tongue man, Professor Norman C. Stageberg of The State College of Iowa, consists for the most part of diagrams worthy of some Dutch doctor's office or jaw-treatment lab. Presumably such is where sound-system studies *pur sang*, phonemics rather than phonetics, belong. It is far from my

[42]There is a slight difference between a slant rhyme and a catachresis, but for all practical purposes they are the same—grief/death, the kind of thing used skillfully by Wilfred Owen. High-school students are sometimes told that the trick comes out of Welsh poetry, where it is called the *cynganhedd,* but since few high-school students know much about Wales, let alone Welsh, this is simply adding another chunk of information, rather than knowledge, and once more reducing poetry to a technique. It is, further, seldom shown how catachresis turns into metaphor (e.g., Latin is Greek to me).

intention to deride them. The importance of speech pathology can hardly be overestimated. In the Trobriands, according to Malinowski, the word *tonagowa* simultaneously stood for both idiocy and defective speech.

The important thing about rhyme is that we like it. Children like it, and the reason is usually ascribed to the pleasurable anticipation set up by any rhythm or repetition. Coleridge remarked on this, and the Romantics were of course highly interested in the treasury of word-wisdom to be found in the child. Not only is repetition pleasurable, however, it also makes a human correspondence, one common to all such devices as alliteration, assonance and so on. Thus "While melting music steals upon the sky," we relax many mutually exclusive tensions and listen to a new construct commencing. We are linked to past and future in the magical manner of a true semantic. As George Beiswanger put it in a recent issue of *Dance Observer,* "man through rhythm ties himself back into the esctasy or terror of a moving universe."

Thus rhythm responds to our entire repertoire of cyclic life—to our heartbeats, to seasonal recurrences, night and day, eating, drinking, sleeping, excreting. It is in league with survival since it is by metabolic repetition that the organism resists decay. Churchill liked to call his heart his *gallop.* So to create rhyme is to duplicate the human; we note that Siegfried Sassoon hung on to sanity in the trenches of World War I by remembering advertising jingles. If "savages" do it with tom-toms, we do it by ads. "DON'T BUY SOAP—BUY HOPE!" "TAKE TEA & SEE!" Or that phenomenally successful British slogan—"DON'T BE VAGUE—ASK FOR HAIG."

Phonological schemes must impress and seduce us by their underlying appeal to living processes. It is for this reason, if no other, that foreigners can perceive the direction of an advertisement, although they may be ignorant of the language in which it is couched. In his study of British advertising, Geoffrey Leech, a Lecturer at London University, sensibly suggests that the human property intrinsic in repetitions "accounts for a use of phonological schemes in television advertising in parts of the message *where memorability is not especially important.*"[43]

Commercial exploitation of such processes has certainly increased. F. Presbrey's *The History and Development of Advertis-*

[43]Leech, *English in Advertising,* p. 189 (italics added).

ing (1929) emphasizes a journalistic trick of the American 1850's, of making up an advertisement with repetitions of a small ad, as a significant turning-point in this increase. Today the repetition of kinesthetic stimuli at regular intervals is standard Madison Avenue rhetoric. Those responsible not only admit the fact, they brag about it.

A New York evening newspaper reports: "Buick this week launched a campaign that includes 4-second (four, that is) commercials in 50 major markets. The complete message, 'It's Buick easy ownership time.' The message will be delivered 40 times a day on each of 50 stations three days a week for eight weeks." An ad from Chevrolet concludes that their cars "are built to keep WORKING AND WORKING AND WORKING. . . ." The words "AND WORKING" were repeated a dozen times on a single page of *Life*. The Anacin TV commercial of 1966-67 repeated *pain* and *depression* so often the consumer needed the product before the end of the commercial. A 1967 Johnnie Walker Red ad was in the same vein.

This language is not to inform us. "TWICE AS NICE AS MICE" scarcely "describes" a cat food.[44] It is intended to come over more on the basis of an orchestral score. Music notoriously stimulates the organism, and of course the making of music for commercials is very big business indeed, chiefly via royalties for re-use (euphemized as *residuals* in the trade). Edward Thomas, President of Forrell & Thomas, Inc., remarks that "Constant performance of his jingle, the client feels, will sink the tune into the average listener's ear." Into, of course, the child's ear so that when radio or television set is switched off, you have a built-in jingle-singer right there beside you.

It is all very well for David Ogilvy, an ex-English impresario of what has come to be known as Madison Avenue (an admittedly inconclusive classification), to complain: "How would you react if you went into a Sears store to buy a frying pan and the salesman started singing jingles at you?" In effect, this has happened, a housewife having recently asked the manager of one large supermarket, "Could you tell me the detergent I'm looking for, please. I don't know the name, but I can hum you the tune."

It is obvious that unconscious responses are stirred up by orches-

[44]"New 9-Lives Cat Food. Fortified with Vitamin E. *All-tuna fish*. Cats love it instinctively. 22.5% protein. . . ."

tral scores of this sort, which are hardly amenable to intellectual analysis on the level of, say, *Modern Philology*. Ernest Dichter's "subliminal" observations were so off the point, innocuous to the semantic of positivity, they could actually be encouraged by Madison Avenue (Dichter's supposedly critical journal *Motivations* was subscribed to principally out of advertising offices). "I'm going to pack the wax and hit the tracks," yodels the disc jockey. You do not look for denotational extension of these terms, and it would be equally immature to do so for PICK-A-PACK-OF-PK-PELLETS, *Filter-Flavor Flip-Top Box*, BETTER BUY BIRD'S EYE—or for that classic of its kind, the lovingly depicted deodorant ad on early TV which I quoted in my *Parade of Pleasure*, TURN YOUR ARM-PITS INTO CHARMPITS.

Defeated Echoes

We must resort once more to Sapir. An entropy is created. When one form of energy is translated into another, there is a loss. The second law of thermodynamics is artificially accelerated in advertising, which arouses an impulse and then runs it down quickly in another direction. We see a bosomy girl, duly slaver, then burn out the energy on a certain brand of gasoline or whatever. The negative nature of the activity is, to my mind, confessed in the very optimism and certainty of advertising, with its frantically smiling models and surreal gaiety. When you hear the chewing-gum ads every morning as an overture to the latest Vietnam casualties (or "losses"), the end result is living sick humor.

Rhythm of this nature is taking a blank check on physical inevitability. Because we must eat and sleep and keep breathing, and because our hearts must keep pumping, rhythm ads appeal to us to accept their entropic inevitables, or syllogisms, *on the same level of consciousness*. You more or less have to buy certain things in the urban world, like soap and matches and detergents, and you are urged to do so on the basis that such actions are absolutes to being. To exploit the human potential of "apparent" language like this is hitting below the belt; indeed, wherever possible, our vulnerability to physical inevitables (receding gums, saggy breasts, "tired" blood) will be insisted on in advertising for this very purpose. Once again man is made over into T. S. Eliot's "human engine . . . / Like a taxi throbbing waiting." One of the most successful ad campaigns of 1966-67 showed a "wound-up" executive fleeing into the distance with a monster key in his back. Today's teen-ager is, we note, "turned on."

Again, "apparent" language of this sort will be invoked from time to time where discourse is properly "transparent." I LIKE IKE had no "meaning," in the true sense.[45] The facile assonance tried to impart the feeling that political absolutes are inevitable, too, and the rival Stevenson campaigners never really came up with a sufficiently physiological substitute (I BELIEVE IN STEVE and GLADLY WITH ADLAI were perhaps the best attempts). So we got Ike, and government by technocratic elite, which presupposes "human engines." The "apparent" slogan ALL THE WAY WITH LBJ was answered by embittered student peace-marchers with the famous "transparent" translation—HEY HEY LBJ HOW MANY KIDS DID YOU KILL TODAY? In late 1967 the Black Power movement passed a resolution on the draft in a rhythmic absolute— HELL NO, WE WON'T GO.

In such uses, or rather misuses, libido is nearly always negated. The phonetic basis of rhyme accentuates what it is to be human. There is a device of ballad poetry called incremental repetition (once again, notice the Romantic interest in ballads). An increment is added after the repetition of several sounds, as in the *Frankie and Johnnie* formula, or that of *Lord Randal* or *Edward*. It is the technique of many tops in pops today. The anticipation is set up . . . then counterpointed by a change. The ear is alerted, aroused by the alteration or defeated echo. In front of "apparent" language we are really no more than children, playing with fire. And, as they say, you can't unburn a match. Exaggerated entropy, the metronomic tick-tock of industrial times, turns us into automata, so many digits looking for the holes in the punchboard out of which we were silhouetted.

[45]This intensely idiotic slogan was well analyzed by Roman Jakobson (see T. A. Sebeok, ed., *Style in Language*, Cambridge, Mass.: M.I.T. Press, 1960, p. 357).

THREE

> How had the ball been? Oh, it had been
> a riot. A what? A panic. Terrific, in a word.
> Had Lo danced a lot? Oh, not a frightful
> lot, just as much as she could stand. What
> did she, languorous Mona, think of Lo? Sir?
> Did she think Lo was doing well at school?
> Gosh, she certainly was quite a kid. But her
> general behavior was—? Oh, she was a
> swell kid. But still? "Oh, she's a doll," con-
> cluded Mona . . . .
>
> Vladimir Nabokov, *Lolita*

HIDDEN LANGUAGE:
THE RITES OF RITUAL

The Trials of Tact

For Walter Bagehot true culture was a state in which the primitive existed in harmonious intercalation with the sophisticated. If
it is essential to psychic health that our lives contain elements of
the presymbolic, we can find examples of such "apparent" language
in those phrases, formulae and utterances, often inane enough if
regarded rationally, which fill out our daily discourse.

These are like so many verbal worry-beads, slipping comfort-
ingly through our fingers—"Hi" . . . "Howdy?" . . . How's it going?"
Another analogy might be to that of someone playing music on an
organ without the air turned on. One observer of the national scene
has suggested that we should employ an automatic tongue to do
this job for us, since about 95 percent of our discourse on an average day is ritual communication. The automatic tongue, pinned in
a lapel, would be timed to make certain such utterances throughout
the day—"Sleep well?" "Never felt better," "I'll give you a call,"
"How's your wife?" and, of course, "How's it going?"[1]

[1] Russell Baker, "How's the Wife and Pass the Sugar," *New York Times,*
May 19, 1966, p. 46.

It is not, of course, "going" anywhere. The individual who chose to answer your cheery morning "How are you?" with a pondered "A touch of leprosy today" would hardly be communicating according to the rules of the game. I can vouch that "Nice day, isn't it" sounds particularly fatuous as a silence-breaking gambit in the tropics, where every day is relatively predictable. In England, where the weather is either unpredictable or predictably bad, it makes a good conversational opener, or agreement-provoker, and as a result a certain amount of tribal wisdom has collected in British weather saws.[2]

Much the same could be said of the varieties of "Good appetite" heard before meals in Europe, notably France. In English-speaking countries, where gastronomic standards are not high, "Good appetite" has not caught on as a sound-procedure since it resists the residue of reality left in such utterances. Indeed, the conventional question mark sometimes included at the close of introducers—like "How do you do?"—is a grammatical artificiality. The event is here what matters, the act displays its token syllables. In fact, J. L. Austin devised the term *behabitives* for such utterances, on the grounds that such language is about 90 percent social behavior, in which the verbalization comes prepacked.

Obviously the informational content of many conversational exchanges in cities is low, vocal sniffings and nuzzlings of the sort parodied in the original *Marty*. (Piaget claimed that only about 15 percent of language is adapted information.) Dorothy Parker had an alert ear for this sort of thing—e.g. " 'Well!' the young man said. 'Well!' she said. 'Well, here we are,' he said. 'Here we are,' she said, 'Aren't we?' 'I should say we were,' he said." It is said that President Roosevelt once found a reception line he had to greet so appallingly long he began to shake hands with each guest, smiling perfunctorily and saying, "I just murdered my grandmother." (Only one man, a dyed-in-the-wool Republican, retorted sourly, "She deserved it.") There used to be a Marx Brothers setup during which one or other of the comedians would bow and smile sanctimoniously to some Russian or Pole who had no English, the while saying "You bastard

---

[2]"Red sky at night, shepherd's delight . . . / Red sky in the morning, shepherd's warning," etc. Chaucer's England is presumably conventional, in the sense that he was drawing on Italian or Provençal weather stereotypes (languidly warm springs, and the like) for a lot of his literature; a pilgrimage through Kent in early April would be wet, windy, muddy and cold, surely even in his day.

. . . you sweet sonofabitch" and the like. The other would bow and grin back, delighted. Such is known as tact.

For Roosevelt was here rightly assuming a form of word-wisdom, in this case that sound conveys sense. Social custom demanded that, caught in a receiving line, he utter a set of given cadences with a fairly point-for-point relationship. A variation in sound, that is to say, would cause more distortion in meaning than a change in vocabulary. One student I knew worked in the Christmas rush at Macy's information counter. He described his task as that of an indoor forest ranger to hordes of bundled clumps of humanity, desiring to know where coffeepots or shoes were sold. Finally, as the umpteenth shopper whispered through frost-bitten lips, "Where's the steam irons?" he calmly pointed nowhere, saying "In the Steam Iron Department, Madam." When asked, "Where can I find a napkin holder?" he'd reply, "Why, in the Napkin Holder Department." He found this completely satisfied the wet mass of shoppers . . . until the day the question came, "Where's the men's room, buddy?" and he heard himself replying, "In the Men's Room Department, of course."

In the same way a girl I knew told me about the trials of life in her office; every time a typist left her desk the grouchy boss would advance, demand an explanation, and conclude, "Well, don't let it happen again." One day my friend got so tired of this tactic that, when he approached her after an absence from her machine, she retorted, "I'm sorry, but my period came on and I had to borrow a sanitary napkin from Mary." The boss went pink, but came right back with his stock gambit, "All right, but don't let it happen again." (Note that Tampax, Inc. announce a *regular* dividend.)

Roosevelt's parody, and that of the Marx Brothers, point up language barriers between countries, which are often no more than misclassification of sounds. For the intonations, or phonemics, of German are other than those of French, and vice versa. You can say the right word in a foreign language without necessarily being understood.

This can be checked easily enough by your degree of comprehension of a French or German sentence as spoken by a compatriot and that same sentence as spoken by a native Frenchman or German, preferably by a heavily accented user in each case, from the *midi*, say, or Bavaria. I hazard the guess that this, too, is why jokes in foreign tongues so often fall flat in translation; the phonemic background is no longer there. Victor Hugo rendered the Firth of Forth as *"le cinquième du quatrième."*

When this happens we say that someone has a good accent in one tongue, a poor one in another. This is but half the story. What is going on is that a foreign speaker fails to use the same allophones as the native speaker. Allophones are "phonetically similar sounds that never get in each other's way."[3] They form part of our instinctive use of the language. It is when they are incorrectly used that we say someone has an accent. An excellent, though tragic, instance of this was given by Micheline Maurel in her book on concentration-camp life, *An Ordinary Camp:*

> Often there were fights merely because people did not speak the same language. Words that were not understood were taken as insults and were answered with blows. When a Frenchwoman spoke to a Russian, the latter would almost invariably reply, *"Nie ponimayu"* ("I do not understand"). Once I saw a little Frenchwoman throw herself against a Russian with fists doubled, furiously shouting, *"Ni-pou-ni maille* yourself, you brute." Fortunately I knew Polish and enough of the other Slavic languages to be able sometimes to prevent trouble. But the fact remains that the natural intonation of some Russians and Ukrainians has a harsh and unpleasant ring to French ears.

When a Corsican is speaking his local dialect, Corse, he nearly always sounds angry to a foreigner.

Elected Silence

The kind of agreement-producers I have mentioned are prolix in America, where it is considered impolite (or "snooty") to remain

[3]This definition is provided by George P. Faust, a phonologist whose article on the subject is brilliantly lucid for a highly technical abstract: "Terms in Phonemics," *College Composition and Communication,* v (February 1954), pp. 30–34.

In all the writings I have studied by speech teachers, the one observation I have not seen made is that allophonic content shapes the mouth. Children can speak any language. But as they grow up, and speak only one, they develop a certain mouth pattern. In these days, when you cannot easily tell a French or American or Dutch or German or Italian tourist apart in the cities of the world, the mouth gives much away. An upper-class Englishman has a particularly recognizable mouth-look.

silent, and such social levers are much in demand. As Johnny Carson once said on *The Tonight Show*, "I just keep talking until I have something to say."

I suppose that by now the French satirist Daninos has kidded the British out of some of their habits of reticence, but in my youth England was still a country in which a child had a sense of penalty for misunderstanding words. Nations with the greatest respect for private property (forced, as doubtless this may have been, on the overcompressed British) are those with the strongest abstinence codes. I would further risk the surmise that an abstinence in speaking results in a lot of writing; up to a few years ago England used to publish annually close on double the number of titles issued in America in a year, while both the number of mail deliveries and the use of the business "note" in England attest to a scriptural culture.

The purpose of the West End club used to be to preserve silence, rather than to break it. Sherlock Holmes' brother Mycroft belonged to the Diogenes Club, where silence was obligatory; though Mycroft was in all senses fabulous, Doyle was hardly exaggerating here. In my own London club, to which I return now and then, some irritated comment from a dining-room table, like "*Must* they put gnats in the flan?" resounds as a distinct breach of decorum.

Professor Alan S. C. Ross, in a double superlative, calls silence "perhaps the most favorite of all U-usages today,"[4] and instances the lack of a drinking salutation, so common elsewhere (*Skål! Prosit!* etc.), in the vocabulary of the British upper class. *Cheers!* (sometimes used in America) used to be so non-U in England it could even be employed facetiously. *Chin-chin!*, preserved for some reason in France though out of date thirty years ago in England, was more convenient still when there was need of some communication to show a foreigner, or non-U interlocutor, that one did not mean to be impolite. As control, silence was one of the highest forms of civilization for the British. One was taught to say nothing rather than something, and if, as Ross suggests, this could be a considerable handicap at times (in apologies, for instance), it protected one from verbal *gaffes*.

A final anecdote might serve to clinch this reminder. On a Caribbean island I visit annually, an unaffected friendliness still prevails.

[4]Alan S. C. Ross, "U and Non-U: An Essay in Sociological Linguistics," *Noblesse Oblige*, ed. Nancy Mitford, Intro. by Russell Lynes, New York: Harper & Brothers, 1956, p. 71. See my footnote 41 to Chapter One, above.

At every turn in the road, on every corner, there are cheery waves and other intimations of exuberance. But a year ago a friend who runs a small hotel there told me of an English couple who had spent their entire vacation confined to the fairly limited bounds of his grounds; this ultra-British couple ultimately confessed that they could not bear to walk out since to do so would involve returning constant greetings. In the same spirit I well remember being taught as a boy that Nelson's last words could not have been "Kiss me, Hardy"—how could a national hero have wanted another male to embrace him?—but "Kismet [i.e. fate], Hardy."

One should also mention that in time of war reluctance to utter becomes functional. To talk about death is to face death, and we are not always as ready to do that as we might like to think. Soldiers and sailors and airmen perforce have to be, however, and to verbalize the death that comes their way daily would be to overload those fuse-boxes of taboo which I shall discuss in my final chapter. I recall such Army avoidances well, verbal shrugs, cynical songs and fatalistic terms thrown up on the spur of some moment, a few still retained—like the word *gong* for the rare medal that came an English serviceman's way. In retrospect, the RAF slang devised to meet this situation, and to euphemize an excess of death during the Battle of Britain, sounds oddly elegiac and touching today—"Quite a prang . . . gone for a burton . . . yes, baled out over bocheland . . . no future at all, old boy."[5]

For the national inhibition had its sources. Surrogating for sociology, the literature of the last century shows England feeling itself increasingly hemmed in; as a consequence there was a romance with the countryside, coeval with the reverse in agrarian cultures, as with the wide open spaces of the—as then—unexplored Empire.[6] "Men like Clive, Nelson, Nicholson, Gordon," wrote Orwell, "would find no place for themselves in the modern British Empire." For my money he could have replaced Gordon with Raffles, but the point is good. England came to be considered overcrowded at an early date (see Kipling's poems, like *Mandalay* and *Pagett, M.P.*), and room was sought by ignoring those who peopled

[5]*Prang* was taken from old Zulu.
[6]"Possibly the centrifugal tendency of English culture, whether the nature-loving example be George Eliot or D. H. Lawrence has been a reaction against its prevailing industrialism. Conversely France, which remained more agrarian, became more centripetal in its fixation upon the metropolis" (Harry Levin, *The Gates of Horn,* New York: Oxford University Press, 1963, p. 37).

space—the populace. In America, of course, "Howdy, partner" filled a need, even a hundred years ago. Today, with every farmer in front of a TV set, the British situation has become the American, and if you walked the streets of New York exchanging ritual remarks with every stranger you met, you would not get very far. The much-publicized "lack of involvement" (resulting in thirty witnesses to a Brooklyn rape, and dramatized years ago in Chekhov's "The Lament") has its roots here. When a year ago a bank robber flourished his gun at a Manhattan teller, the latter retorted "Sorry, sir, this window's closed."

S. I. Hayakawa reports on a typical ritual situation as follows: "A not-very-bright-looking but friendly youth comes up and asks, 'Got a flat tire?' If we insist upon interpreting his words literally, we will regard this as an extremely silly question and our answer may be, 'Can't you see I have, you dumb ox?' "[7] The youth, that is, is making so many "apparent" sounds, and we would be miscommunicating to construe these as "transparent."

Karl Menninger comments on Hayakawa's commentary in a long analysis, which, useful as such thinking may be in the clinics, seems to me actually to damage word-wisdom by its naiveté.[8] For today such ruptures of silence in grammatically phrased, though basically nonverbal, utterances of this nature are far from always on the side of the angels.

The Smilers

The very large category that exists in America (and also, to an unexpected extent, in England) of inspirational or uplift books nearly all counsel continual friendly discourse. Such "consent" books would include Norman Vincent Peale's *The Power of Positive Thinking*, three years on best-seller lists and going through four printings in its first three months, Dale Carnegie's multimillion seller *How to Win Friends and Influence People*, Rabbi Joshua Liebman's *Peace of Mind* and the successful uplift books of

[7]S. I. Hayakawa, *Language in Thought and Action,* 2nd ed., New York: Harcourt, Brace & World, 1963, p. 78.

[8]Karl Menninger, *Love Against Hate,* New York: Harcourt, Brace and Company, 1942, pp. 268 *et seq.* Alas, in this chapter on something called "Love," Menninger seems to understand as little about semantics, seen as the crudest form of "adjustment," as about his title subject ("liking and loving differ only in intensity," p. 271).

"Smiley" Blanton, Marjorie Hillis *(Orchids on Your Budget),* Fulton J. Sheen and others.[9]

In such texts, and their successors, silence stands for nonparticipation. It represents a questioning of the Great Society. After all, taking the Fifth is an elected silence now considered close to a crime. So silence has to be disrupted in a variety of ways, including those proposed by Dale Carnegie as rules, viz. "Smile," "Make the Other Person Feel Important," "Never Tell a Man He Is Wrong," "Don't Criticize" (notice, in this last, the pejorative connotation of *criticism*).

In these manuals on How to Today, the chapter heads themselves indicate a sort of concertina-ing of spiritual and financial practice ("Put a 'Stop-Loss' Order on Your Worries"). Peale's case histories preach similar herdism, but lack the brashness of Carnegie, which was, in its way, sort of endearing. Of course, Peale is more definitely in the pulpit, albeit a conveniently nondenominational one. His *Guide to Confident Living* (twenty-four printings in three and a half years) retreats before every problem to "faith." Prayer cures all. A "cranky" student is told: "Who wants to be an old bookworm anyway? ... In class, when the teacher calls on you, quickly pray before answering." When you sink a long putt on the links, you should thank God. We are told that religious people get no neuroses.

These books, with their strongly directive titles, show the most elementary use of silence-breaking. If you say it, it will happen. Repetitive restatement produces the reality. This was a principle of primitive magic, as it was of the institutionalized optimism of Coué ("Every day in every way I am getting better and better"). In this sense the spate of American uplift literature, almost entirely ignored by the intelligentsia and dashed of late by the adjustments to reality that have had to be made within it, is the contemporary supply of Puritan pamphlets. Here was another attempt to organize

[9]It must be said that this industry, too, has its incest, as must any words that ignore the world. In *Positive Thinking* Peale refers to his former collaborator, "Smiley" Blanton, as an "eminent psychiatrist." Carnegie recommends David Harold Fink, author of *Release from Nervous Tension,* who in turn praises Peale. "How to Overcome Worry," "How to Analyze and Solve Worry Problems," "How to Avoid Getting Upset" are chapter titles from three "different" uplift books (*I Can* by Ben Sweetland, *How to Stop Worrying* by Carnegie, and *Confident Living* by Peale). Even so I was somewhat startled to see a book emerging recently called *Positive Thinking* by Melvin Powers.

optimism against the impossible. As Malinowski put it, "Organized magic always appears within those domains of human activity where experience has demonstrated to man his pragmatic impotence." *Lift Up Your Heart* by Sheen, *Hope for the Troubled* by Lucy Freeman, such echo the innumerable *Profitable Meditations*, the *Sighs from Hell*, the *Plaine Mans Pathway to Heaven*, and the like, of the British seventeenth century. The gimmick title was common to the Ranter of this period, too, like Joseph Salmon's *Heights in Depths and Depths in Heights*, or Abiezer Coppe's *Fiery Flying Roll*.[10]

Too, there is the same *Realpolitik* of that Puritan ideal, busyness. In his *Autobiography* Benjamin Franklin formulated rules for life which we find vulgarized by Carnegie and Peale. Franklin checked his adherence to these on a chart. They were based on the principle "Imitate Jesus and Socrates," precisely the two preceptors Carnegie chooses, though to imitate Jesus and Socrates today would, as recent peace-marchers have observed, land one in extremely warm water with Western officialdom. Like the celebrated maxims of "Your Servant, SILENCE DOGOOD," Franklin's rules may have given Carnegie and his fellow crusaders a tip or two.[11]

But the facile synthesis of moral and material in this semantic is precisely what the West is contesting, in the death-throes of Marxism. (It is not for nothing that Bacon has been canonized in Russia.) Power, Energy, Efficiency—this is the same troika that rushes the Russians on. *How to Get Things Done* (Seabury and Uhler), *Make Up Your Mind* (Wilson), *Keeping Mentally Alive* (Cotton), this huge uplift industry implies a verbal relationship with reality

[10]For a fuller consideration of this comparison, see my article "Inspiration for Conformity," *Chicago Jewish Forum,* 15:1 (Fall 1956), pp. 16–23. Though this article was written over a decade ago, its criticism still seemed valid for Alan Harrington's delightful parody of Carnegie-ism in *The Revelations of Dr. Modesto,* whose doctrine of Centralism is pure Carnegie—"an ecstasy of Mediocrity."

[11]Cf. Franklin: "Lose no time; be always employed in something useful; cut off all unnecessary actions." Carnegie's Rule 1 (or First Commandment) says the same, throwing in some pietistical phraseology for good measure: "Rule 1: Keep Busy. The worried person must lose himself in action, lest he wither in despair." Peale also counsels constant activity as a social bromide in the manner of Franklin's *The Way to Wealth,* which was first printed as an opener to *Poor Richard's Almanac* for 1758. *"Trouble springs from Idleness,"* Franklin observed here, *"and grievous Toil from needless Ease."* The *needless Ease* to which such busyness led is now, of course, the subject of a literature, or sociology, to itself.

that lags almost consciously behind the social destiny. We are here simply invited to extend the advertising we see into real life, and suddenly everything will WORK! Fortunately, forcible conformity is not everyone's recipe for the good life, nor has the human animal found true deliverance through the opium of forced labor.

Social Redundancies

One emphatic way of disrupting silence is, of course, through social jargon. The result must usually be to cast suspicion on words in general, in common with any cheapening of articulation. We note that one of the first things the Chinese captors of GI's taken in Korea did was to get their prisoners to verbalize. This was particularly damaging since, in their case, they had no world to check against their words. Mail was either cut off or censored to assist this process. Those who refused to speak at all were labeled *reactionaries* and given up as a bad job, like art critics with us; for the *progressives* a confessional autobiography was the first step in the breaking-down process. Every schoolboy knows that a falsification he repeats often enough to himself becomes increasingly acceptable as truth.[12]

Without a phonetic alphabet one cannot easily transcribe voice accents on a printed page; and it is largely by accent that social jargon is conveyed.[13] I have, for instance, listened to one end of a telephone call during which a man said "Okay" eighteen times, each time in a slightly different intonation; I have heard much the same in Germany in the use of the word *so*. Still, I wager that most city Americans would spot the ethnic origins of the two greeting exchanges I heard yesterday:

1. Joe: Hello!
   Jake: Say, hello!
   Joe: So what's new?
   Jake: Ach nothing. How's by you?

[12]See my article "Semantics as Therapy," *Twentieth Century,* 164:977 (July 1958), pp. 44–50. This article was based on what were thought to be facts, as given in Eugene Kinkead's *In Every War but One,* a series of *New Yorker* articles gathered into a book; Albert D. Biderman's *March to Calumny* challenges the picture Kinkead gives, and I would have now to qualify my article accordingly.

[13]The Monotype keyboard presently boasts, of course, seven available alphabets—roman capitals, roman lower case, italic capitals, italic lower case, small capitals, bold capitals, bold lower case.

Joe: Well, I got my health.
Jake: That's the main thing. How's business?
Joe: It's a living. What could I tell you?

2. Joe: Hey baby!
Jake: Hey hey what's hopping?
Joe: Nothing much. Still seeing Betty?
Jake: Man!
Joe: Where you going?
Jake: Home.
Joe: See you, man.
Jake: Cool!

Henry Roth's *Call It Sleep*, originally published in 1935, has one passage describing the language of a lower East Side crowd that gathers round the body of a victim of electric shock in the subway:

"Holy Mother O' God! Look! Will yiz!"
"Wot?"
"There's a guy layin' there! Burrhnin'!"
"Naw! Where!"
"Gawd damn the winder!"
"It's on Tent' Street! Look!"
"Oy! Oy Vai! Oy Vai! Oy Vai!"
"Git a cop!"
"An embillance—go cull-oy!"
"Don't touch 'im!"
"Bambino! Madre Mia!"
"Mary. It's jus' a kid!"
"Helftz! Helftz! Helftz! Yeedin! Rotivit!"

Recently the British *The Use of English* observed that " 'Excuse me' is only one of the phrases current today which has lost its original meaning. Today it means 'Get out of the way.' 'Can I help you, sir?' means 'What the hell are you doing here?' 'With due respect' or 'In all respect' means 'I have no respect for your opinions at all.' "

To Americans, needing silence less, and thus developing a considerable rhetoric of social redundancies, such examples seem all too mild. What, it might be asked, are the informational meanings of the following passages in italics?

1. By *popular* demand we present *in person* Jayne Mansfield.
2. *Get out of here!*
3. *To tell you the truth,* I find him a bore.
4. *Whaddya say?*
5. *Do you want to* open the window?
6. It's pot-luck, but *we knew you wouldn't mind.*
7. Judy, *what a gorgeous dress!*
8. *To be frank,* I'd rather not.
9. *The simple fact is. . . .*
10. You're *perfectly welcome.*
11. *Nice party, huh?* How 'bout a drink?
12. I just don't like him, *see.*
13. Of course I'm liberal. Why, *some of my best friends. . . .*
14. *Take it easy!*
15. *See you.*
16. *Have fun.*
17. Sorry, but *I think* you have the wrong number.

If you "present" Jayne Mansfield you are compelled to do so *en persona.* Just as someone who gives birth to a girl has to give birth to a *baby* girl. I once caught a movie ad for *The Spiral Staircase* "with Rod Steiger in the title role," i.e. as a winding stair. The British locution "to do *damn all*" means to do nothing. The same reverse redundancy is seen in "He's *had* it," meaning that, in fact, he hasn't had it.[14] (The point seems proved when the idiom is transposed: I have seen this translated in German as the positive, and non-selfcontradictory, *Das ist im Eimer.*) The same confusion was manifested by a new hotel in Puerto Rico which advertised "Two World Famous Dining Rooms" before opening. When a character in Lewis Carroll's *Sylvie and Bruno* is asked what kind of a night he's had, he replies: "There's only been *one* night since yesterday!"

I once tried my hand at weaving such mislocutions into a story. Here is part of it. The harried freshman T. C. Mits, Jr. is on his way to give his girl friend a present, a box of chocolates.

Mits crosses to a newsstand, whose wares he peruses to see if the latest issue of "Thrush" has come in.

[14]This and other ironies of expression of RAF slang in the last war are briefly discussed by Eric Partridge in his *Words at War: Words at Peace* (London: Frederick Muller, 1948).

"Lookin' fer sumpin', bub?" asks the vendor.

Nervously Mits turns and crosses the street back to his bus-stop. A speeding Chevvy knocks him sprawling.

"Didja see that?" a woman runs up to him and cries.

As he writhes in pain, a man inquires, *"You hurt?"*

Mits recovers and with the now somewhat battered box of chocolates in one hand catches his bus. Finally he gets off and makes for his girl friend's apartment. It is pouring with rain and long after midnight. His girl friend's father doesn't ap-preciate visits to his daughter after ten. But Mits manages to avoid the ogre and is tiptoeing down the passage after his be-loved, when the father appears and pointing to a huge grand-father clock shouts out, *"Do you know what time it is?"*

Mits shrugs and follows his girl into the room, where he stands disconsolately dripping.

"Gee, *is it raining out?"* she asks.

Shyly he pushes the box towards her.

"For me?" she squeals.

"No!" Mits roars suddenly. "For Rover."

A communication has proceeded since in human conversation emotion sometimes fractures reason and sound can precede sense. No one—outside an asylum or that other form of it, a university—responds to these ritual utterances on a grammatical level. In Eng-land someone says, "Would you open the window?" In America, "Do you want to open the window?" But volition is no more at is-sue than it was when my Sandhurst Sergeant-Major used to bellow at me on parade, "You wanna wake up, you do!" When a Scots housewife says to her grocer, "I was wanting a lettuce" or "Who will that be now, at the door?" she is getting her meaning over by means of old modal forms which are themselves "ungrammatical" in the context concerned.

Dr. Eric Berne, of psychological games fame, reduces greeting rituals to a rather arch scoring system, and analyzes their psycho-dynamics. You intuit, Berne proposes, that you owe your neighbor a certain number of greeting "units" (or pointless points) daily. If he has returned from a vacation, you owe him more, and so forth. Distortions in such transactions can cause suspicion:

Mr. E and Mr. F have set up a two-stroke ritual, Hi-Hi. One

day instead of passing on, Mr. E stops and asks: "How are you?" The conversation proceeds as follows:

1E: "Hi!"

1F: "Hi!"

2E: "How are you?"

2F *(Puzzled.)*: "Fine. How are you?"

3E: "Everything's great. Warm enough for you?"

3F: "Yeah." *(Cautiously.)* "Looks like rain, though."

4E: "Nice to see you again."

4F: "Same here. Sorry, I've got to get to the library before it closes. So long."

5E: "So long."[15]

Joyce poked fun at the stereotypical nature of such rituals years ago, when he closed his party in "The Dead" with a butcher's dozen "Good-night" 's.[16]

Sound Before Sense

We need to be reminded that we are making sounds in this way Shaw so reminded an Irish audience heckling him at a time when nationalistic aspiration was using Gaelic as a tool. "If you don't shut up," said Shaw, "I'll deliver the rest of my speech in Gaelic and not one of you will understand a word." Nationalistic passion for Gaelic, meanwhile, recently resulted in the inscription *Déanta sa t-Seapain* on plastic leprechauns, recently sold in Dublin; I doubt if all the tourists who carried off these souvenirs knew that this morsel of old Erse meant "Made in Japan."

These erosions have been fructifying. We know we do little more than make sounds when we swear . . . when we bark an orally incomprehensible drill command. Our thoughts are shaped by physical presence, and, thanks to physical rhythms, a word with long vowel sounds will always suggest slow rather than rapid movement in our minds.[17] When breath passes through a narrow rather than

[15]Eric Berne, *Games People Play,* New York: Grove Press, 1964, p. 39.

[16]*The Portable James Joyce,* New York: Viking Press, 1949, p. 230. E. M. Forster has a similarly ritualistic leave-taking in which nine "Good-bye" 's are exchanged (*A Passage to India,* New York: Harcourt, Brace and Company, 1952, p. 79). Compare also the last lines of the second section of T. S. Eliot's *The Waste Land,* also with somewhat the same semantic effect and, no doubt, intention.

[17]See Henry Lanz, *The Physical Basis of Rhyme,* Stanford, Calif.: Stanford University Press, 1931.

a large opening, appropriate ideas (of weakness, slenderness etc.) accompany the sound. The motor activity (respiration, pulsation) impresses the experience.

Onomatopoeia is Greek for name-making. The Greeks meant by this that a noise makes its own name (e.g. *ping-pong*). There are, of course, thousands of such basically imitating words—*whip, fizz, hum, buzz*—everyone can think of his own favorite in the field. What is important to realize in this root creation, however, is the degree of word-wisdom or echo symbolism that enters into the process of coinage. Henry Bradley, in *The Making of English*, puts his finger on this when he points out: "the rendering of noises into the sounds of human speech involves some play of fancy, like that which is exercised when we see faces in the fire, or landscapes in the clouds." Which is to say that in onomatopoeia we are producing a mental picture first and foremost; this can be instanced in Carroll's *Alice* books and *The Hunting of the Snark*.

Unfortunately, onomatopoeia—like assonance and consonance and other sound effects produced by the human oral system—is today learnt by rote as, principally, an element of poetry. But animals imitate inarticulate by articulate sounds, with organs similar to our own; vocalic repetitions are audible to animals, as well as in English Departments, thus suggesting that phonetic symbolism provides the origin of a considerable word store. "And the silken, sad, uncertain rustling of each purple curtain," wrote Poe—and one can debate how much sense, rather than sound, one gets out of this line. John Crowe Ransom has composed a nonsense rhyme of sheer sound to reply to Tennyson's famous "murmuring of innumerable bees."

Thanks, chiefly, to Tennyson generations of college graduates today associate such effects with poetry. "With lisp of leaves and ripple of rain" (Swinburne); "With throats unslaked, with black lips baked" (Coleridge); "And by her in a line a milke white lambe she lad" (Spenser)—the examples could be prolonged indefinitely, liquid sibilants soothing and hushing one half to sleep. Browning's celebrated "*Hy, Zy, Hine* . . ." at the conclusion of his *Soliloquy of the Spanish Cloister,* much discussed, is probably a tintinnabulation. But the sound is realized in terms of content. Such is of major importance whenever the word defines itself by sound. Intrinsic expressiveness of this sort has been toyed with by Felicia Lamport, in "poems" like *Hmm* . . . :

Nothing gives rise to such wild surmise
As the peachable widow with consolate eyes.[18]

In fact, we support our sense daily with alliteration, assonance and the rest of the technical tricks of the poetry classroom. Because we learn them out of famous authors of the past, we often fail to recognize them in everyday life, describing cars, jets, the like. When we see such tricks in advertising, we conclude that a debasement has automatically taken place. To deride the onomatopoeia of advertising may show a certain semantic sensitivity, or it may not; communications mechanics are the issue. As Clyde Kluckhohn put it in *Mirror for Man,* "The meaning of a word or phrase is not its dictionary equivalent but the difference its utterance brings about in a given situation." In his *Language and Psychology* Samuel Reiss consorts with this opinion, finding the imitative quality psychological, rather than physical. Thus the word *creak* does not well represent the sounds we hear when opening a door; rather, a process of *creakiness* is attached to the word-sound.

When Milton ended Book II of *Paradise Lost* (itself a verbal lost paradise, of course), he made his famous line predictive of Satan's eventual descent to a serpent, as the devil is seen ascending from Hell to the created universe—"Accurst, and in a cursed hour, he hies." We hear a hiss. Our culture, unlike the Japanese, associates this sort of sibilance with dislike. It is our ear that here reads the pejorative for us. The whole subject has taken on a new dimension in an age which now tests sounds by decibels and kills horses by sonic boom, animals having been driven to eat their young by the noise of passing jets, and so on.

What is true of Milton's line applies to the parlance of disc jockeys. For this reason, parodies of poets strong in sound-wisdom, like Milton or Hopkins, tend to misfire since the parody utilizes the effects at work behind the sense being spoofed. In the same way, we seldom judge the words of someone introducing a famous speaker by the same syntactical standards that we use when listening to the eventual speech that follows. We assume a set of polite sounds, so many verbal pats on the back, before the great man opens up "in person." Strong sounds and rhythms accompany all

[18]From Felicia Lamport, *Scrap Irony,* Boston, Mass.: Houghton Mifflin Company, 1961. This is actually Jabberwock, which I discuss in the first chapter of Part Two.

forms of ritual address, from a marriage ceremony to a judge's sentencing. In fact, the black cap is really a word.

So true is this of religion, which is primitive in origin and taboo in discourse and to which we therefore concede a lot of musical leeway, that when I was a boy some of us used to recite the Lord's Prayer in chapel to a parody that held to the sound before the sense. One puzzled newcomer to this rite believed for quite a while that God's name was Harold ("Harold be Thy Name . . ."); sitting in their stalls, the masters knew no different.

Similarly, when Art Linkletter asked one American kid who the most important man in the country was, the answer was returned, "Dick Stands" ("the Republic for Richard Stands"). Autographing copies of a new novel in an Australian store, Monica Dickens wrote, in response to one lady's twang, "For Emma Chisitt." The woman replied that she was not giving her name, merely asking the price (London *Evening Standard*). The use of vernacular in the Mass has been the Catholic Church's somewhat tardy recognition of this word-wisdom. Similar concerns have, however, been voiced about Hebrew in Jewish synagogues, Sanskrit in Japan.

The Shape of Words to Come

At this point it is worth pausing to remind ourselves that a word is written as a construct of letters. Written English, as we know it, has a history of but some fifteen hundred years, the Roman alphabet being introduced into Britain by Christian missionaries. It is hard to overemphasize the alteration in semantic ratios that something like this can cause for the conscious life of a people. For there is nothing intrinsically closer to, say, the object I am sitting on in the written word *chair* than in the spoken syllable for it. Or vice versa. Both are conventional tokens.

For this reason the recent spread of auditory media, in telephone, loudspeaker, tape-recorder and the like, must to some extent be welcomed, if only because such techniques restore an emphasis which, in the eighteenth century at least, came into disrepute. We must not let ourselves forget that the spoken language came first, that speech is a direct physiological transmission of personality, and that it is primarily a speech sound which marks and makes an instinctive difference in meaning for man. This is what a phoneme does. The idea that it perishes rapidly on the zephyrs, unlike *lettera scripta,* is what has given such authority to the latter.

114

In fact, the printed representation of speech has become so unsatisfactory that an entire science (that of phonetics) has grown up in an effort to transcribe sounds with greater accuracy to the eye; there is thus an International Phonetic Association, with an official publication, *Le Maître Phonétique*. This science has found sympathy in America for if the Roman alphabet served to carry the thought of Christian missionaries fairly directly, it is less satisfactory for the purposes of a polyglot nation of nearly two hundred million relatively recent immigrants. "Thou whoreson zed! thou unnecessary letter!" cries Kent in *King Lear* of the then dubious final sign of the alphabet, a Latin ampersand pronounced *zee* in America. He finds an echo in modern education.

When I first came to America I was confronted with the public use—brazen in neon—of phoneticisms like TONITE . . . DEE-LUX. This appalled me. Surely such spellings were glaring illiteracies. Or illiteration. They probably were and are (since they do not form part of any intelligent system), but the doubling of vowel letters to indicate vowel length (*bōk*—book) was standard ME (Middle English) practice, and Chaucer varied the identical *i* sound several times in a matter of lines. He spelt island *iland,* which, put into today's neon, would be taken as another barbarism. The *s* was inserted into this word by knucklehead scribes, or "inkhorns," of the same ilk as the pedants I have scoriated above, who wanted to show Latin ancestry in all English words wherever possible, and erroneously chose *insula,* rather than Anglo-Saxon *ig-land,* as the source word. Here pronunciation did not, incidentally, follow orthography, but often it did. The supposedly genteel Latinate *th* imported into *autor* was followed by the speaking public (the introduction of Latinate *b* into *det* and *dout* from France similarly cast aspersion on direct spelling).

Some of the written-English pedants of my youth ought to have done a stint in the free-ring circus of an American city college. Even in the Ivory League I wager they would soon take for granite, in Freshman themes at least, coinings like the Sermon on the Mound, Albert Ross (of *Ancient Mariner* fame), Leonard Duvinsky (the Leonardo Da Vinci of the *garment centre*), psychoceramics (the study of crackpots?) and so on. I wager my prepschool headmaster would have turned white as a sheik at some of the temptation marks I've had to correct in my day. Much adieu about nothing, in short.

These are not truly illiteracies. Or at least we are misdirecting our pedagogic energies if we correct them *only* as such. They simply mean that people are not looking when they're writing. Harassed students, under the pressure of contemporary invigilation, increasingly fail to differentiate spoken from written words. The emphasis on the latter has by now come to be yet another dead hand in our education—principally so for social reasons.

A letter suggests a sound. At the start of its career Roman letter usage was phonetic. After printing began, certain forms of letters appeared and certain others disappeared. According to John S. Kenyon, whose *American Pronunciation* is an acknowledged classic in this field, Milton—a study man, note, and finally blind—was one of the first great English writers to help standardize certain spellings for posterity. Thus the 1611 Bible has "I am iealous for Ierusalem. . . ." Milton generally used *i* for vowels and *j* for consonants, but the British Museum didn't separate *i* and *j* in their catalog until about 1930.

With the change in speech, particularly in certain vowel sounds, our alphabet became less phonetic. There was an ever greater rift between sound and spelling—until you reach the well-known eccentricities of English pronunciation famous among foreigners (according to the "Phonetics" article in the eleventh edition of the *Encyclopaedia Brittanica*, "English shows the maximum of irregularity and arbitrariness").

Staff/laugh/graph . . . laughter/daughter/slaughter . . . seize/squeeze/grieve . . . singer/ginger/finger . . . novel/oval/shovel . . . city/cat/vicious (for disparate *c* sounds)—the list could be prolonged indefinitely, and has given rise to various rhymes.[19]

A foreigner, or American, arrives in England, tries a broad *a* in

[19]One particularly appropriate example by Katherine Buxbaum in a 1945 *Word Study* includes the following:

> I came beneath a pine tree bough
> When I was searching for my cough.
> I could not reach the pine cones, though,
> The branch was high and I was lough.
> "Ah, me," I cried, with rueful laugh,
> "Would that I were a tall giraugh."
> Just then a wind came hurtling through,
> The branches cracked, so fierce it blough. . . .

general, but comes a cropper on *classic* and *regatta*. Orwell complained that to spell *toe the line* as *tow the line* twists the original metaphor out of shape, but how is a foreigner to know? Shaw's remark about England and America being separated by a common tongue was bang on. His suggestion was that *fish* be spelt *ghoti* on the basis of the *gh* sound in laugh and *ti* in *ambition*, the *o* being taken from *women*. The spelling of the word *minute* conveys little about the sense in which this collection of letters is to be taken ("Wait for me a minute minute, would you"). Add to this that in actual fact no one speaks quite like anyone else, and you will be forced to goggle at the temerity of those who try to preach standards in this regard.

Until recently any diversity of pronunciation was to be deplored in upper-class English education. There was U-English, then accents—rather as there was Eton, and then the rest. To pronounce *Arctic* without the central *c*, or *library* without the central *r*, was sheer slovenliness, just as it was considered outright laziness to say (as did almost everyone else in England except prepschool headmasters) *goverment*. This was poor pron*oun*ciation. Such habits led to an evil life and, worse, to bad grammar—like *use to*.

Pointless to point out how Kenyon showed that the *a* in *sofa* could be represented by dozens of spellings (*e* in *fallen, o* in *gallop* etc.) or that George Faust faulted stress dictionaries for not marking the second syllable of *cargo* although it carried more accent (more stress cargo) than the second syllable of *sofa*. Such men were Americans. The American "twang," so offensive to U-speakers of my youth, is, according to Norman Stageberg, "caused by the habit of slightly lowering the velum for sounds that are normally oral, thus permitting some of the air to go out through the nasal cavity."

The air that went out through the oral cavities of my first spelling instructors was originally blown with authority in the eighteenth century, when lexicographers held that the speech actually heard was usually rather barbarous and "embarrassing," and that written English, as much less painful, was the authoritative standard for formal pronunciation. Dr. Johnson acknowledged that "language was at its beginning merely oral" (note the *merely*), but that just too much of it was presently spoken: "When I took the first survey of my undertaking, I found our speech copious without order."

About as far as he would go was to begrudge, "In settling the orthography, I have not wholly neglected the pronunciation." He further specified: "For pronunciation, the best general rule is to consider those as the most elegant speakers who deviate least from the written words." He would not, then, have got to Cirencister, which is pronounced in England *Sissister,* nor even to Salisbury *(Sawlsbury),* or Greenwich *(Grennitch).* Nor would he have ridden to hounds with the Belvoir *(Beaver).* But in no case would he have done so.[20]

Of course, Johnson is not to be blamed. His achievement, in the time, was heroic, but he was no more than a man of his times. He was paid to "fix" language, and he tried to fix it. In 1712 Swift had suggested a plan for such fixing of "correct" English to the Earl of Oxford. Johnson was given a cruelly short schedule, and the way he worked itself shut the door on pronunciation. He simply read books, underlining words and slipping them to his underpaid amanuenses (one of whom, a Scot called Francis Stewart, explained "low cant phrases"). James Clifford's *Young Sam Johnson* illustrates this clearly. Johnson's manner was his matter, and from all accounts it seems that he tried to rationalize work habits forced on him by want, in stressing the difficulty of "fixing" so many conflicting views of pronunciation. And it must be admitted that the method was Voltaire's—"when one has a sufficient number of approved authors, a language is fixed."

Moreover, although the Johnsonian method emphasized the authority of the past (to the extent that archaisms were often preferred to contemporary definitions), it showed that language is built on usage. The *Preface* confesses this, perhaps a trifle reluctantly. The word is its world. Johnson knew language too well to be faithless to it. For, furthermore, the legislative or "fixing" intention was forced to yield to objective recording. Such is admitted in Johnson's remarks about speech. Today it is estimated that if all speakers used the full English word stock, the lexicographer would have somehow to reflect 112,500,000,000,000 individual pronunciations.[21]

---

[20]There is, of course, the celebrated Berkeley *(Barclay)*/Derby *(Darby)* syndrome. Americans pronounce Berkeley *Burkly* (cf. clerk-*clurk*). But this is how quite a bit of England pronounces it, too, and a *burk* in Cockney rhyming slang depends entirely on the US/non-U pronunciation. For from *burk* you go to *Burkly 'unt* which naturally rhymes with *cunt.* Which is what a *burk* is.

But it was out of the legislative side of Johnson's efforts that there came three pronouncing dictionaries in the following twenty-five years. Such were, like my headmaster, socially legislative. An emergent bourgeoisie wanted to know what was their equivalent of U-speech. (This is Johnson's emphasis on "the most elegant speakers," or polite society.) These early pronouncing dictionaries indicated accent by superscript numerals and the like. But this conferral of powers to various sounds lets in still more individual difference.

For this reason practically no recent dictionary makes such pretensions, and if it does so it is wrong. (The intentions of Webster's editors should not be confused with those of their advertisers.) "The simple solution of the whole difficulty," wrote the late Professor T. R. Lounsbury of Yale, "is that in the matter of pronunciation there is no standard of authority at all. Nor, as things now are, can there be." One has only to contrast the words of John Walker, in his Preface to *A Critical Pronouncing Dictionary and Expositor of the English Language* of 1791: "If the analogies of the language had been better understood, it is scarcely conceivable, that so many words in polite usage would have a diversity of pronunciation which is at once so ridiculous and embarrasing."

This idea, that there is some "true" sound of words, some fixable "purity" of diction and language, has done irreparable damage. Even in my lifetime, even in the relatively advanced communities in which I have lived, it has meant the loss of much poetry. It has meant that troops of children with slates and/or schoolbooks under their arms have traipsed over muddy fields to schoolhouses to get rid of their "embarrasing" idiosyncrasies of speech. In other words, of their mother tongue. The Scots boy was told that the Doric was not "polite usage," and learnt how to say Old Long Since for Auld Lang Syne with the best of BBC announcers. Mexican Maria similarly lost much of the magic of her language when she went to Spain and found the bourgeoisie aspirating the *h* and giving *c*'s a *th* sound. Corsican Davia learnt to lose the language she used at home—again the only one that could express shades of reality endemic to her native island; she learnt the "polite usage" of French. No one would be "embarrassed" by her Corse any more. Meanwhile Virginia Woolf (whose letters to Lytton Strachey cannot be

[21]Albert H. Marckwardt, "The Dictionary as a Guide to Pronunciation," *College Composition and Communication,* IV (May 1953), p. 35.

read by any language lover without cringing) complains of the way in which W. J. Turner pronounces *count*.[22]

Although my Corsican analogy may be shaky (since, in some respects, Corse is a corruption of a mother tongue), it is certain that this genteelizing attitude has lost us minority language after minority language in the past two centuries. Sapir—and he is joined in this by Lévi-Strauss from Brazil—says as much: "I found that it was difficult or impossible to teach an Indian to make phonetic distinctions that did not correspond to 'points in the pattern of his language,' however these differences might strike our objective ear, but that subtle, barely audible, phonetic differences, if only they hit the 'points in the pattern,' were easily and voluntarily expressed in writing."

If only they hit the points in the pattern. What a statement of magic, as well as of the physicality of words. I would even suggest that the Johnson-Walker position has come to stand so strongly for conservative values in general that England now actually treasures her involved eccentricities of spelling. Emblems of English apartness, and independence, they are like the comic uncles and eccentric aunts of her "smart" fiction.

For instance: Why *an* historian? Fowler condemned this habit (since the haitch was by now aspirated) in the very first entry of his usage. However, Fowler was non-U. Thus, hotel has an unaspirated haitch with British U-speakers, who would have to put *an* before it for the purpose of illision.[23] Such speakers would never spell laundry as they say it, namely *larndry*. Nor would they be likely to respect the fact that most inhabitants of Cirencester today pronounce their home town to conform with the spelling, anyway.

It is, rather, the secret code of a class, what German calls a *Geheimsprache,* and either you know it or you don't. Etymology can be no guide. The code is especially cherished in names, like the celebrated Cholmondeley *(Chumley),* or Caius College *(Keyes).*

---

[22]"A very small bird-like man with a desolating accent . . . but really a nice little fellow, when one has got over the way in which he says 'count' " (Virginia Woolf and Lytton Strachey, *Letters,* ed. Leonard Woolf and James Strachey, New York: Harcourt, Brace and Company, 1956, p. 143).

[23]Whether or not an *a* or an *an* should precede *hotel* was lengthily debated in the House of Lords during June 1956. The U *an* won out. Lord Conesford suggested that "every one of your Lordships would say 'a Harrow boy' but would also speak of 'an Harrovian.' " But would they ever mention the topic at all?

I soldiered with a man whose surname sounded *Fanshawe;* it was spelt Featherstonehaugh. There is no rationale and part of the point is that there should not be any. Social taste must remain the sole arbiter. Thus Beaulieu is pronounced *Bewley.* By the same token it would not be incorrect to pronounce Fontainebleu as the hotel of that name in Miami is heard there—*Fountainblue.* But it is incorrect, partly because Americans do it, but principally because U-speakers don't.

The moment at which you incorporate into your native pronunciation some foreign word seems similarly arbitrated; it is considered affected to speak French words in a French way in an English sentence (though a slight stress on the second syllable of *garage* will not go amiss). This is again a matter of a secret style, and has little to do with linguistics. What now seems apparent in England is that the old minutiae of such parlance are too tied to a vanished social order.[24] Certainly something more comprehensive and more innocuous must be chosen for radio and television; commercial advertising seeks a neutral norm, or what is called "register." In practice this presently works out to be pseudo-American, middle-Atlantic or "Canadian." Especially is this true of sportscasting.

Frenetic Spelling

It is one thing for Britons to waive the rules and evolve a synthetic amalgam for radio usage; it is quite another for genuine Americans to give *herbs* a properly U inaspiration, to pronounce schedule with a *sk* that is closer to its classical origin; they are still "Ameddicans."

We are not dealing here with more than a method of social discrimination, and so much has this become the case that in certain circles spelling phonetically means spelling inaccurately. *Tonite* is incorrect, on the same terms that *iland* is incorrect (or *hite* for height). Furthermore, though the *i* in all three words reports the spoken reality more accurately than what we now have, *hite* would usually be considered a more damning crime in a child's essay than the misspelling *heighth.* There seems at times to be a conspiracy of "elegance" to prevent spelling from molding itself to English

[24]"A man who speaks in what would have been called an educated way can hardly any longer appear in a play or film except as a figure of fun" (*Daily Telegraph,* August 23, 1966).

pronunciation. What Johnny finally learns is that the only way to spell right is never to spell wrong.

A great deal has been written about the difference between British and American speech rhythms,[25] and this is not the book in which to add to the subject. As one who was educated in England and now educates in America, however, I have had to learn the hard way, turning my æ diphthongs into e's, banning the hyphen when in doubt, and knocking the u's out of my -our suffixes and the ue's out of my -ogue's. Noticing, too, that when certain spurious British glamour is to be attached to a word, like *Glamour* on the cover of the magazine of that name, logical grammar is neglected; Third Webster still retains the u in this word. No one is to blame for this, but the mechanics must be understood for what they are.[26] With any luck advertising and allied forces will compel written symbols with genuine impressions of the words concerned upon even our dictionaries.

Before passing on, however, I might mention one Anglo-American difference of interest here; that is the heavy accenting of syllables in sequence which so strongly differentiates the American from the British. Try *Hampshire, mountain, blackberry* either side of the "big drink." Or *military, miscellany.* The Englishman nearly always stresses one syllable pre-eminently, e.g. *mìll-try,* rather than *mil-it-àry. Miscellany* is the same, with the limey hitting the central syllable hard and letting the rest go hang. The American emphasis on each syllable sounds to the English as a "drawl" (and since it is a variation from their prevailing standard it sounds substandard). Allen Walker Read suggested to me that American nineteenth-century alphabet primers may have been responsible for much of this effect of "drawl," by requiring children to linger carefully on each syllable. This practice is sometimes called correct enunciation and was more recently propagated (in America, at least) by F. H. Vizetelly.[27]

[25]See Eilert Ekwohl, "American and British Pronunciation," *Studia Neophilogica,* Oppsala: Lundequist, 1946.

[26]For a thesaurus of such oddities of spelling, see Michael West's excellent *A Dictionary of Spelling (British and American),* London: Longmans, 1964. The second edition of H. W. Horwill's *American Usage* (Oxford, 1944) was good for its day, though written for the British.

[27]Cf. "We ought to let every syllable come out round and full like a golden bubble" (Robert Hillyer, *In Pursuit of Poetry,* New York: McGraw-Hill, 1960, p. 45).

All the same, it is interesting that "better speech" books for American schoolchildren still agree in making a rule of careful stressing of the final syllable. Charles Fries cites one such instructional text of recent years that requires stress on the final syllable in such words as *Boston* and *pupil*. No American I know says *Bostòn*. Moreover, I am not myself sure that preaching against illision (i.e. to say *snow and ice* instead of, as everyone does, *snow'nd ice*) is good language practice. It certainly hinders you when you speak French. Again, with any luck, popularisms (like *His 'n' Hers*) will insist on introducing reality. As Wittgenstein put it, in his *Tractatus* (4.015): "nor does our phonetic spelling (letters) seem to be a picture of our spoken language. . . ."

Sly Twitch or Slight Witch?

As regards hidden language, then, we can advance the following: (1) the human voice is today more widely heard than at any time in history; (2) standards of pronunciation are based on heard voices; (3) English lacks on accurate conventional spelling.

By contrast, Italian, Hungarian, Korean and Finnish are said to have simple spellings, or word physiques. Spanish letters and digraphs are also claimed to correspond more closely to what a kid is actually asked to transcribe (a lot of our digraph forms come from the French, anyway). Again, sign and sound are said to match cogently in Russian: so much so that we are told that in the first grade happy little Ivans are working on passages of Tolstoy after only a few months of learning a vocabulary based on the thirty-three characters of the Russian alphabet. This, it is suggested, is why Russia is ahead in the space race.[28]

I can't confess that "overtaking Russia" appears a particularly succulent carrot to hold in front of the donkey of spelling reform. Indeed, phoneticists exaggerate the attractions of precision and order which are supposed to make Vanya's eyes light up with joy whenever he sees a word. Arithmetic is arithmetic. But it seems useless to deny that Anglo-American spelling is fantastically wasteful of our children's energies; it is also tied to social attitudes of which the best that can be said is that they are impractical. The physique of his word no longer gives Johnny his world.

The official reply to such semantic criticism is that there are per-

[28] See Helen Bowyer, "It's Not Johnny!" *Phi Delta Kappan*, xxxx (June 1959), pp. 378–380.

fectly good reasons for spelling English words the way English words are spelt. And anyway the system "works." (This latter is a familiar catchphrase of the indolent; in one sense, everything "works," like the Ptolemaic system of old.) The difficulty, we are told, inheres in the very character of the language. Moreover, to make our alphabet more "phonetic" would be to cut off our young from much great literature of the past. To follow these defenders of the faith, or orthographic *status quo,* our task with Johnny is to give him proper grounding in Saxon, French, Roman, Egyptian, Phoenician and Arabic derivations of his word store. Naturally he should, like the young Montaigne, know Latin before his own tongue. Today a short course in Japanese would help, too. After which, all he has to do is get up the habits of fifteenth-century printers, and he'll never go wrong. He will then be able to tell you that Yorkshire *riding* really comes from Danish *thrithing* or, if you wish, that the word *spell* itself has four etymological origins, each with variant histories converging into one. Eventually, when Johnny becomes a man, he may be able to write a book like *The Mother Tongue,* by the Vice-Chancellor of the University of Guiana, Lancelot Hogben, who can even impart such vital information as how his own name came into being. I am not at all sure that a more phonetic spelling would not simply be a utilitarian spelling, a new newspeak. It might even be harder! But if this is the best the academy can do to detract from phonetic proponents, then I hand the palm to the reformers, for they are at least in touch with child and student life.

In England, one particularly successful intermediary alphabet has been devised, and its effects studied in the Reading Research Unit of London University and at Leeds University (the former closed in 1967 for lack of funds though 300 schools used the method). This is the "augmented Roman" or Initial Teaching Alphabet, devised by Sir James Pitman and utilizing forty-four letters and digraphs. Shaw's idea, if you remember, was for an alphabet of forty letters. (Chinese has 8,000 character-words.) The phonetic consistency of ITA helps children get going, and secondly, it allows a fairly smooth switch to normal print with increased comprehension. Since a digraph is a combination of letters, it retains some phonic character and should satisfy multiperceptual addicts like Marshall McLuhan, while the whole treatment of reading as a progressive sophistication, not simply something to "learn" and get out of the way early on, is surely most healthy.

For it must be said that the apogee, or nadir, of antiprint mania is to be found in Marshall McLuhan's wide-ranging *The Gutenberg Galaxy*, already mentioned. This book presupposes that "the eye has none of the delicacy of the ear" and that "speech is an outering (utterance) of all of our senses at once." It is an attack, a fairly bloodthirsty one, on the habits of printed literature in favor of something called the ear, which is always axiomatically excellent. (As Harry Levin has put it, "oral literature" is really a contradiction in terms.) The Initial Teaching Alphabet would seem to show the child the phonic possibilities of script, emphasizing—with the change-over to ordinary print—that the word still contains its world.

Since McLuhan's confusions are rapidly becoming institutionalized in communications study, it is worth considering this work of his in passing. "The auditory field is simultaneous, the visual mode is successive." Yet McLuhan had just told us that savages cannot generalize their visual experiences, a prerogative of the sophisticated; therefore, the "mosaic" of the latter is not "successive." It is highly debatable, to say the least, that the eye is any more "successive" than the ear, and to go on to say that " 'writing' to a medieval student was not only profoundly oral but inseparable from what is now called oratory" is quite another tack altogether. That the Chinese "written character does not separate speech and visual code in our way" may be an equally unexceptionable (and unexceptional) statement; I do not know Chinese well enough to say, and doubt if McLuhan does, either. But the Chinese students to whom I have put this theory do not seem particularly galvanized by it, and of course China itself is happily alphabetizing its script, no doubt making it "visual, sequential, uniform, and lineal," in common with the Koreans who are said to have had cast-metal type by 1403.

Nor is it at all clear that McLuhan understands the printing process at all. He talks about something called "print" and that is that: in fact, the first wood blocks, laboriously cut to simulate the writing of scribes, barely speeded the process of script. Moreover, although presumably "sequential," the Linotype machine (commonly used in newspaper work) casts individual *lines* of type, while the roll taken off the Monotype machine to the caster is nonpredicative since it "plays back," unwinding backward.

Although McLuhan ducks out from specific evaluation, everywhere asserting that he is only studying what is happening to us in media, the "visual, sequential" is, we note, *uniform* and undoubtedly disliked. "We have spent much energy and fury in recent centuries in destroying oral culture by print technology so that the uniformly processed individuals of commercial society can return to oral marginal spots as tourists and consumers, whether geographical or artistic." It is hardly likely that man would have proceeded with this "destruction" for century after century if it were not in some way necessary for him to do so. And indeed, McLuhan has to admit that it is print that has kept principles like *freedom* in the forefront of man's social and political dialogs.

Once again the truth is that McLuhan's terms "visual" and "oral" are, like his terms "hot" and "cool" in *Understanding Media,* so hypergeneralized as to be applicable at will, and even interchangeably. As Kenneth Burke has put it, "We here confront a mere matter of terministic policy." (The "hot" and "cold" analogy was, incidentally, used many years ago by Lévi-Strauss.) We are told that unlike "visual" English and American audiences (watching *The Bridge Over the River Kwai*), Frenchmen are "oral." Ah, come off it! *Is* the ear more sensitive and multiperceptual than the eye? Who says so? McLuhan says so, just as he decides at the end of this study that "lineal specialisms and fixed points of view" are dissolved in 1905, with, presumably, Einstein and Planck.

Similarly, we are told that "with film you are the camera. . . . But with TV you are the screen." This sounds delightfully adroit, smooth cocktail patter indeed, but it was written at a moment when about 80 percent of most TV consisted of film, and the remainder of filmic techniques.[29] However, we are reminded of the heresy of such an objection—"This, of course, is to consider only the 'content' of new theories." TV soaks up dud film, McLuhan alleges, because any new medium needs matter; the early printing presses pleaded for manuscripts.

This argument, and others, are so many schoolmen's tricks. We are assured that form produces its own content at will. Thus McLuhan answers himself by his own question; he confuses origin and import, cause and effect. His tautology on television boils down to this. Bad TV is merely the "content" of a past form—being borrowed, as it were, by the new form—until it throws up new content itself. As there is virtually no other content available to examine,

[29]In the strike by AFTRA (American Federation of Television and Radio Artists) of April 1967, it was shown that 85 percent of programming was still produced on film—only the remaining 15 percent being live or taped.

however, one is left to speculate on the basis of form alone. We end up by conceding that only McLuhan can predict the future.

A similar aheadofness race can be discerned in modern art. ("Works of art aren't eggs," T. E. Hulme objected.) Only the pundit is supposed to know what is *avant-garde*—that is, in the position of possibly being great art at a future date. But the pundit is part of his time, and his criteria of prediction could be made to fit, too, the dreariest academic realism of its day.[30] McLuhan reminds me of that moment in a Marx Brothers movie showing the comedians in an operating room, dashing about madly with stethoscopes and scalpels, their white coats covered with blood. A real doctor looks in and cries, aghast, "Hey! You guys must be crazy." One of the four turns on him with beatific grin—"That's what they said about Pasteur."[31]

This confusion of form and content, which in fact comprises a harmony like word and world, is dangerous epistemology and needs exposing, since it leads to excitable action. As Alfred North Whitehead gently put it, "Error is the price we pay for progress."

For speech is *not* purely "oral"—whatever that may be—one cannot form close categories out of human senses. Literacy itself is multisensory, as the use of Pitman's "augmented Roman" shows. Speech, too, is very largely sequential, and is only fully speech in a contextual situation of which it takes full cognizance. The sounds of foreign words give no clue to their meaning. Here I am of course talking about symbolic or "transparent" words, not the kind of word-signs discussed as onomatopoeia, which are tonal forms instinct with the cuckoo's cry, the owl's hoot and the like. Thus the word for mother—especially the child's diminutive—is close in a

[30]Notably the criterion of newness. "Beaujolais 1964 is here!" yodels a Bordeaux Wines & Liquors Corp. ad . . . in 1964.

[31]The misreading of literature in this text also attains at times a kind of genius. What does the repeated catchphrase "Hopkins and the symbolists" mean? Which symbolists? When? Well, we mustn't forget that "Symbolism is a kind of witty jazz." Nor that Freud would "have carried no interest" unless "the West had long been processed by print." The seventeenth century "emerged into a merely visual science in its conscious life," and the "painterly strategy" [*sic*] since Cézanne has been "to paint as if you held, rather than as if you saw, objects." There is space but for one final clobbering of truth by these kinship terms: "The miseries of conflict between the Eastern and Roman churches, for example, are a merely obvious instance of the type of opposition between the oral and the visual cultures, *having nothing to do with the Faith*" (italics added). And McLuhan can still quote Sidney's sonnet which concludes, " 'Fool,' said my Muse to me, 'look in thy heart, and write!' "

number of languages and obeys Maurice Grammont's theory of sound-metaphor; it no doubt responds to the sucking sound of a breast-fed infant. But the word for woman varies considerably.

In *Scientific American* for June 1960 James Cooke Brown writes on a synthetic language called Loglan. This goes beyond mere revision of the alphabet into the kind of differentia of meaning which that early semanticist, Charles Peirce, tried to organize under a complicated system of qualisigns, legisigns, semes, phemes and so forth. Loglan's grammatical apparatus is determined by 112 operators (Peirce boiled things down even further) and is predicated on the phonetic familiarity of a word. Thus Loglan for blue is *blanu,* containing 100 percent of the phonemes of the English blue, 100 percent of those for the Chinese *lan,* 50 percent of the Hindi *nila* etc. Loglan eschews nouns and verbs as such. It is what McLuhan might well call "oral." You take the phoneme percentages, multiply them by the percentage of the population employing that particular language, and come up with a total learnability score of .76. Interestingly, under this scheme, the most readily learnable word in the language is *matma,* which has a score of .94 and means guess what? Mother.[32]

After all, German *Gift* is almost the reverse of English *gift,* though pronounced practically the same. If I ask for *pétrole* in my local *épicerie* in France, I will not get petrol, or gasoline (which is *essence*), I will be poured a quantity of paraffin or kerosene oil for use in lamps. The word-sound *rock* means a jacket in German, a year in Czech, and fate in Russian; and this is a useful example since in England a rock is not a stone, as it tends to be in America. You could not hurl a rock at someone in the British Isles. The popular song group would have missed the point of its nomenclature by calling itself the Rolling Rocks.

The only writing I know which appeals wholly to the eye is mathematical. (Perversely, McLuhan finds number "an audile-tactile code.") Phonic character, like song, derives much of its richness from its slower speed. Seventeenth-century punctuation was "for the ear and not for the eye" perhaps. It was also much less

---

[32]Anyone wanting to follow the intricacies of phonetics should certainly consult Daniel Jones, *An Outline of English Phonetics,* New York: Dutton, 1956. There is also, of course, Sweet's *Handbook,* nearly a century old by now.

consistent than ours, and so slowed and varied the pace. No, as Susanne Langer has properly put it, "A sentence is a symbol for a state of affairs, and pictures its character."

Nonsound

Yet, when all is said and done, McLuhan strikes responsive chords. Student conversation is growing less and less verbal—though no more "oral" than "visual." Students have words slung at them all day long, day after day. The homogenizing effect of our school and college education is well identified by McLuhan: "The school system, custodian of print culture, has no place for the rugged individual. It is, indeed, the homogenizing hopper into which we toss our integral tots for processing." In *The Vanishing Adolescent* (Boston: Beacon Press, 1959) Edgar Z. Friedenberg agrees: "The process of becoming an American, as it goes on in high school, tends to be a process of renunciation of differences." Violation of language "rules" is seen as error rather than variation, and this pattern builds itself into a student's word-world.

Thus a contemporary student will often initiate a phone call with a neo-Neanderthal grunt or groan, whose shock value is intended to awaken "the other" out of the lethargy induced by the kind of ritual communication and formulaic discourse we have examined. Only by so doing can the door be opened to genuine communication. A groan has become a student's stock answer to a whole lot of questions. The letter from Salinger's Esme which prevents the suicide of Sergeant X in "For Esme—With Love and Squalor" appeals to the young on precisely this level, as does the note from the same author's Seymour Glass to his parents from his (rather camp) camp—"As you know in your hearts and bowels, I miss you like sheer hell." By the age of seven Sey can boast he's never once been guilty of saying, "What a nice day."

Such semantic disaffiliation is an insistence on honesty in discourse. The new generation, with its propensity to hide, play roles, "drop out," sees presymbolic utterance as part of the texture of the old. Among the young, ritual phrases of Dr. Berne's type are out. "My love, she speaks like silence," grates Bob Dylan, "without ideals of eyelids. . . ." Rimbaud boasted that he wrote silences. "Bob Dylan's songs and lyrics," declares Ralph Gleason, "changed my life because they provided a new nonideological basis for an attack upon the evils of our society."[33]

In Dylan's words this generation knows there's no success like failure, and are quite out of key with Rock Hudson or Dean Martin chasing Doris Day around a bed.[34] For a while Bogie even came back, as icon for those who rode Hondas in boots and sheepskin coats. The college mixer is gone for good. Question and answer alike are tongue-in-cheek. (Autistic children find it difficult to say "Yes.") Describing her sensations at one of the new multiperceptual nightclubs, an eighteen-year-old Vassar girl moves beyond words—"I give everything that is in me. And when I get going, I'm gone. It's the only time I feel whole." Fashion boasts the *no-look*.

In an odd way my own British upbringing of a generation ago was a concomitant of this. Nonsound was self-protection. With its ideal of the "stiff upper lip" (i.e. nonarticulating mouth), such education was predicated on the basis that the presymbolic is *per se* barbaric. (And I include in *barbaric* the old Greek sense of this term, as applying to sounds made by non-Greek-speaking foreigners.) The height of human intercourse was seen as the antithesis of the primitive—calm control, the kind of nonutterance of the men's club I have mentioned, or the prewar railway carriage.

In such a civilization you are allowed to sing in the bathtub, but never—like Latins—on the street.[35] D'Annunzio's airmen, on the other hand, were ordered to utter war cries when dropping their bombs; such atavistic shrieking was totally symbolic since it was unheard by their enemies. I remember how difficult Sergeant-instructors found it to get us to yell when plunging our bayonets into dummies on training. Religion, meanwhile, provided a safety

[33] Ralph J. Gleason, "The Children's Crusade," *Ramparts,* IV (March 1966), p. 28.

[34] Writing of a TV show in the *San Francisco Chronicle,* Ralph Gleason says: "The costumes are a dissent from the Ed Sullivan slick. . . . These performers NEVER have a nose-bob or cap their teeth. Instead of hiding a so-called bad feature, they accentuate it, like a living caricature." The flawed Venus of the symbolists (Poe's consumptives, Baudelaire's prostitutes and amputees) is truer to life than *Life;* when Bloom's Gerty McDowell got up, she was lame. For an opinion that corroborates mine, see Leo Hamalian, "The Loss of Tragedy," *The Nation,* 202:23 (June 6, 1966), pp. 676–679.

[35] "How we used to laugh at male foreigners for kissing each other on greeting!" (Alison F. Blood, Letter to the Editor, *Daily Telegraph,* August 9, 1966, p. 12). Lady Blood is here lamenting the spectacle of British soccer players hugging each other after a goal.

valve, with emotional chants and vituperative sermons. It will be long before I forget the satisfied manner in which my uncle, beside me in the pew, used to pronounce the final word of the *Te Deum*— "confounded!"

The basis of British "reserve" meant that volubility was suspect, and usually Latin ("Dagoes begin at Dover," the saying went). Tactile communication was minimal. The consequence was a sense of release for the Englishman when he first left home and was allowed—nay, encouraged—to indulge in presymbolic ritual in Italy, Spain, France. Now a thing of the past thanks to technological stereotyping, this liberation from the inhibitions of native semantic gave rise to a literature of British infatuation with Italy; any romance with another culture is usually a confession of insufficiency in one's own.[36] The code had, of course, considerable political repercussions.

To treat British U-usage, therefore, in anything other than the light whimsy of Professor Alan S. C. Ross has a most painful effect. Before the latter sections of *Noblesse Oblige*, contributed by Nancy Mitford and Evelyn Waugh, one longed to be voluntarily deaf, like St. Augustine's adder; for actually to discuss U-usage is, of course, the most non-U activity of all. Parenthetically, however, it is interesting that when Clifton Fadiman followed this treatise up with observations on American U-speech, the criteria given turned out to be no more than those for some successful public speaker or Dale Carnegie graduate ("avoidance of language fidgets" and other such irrelevancies). At the end of the eighteenth century William Cobbett set down in his *A Year's Residence in America,* that least baffled of British books on "the States," "There is no *brogue,* no *provincial dialect.*"

London, in U parlance (a non-U term), is always London in full, never *town*—which was of course U in the eighteenth century. Essentially, as observed, this dislike for abbreviation was a semantics of control. Abbreviations save time and the gentry do not need to save time. It involved an ostracism more potent than block or rack—the Gileadites slew everyone at the passage of Jordan who

[36]"Traditionally prone to attribute loose morals to the inhabitants of warm countries, British novelists are seldom able to imagine in convincing detail the relaxed depravity that so attracts them" (Glendy Culligan, "New Fiction," Book Week, Sunday New York *Herald Tribune,* March 6, 1966, p. 16).

said *sibboleth* rather than *shibboleth*—and young Brigade of Guards ensigns never had to be punished, by extra Picquet duties and the like, for infringements.

In this sense, as Malcolm Muggeridge put it, the only true Englishmen left today are Indians. (Or certain eastern Americans?) Dostoevsky's Stavrogin, Conrad's Schomberg, Turgenev's Bazarov, Hamsun's Glahn (who spits in a Baron's ear rather than go through polite discourse at a ball), such characters tried to break up this bridge game of "real" society to probe to the essence of things. Ginger men and Lucky Jims and Billy Liars were nerveless substitutes by comparison.

Besides irrelevantly saving time, to abbreviate—a crime Wilde claimed at his trial never to have committed—is to infringe, to invent, to play, and therefore to relax the emotional. But a desiderated omission, or ellipsis, is, in the main, a semantic reluctance; and since the word is its world, it is politically indicative.

Ellipsis and Litotes

Verbal understatement is a symbol of psychic security as much in an American "drop-out" of the sixties as in a British officer in India a century ago. When Ford Madox Ford titled the first volume of his tetralogy of "the last English gentleman," he did so with an ellipsis at the end—*Some do not. . . .*[37]

Now I have counted up to twenty ellipses per page of this work. Some do not—what? The omission is the point. For an ellipsis is a refusal to utter, something also operating in taboo.[38] It is unspeakable. A gentleman just doesn't. What he doesn't is precisely that undifferentiated of which Ford went on to write elsewhere: "It has been remarked that the peculiarly English habit of self-suppression in matters of the emotions puts the Englishman at a great disadvantage in moments of unusual stresses." Paradoxically, this

[37]Benjamin DeMott's 1966 study of American inhibitions was called in the same spirit *You Don't Say.* DeMott surveys patterns of inhibition which today veto "certain ways of feeling and talking that once were acceptable."

[38]"Give me a few well-placed dots, asterisks and dashes and leave a little to my imagination. Give me a wink instead of a straight stare. And preserve me from the pedantic scholarly zeal of the Sagarins and Youngs. They may consider themselves the comrades-in-arms of the grand daddy of American four-letter-word literature, Henry Miller, but they are in reality his antithesis" (an example of verbal playback from Felix Pollak, Letter, *Evergreen Review,* August/September 1964, p. 94).

suppression did provide a queer kind of psychic protection, too. If today we see the "pukka sahib" as a caricatural absurdity, he himself was able to reduce reality to a sort of last mad movie reel, and death to a dream. Check this in Rider Haggard's Zulu fiction.

In the very first chapter of his whole, Ford reflects of the hero, "As Tietjens saw the world, you didn't 'talk.' "[39] The parody of taciturnity makes its point. Much of England's greatness owes it a debt, from the telescope put to Nelson's blind eye to the purposeful ignorance of orders which led Raffles to Singapore, and British dominance of the Malay peninsula. Political glory was the obverse of a collective hushing-up of the national psyche. So the celebrated British understatement comes out as a sort of double negative. And if the ellipsis is one figure for avoiding utterance, that known as the litotes is its twin, or mirror image, and an equally important tool in the ritual of reserve.[40]

For this rhetorical form expresses an affirmative via the negative of its contrary (or by denying or refuting its opposite). OED cites "a citizen of no mean city." Satan's "not inglorious" strife in *Paradise Lost* is another instance. In the same poem Eve is seen as "Not unamazed." British U speech is, or was, full of this locution. Something hilariously funny will be termed *not unamusing*. Henry James used the litotes continually, and successors of James to such an extent that one sometimes wonders what meaning is thereby being passed, if any.

Thus some of Elizabeth Bowen's later fiction seems an essay in keeping the reader from reaching meaning at all: "Yet a hampered anger, anger at being hampered, rose in her breast. What she'd done—and what *had* she done?—was being made unspeakable by not being spoken." What is being conveyed here? Is the character

---

[39]For a fuller consideration of Ford's use of the ellipsis, see my article "Ford Madox Ford: The Honest Edwardian," *Carleton Miscellany,* VI:2 (Spring 1965), pp. 12–27.

[40]This book is not the one in which to identify the "out-of-context" use of the ellipsis. Bosley Crowther, of the *New York Times,* wrote in review of a recent French film: "While sparkling and penetrating in flashes, it is rather laboriously contrived." The ads here did not even have to distort by ellipsis, merely quoting Crowther's "sparkling and penetrating."*MAD Magazine* went to town on this habit. But when Jerry Tallmer panned a play in the New York *Post* as follows, *"The Pocket Watch* is a triumph of platitude and Jewish laughter and typical soap-opera anguish skillfully applied, and if they quote 'a triumph' in the ads you will know it isn't meant quite that way," why, the next day's ad read, " 'A TRIUMPH' . . . Tallmer, *Post."*

in question hampered by being hampered? It is not by any means the truism expressed by the grammatical apposition that, while a "hampered anger" may be "anger at being hampered," the latter is the former. In fact, the reverse would be more likely.[41]

Obviously there must be discrimination in such nuances. In the same book Miss Bowen writes, "Mush for the chickens, if nothing else, was never not in the course of cooking." This is certainly different from "Mush for the chickens was always cooking." But if used equally of cooking mush for chickens *and* deep emotional states, the litotes loses force as a verbal structure and becomes a mere mannerism, style in decay. Similarly, it can be seen that in advertising the ellipsis often loses its power as an absence.

I suggest it was partly for this reason, for this collective and substantive litotes, that England was unable to diagnose the semantic of Nazi Germany. Revivalism never took strong root in Britain. Hitler's noise orgies were seldom understood for what they were. Yet, if we cannot live as animals ("It is not granted us," as Lawrence put it in *The Plumed Serpent*, a fiction packed with knowledge of expressive noise), it is our duty to identify the presymbolic in our midst.

If those who showed such aversion to the first waltzes had understood the semantic of this dance, they might have had more chance of controlling military history, and saving their own necks into the bargain. Presumably the same can be said for the frugs, jerks and watussis of today, where we enact Wyndham Lewis' "dithyrambic spectators," the participating audience of Frye's *auto*, in tribal returns extending sound. The whole face of cricket was altered, after all, when a few years ago the West Indians invaded Lord's and, instead of politely clapping at the fringes of the game, often tried to enter into it.

As the onomastic excursions of Socrates in *Cratylus* suggest, there is a mission or destiny in words that arises from their sounds

[41]My examples are drawn from Elizabeth Bowen, *A World of Love*, New York: Alfred A. Knopf, 1955. In my article "Elizabeth Bowen and the Artificial Novel," *Essays in Criticism*, xiii:2 (April 1963), pp. 155–163, I explore this tic in Miss Bowen more fully, e.g., the litotes as double negative, in "he *not unreasonably* asked," "the ironic love for Antonia she had *seldom not shown*," "*not ungently* putting aside the tumble of hair" (all italics added). The reader can make his substitutions—*reasonably, often shown, gently*— and by seeing the loss involved in each case understand the force of this figure.

and shapes. A linguist tells us that the very word *Caligula* "strikes us as uncanny, almost fiendish," a combination we hear again in ghoul, Dracula and so on.[42] Today the literary intellectual frequently envisages new developments in popular culture with misplaced gloom, for he applies norms of symbolism to signs.

It seems long ago since the first shock waves of the Elvis Presley phenomenon swept over America and Europe. Members of the so-called intelligentsia performed little-magazine acrobatics to show that such inarticulation symbolized lack of social control, and thus accordingly appealed to the young. But this was to ignore the non-verbalized yet eurhythmic caterwauling of dozens of similar singers in the twenties and thirties (e.g. the "scat-singing" of Calloway, Waller, Gonella). It was also to misunderstand the nature of Presley's popularity at the time in European jukebox joints, where he would not have been understood (any more than Dylan is there now) even had he verbalized and from which he produced, as if out of his commodious coat pockets, his own imitation, the French Johnny Hallyday. It was to misrelate the word to its world.

For this kind of reflexive relationship—America sends rock-and-roll into England and gets back the Beatles, France sends fashion to London and then falls victim to Mary Quant and the *minijupe*—is man talking to his most enchanted listener, himself. The tape-recorder is technology's parody of this noncommunication, or auto-hypnosis. The University of California anthropologists go to the Bronx Zoo and record the cries warning of an approaching storm by the monkeys there. Later, on a fine day, they play back the tape to the monkeys—who rather obviously run off to hide from the nonexistent rain they think they have just announced to themselves. Mediums and spiritualists, when losing their power, "produce" spirit messages which they have read in the literature of the subject. French *savants* in the field have found Haitian voodoo rites to be full of trash picked up from imported occult literature, cheap French "magic" books, *grimoires*, as they are called. Recent scholarship has shown that in recording his hallucinoses in *Aurélia* Gérard de Nerval often failed to distinguish between what he had genuinely fantasied and what he had read of and imported from the fantasies of others. Wendell Johnson called this sort of thing

---

[42]A. A. Roback, *Destiny and Motivation in Language*, Cambridge, Mass.: Sci-Art Publishers, 1954, p. 66.

semantic thumb-sucking. As Blake put it, "they became what they beheld."[43]

In significant harmony with the little-magazine intelligentsia, New York's WMGM survey regularly panned Presley at the height of his popularity, as they panned Anka, the Beatles, Dylan and dozens of others on their first shouldering into the surveys. Most of these differed from the established norm, and the average disc jockey is supported by advertisers to maintain the norm, and eulogize success. Although he can, then, tell his public what to like, he cannot tell them what they like; this they feed to him. And what they feed back is their own image.

More recently, WMCA in New York was accused of ideological screening of its tops-in-pops surveys, Allen Ginsberg in particular claiming that the new folk-rock groups have made "contributions to American language" (*Village Voice*, September 26, 1966). R. Peter Strauss, the station president, replied: "We don't broadcast material that's likely to lead people to injure each other or themselves. That applies to toxins as it applics to incitements to riot. . . ."[44] A station director like this is forced to comply with his public's wishes. The "Good Guy" DJ Jack Spector of this program wouldn't play the Fugs because he allegedly didn't like their names, yet despite deprivation of New York air space, sales of records by the Fugs rocketed. Though Spector didn't think Dylan's *Eve of Destruction* "worthy of airplay," it still became a superhit. The Beatles' LP *Revolver* sold a million copies in America within two days of its release despite deejay panning of this group after their remarks about Christ. *Eight Miles High*, by the Byrds, was banned by Cleveland cops but still sold hundreds of thousands.

According to their own statements, the Beatles were bred on colored American groups. The Stones found records in London by blues singers like Muddy Waters, Jimmy Reed, Howlin' Wolf, little

[43]Compare, too, the Western. In 1955 Hollywood produced a Western a week. Today it issues thirteen a year. Yet there are twice as many Westerns produced today as in 1955. Most of these are Italian ("spaghetti Westerns"), with unemployed Calabrian peasants daubed to play Indians. There are five Tombstone City's in Spain, three in Yugoslavia, and one on the outskirts of Rome. The fact that Italy made realist Westerns in theme, like *La Strada* (with its hero named Zampano), shows how the copy is preferred to the real in the relationship I mention.

[44]Strauss' attitude is available, in a more intelligent form, from David Holbrook, "Folksong and the Culture of Hate," *The Use of English*, XVIII:1 (Autumn 1966), pp. 3–11.

known in America. They and the Animals (who evidently un-
earthed Tampa Red and John Lee Hooker) played America back
to America. A reflection often moves ahead of its image. According
to Nat Hentoff, when a reporter asked John Lennon if the Beatles
planned any antiwar songs, John is said to have answered, baffled,
"All our songs are antiwar." Staying at the same hotel in the West
Indies as the Beatles once, I got a big kick out of watching chutney-
cheeked retired British Colonels approaching their table from time
to time. Almost weeping with shame, they would shove an auto-
graph book under Paul's or John's or Ringo's nose and ask for a
signature for a daughter. The feedback was annulling itself. They
became what they beheld. A study of Tyneside speech is in progress at Newcastle University as I write.

In Europe such singers were enjoyed without the stigma of what
they stood for. At the height of Presley's popularity in Europe, I
watched him parodied in a St. Trop' *boîte,* but the butt was a style
of communication, not what that style was said to stand for. In
Europe, that is, such sound could be recognized as ritual, as "apparent" language. It was not something other than what it was. For
this reason a much higher social milieu, including Upper Bohemia,
found Presley "advanced." You talked about playing *un rock, un
hot,* finally *un Elvis.* Reciprocally, American symbolic brashness is
"transparent" and has often baffled the most discriminating French
minds—from Marcel Duhamel translating *Tobacco Road,* and
Boris Vian fabricating American thrillers, to André Gide (just after
the war) equating in significance Kathleen Winsor and Katherine
Anne Porter. After all, the Beatles did not really sing "better" than
native groups; but they mirrored a style. Sightsinging.

Imported Wines and Rats in Ruffs

Speech sounds, we have seen, are predicated on silence. It is the
province of the literary intellectual to hear all such barbaric yawps
as vulgarisms. This is really a bit like the American lady who ordered a little-known Californian wine at La Tour d'Argent. When
her husband remonstrated, objecting that they had hardly crossed
the Atlantic to drink American wines, she replied: "But I was always told that *imported* wines were better." The expert on Pope or
Dryden shudders in dismay at the greedy jukebox hues and pinball
flashes of The Strip, whereas an American poet, Vachel Lindsay,

singing and swinging across the continent, saw the Great White Way as a "new Zodiac, guiding the wise."

Ritual communication diagrams the world for us. There is a theory of language origin (Paget) which has it that speech literally *is* gesture. Man first used his hands to speak, but, as he evolved and found his hands increasingly tied up in work, he reproduced his hand movements inside his head, with his tongue. This would make nonverbal responses nicely "operational," in Anatol Rapoport's useful term. It also illustrates, or emphasizes, how any impairment of presymbolic aliveness wounds all communication today. For the presymbolic is not invariably a reversion, nor is—*pace* the British upper classes—volubility a crime. It may not be "given" us to be animals, but knowledge of nonverbal ritual can operate as a means of protection and survival.

Studies of tactile communication are, in fact, repeatedly emphasizing exactly this. Recent tests with juvenile delinquents showed a much higher criminality rate in those who had had upbringings robbed of the tactile. There are the well-known studies showing the psychic health of babies carried on their mothers' backs. Experiments with rats made to wear ruffs round their necks, so that they could not lick themselves, proved how disturbing such deprivation could be. Kinesic communication is evidently essential to the young of all species, and most of all to a young mammal emerging from a rhythmically pulsating environment. "Denial or deprivation of these early tactile experiences may compromise his future learning, such as speech, cognition, symbolic recognition, and his capacity for more mature tactile communication."[45]

There is, lastly, the direct application of such findings. In the July 1961 issue of *ETC.* two Carnegie Institute of Technology researchers, B. Von Haller Gilmer and Lee W. Greg, reported on experiments likely to help those whose normal receptors had been artificially impaired. One thinks at once of astronauts or frogmen, with their special uses of "apparent" language, but when radio broke down in tanks in early Libyan campaigns in the last war, tank regiments were obliged temporarily to resort to old flag signals from turrets. Heavy artillery units had their own sign language, and, indeed, the passing back of a message in an infantry patrol was effected more accurately if a sign could be substituted for a sen-

[45]Lawrence K. Frank, "Tactile Communication," *ETC.*, xvi:1 (Autumn 1958), p. 49.

tence, in the manner of Mrs. Bentley's snuffbox. Genghis Khan was said to have sent his battle orders in rhyme. The Carnegie team made a careful study of electric pulse stimulation of the skin as a kind of Morse Code of the psyche.[46]

No literary intellectual I know would share the word-picture of the high-spirited girl who said she must have been born in a hurricane. In the next chapter we shall inspect the need of "apparent" language for the purpose of comprehension, as well as the abuses of such meaning transmission. Indeed, the "adaptability" of an amputee is perhaps the most telling parable I can think of at this point for modern man confronted with an ororverbalized culture, of Mr. Mits wondering what it all means.

[46]Compare with these comments two books: E. Lynch and Harold C. Crain, *Projects in Oral Interpretation*, New York: Holt, Rinehart and Winston, 1960; Jack Vernon, *Inside the Black Room: Studies of Sensory Deprivation*, New York: Clarkson N. Potter, 1963.

FOUR

> What indeed are faculties? We talk of
> faculties as if they were distinct, things
> separable; as if a man had intellect, im-
> agination, fancy, etc. as he has hands, feet
> and arms. That is a capital error. Then
> again, we hear of a man's 'intellectual
> nature,' and of his 'moral nature,' as if
> these again were divisible, and existed
> apart. Necessities of language do not per-
> haps prescribe such forms of utterance; we
> must speak, I am aware, in that way, if we
> are to speak at all. *But words ought not to
> harden into things for us.* It seems to me,
> our apprehension of this matter is, for most
> part, radically falsified thereby. We ought
> to know withal, and to keep forever in mind,
> that these divisions are at bottom but
> *names* . . . .
>
> Thomas Carlyle,
> *On Heroes and Hero Worship*

ON EATING THE MENU:
KICKING WORDS

Words in Good Shape

"When *I* use a word," said Humpty Dumpty in his famous formulation, "it means just what I choose it to mean—neither more nor
less." He echoed Thoreau—"It is the man determines what is said,
not the words."

The feedback quality of "apparent" language results all too often
in signal reactions, when symbols are taken as objects, and words
as things. Such is by now a truism of semantic study. In a nutshell,
you might say that we talk to dice . . . but we do not eat the menu.

To the so-called primitive mind, words *are* things. In *Myth,*

Ritual and Religion Andrew Lang tells us that the savage "assigns human speech and feelings to sun and moon and stars and wind, no less than to beasts, birds and fishes." Conrad dramatizes this human legacy when he has Tamb' Itam, Lord Jim's faithful servant, entrusted with a verbal message. The man demands a token, or thing —" 'Because, Tuan,' he said, 'the message is important, and these are thy very words I carry.' "[1] Jim gives him his ring.

Words undoubtedly do have a physical dimension, occupying units of time (when spoken) and of space (when written)—though the two form a harmony. The physiology of the latter assumption was evident in the old Stoic theory that the visual impact of a word carried much of its significance. Though this theory is now smiled at, a word's physique cannot be entirely dissociated from its meaning without loss. We know that Dante supposed that his word for man, Tuscan *omo*, stood for a man because it looked like one, the *o*'s being the eyes and the *m* the nose (and/or mouth?). (Spenser did somewhat the same in his House of Alma.) Oddly enough, the Omo detergent advertised so hectoringly all over Italy today utilizes exactly this as a "modern" sales pitch.

In 1966 the New York City Board of Education's Law Department played Tamb' Itam by disallowing yarmulkas in public schools on the grounds that the wearing of such a skullcap violated separation of church and state. The Law Department concerned was here saying, of course: Skullcap = Religion. On this basis Hungarian scholars have claimed especial antiquity for their tongue (e.g., Hungarian *olló* looks like a pair of scissors). Greek claims to the genesis of democracy on the same score are well known,[2] and equally insecure, while the very size of words often provokes a feeling of indigestibility. Theories like *transsubstantiation* or *existentialism* are readily imagined difficult, since so physically impressive.[3]

[1]Joseph Conrad, *Lord Jim*, New York: New American Library, 1961, p. 293.
[2]"By definition we Greeks love liberty and will do everything to oppose force and tyranny" (from a letter from George P. Piperopoulos to *The Campus* [a CCNY student newspaper]). If democracy comes by name from Greece, so do monarchy (*monarchia*) and tyranny (*tyrannis*) and despotism (*despotes*).
[3]Not long ago Charles W. Ferguson brought out the *Abecedarian Book*, an attempt to introduce children to big words via a conventional ABC book: thus, A is for antediluvian, B for bioluminiscent, and so on. Ferguson's point was that if a child learnt a big word, it learnt about half a dozen other words along with it.

After all, our first true dictionary, that of Cokeram in 1623, was sub-titled "An Interpreter of Hard Words." Shakespeare gives us *honorificabilitudinitatibus* in *Love's Labour's Lost*, the *OED* provides *floccipaucinihilipilification*, and Peacock, in *Headlong Hall*, comprises the human frame in *osseocarnisanguineoviscericartilaginonervomedullary*. The recent *Random House Dictionary* adds Mary Poppins' *supercalifragilisticexpialidocious*.

Certain Polish names look like so many eye-chart tests to foreigners—as Chesterton put it of the French kings, "We liked their smiles and battles, but we never could say their names"—and I know I often long for a short simple Chinese name to pronounce, i.e. mispronounce. There was an Arabic undergraduate up with me at Oxford, whose name used to cause havoc in student rolls since, alphabetized, it turned into a comma.

Alphabet symbolism has an ancient history, Talmudists of old utilizing such for homiletic purposes. There is a respectable repository of this primitive respect for word physiques in our contemporary superstition and child play, for kids love to monkey around with names. There are alphabetic poems, where each succeeding line begins with the next letter (Shakespeare hiding an obscenity in one such); palindromes which read the same backward as forward, in both names (Kabak) and sentences (Lewd did I live / Evil I did dwel);[4] poems like axes and bottles (Theodoric), like altars (Herbert), like goblets (old drinking songs), like the Cross (a mannerism recreated by Dylan Thomas), even like a mouse running across a page (cummings); macaronic verse, malapropisms, and refractory rhyming.[5]

We still use letter shapes metaphorically—e.g. the O of his mouth (cf. Shakespeare's "wooden O" to describe his theater). Pauline Réage's *L'Histoire d'O* featured a heroine called O to signify her obedience, and general availability. Lalo's opera *Le Roi d'Ys* could be instanced in this connection as could Stephen Dedalus' prophetic suggestion of novels with letters for titles—"Have you read his F? O yes, but I prefer Q" (prophetic because it anticipates efforts like Thomas Pynchon's *V*). Everyone can make his own list.

[4]Cf. WYBMADIITY, seen behind a London bar. Will You Buy Me A Drink If I Tell You? In reverse, You Thought I Intended Drinking A Mild But You're Wrong.

[5]The specialist in semantic curiosa of this sort was Charles C. Bombaugh: see a recent selection edited by Martin Gardner as *Oddities and Curiosities of Words and Literature*, New York: Dover, 1966.

And of course the entire "superstition" of a period, or cultural cycle, was based on a shape, on respect for the circle.[6]

In *The Psychology of Your Name* (1924) a self-help writer *avant le jour,* one Nellie Dewey, sets up an entire system of character analysis, or do-it-yourself fortune-telling, via this emphasis. A, for instance, is the lion of the alphabet since the angles and straight lines of which this letter is composed indicate energy and organization; numbers and colors are accorded each letter, as in Rimbaud's sonnet·on vowels, which was probably based on French children's alphabet books of the time. In 1967 a British doctor, Trevor Weston, put forward a theory of "alphabetic neurosis," people with names beginning at the end of the alphabet, like myself, supposedly having three times as many ulcers as those at the start.

In this sense, too, we can note the courtesy expressed by capitalizing address-words, like *Sie, Du, Lei, Usted,* as against the more democratic French and English characters for the same. Critics recently complained that Proust gave a large number of characters names beginning with an S, in the posthumous *Jean Santeuil.*[7] Faulkner repudiated "easy reading" by naming two characters in the same book Quentin. In calling his characters by letters the French novelist Alain Robbe-Grillet is only doing what Joyce, Kafka and many others have done before him. "This novel is not written," runs World Publishing Co.'s ad for a recent fiction "told" in woodcuts. "It's carved."

Plato believed that the word tended to express in its sound the inner nature of the thing it described. We would seem here to be back at onomatopoeia, that words should sound like their spatial reality—English *whisper,* French *chuchoter,* German *flüstern.* Not quite. Sound imitation by lettristic physiognomy is to my mind onomatopoeia *pur sang.* But Plato's theory was not so much a matter of exact imitation as, rather, what the philologist Henry Bradley

[6]Feeling the end of the world at hand, seventeenth-century England was constantly looking for figures, or "signatures," expressive of the universe; the Cross was an obvious one, to be sure, but there was Thomas Browne's quincunx among others. The circle was a particularly pervasive pattern since it was also the shape of a letter, a point missed by the point-missing Marjorie Hope Nicolson in her *The Breaking of the Circle* (Evanston, Ill.: Northwestern University Press, 1950).

[7]I counted: Santeuil, Surlande, Sureau (Jean's great-aunt), Sercier, Savinieu (the lawyer), Saurin, Savin, Saural, Sandré, Sauvalque, Saureau (the Commandant once misspelt in the Anglo-American text as Seureau), Saintré, Serran, Servier, Saylor (with whom Jean duels), Scipio, Savone, Servais.

hit off when he said that onomatopoeia "consists not so much in similarity of impression on the ear as in similarity of mental suggestion."[8] This is far more truly physiological and shows the crudity of McLuhan's claptrap category of "oral." In instance of Bradley here one could cite Maurice Grammont's feeling that clear vowels will always express smallness, and rapidity (and *élan*).

However this may be, if today we shrug off these old Greek and Latin debates about the relation of sounds to things, as yet another discredited notion on the part of the less enlightened, we are in danger of cutting ourselves off from the sources of word-wisdom; it was part of language, long before program music, to respond by imitation to the sounds about us, to bells, brooks, clanging hammers, and ringing hoof-beats (as in the wonderfully representational opening sounds of Burns' *Tam O'Shanter*). To lose this would be to lose a healthy ratio between the senses. There are new sounds in our lives today. Words should be both looked at and heard to be "felt." They are brands on our consciousness.

Computer Control—It says, "Cogito, Ergo Sum"

Tamb' Itam was happier pointing to real things when speaking since, for him, words were simply direct substitutions or signs for those things, as when Eskimos recently labeled a new credit union in their village a *qikartissivik* (the place where the money stopped). Somewhat the same verbal relationship to reality can be observed in the fact that, until recent years, Scots *toun* and Gaelic *baile* both included in their meanings "farm, homestead" as well as town.

Belief in this relationship was taken into lexicography by the seventeenth-century British Bishop Wilkins, who tried to set up a unireferential, word-thing dictionary.[9] Similar attempts crop up from time to time, reminding us that here lies a basic human need (sometimes called reification). Work toward the fixing of connotations, and semantic differentials in general, has been made of late in the same spirit by the French Academy.[10]

[8]Henry Bradley, *The Making of English,* New York: Macmillan, 1904, p. 156.

[9]See Ralph Renwick, "Seventeenth-Century Semanticists," *ETC.,* xix:1 (May 1962), pp. 85–93.

[10]See also the work of Charles W. Morris, George J. Suci, Percy Tannenbaum and, of course, Ogden and Richards. David K. Berlo's *The Process of Communication* (New York: Holt, Rinehart and Winston, 1966) takes up this matter toward the end, and supplies useful bibliographical references.

The Appendix to Orwell's *1984* was a rather uninspired attempt to show that computer language, on the one-word-one-meaning level, is the first step to dictatorship. If so, it suggests that technocracy is such. For Orwell's Newspeak was a parody of reduced connotations[11] and by no means dissimilar from the system already perfected by the US Patent Office as a means of checking new patent applications. In this case, electronic engineers have evolved fairly foolproof word-thing terms to feed into their machines: e.g. *compor* (from *common portions*—i.e. inventions having one or more portions in common), or *sepfrom* (from *separate* and *from*—i.e. having nothing in common). But the vocabulary of the Patent Office is unusually successful since it does not, unlike Orwell's Newspeak, have to operate in context. Directly you move into context, new language laws must operate. A *ring* is circular on a finger, rectangular when you box in it, and resonant when you hear it.

It may have been in response to such Royal Society empiricism that Swift inserted his celebrated satire concerning the Academy of Lagado into Chapter V of the Third Part of *Gulliver's Travels*. Actually, it seems more likely to me that Swift was responding universally, to man's whole semantic heritage. The scheme was to purge language of misunderstanding, not by Newspeak, but by confining discussion to what you could physically exhibit. This was roughly the manner in which Robinson Crusoe taught Friday his English. Swift writes:

> An expedient was therefore offered, that since words are only names for *things,* it would be more convenient for all men to carry about them such things as were necessary to express the particular business they are to discourse on. . . . I have often beheld two of those sages almost sinking under the weight of their packs, like pedlars among us; who, when they met in the streets, would lay down their loads, open their sacks, and hold conversation for an hour together. . . . Another great advantage proposed by this invention was that it would serve as an universal language to be understood in all

[11] I should state at this point that I refer to John Stuart Mill's famous theory of *denotation* and *connotation* with the customary GS variation. By *connote* Mill meant *imply*; general semanticists usually use this term to describe the aura around a word, reserving denotation for a strict sense of meaning, dictionary definition, etc. In his lecture on "The Theory of Meaning" Gilbert Ryle shows the weakness of Mill's reasoning in this regard.

civilised nations, whose goods and utensils are generally of the same kind. . . .

Language literature too often chuckles at this passage without catching the backlash in Swift's satire. For when meaning becomes flawlessly unattached, and politics is conducted in the spirit of a graduate seminar on the higher esthetics, then we need Lagado, reification ("Because of this divorce between words and actions Kennedy failed to move us as did Roosevelt and Churchill"[12]). Bacon rejected the syllogism precisely because of its removal from reality. In short, we sometimes have to communicate by things to keep sane. Ours *is* the Academy of Lagado, which in one sense has come to pass in the 1966 French publication of Lionel Chouchoun's novel offering the "reader" the objects that are the subject of the text, glued to the pages of each copy—a bus ticket, a hairpin, a detergent sample, and so on.

Anatol Rapoport's *extensional definition* ("definition by pointing to, or exhibiting, that which is defined") is not startlingly different from Sir Ernest Gowers' game of semantic musical chairs, with each idea looking for a word to sit on. Extensional definition has long been a principle of legal evidence. It is a principle of habeas corpus. Of much medical practice. It is there when firms send out free samples.

Today the teaching of increasingly abstract subjects has more and more to be accompanied by some sort of physical entities. Painting and drawing, of course, could be (have been) taught by a sensitive mute. The same is doubtless true of carpentry. But in modern math, physics and chemistry the teacher is repeatedly obliged to refer to "reality" in the form of models—such as the now conventional system of interlocking plastic beads for molecular structures, or the colored lucite cones, appropriately sliced, used in math to demonstrate parabolas, hyperbolas and the like.

Such must remain reductions, however. As Einstein put it in *Geometry and Experience,* "As far as the laws of mathematics refer to reality, they are not certain and as far as they are certain, they do not refer to reality." Geologists have lately learnt that one of the most accurate tests for seismic tremors is direct human reaction. One engineering professor reports:

[12]Hans J. Morgenthau, "Monuments to Kennedy," *The New York Review,* January 6, 1966, p. 8.

In classical thermodynamics we take a wholly operational point of view. We begin with operational meanings of length, time, force, and mass and then proceed to temperature, heat, work, and other thermodynamic quantities. We present the First and Second laws as matters of operational experience, the "laws" being generalizations from a large number of experiments.[13]

As Einstein knew, the computer button falsifies the word-world relationship. When we set off a signal reaction of this nature, we get the man who slam-bangs his car because he's irritated with it,[14] or (as recently happened) sets fire to a vehicle that sideswiped his, or shoots his TV set, or yells at the parking meter which has betrayed him, "You stool pigeon!" Sometimes we start a war.

Allergies and Alkalis

"The sign," Susanne Langer reminds us, "is something to act upon, or a means to command action; the symbol is an instrument of thought." The reaction triggered by the sign short-circuits thought and can be studied in the clinics in allergy sufferers. It can also be seen, of course, in animals like monkeys, whose semantic is a kind of cradle of "apparent" discourse. R. L. Garner's *The Speech of Monkeys,* published in 1892, claims a monkey vocabulary of about forty words—which happens to be the exact total learnt after six years with humans by Kamala, one of the several Indian "wolf-children" studied (perhaps unreliably) in the twenties and thirties of this century. Wolfgang Köhler's *Gestalt* experiments with chimps in the early twenties are reinforced, but not fundamentally altered as regards ritual semantic, by the tests in the sixties of such as Washburn and DeVore, of the University of California, or of the German zoologist, Walter Hoesch, working in South West Africa.[15]

[13]John R. Dixon, "Symbols in Engineering Education," *ETC.,* xix:3 (October 1962), p. 270.
[14]"More than one motorist has secretly wished he could do what Samuel Rios, 30, was accused of doing yesterday. Driving at 12.30 A.M. through Williamsburg, he swung around a corner and accidentally sideswiped a sedan parked at the curb in front of 141 Hopkins St.
"Furious, police charged, Rios stopped, took the jack handle from his car trunk and slam-banged the offending obstacle from windshield to tail lights" (New York *Post*).
[15]See also Ramona and Desmond Morris, *Men and Apes,* New York: McGraw-Hill, 1966.

Although Hoesch found a female baboon, Ahla, trained to be an effective shepherd, or shepherdess, none of these researchers gives any evidence of "transparent" language among animals. Phobias in humans are very largely signal reactions on the "apparent" level.

Thus tests with vasodilators (in the skin) have established beyond much doubt that you blush when your society tells you to blush, whether—in the case of ladies—at exposure of ankle, knee or thigh. The University of California team mentioned showed that monkeys blush with their backsides, females turning and blushing in this manner at the male of their choice.

There are dozens of instances of etymological origins for *idées fixes* and for phobias (which are fixed ideas carried, in a sense, into neurosis). Rapoport cites the story of the professor walking out of one of Freud's lectures on hysteria in dudgeon, since Freud was being impertinent enough to suggest that men could be subject to this affliction also—"Why, the very word 'hysteria' is derived from the Greek word for womb!"[16] Soldiers in the holds of ships have been known to be violently "seasick" when imagining they were at sea, only to learn later that they were still tied up in port. Beatle-fainting is presently another case in point.[17]

A few years ago tests with a woman allergic to milk dramatized this distortion. Researchers would pour water into this sufferer's stomach telling her it was milk, and the lady would be ritually sick. Dr. Stewart Wold, head of the Department of Medicine at the University of Oklahoma, aptly summarized the case—"That woman was about as sensitive to milk as you can get, except that her sen-

[16]The *womb* story has had much retelling by now. I accept Anatol Rapoport's attribution of it to Freud, in *Science and the Goals of Man* (New York: Harper & Brothers, 1950); but the fallacy, one of origin-as-meaning, was quoted by Francis L. Wellman in *The Art of Cross-Examination* of 1911, concerning a doctor's diagnosis of *hysteria* in court. This is taken up more recently in F. A. Philbrick's excellent *Language and the Law* (New York: Macmillan, 1951). The ridicule to which Freud's theories about hysteria in the *Studien über Hysterie* of 1895, on) were subjected can be seen in Ilza Veith, *Hysteria: The History of a Disease,* University of Chicago Press, 1966.

[17]Cf.: "Eleven girls were taken to hospital lately at Nottingham for fainting attacks after a hockey match; carbon-monoxide poisoning was at first suspected, but later one of the hospital staff diagnosed hysteria. Some of the parents were angry: the father of one of the girls protested that it was ridiculous to talk of them 'putting it on.' Another father said, 'Girls don't go fainting all over the place just for the fun of it' " (Miles Howard, London *Spectator*).

sitivity was to the word 'milk.' "[18] Korzybski used to cite a similar instance of hay-fever allergy to roses, the symptoms being induced even when paper roses were substituted. The huge sales of arthritis literature owe much to this misevaluation. In *The Observer* Cyril Ray nicely summarized our situation as regards such signal reactions, as follows: "I have seen a letter recently in the magazine *Wine* from a chemist who wrote that effervescent alkalis *don't* cure hangovers; that it is purely psychological. So, very often, is a hangover; if I seem to have a hangover, I should be quite pleased if it only seemed to be cured." Hospital etiquette now works in much this spirit, combating such superstitions by relabeling certain diseases in order to make them more bearable to sensitive patients.

By far one of the most famous cases of mass hysteria, however, perhaps because it was subsequently investigated by one of the foremost social psychologists of our day, was that initiated on the evening of October 30, 1938, by Orson Welles' broadcast, purporting to describe an invasion of Martians.[19] In fact, this oft-cited case was far less extreme than examples of prowler phobias and the like, afflicting American townships, as frequently exposed in *Public Opinion Quarterly*. Welles' Hallowe'en broadcast coincided with a number of things, particularly the new power of radio ("We have so much faith in broadcasting," was a typical comment of Newark residents at the time). It was successful enough, however, to make a number of Manhattanites wink knowingly at each other when they subsequently heard of the bombing of a place called Pearl Harbor.[20] It has been said that Hitler took Austria by radio. Certainly early German tank warfare was as successful as it was thanks to a sensitivity to radio techniques. Today one can stifle much of a country's political consciousness by state-owned radio; Americans had a grim reminder of the condition of France in this respect when a leading radio and TV executive recently resigned owing to ex-

[18]Richard Carter, "Mysterious Stomach," *Life,* xlv:20 (November 17, 1958), pp. 148–160.
[19]See Hadley Cantril, Hazel Gaudet, and Herta Herzog, *The Invasion from Mars,* Princeton, N.J.: Princeton University Press, 1940; also John Houseman, "The Men from Mars," *Harper's Magazine,* 197:1183 (December 1948), pp. 74–82.
[20]The full text of the Wellesian "invasion" was for long notoriously hard to get hold of; congratulations, then, to Groff Conklin for reprinting it in toto in his *Invaders of Earth* (1952).

cessive interference from Washington (chiefly over the Vietnam war).

Unlike the academic scientist, Mr. Mits has to describe things for the purpose of daily living and, by using words for things, he finds himself placed outside things.[21] Once again, as in the Martian "panic," the word swamps the world, and proper semantic harmony is shattered. The most outrageous example of recent times of thinking *inside* things, as of "apparent" language run amok, was exhibited by Herman Kahn, author of *On Thermonuclear War* (Princeton, N.J.: Princeton University Press, 1960). For here is the assertion that to lose sixty million American lives in a first thermonuclear attack would constitute something called *defense*. Sixty million simultaneous deaths represents something more than our sign-symbol, or word-world, equipment can absorb. You could add a few zeros to the total without much difference to our minds. It is like the Roman talking to the new Arab mathematician: "If 0 means nothing, what is the purpose of writing it? . . . You explain that the mark − 1 means ONE, yet on the very same page you show it to mean TEN in 10, and one HUNDRED in your 100."[22]

Thin Symbol-Skins

In Volume I of *A Social History of Art* Arnold Hauser demonstrates that to paleolithic man "art" was so much an extension of homocentric reality, of a world *within* things, that the celebrated cave drawings may have preceded speech. Such iconography was, in short, but a practical means for procuring food. The fact that most such pictures were concealed in the unlit interiors of deep caves indicates that the intentions of the "artists" were far from purely decorative. It was proper magic, and the caves were holy places. More direct evidence that prehistoric man failed to distinguish between his paintings and his reality lies in the fact that he killed his prey in effigy, as the still perceptible spear marks on the bare walls testify. In A. D. 1967 three major airlines received anon-

[21] I am more than aware that the term *thing* is not a happy one here, since it suggests necessary material substance, not invariably a property of semantic "things." Ogden and Richards, I note, prefer *referent* and in an academic context they are doubtless right (C. K. Ogden and I. A. Richards, *The Meaning of Meaning,* New York: Harcourt, Brace and Company, 1923, p. 9). My choice is for Mr. Mits.

[22] "In Military, as Ever, It's by the Numbers . . . But Arabic System Made No Sense to Romans," [US] *Army Research and Development Newsmagazine,* July 1964, p. 42.

ymous telephone threats of bombing after an NBC television show dramatizing a fictitious plot to bomb an airliner.

Parallel passions come through in the floods of letters poured in on TV characters. "Grandpa Hughes" (portrayed by actor Santos Ortega) thus received 180,000 greeting cards, two tons of mail in all, on his seventieth CBS "birthday." The actor himself was but in his fifties at the time. Sean Connery's similar trials as the filmic James Bond were related in *Playboy,* and when one Civic Theater group decided to stage Maugham's *Rain* in its repertoire there were letters to the local paper protesting the appearance of Sadie Thompson ("Miss Thompson herself has a questionable background and a too well-known reputation"). George Sanders' *Memoirs of a Professional Cad* cites many instances of this sort of misevaluation, a more serious study of which can be seen in Henry James' story "The Real Thing" (as also "Paste"). When the House of Lords debated *Lady Chatterley's Lover,* one noble Earl, referring to another fiction by Lawrence, fulminated: "Let us get down to the realities and the origin of this deplorable book. It emanates from the warped mind of the author. The story he tells is pure invention; it never actually happened."[23] As a fringe benefit of this we have the old fictional trick of sketching a character by means of a thing, probably taken to a peak in Melville's Stubb, who virtually *is* his pipe.[24]

Magic of this nature, assuming that words in ritual order will influence the order of things, is still with us, then. General MacArthur refused to take down the American flag on an occasion in the last war when it was actually endangering and costing lives, as a marker for raiding enemy pilots. This is defending the flesh and blood of your country by means of its symbol. The concatenation is exact. In 1967 a teacher of elementary semantics was suspended by Indiana State University for burning a small American flag before his class, although he had done so, not out of disrespect, but as

[23]*Hansard,* 227:23, col. 528.
[24]"What, perhaps, with other things, made Stubb such an easy-going, unfearing man, must have been his pipe. For, like his nose, his short, black little pipe was one of the regular features of his face. You would almost as soon have expected him to turn out of his bunk without his nose as without his pipe. He kept a whole row of pipes there ready loaded, stuck in a rack, within easy reach of his hand; and, whenever he turned in, he smoked them all out in succession . . . when Stubb dressed, instead of first putting his legs into his trousers, he put his pipe in his mouth."

instruction in symbolism. (In defending David J. Miller for burning his draft card, the New York Civil Liberties Union argued that Miller's act was "symbolic speech.") Similarly, we are told that, just before World War I, French Generals refused to eliminate the vulnerable wearing of red trousers by troops because *"Le pantalon rouge, c'est la France!"* Such is the semantic of the Victorian parent swilling out a child's mouth with lye in order to stop it using bad language. And this, too, was surely a hangover from bygone punishments designed to fit, or dissuade from, the crime. A man's hand was cut off if he stole, Chinese poured mortar into the open leg wounds of prisoners who had tried to escape, while Peter the Great's father ordered smokers' noses to be cut off (in this spirit a recent Kentucky judge made traffic law violators visit funeral homes). Nor are you far here from the Japanese teachers of less than a generation ago committing suicide because the mere picture of the Emperor in their classroom had been defaced.[25]

In *The Informed Heart* Bruno Bettelheim, Director of the Sonia Shankman Orthogenic School at the University of Chicago, shows in the business-as-usual mentality a kind of accumulating philosophy of life as a *thing*, eventually making enforced suicide possible and grotesquely "acceptable." Out of a group of naked prisoners about to enter the gas chamber an SS officer selected one woman who had been a dancer. He made her dance. And it was a dance of death since this incredibly courageous woman seized his gun and shot him down. Bettelheim comments: "No longer was she a number, a nameless, depersonalized prisoner, but the dancer she used to be." She was transformed from a thing to a person.

The thinness of symbol-skins can account for the most dangerous, as well as tragic, transformations. One of these was identified recently by John Kenneth Galbraith as the *wordfact*. "The wordfact," Galbraith wrote, "makes words a precise substitute for reality. This is an enormous convenience. It means that to say that something exists is a substitute for its existence." Thus a disastrous diplomatic visit of an American President to an Asiatic country goes down in history as a *success*, thanks to wordfact. Dictatorship in South America turns into its opposite in Washington via wordfact, and (Galbraith suggests) "Flying planes over other countries became a kind of fifth freedom. . . . The flights were then

[25]S. I. Hayakawa, "Suicide as a Communicative Act," *ETC.*, xv:1 (Autumn 1957), p. 47.

suspended, and this became an act of wise restraint." More recently, words like *commitment* and *obligation* have been used as fact in this way. We are committed because we say we are committed.

Adult Child-Language

A few years ago a child of ten was asked to describe a cow. There were no true "referents" in the resultant description, which ran as follows:

> It has six sides—right, left, an upper and below. At the back it has a tail on which hangs a brush. With this it sends the flies away so that they do not fall into the milk. The head is for the purpose of growing horns, and so that the mouth can be somewhere. The horns are to butt with and the mouth is to moo with. Under the cow hangs the milk. It is arranged for milking. . . . The cow has a fine sense of smell—one can smell it far away. This is the reason for the fresh air in the country. *(Atlantic Monthly)*

The strong sense of function in this passage could be duplicated from the writings of the Piagets.[26] There is no real need of words in this innocent Lagado. Happiness is a warm puppy . . . or a fuzzy sweater . . . or a pile of leaves to play in. A rose is a rose is a rose. Business is business. And boys will be boys.

But to live in Lagado for life is to inhabit a semantic asylum, of sorts. This is the world of the New York State Senator who opposed a bill to regulate syphilis because the term itself should not be given currency (creating "a shudder in every decent woman and decent man"). It is the world, too, of the Massachusetts City Council making it illegal to use the word Lenin or Leningrad in

[26]E.g.: "Could the sun have been called 'moon' and the moon 'sun'?—*No.* —Why not?—*Because the sun shines brighter than the moon* . . ." (Jean Piaget, *The Child's Conception of the World,* New York: Harcourt, Brace & World, 1929).

The supposedly "invariant" responses of the child in such instances may well be due, it seems to me, to a misunderstanding or misevaluation of the question. Movies of such children answering test questions like the above show them following their invigilators' faces rather than the objects displayed: i.e., they are striving to understand a process of reasoning (called, on higher levels, "what the teacher *wants*") and generally to keep out of trouble. Actually, I have quoted the above example since the etymological equivalent of Albanian *sun* has today turned into *star.*

printed literature.[27] A hammer and sickle in a Californian's painting recently resulted in the artist being hauled before the usual committee of superpatriots, the irony here being that the emblem appeared on a boat and was found to be part of a local boatbuilder's trademark (hastily altered, needless to say). A low-number license plate might be a sign of high status in New York, and mean nothing in, say, Ghana. In *The Age of Jackson,* Arthur M. Schlesinger, Jr. tells us that such was Calhoun's fear of capitalism "he flinched even from the name."

In one sense, of course, each thing is its symbol. The Cross is both its reality and its surreality. But since language contains the thing and its extension, verbal experience can be said to comprise all others. Tattooing is supposed to make us yield a standard reaction, like so many Pavlovian dogs.[28] In fact, when *MAD* went mad over the famous Marlboro cigarette ad, with its tattooed male personifying virility, and converted the mark to a hammer and sickle across Khrushchev's right knuckle, the result could have been taken quite seriously in Russia. Sailors have had the letters "H-O-L-D F-A-S-T" tattooed on the backs of their hands, in order to keep them from falling off yardarms. But the latest instance I have seen of extending words in this manner, on the skin itself, referred back to reality with a vengeance. The Vietnamese took to tattooing *Sat Cong* (= kill Vietcong) on the chests of their men. They did this to boost morale, but it turned out to have a literal application, since it discouraged defectors to the other side.

Anthropomorphism

All early religions expressed man's natural desire to see the universe as a man. After all, the primitive knew more about the human body than about the universe, and this knowledge he held in trust with his fellows. The best way to explain something that has an

[27] 'Mrs. Bradshaw, are you maintaining that the mere use of the word "homosexual" is obscene?'

" 'Yes sir.' "

This courtroom exchange was not taken from a Victorian novel, but a proceeding brought before the Ninth Circuit Court of Connecticut in 1966. Mrs. Bradshaw there appeared as an "expert witness" on obscenity.

[28] See the tales of cabalistic tattooing in George Burchett, *Memoirs of a Tattooist,* compiled and edited by Peter Leighton, London: Oldbourne, 1958. An irony of the virility signal transpired when a New York health inspector recently concluded that tattooing resulted in hepatitis; the practice—or art— was locally forbidden.

effect on you (like winds or trees) is to attribute human qualities to it. It has become a cliché to say that the assigning of human attributes to nonhuman entities fades, or becomes artificial, as the breach between man and nature intensifies; that the primitive's close identification with his world is no longer with us today.

For who is this "primitive?" The answer is—a human being. His reciprocity of perspective is truly a form of synecdoche (for Littré, metonymy), since it includes the object under scrutiny within the human species, suggesting that (say) cats and dogs called Jane and Fido have a sort of lesser human rank. They are therefore part of a metaphoric human society. French has a rich system of human names for birds. Iroquois naming was apparently of this nature. However varied in levels of generality, our penchant for linguistic equivalents (or mirror transpositions) in naming little humanized areas—calling a dog *Rover* or a flower *Marigold*—testifies to our desire not only for appropriation but also for a bygone ratio in discourse, for small-scale models or paradigmatic chains within communication, so as to be able to pass easily from species to category.

Man wanted words for his world. The forces of nature were personified. Early poetry is full of the anthropomorphism of boats (anticipating modern man's hymns to his car—"She's a honey to handle"). Such was metaphor in the true sense, for as Richards put it, in *The Philosophy of Rhetoric,* "The mind is a connecting organ." Anglo-Saxon riddles form a famous case in point. From Thales on, a number of intelligent human beings believed the world to be animate. And so instructed. The visible world lived like man and the more you understood of both, the more ingenious —and thus convincing—became the resultant correspondences.

Crinkled mountains were the earth in its "senior-citizen" aspects, a volcano was a belch, and fresh-water streams corresponded to the sea as did the newly discovered stream of white to red corpuscles in the blood of man (Harvey). Metaphor was thus a kind of constant truth. Finally, you could personify abstractions, in the manner of Dr. Johnson or contemporary incorporated companies. This is not imitating reality so much as allowing it to collaborate with you. Shelley—despite hair-splittings about tone— effectively exclaims that *his* leaves are falling. Coleridge is said to have looked out the window one day and turned to Wordsworth— "Look, *I'm* snowing." Gaelic literature, one of the last with an intensive animism, made of man's environment such a living force that a Gaelic writer could think of himself as "You," thus retaining a rich residue of psychic control.

R. G. Collingwood argues that today we have just about reversed this process, seeing change as axiomatically progressive, and thus meliorative. The effect is to downstage nature, while upgrading economy. "To most people," writes Susanne Langer, "the ancient, obvious symbols of nature have become literary figures, and to many these very figures look silly." Every summer I live in an island community where it is extremely important—a matter of livelihood—as to: the direction of the wind; the state of the moon; the extent or likelihood of rain. I very much doubt that if I stopped a New Yorker or a Londoner on the street in the next five minutes and asked him the direction of the wind he would be able to answer with any accuracy. His water is brought in by mains, and stoppages in its flow are artificial. In a city like New York the moon is so purely artificial in influence it really looks like something lobbed into the sky by a playful prop man, in contrast to the street, shop and auto lighting.

Thus, relying on a rapid turnover of technological trends, we reproduce this relationship (or misrelationship) in art and other mythic symbols. Concepts of stability were clearly more fitted to assisting "stable" regimes. When now we touch the natural world in this way, it is rather in the spirit of condescending simile than as a source of truth. To see the branches of a tree outstretched to heaven like arms was an easily available primitive metaphor (as when a warrior, in *Beowulf*, was laid "in the ship's embrace"). As in Greek mythology the world was made thereby more livable by the metaphoric or imagistic extension.

But in a technology like ours, where it is incumbent to celebrate our constant dominion over nature, this becomes paradoxically unnatural. So when Nabokov, let us say, writes that "the train stopped with a long-drawn Westinghousian sigh,"[29] the relationship is rather one of simile. The distinction implies that we have conquered our world. I have not yet met with a single young American who "believes in" ghosts.

So this ability to see man everywhere, a sort of sensory complicity with the universe, far from being a *raison d'être*, has be-

[29]Vladimir Nabokov, *Speak, Memory*, New York: Grosset and Dunlap; 1951, p. 97.

come suspect to the electronic age; anthropomorphism is usually sidelined to fashion, rather than leading art. To imply a common quality between man and the natural world (as by referring to a boat's "embrace") is to run counter to the supremacy we desiderate over the reality around us.

It is hardly necessary to point out that this shift in personification habits has involved a loss of intensity in language. When Shakespeare wrote, "the morn in russet mantle clad" (*Hamlet,* I, i), or Ben Jonson that "the house is so stored with jealousy, there is no room for love to stand upright in" (*Every Man in His Humour, IV,* viii), there was an emotional movement in the ascription of human characteristics to elements nonhuman. Almost every mythology has categorized a rainbow as a young girl. This metaphoric transfer grows decorative in industrial civilization, and has today declined to a pseudopantheism almost purely designed to persuade.

To say that an engine *purrs,* or that a car's *body* has a graceful line, is an end-product of valid anthropomorphism. The belching cannon and climbing moons of old are replaced by Porsche's claim that their brakes "shrug off road water," or the "RESILIENT DOLLAR" of a recent ad. Modern man's sexual car fantasies were prefigured by the tenderness Zola's Lantier lavished on his train engine, "La Lison," as by Huysmans' adulation of locomotives, through his Des Esseintes, as adorable seductresses. Today we talk about *what makes him tick,* and *turning on.* Our machine metaphors are largely complimentary (He's a *dynamo,* a real *powerhouse*).

Yet nothing is added to the dimensions of our existence by advertising personifications, whose chief errand is in fact duplicity. To see a tree as a man, or a sun smiling, were synesthesic experiences that enriched and extended life. But to envision clothes dryers and refrigerators and sump-pumps as human is ultimately depriving in effect, for the man-nature relationship is reversed in another elevation of mammon. "This new Maytag Dryer with Electronic Control that feels the clothes for moisture as they dry. Just as you often do"—such is a reduction. Man is mocked. True anthropomorphism was an enlargement. Man was magnified.

Actually, food and wine vocabularies have been traditionally strong in such figures, and perhaps legitimately so; thus a "sturdy" wine (with, note, "body") leads to Seagram's whisky "light in character" and on to Lipton's "robust" soup, and so forth. In fashion, this humanizing of the inanimate includes class consciousness, as Mary McCarthy has indicated. In a 1950 article entitled "Up the Ladder from *Charm* to *Vogue*" this shrewd observer remarked that "In the upper world of fashion, the notion of fashion as fun acquires a delicate savor. The *amusing,* the *witty,* the *delicious* ('a deliciously oversized stole') evoke a pastoral atmosphere, a Louis Seize scene where the queen is in the dairy and pauperdom is Arcadia."

Today, since Marie Antoinette is even less likely to tip up at your surprise party than a decade ago, a certain frantic insecurity —if not an epithet store of outright insanity—clogs the verbiage concerned. In this vein consider the following, extracted from a single paragraph of an article called "The Go-See Scene" in the New York *Herald Tribune,* for February 28, 1965:

> . . . four outfits to be shot for an ad in the *New Yorker.* They are a silver lame evening outfit with *crazy* pants, a long, black thing with a cut-out at the cleavage, a beach set with medieval cap of dotted swiss [cheese?], and a zebra stripe cut-out sun dress. Very *nutty.* "We wanted Carita because she's the right type," enthuses Bruce. . . . "She's *kookie* looking. . . . We saw some pictures of her that are *wild* and very sexy looking. Our clothes are very proportioned and terribly short and *bouncy.* This one, for example" (he points to the silver lame) "is a *mad* dress. . . ."[30]

Thingishness

This ability to see man everywhere, and attribute feelings to things, was called the "pathetic fallacy" by Ruskin. It was playing itself back as it was playing itself out, so that in something like Gothic novels scenic conditions reciprocally defined the consciousness of a character. In some of Mrs. Radcliffe's fiction it is quite easy to identify the suppressed sexual state of a heroine by reference to the landscape about her (torrents, gorges, etc.). In her

[30]Excepting the title of a magazine, my italics throughout. "Proportioned" would seem to be a euphemism for tight-fitting here (cf. the old Sanforized ads). As I write, Italian radio is screaming itself silly about something called *La fibra viva.* One recalls the protagonist of Poe's *Ligeia:* "Alas, I feel how much even of incipient madness might have been discovered in the gorgeous and fantastic draperies, in the solemn carvings of Egypt, in the wild cornices and furniture, in the Bedlam patterns of the carpets of tufted gold!"

book *Pathetic Fallacy in the Nineteenth Century,* Josephine Miles cites *the trees were gay* and *the proud fields laughed* as typical pathetic fallacies. But these metaphors are too tired to serve any literal meaning and, in context, they could usually be translated: *she felt gay as she ran past the trees,* or *she walked through the fields proudly smiling,* or some such. This lyric ratio can of course be seen in the novels of Hardy, Lawrence and Faulkner. It was in the spirit of revolt against this rhetoric that a new school of French fiction arose some years ago.[31]

This school has been given a variety of names, including *chosisme*—thingism; and it involves a discrepant group of writers, from Alain Robbe-Grillet through anovelists like Claude Simon and Marc Saporta (whose main effort in this field was a multinovel in the form of a deck of cards, with pages to shuffle, a box rather than a book), traditional experimenters like Michel Butor, down to the monumentally boring theorist of the movement, Nathalie Sarraute, who spreads the gospel *outre-mer.*

It is not fruitful to attend only to the pretensions of this school as expository of its aims, for such can be irritating enough. One ends up, doing so, with such oversimplifications as that of Storm Jameson that "the New Novelists devalue man, rob him of his identity, as fatally as does the most menacing product of technology."[32] This is to confuse the achieved result of the novels with the intentions of the novelists concerned. In actual fact, we find a symptomatology of our times. "This is a world without a past," writes Robbe-Grillet of his *Marienbad* movie; to a semanticist this means that it is denied a future.

Indeed, in the New Novel the thing is asymbolic, totally "apparent." Metaphorical descriptions and relationships are eschewed, the pathetic fallacy banished; nothing human must intervene between us and the activity of the trees or fields. The idea is to make the reader see again, perhaps in the spirit of Conrad's belief that "art itself may be defined as a single-minded attempt to render the highest kind of justice to the visible universe"; unfortunately, or rather fortunately, Conrad added the rider "by bringing to light

---

[31]For a fuller consideration of this group of writers, see my article "Freedom to Be a Thing; The 'New Novel' and Reality," *The Intercollegiate Review,* 3:1 (September-October 1966), pp. 23–29.

[32]Storm Jameson, "The Writer in Contemporary Society," *American Scholar,* xxxv:1 (Winter 1965–66), p. 72.

the truth, manifold and one, underlying its every aspect."[33] There is no "truth" underlying the aspects of *chosisme,* that is its point.

That this new, though scarcely novel,[34] epistemology reflected our times was evinced in the welcome found at once for it in the cinema, where mere presence on a screen lets objects make, as it were, their own statements. Physical facts are invited to speak their own language, "uncontaminated" (the slanting is significant) by the human. The reflexive nature of the whole was such that Robbe-Grillet's text might have been taken straight out of the esthetic camp he opposes, that of Marcel Proust: "Perhaps the immobility of the things that surround us is forced upon them by our conviction that they are themselves, and not anything else, and by the immobility of our conceptions of them."[35]

So in the New Novel of this nature objects are divorced from any association with emotional states. "For Robbe-Grillet," writes his enthusiastic expositor Roland Barthes, "the function of language is not a raid on the absolute, a violation of the abyss, but a progression of names over a surface."[36] Robbe-Grillet summarizes his motives himself best as follows: "Drowned in the *depth* of things, man ultimately no longer even perceives them: his role is soon limited to experiencing, in their name, totally humanized impressions and desires."[37] Thus in this mystique the thing is to be cleared of the word, cleansed of all signals, especially of those in any way oriented toward judgment (and, according to this creed, function is a form of judgment):

---

[33]The citation is taken from the famous Preface of 1897 to *The Nigger of the "Narcissus,"* in which Conrad claims that the task of art is to make man see again. Note that in *Victory* Heyst tells Davidson that he is "done with observation," while in the same book Mrs. Schomberg, who helps Lena and Heyst to escape, is observed as follows: "Nobody had ever suspected her of having a mind. . . . One was inclined to think of her as an It—an automaton, a very plain dummy. . . ."

[34]Actually, the whole bit can be found in Langer, notably in Chapter 6 ("Life-Symbols: The Roots of Sacrament") of *Philosophy in a New Key;* cf. "The image of a rose symbolizes feminine beauty so readily that it is actually harder to associate roses with vegetables than with girls" (p. 128).

[35]Marcel Proust, *Swann's Way,* translated by C. K. Scott Moncrieff, New York: The Modern Library, 1928, p. 7.

[36]Roland Barthes, "Alain Robbe-Grillet," *Evergreen Review,* II:5 (Summer 1958), p. 114.

[37]Alain Robbe-Grillet, *For a New Novel: Essays on Fiction,* New York: Grove Press, 1966, p. 68.

A slice of tomato in an automat sandwich, described according to this method, constitutes an object without heredity, without associations, and without references, an object rigorously confined to the order of its components. . . . For example, we would ordinarily say, "So-and-so's dinner was ready: some ham." This would be an adequate representation of the function of an object—the alimentary function of the ham. Here is how Robbe-Grillet says it: "On the kitchen table there are three thin slices of ham laid across a white plate." Here function is treacherously usurped by the object's sheer existence. . . .[38]

This rephrasing or parody of Heidegger ("The human condition is to be *there*") is a sharp lesson in word-wisdom, for it is a mirror to our times, in which (as Storm Jameson suggests) man is in danger of being devalued to Conrad's It. For this is the "reality" as seen by the technocrat, or rabid engineer, roughly Robbe-Grillet's own trade, before that of New Novelist. The innovator once again fails to understand the force of his Frankenstein, and the world of the New Novel is precisely that of (the more elementary or fanatic) engineering students, who proceed in a steady rote from Physics, Chemistry, Drafting back to Math, Drafting, Chemistry, Physics, day after day, and who do not, in fact, find Robbe-Grillet's fiction or his movies difficult at all.

In this world man is *there* . . . with a vengeance. His human function is tragically usurped. He lives symbol-less, in that iron world of elevators, subway cars, gas-mains and electrical outlets that Susanne Langer sees as the end of man as a sentient being at the close of her *Philosophy in a New Key*. Like an object, man has no being beyond that of phenomenon. The "business-as-usual" philosophy described by Bettelheim culminates in phenomena. It is then but a step to what are now called "human engineers," like Herman Kahn, who could write the following passage about the results of an atom-bomb attack resulting in sixty million American phenomena or objects dead, in his now celebrated *On Thermonuclear War:*

Under these conditions some high percentage of the pop-

[38]Barthes, *Evergreen Review*, II:5, pp. 115–116.

ulation is going to become nauseated, and nausea is very catching. If one man vomits, everybody vomits. Almost everyone is likely to think he has received too much radiation. Morale may be so affected that many survivors may refuse to participate in constructive activities, but would content themselves with sitting down and waiting to die—some may even become violent and destructive. However, the situation would be quite different if radiation meters were distributed. Assume now that a man gets sick from a cause other than radiation. Not believing this, his morale begins to drop. You look at his meter and say, "You have received only ten roentgens, why are you vomiting? Pull yourself together and get to work."

This methodological exposition, coming not out of *Dr. Strangelove,* nor even Robbe-Grillet, but from a man who has advised Air Force Generals, shows such a terrifying distortion of word-thing semantics it can be offered as a gallow's-humor version of truth. For the world *inside* things this is logical enough. The new scholasticism asserts that thermonuclear war is inevitable; but if it is inevitable, we cannot live. This is where Swift said we would end up if science was to solve everything. And, of course, if the radiation meter doesn't work, science will unearth some new artifact to protect man ·(after sixty million dead).

It is the almost total lack of reality in such words—by which I mean human reality—that is staggering, and is best attested by Kahn's "answer" to the reporter who pressed him as to how anyone could lead a happy or normal life with a third of the nation dead—"I guess I shouldn't have used the words happy and normal. But I meant that the quality of life after a thermonuclear war would not be much different than before. And who the hell's happy and normal right now?"

Precisely. A distorted word-thing orientation is not conducive to happiness. This kind of faith in science reminds one of the pitiful Victorian assurances—that God is watching you. Your father in heaven has called Mommy to his bosom. She trod on the accelerator instead of the brake, you see, but she has passed over now to a better land. Meanwhile—and here the headmaster joins the jovial chorus—"Pull yourself together and get to work." As Carnegie and his cohorts advised, keep *busy.* By doing so, you will not only help yourself, you will—more important—support the System.

The truth is that you do not remain an engineering student all your life, and most of Robbe-Grillet's "heroes" are mad, or disturbed to the verge of pathology. To those for whom the world simply *is* (to paraphrase Robbe-Grillet's own paraphrase on the subject), the connection between symbol and thing is nonexistent. We have the dissociation predicated in Sartre's *La Nausée*. As in Faulkner's *The Sound and the Fury* time is dislocated only by space, and shapes carry their own meanings, or nonmeanings. Images are phased like cinematic "frames," cut up, imposed beside, and/or over each other. The legs of one girl can adhere to the body of another in a narrator's memory. Time shifts are made by shapes, like O's and Y's and V's. As Lionel Trilling well put it, though in another context, "The obsessive contemplation of the objectivity of objects, the thingishness of things, is a step toward surrealism, perhaps toward madness."[39] Right. Rather than the Gaelic "You," you become an It. *He walked into the room. He picked up the knife. He plunged the point of the knife into the chest. . . .*

I improvise, but note that nearly all Robbe-Grillet's fictions to date are centered on murder. Man is simply *there*. Bettelheim emphasized that phenomena could be exterminated (forcibly reduced from Jews to digitary end-products of capitalism). Anthropomorphism is ultimately reversed. Man is seen as a clothes dryer, rather than vice versa, which is saying that he is an analog of the machine, Eliot's "human engine." For Herman Kahn this means that sixty million It's can be wiped out and we have had a successful *defense*. Our actions are exonerated from the meaningful, since the universe has no meaning. We are in the world denied a future.

If I have overelaborated on a literary movement, it is that our discourse gathers more and more into the Academy of Lagado. I think that in Robbe-Grillet's very first novel he innocently gave us this warning. The story concerned a private detective, a modern Oedipus, and while this man was not specified as actually insane (like the homicidal watch salesman or the pathic banana planter to come), his semantic relationship, his word-world harmony was a paradigm of our own. Any exclusive concentration is an unnatural activity for the human being, who has seen one thing in relation to another since the dawn of time. So the New Novel gives us this nightmare of science, an extension of Huxley or Wells,

[39]Lionel Trilling, *A Gathering of Fugitives,* Boston: Beacon Press, 1956, p. 15.

with every crime "forgiven" in the amorality of attention to *things* . . . pardoned by the First and Second Laws. We praise the Lord for C. P. Snow, heap him with honors, and send his son to Eton.

To me, the New Novel suggests that if the human condition is simply to be *there*, we won't be here very much longer. This frightful freedom to be nothing is what Robbe-Grillet wisely called man's "fatal complicity," his final tragic flaw, that of not being able to leave the universe alone. The 1966 Xmas truce in Vietnam was terminated by a shell marked "To Charlie, with love, Chris." Charlie was local soldier slang for Vietcong, and Chris was Chris Noel, a giggling female deejay who saw it off—reminding one, in between her bursts of hilarity, that by the start of 1967 a million children had been killed, burned or wounded in the war in that country.

"Intentional" and "Affective"

By now, thanks to studies like that of Miss Miles, the pathetic fallacy has been pretty well talked out. Yet no book on word-wisdom should omit to re-emphasize that, contrary to common conception, the Romantics wanted to correct (reify), rather than make more subjective, the excessive abstraction of the Enlightenment. They wanted to break out of what Wordsworth called "the increasing accumulation of men in cities" and perceive the world of things anew. As John Rosenberg puts it, "Experience revealed to the Romantics, as it did to Ruskin, a multiverse rather than a universe. Hence their stress on the concrete over the general, the 'real' over the ideal. Hence, too, their faith in feeling and distrust of the tidiness of reason."[40]

Only by reification could man reciprocally abstract and perceive the "glory" in the "flower." Coleridge's insistence on the organic unity of the esthetic vision ("nothing permanently pleases which does not contain in itself the reason why it is so, and not otherwise"), the participational harmony Shelley proposed (calling Bacon a poet), Keats' synesthesia and conception of the poet as chameleon ("because he has no identity"—viz. all identities)— such beliefs were articulated in the teeth of abandoned magic. Arnold's scholar gypsy characterizes "this strange disease of modern life" as having "divided" aims. The indictment is exact. Divided life is death.

[40]John D. Rosenberg, *The Darkening Glass,* New York: Columbia University Press, 1961, p. 16.

The distortion of ascribing intentions to objects, of kicking words, is but the mirror error of depriving the symbolic, or "transparent," of all intentions. In a curious way, by its insistence on trying to be "scientific," much contemporary literary criticism is really in league with the madness of method of Lagado, above.

It does not matter, says Yale Professor Cleanth Brooks, what Hemingway himself intended in a work under scrutiny, the critic's duty is to examine the result. In Brooks' words, "he assumes that the author's intention *as realized* is the 'intention' that counts, not necessarily what he was conscious of trying to do. . . ." The critic thus decides what the author decided to do and, as the syllogism closes, becomes more the author than the author. This is eating the menu with a vengeance.

In *The Verbal Icon* W. K. Wimsatt, Jr. pours scorn on what he calls the "intentional fallacy," a sort of offshoot, then, of the pathetic fallacy, and of the affective fallacy mentioned. Such policemen of the intellect are like the magistrates of old, who refused to consider an author's intention at all when judging libel or obscenity in a book; it was the achieved result, the "intention *as realized*," which counted. Until quite recently it was held libelous to burn a man in effigy in England. "Judging a poem is like judging a pudding or a machine. One demands that it work," claims Professor Wimsatt. Alas, this means little. A pudding does not "work" in the way a machine works; and that a pudding works at all (tastes good, presumably) is highly subjective. Some like suet pudding, some like treacle tart. Wordsworth put his finger on the poem-as-pudding (or -as-sherry-wine) heresy, at the end of his Preface to *Lyrical Ballads*.

Fattening off "fallacies," the confusions of such literary critics, each trying to be more severe than the last, are considerable. Cleanth Brooks, heavily responsible for much New Criticism, advanced something called paradox as a touchstone of great poetry. Apart from the fact that Brooks' terminology would not hold water in a freshman Philo course, he brings forward, from a sonnet by Wordsworth, a word like *breathless*, declaring: "The adjective 'breathless' suggests tremendous excitement." It may do so to Cleanth Brooks, but it might have rigorously other connotations for a runner at the end of a race, an underwater diver, or astronaut. In this same essay Brooks claims that certain figures "have sharpness and bite." In another article, on Keats, he discusses the "falling-off" of a certain stanza, and "one of the most moving passages in the poem." In the same way Wimsatt (Son of the Well-Wrought Urn) adduces the "suggestive power" of certain allusions.

Now these are "moving" and "suggestive" to the critics concerned. And the purpose of this glance at literary criticism is to identify yet another pretension to science which, in terms of literature, must be reductive. New Criticism is shot through with subjectivity, yet is at heart the reverse of Robbe-Grillet's coin, or, in other words, what he is parodying. Both are morphological equivalents of science.

Reification

To *reify* is to confer objective reality on symbolic constructs (note Wordsworth's insistence on rocks and trees and . . . things). Ten minutes ago I made a call in a pay-booth. The place was disgustingly dirty, stuck with gum, and littered with butts. On glancing up to dial, I chanced on the company's ad—"Gee, what a wonderful place to be!" Outside, in the street, a bus with a picture of gamboling lambs on its side above the legend "BE KIND, BE GENTLE" honked a blind man off a crossing.

Dickens' *Martin Chuzzlewit* has always seemed to me to anticipate Korzybski's point that words stand like maps to the territories we inhabit, in a parody of European optimism about the American utopia of the time (disfigured as Martin finds this to be by the symbolic stains of spat tobacco juice). Today the expectations-reality contrast is everywhere, from the *Let's Mail More Often* posters, with their smiling mailmen, to the harassed husband before his TV set calling through to his equally harassed and dishwashing wife, "Honey, here's wonderful news from the world of detergents." Like those of advertising, the appeals of our society are less by attacks on rival brands than by ever larger and more certain promises.

The anthropomorphic dreams of TV ads, with their animated inanimates, and gadgets come to sudden life, are "horizontal" fantasies. They look silly when confronted head-on with the rational world. Married couples do not sing duets at the breakfast table, nor does a housewife do her vacuuming in a tight sheath and high heels. A refrigerator door is not left open to display its contents. Still, there are times when we should like to sing ("to reach the secret spring of responsive emotions"), and treating the vacuum

as partner in a dance is not a bad way of dithyrambically enrich-
ing the single-level experience with which science presents us
daily. When a TV adwoman gestures at the family wash and it
hangs itself against a line of cypress trees, or when an overworked
mommy sees her luncheon sandwiches wrapping themselves, we
should perhaps search the semantic of fairy stories before hauling
in the FTC. "Coffee may have that dark, winy look simply because
the cup you see is actually filled with hot wine rather than coffee.
The dress that clings to a model without a crease or sag may be
pinned up in a dozen places in the back."[41]
 There is no doubt but that the Federal Trade Commission "protects" the public in many ways. But its zeal at present writing
seems to me occasionally misplaced, directed against specific sets
of tricks, usually spurious mock-ups, like the order against Colgate-
Palmolive Co.'s "sandpaper test," which showed what purported
to be sandpaper shaved smooth with the aid of Palmolive Rapid
Shave Cream (the FTC charged that what was used was a plexi-
glas sheet to which sand had been applied). In the famous action
against Mennen Co. the Feds pounced on another "test" showing
the alleged superiority of Sof' Stroke aerosol shaving cream by
having a skin diver shave under water, first releasing the cream
of a competing brand into his palm. The latter product dissipated,
while Sof' Stroke stayed firm. Charging that Sof' Stroke was doc-
tored with toothpaste the FTC got its customary "consent" decree,
whereby a company makes no admission but agrees to stop the
commercial.
 Life would be dull without these fairy stories, into which considerable ingenuity has poured. No one I know is proposing to
shave under water, so the *shavingness* of the cream is not in issue
on the transitive level. And by constantly attacking the language of
advertising, we are, of course, pushed into attacking language (not
all cigarettes can be healthy). To my mind, there is a more valuable area for the FTC to explore in the discrepancy, or anomy,
between the public's social needs and means. There is a dangerous
stratum of nineteenth-century *ennui* lurking in the ground between
the "map" of good living so glibly handed out (including the family plan for its cemetery plot and college insurance program) and
the actual "territory" of minority group families.

 [41]"TV Commercials: Wonderful World of Make-believe," *Changing Times:
The Kiplinger Magazine,* May 1962, p. 25.

It is in the field of abstract knowledge, especially politics, that Korzybski's code does most good. The verbal "maps" describing Fascism before the last war, or China after it, were obviously inadequate. The Maginot Line mentality still leads to tragic misevaluations; even today few Westerners seem aware of the austere existence led by hundreds of millions of Asiatics. Or even of who these Asiatics are.[42] According to an Army spokesman, the average GI prisoner in Korea "seemed lost without a bottle of pills and a toilet that flushed." An Army doctor taken captive at this time recalls:

> during those early marches in Korea I saw sick prisoners lying down at the side of the road and waiting to be picked up by ambulance. They thought that just because our Army had ambulances for picking up straggling prisoners, the Communists would have them, too.

Among survival kits issued to pilots in the Vietnam war was a US Armed Forces phrase-book of what to say on being taken prisoner.[43] One of the phrases was: "Where is the nearest telephone?" The chief concern of Mexican movie censors has been to check the image of Mexico fabricated in Hollywood, as a land of villians with mustaches dripping over their chins and hoop-earringed cantina girls eternally masticating roses.

The many books of Bergen Evans collecting follies, from the eating of beaver's testicles in order to bring on an abortion to shaving so as not to divert nourishment from the scalp,[44] all attest to a human desire not to be dominated by the rational; and there are times when we not only enrich experience, but actually collaborate more with reality, by breaking out of the maps-territory straitjacket (cf. Gregory Corso's *fried shoes* philosophy). In a small but long-lived book, *The Standardization of Error,* the Arctic authority Vilhjalmur Stefansson lambasts our metaphoric use of birds like ostriches and storks. Unlike him we do not see these birds in

[42]"Japanese in Moscow Complain, Mistaken for Chinese, Abused" (headline in San Francisco *Nichi Bei Times,* October 1, 1963).

[43]This booklet was condescendingly called *Pointee-Talkee.* In fact, pidgin English has a pedigree; Melanesian Pidgin has been the subject of serious study by Professor Robert A. Hall, Jr., a Cornell linguist.

[44]Bergen Evans, *The Natural History of Nonsense,* New York: Alfred A. Knopf, 1946, pp. 30, 157.

daily life, and their "transparent" use, as that of the roses Miss Langer mentions, has almost drowned out their reality. Storks bring babies and ostriches hide their heads in the sand. The zoological definitions, or "territories," are less picturesque in both cases. Enid Bagnold's "ponies" were a similar case in point to a number of teachers contributing ideas to *The Use of English* on how to get British girlhood off the hook of this unreal writer; the best suggestion was to introduce children to real ponies.

The End of Anomy

Today an overscientized community fights to hold on to some last flicker of the irrational. Our preoccupation with sex perhaps reflects this. Some hotels still resolutely abandon the idea of numbering a floor 13. The recent Kilander Health Knowledge Tests uncovered a host of popular superstitions in the most advanced technological community the world has ever seen. It seemed needlessly governessy to hold up hands in semantic shame, as did Dr. Kilander at the fact that "About half the public still thinks that raw meat such as beefsteak will reduce a swelling or 'black eye' due to a bruise." (Actually, if the cut is cold enough, it will.) In England there are almost perennial proposals to abolish the House of Lords. But what is the "territory" here? The House of Lords *is* abolished. For years they have been powerless to do anything more than delay the passage of a Bill; in 1966 the Government was "defeated" in the House of Lords shortly before the election of that year, but this action was considered so futile two London papers even failed to report it. Scientific rationalism is not reason; indeed, it can be unreason.

Joyce saw our world enclosed in our words. When Jacques Barzun presented his pathology of "the anti-intellectualism of the intellectual," he suggested that Intellect (with a capital) consisted of certain "habits of discipline, signs and symbols of meaning." It was a sort of social shorthand by means of which we civilize. He cited the alphabet as a harmony, a set of ground rules on which and with which we construct meaning.

Barzun's Intellect is Langer's "proposition," a group of symbols syntactically combined for the purpose of conceptualizing. It is a pity; Barzun nearly understands his own theory here. But the burden of his argument, as it continues, presses the role of imagination into "anticerebration." We get the early Nietzsche misread once more. This is what produces social anomy. In true word-wisdom imagination works rationally and vice versa. To be explicitly systematic is not necessarily to be rational. To add Wit to Fancy, or check Dionysos with Apollo, is not automatically to produce an esthetic.[45] These are man's self-consuming dreams.

A final reminder of the limitations of Korzybski's maps-territories semantic can be seen in the theories of David Riesman. For Riesman coined the term *inner-directed* of a culture force which presumed that "maps" (ideals, demands) were internalized by opinion-formers, particularly of the last century. But he found that it was not so much that these "maps" played false to the reality of our times for the young—in, say, the collapse of the old parental demand for the energetic personality—as that the children of our technology saw *no need for "maps" at all.* Riesman writes, "Little energy is directed toward finding new solutions of the age-old problems. . . ." To which could be added Aldous Huxley's belief, expressed in one of his last books, that in the United States,

> recent public opinion polls have revealed that an actual majority of young people in their teens, the voters of tomorrow, have no faith in democratic institutions, see no objection to the censorship of unpopular ideas, do not believe that government of the people by the people is possible and would be perfectly content, if they can continue to live in the style to which the boom has accustomed them, to be ruled, from above, by an oligarchy of assorted experts.[46]

If the young became *other-directed* in the fifties and sixties it was in a social shrug at the transitive relationship of a scientized society. Their very vocabulary showed this. Their god was acausality. Zen. They had been lied to enough. *Terrorism* was an attack on a U.S. Army unit, while the napalming of a peasant was an *accident.* Even computers might revolt, or throw up, one feels, after a diet of several years of this semantic. The laments over

[45]Sartre's distinction between poetry and prose is parallel to Barzun's between intelligence and Intellect, in this case as between a "transparent," informative medium (prose, or intelligence) and "apparent," opaque intuition (poetry, or Intellect). See my review of Barzun's excellent book in *The Use of English,* xi:4 (Summer 1960), pp. 252–255.

[46]Aldous Huxley, *Brave New World Revisited,* New York: Harper & Brothers, 1958, p. 144.

laxity in teen-age morals have been but a confession of lack of reification on the part of the old. The 1967 British Latey report confirmed as much, advocating majority at the age of eighteen. In fact, the knowledge of contraception possessed by most American teen-agers is a tribute to their understanding of the world. Their parents should know so much.

Lost in the "darkness" of the Congo, Conrad's Marlow stared gratefully at a bucket of rivets. (And we remember that he thought of Kurtz, in an anticipation of Hitler, as a *voice*.) As Frost put it in a poem, "It's knowing what to do with things that counts." Anomy is the malaise of automata. The dubbed "audience" and canned laughter on radio and TV is technology's parody of present word behavior. In this chapter I have tried to lead up progessively to such verbal suicide, the world within things, the finale of technique. I will devote a brief excursion to names, as a last mannerism of "apparent" language, and then proceed to similar comedies of misapplication in "transparent" language. For these distortions delineate social goals. We note that in *The Taming of the Shrew* it is when Katherine decides to *give up* against Petruchio, her Humpty Dumpty here, that she abandons the wisdom of words:

> Then, God be blessed, it is the blessed sun.
> But sun it is not, when you say it is not,
> And the moon changes even as your mind.
> What you will have it named, even that it is,
> And so it shall be so for Katherine.

FIVE

I asked my fair one happy day,
What I should call her in my lay,
 By what sweet name from Rome or Greece:
Lalage, Neaera, Chloris,
Sappho, Lesbia or Doris,
 Arethusa or Lucrece.

"Ah!" replied my gentle fair,
"Beloved, what are names but air?
 Choose thou whatever suits the line:
Call me Sappho, call me Chloris,
Call me Lalage or Doris,
 Only, only call me Thine."

Coleridge's translation of Lessing's Namen

NAMES: THE EMBLEMS OF IDENTITY

What's in a Name?[1]

"Names are sound and smoke," said Faust, but he was referring to the impossibility of naming God. Calling something by some word or term is to set up an anticipation—or, more bluntly if more technically, it is to require an accusative. A name is thus popularly supposed to connote. Like a botanist you write a quality into it. We have all heard the equivalent, at some party or gathering, of the comment—"She doesn't look like a Suzy to me, she looks like a Sally." In a short called *The Pharmacist* W. C. Fields asserted that all Cuthberts were "sissies." On the other hand, Joey (Adams, Bishop, E. Lewis) seems always to carry a folksy and meliorative

---

[1]In this highly elementary chapter I mean *proper names* by "names"; an intentional grammar was involved when your parents decided your name— June, Eleanor, Bill, Harry, whatever. But language had already conventionalized a whole host of other names for you—thus you might have been born on *Monday* in *Athens*.

ring in America. Interestingly, Jewish law prescribes that if some-one marries another with the same first-name initial as the former's parent (of the same sex as the latter), the parent concerned will die. People find names infringements on their individuality, and indeed often change them.

This is presymbolic use become popular error. As Ryle has writ-ten, "Proper names are appellations and not descriptions. . . . Proper names are arbitrary bestowals, and convey nothing true and nothing false, for they convey nothing at all." Langer says the same, "a proper name has no connotation at all," adding that it can some-times connote a gender, like Blanche or Jeanne (the feminine of Jean). But surely even this extent of connotation breaks down, particularly in America, where a Bobby, or Leslie, or Terry may be masculine or feminine (cf. in England Alison, Jocelyn, Evelyn). You could also argue that English George reads to a German as a plural of Georg. My grandfather was called Christian; he was certainly the least Christian member of his family I have known. (The case in France is a little different since there the Ministry of Justice controls the names allowed to be given in birth registration offices.) Melville was always giving allegorical names to his ships. But, as we know, the actual name of a missile or motorcar conveys nothing intrinsic about it at all. Despite this, companies spend millions of dollars a year picking names for products, even hauling in, on one celebrated occasion, America's most distinguished poetess to help out.

By the laws of language a name "means" nothing. It is a sign. It stands for something. The stray dog you adopted last year and called Rough was actually called Rover in its first home; but the quadruped remains the same. Frankly, the sooner we recognize this rule of "apparent" language the better: a name cannot imply anything.

Thus what is going on when an auto is called a Thunderbird or Cyclone or Tempest is a semantic violation; for it is to claim that the name both simultaneously denotes and connotes—and does so reciprocally. Rough, that is, not only stands for your quadruped, it stands for what he signifies. Like Negro, or Jew, or limey, or yank. I will return to this distortion when dealing with classes.

The connotations of thunder, as in Thunderbird above, are im-ported over and over again in this falsely transitive ratio—cf. the F105 Thunderchief currently blasting the outskirts of Hanoi as I write.[2] We smile when a stripper nicknames herself Fury, but not when a plane or sonar torpedo or even a car is christened such. Naming of this nature says more about the namer, or nominative in the relationship, than anything else. It should finally suggest that for a word to mean, rather than simply to stand for, it has to be used in a context or situation.

Shakespeare showed up this semantic in Act III, scene iii of *Julius Caesar:* the mob are out to kill. They seize on Cinna the poet rather than Cinna the conspirator. He protests, but it makes no difference to the mob—"It is no matter, his name's Cinna; pluck but his name out of his heart, and turn him going." What a jest. It is the final fallacy of totemic misclassification, onto which Cinna desperately grafts another, protesting that he is a bachelor rather than a married man, and so forth. It does not suffice. The name is the same. He is what he is.[3]

Rumpelstiltskins

The misrelation mentioned is primitive in origin, and hence slow to die. To surrender your name was thought to be to give up part of yourself (cf. Army instructions to potential prisoners of war today). In Freud's words, "A man's name is one of the main constituents of his person and perhaps a part of his psyche."[4]

Australian aborigines used to give their children secret names, symbolic of each child's unique spirit, and so that this aspect of personality might never be impounded by another, the secret name was never uttered. Among the Iroquois names were closely guarded clan possessions. There is a comic reduction of this in Faulkner's family of poor whites called Urquhart, who did not know how to spell their name and consequently got called Workitt.

The French ethnographer Claude Lévi-Strauss demonstrates

[2]The nomenclature of British aircraft in the last war deserves an article to itself. Spitfires (fighters) were presumably named in the same spirit as Thunderchiefs, though they literally spat fire; the Hampden (bomber) must have been named after a great British dissident, and liberal, of the seventeenth century, but I don't recall a Pym. Wellingtons and Blenheims went back to more obvious military allusions.

[3]Shakespeare gives what is perhaps a complementary example of this misreading in Falstaff's famous speech on honor anticipating what some sociology professors call the "mashed-potato menace" (e.g. 97 percent of all murderers have eaten mashed potatoes).

[4]Sigmund Freud, *Totem and Taboo,* Authorized translation with an Introduction by A. A. Brill, New York: Random House, 1946, p. 145.

that prohibition on pronouncing the names of the dead becomes an actual structural property of certain "savage" systems of naming, and indeed this gets carried to such lengths in some societies that a man cannot boast a name until his mother's death. The Wik Munkan, he informs us, forbid the mention of a dead man's name for three years after his death. A highly complex system of necronyms (expressing kinship relations with the deceased), teknonyms and autonyms consequently develops, and spawns to such an extent that it can actually inhibit marriage, viz. the very bond of relationship that it was originally concocted to conserve!

In *The White Goddess* Robert Graves finds that two medieval Welsh poems, the *Cad Goddeu* and *Hanes Taliesin,* yield a hidden alphabet of trees and seasons, which in turn protects the secret name of God. (There are pious Jews in New York today who refuse to throw out any paper on which the name *God* is written.) The semantically astute Lewis Carroll presents similar timidity over yielding up one's name when his Alice is accosted by the caterpillar in Wonderland. Today the rupture of orthographic rules in order to acquire a unique image is largely the preserve of trademarks, which thus attempt to be "deictic"—"Particularity, or uniqueness, of reference is a semantic property of proper names."[5]

In *The Romance of Words* Ernest Weekley lists a veritable path of civilization by words that came out of place-names—*millinery* from Milan, *calico* from Calicut, *damask* from Damascus, *muslin* from Mosul. One thinks of *worsted* from little-known Worstead in Norfolk, not to mention that grotesque playback, the *bikini.* But many companies try to substitute their trade for generic names in popular usage, as in tampax, kleenex, bayaspirin, orlon, terylene. One forgets that vaseline was once a trade name, as were formica, zip (fastener), jello and scotch tape (in France one asks, "*Vous avez du scotch?*"). Coke has become fairly generic, at least in Europe (in France Pepsi may be given if you ask for *un coke*), while frigidaire and band-aid beg for similar adoptions. Weekley also observes that many forgotten individuals are lexically remembered—mackintosh, brougham, derrick, guillotine, hansom, mesmer(ism), zeppelin, shrapnel; Wellington had boots, hats, coats and trees named after him, and the fictitious Emma Bovary a perfume. In America Cadillac founded Detroit, Pontiac was an Indian Chief, and Olds built his Oldsmobile.

[5]Leech, *English in Advertising,* p. 156.

When names, then, are designative language, they attempt a form of primitive control. As Faust says to his famulus, *"Wer darf das Kind beim rechten Namen nennen?"* Frazer tells us that the Abipons of Paraguay repeatedly altered the name for jaguar, owing to sundry interdictions and obviously in an effort to effect better environmental control. We call cars Jaguars, Mustangs, Cougars. To infringe on the name of the divine has always been highly taboo, and Moses was rebuked for inquiring after God's name. In this way also could be seen the reluctance of the early Hebrews to be counted, another control-activity we syphon off on money today. There is a Jewish tradition of changing a sick person's name in order to confuse the Angel of Death. Adam named his animals, and had power over them. Thomas Mann dramatized this power in *Joseph and His Brothers:* "And the beasts too they are ashamed and put the tail between their legs because we know them and have power over their names and can thus render powerless the roaring might of the single one, by naming him."

We laugh at two children being named John Glenn (and one Orbit, in a similar desire to launch him on an upward path in life) the day after that famous astronaut thrice circled the earth.[6] But is this much different from the British believing that England would prosper once more with a second queen *called* Elizabeth? We must not forget that no British child could be christened Oscar for sixteen years, or that no Austrian baby has been named Adolf since the German invasion of that country. Joyce mocked this semantic at the start of *A Portrait of the Artist as a Young Man* with the young Stephen reflecting:

> It was very big to think about everything and everywhere. Only God could do that. He tried to think what a big thought that must be but he could only think of God. God was God's name just as his name was Stephen. *Dieu* was the French for God and that was God's name too; and when anyone

[6]"LOS ANGELES, Feb. 24 (AP)—A coat-of-arms specialist said today that the motto of Lieut. Col. John H. Glenn Jr.'s ancestors for more than 500 years had been 'Alta Pete,' which he translated from the Latin into 'Aim High.'

"The expert, Joe T. Boyes of Burbank, Calif., said his research showed that for the last two centuries the motto has included this additional phrase: 'Ad Astra,' or 'To the Stars.'

"Colonel Glenn orbited the earth three times Tuesday" *(New York Times).*

prayed to God and said *Dieu* then God knew at once that it was a French person that was praying. But though there were different names for God in all the different languages in the world and God understood what all the people who prayed said in their different languages still God remained always the same God and God's real name was God.

There is tribal wisdom in this desire to have the world respond to the word in this way. When Oscar Wilde signed *The Ballad of Reading Gaol* with the pseudonumber, that of his cell, "C.3.3.," he was protesting against the namelessness of technocracy to come. We have a hint of the horror of anonymity in prisoners, soldiers and even, so it is said, hospital patients. The patient too often becomes a sign vehicle—"What does Forty-five want now?" says the nurse.[7]

Welsh nomenclature is extremely limited, like Corsican nomenclature. Russell made a parable out of this:

> There was once upon a time a census officer who had to record the names of all householders in a certain Welsh village. The first that he questioned was called William Williams; so were the second, third, fourth. . . . At last he said to himself: "This is tedious; evidently they are all called William Williams. I shall put them down so and take a holiday." But he was wrong; there was just one whose name was John Jones

You could well find not only eight Bowens or Davies in a single company of a Welsh regiment, but three or four Hugh Bowens and David (Dai) Davies. The man is then referred to by the last two numbers of his Army numeral—Thirty-eight Bowen, or Oh-four Davies. This apellation is invariably resented, as a loss. For the human is here sensed mediately. One father of an American enlisted man recently sent his son a letter addressed wholly by numerals, beginning with the boy's Army number, followed by that of his camp, and concluding with the so-called Zip code. It took three weeks longer than another letter, consisting only of names, posted on the same day.

Science-fiction had warned us long ago of this reduction to non

[7] See Anna Teresa Baziak and Robert Knox Dentan, "The Language of the Hospital and Its Effects on the Patient," *ETC.*, XVII:3 (September 1960), p. 264.

entity, but the semiosis was nowhere better illustrated than in the efforts of the late, and lamented, Anti-Digit Dialling League, which rose in California to oppose the substitution of telephonic code numbers for area names. Ulster . . . Mayfair . . . Circle—these were at least identities, it was felt, and their destruction for a sign yet one more constriction of the human. Reduced to a digit, indeed, man becomes little more than an accident; he is superfluous or *de trop* in the manner experienced by Sartre's Roquentin, a being sundered from his artifacts and (in our own case) with little control over his weaponry. Gary Youree's poems about his social security number protest against this.

Exactly the same resistance was mooted in France recently, resulting in the enlarging of the repertoire of first names allowed to be given by the official gazette. A friend of mine had a suit against the government to call his daughter Vanina. Although Vanina was not then officially permitted, his lawyer won the case since he showed the name common in Corsica, and thus in "Christian history." Yet the new list still bars "things, animals or qualities" as names. Nor may you call your child Israel in France.

In England similar sentiments have been seen in the revolt against the reduction of the pound to decimals. The proposal to divide the pound sterling into 1,000 octal subunits by 1971—the Octal System being even more limited than the standard—would do away with such pleasures of coinage as guineas, florins and half crowns. Soon LSD will no longer mean money in England, only the drug. There is the story of the kid from St. Paul who asked a buddy what Minnesota meant, and got back the answer, "It's the last name of all the towns around here." There was a well-known World War II anecdote (quoted in S.L.A. Marshall's *Night Drop* as well as elsewhere) concerning the American Colonel vainly trying to get some French peasants to read his map, after he had dropped from the skies over Normandy. All French peasants I know are as bad map readers as they are good territory readers. Finally, the Colonel gave up—"Gee, these people have been living here all their lives and they don't even know the name of the place."

Word-branding

Digitary encroachments were highlit by the late leader of the Black Muslim movement in America, Malcolm X. "The X means that I don't know who I am," he is reported to have said. "No one knows who these Negroes are—their identity was destroyed during slavery. All of the Muslims take X—the unknown. Sixty-seven brothers in our mosque alone have the name James X with the number of their sequence—James X-11, James X-12 etc. We have done this deliberately. I feel more intelligent saying my name is X" *(New York Times Magazine)*. One wonders if, by the same token, Xmas is the birthday of Jesus X.[8]

Initially the objection seems fair enough; it was the same loss of identity suffered by southern slaves—Faulkner gives us Tenny's Jim, and the like. Yet the word-wisdom here is unfortunately low. Malcolm believed his foreparents to have been slaves owned by a man called Little, "and it would be an insult to call me by that name." Malcolm, and or X, resented this verbal brand-mark, as he saw it, and in the same spirit would refer to "so-called Negroes." He explained this as follows: "Not content with stripping us of our names . . . the white man, in his evilness, stripped us of our humanity. . . . So the white man made up a special name for his slave-animal—'Negro.' It's a synthetic name that means low, filthy beast. We want no part of it" (*Saga* magazine).

It means, of course, what you say it means. And by and large the use of initials for heroes in modern fiction is another voice out of this protest, though a more knowing one. Joyce and Kafka underlined the anonymity of mass man thereby. But they reciprocally forced the reader to identify the human in such characters, rather than passively accept a bell-cat emblem, loaded with connotations (Suzy, Sally, Cuthbert). In comes Dickens' Pumblechook and we are all set for a bumbling, pretentious bore. Here strides Fielding's Heartfree, how can he be anything but a good chap? This allegorical tagging has run through English literature from Shakespeare (Malvolio, Hotspur, Blunt), and before, to our own times (Wells' Lord Boom, Waugh's farcical names). Congreve has a Fondlewife. Ronald Firbank's characters include: Countess Medusa, Dr. Cunliffe Babcock, Llewellyn Tird, Noel Nice, Lady Parvula de Panzoust, and Whipsina Peters. These exceed Peacock. More recently,

[8]For a comparison of the rhetoric of Malcolm X with that of Cicero etc. see John Illo, "The Rhetoric of Malcolm X," *Columbia University Forum*, IX:2 (Spring 1966), pp. 5–12 ("Cicero would have approved Malcolm's discourses as *accommodatus, aptus, congruens* . . ."). Meanwhile, synonym-chasers have pointed out that Roget's *Thesaurus* lists 134 synonyms for *whiteness,* all except ten positive, 120 for *blackness,* half of which are distinctly unfavorable.

Ian Fleming filled his Bonded fiction with such heroines as: Honeychile Rider, Pussy Galore, Vesper Lynd, Tiffany Case, Tatiana Romanova (when these ladies are German, they are usually bad as well as exotic, e.g. Lisl Baum, Rosa Klebbs, Irma Bunts). Such characters *are* their names. Or, as Lévi-Strauss puts it of embodied naming of this nature, the name becomes "the signifier of his signified being."[9]

Pantomimic imagery of this nature belongs principally to folk anthropology. It was not for nothing that Matthew Arnold identified an entire national ugliness in a name—Wragg, adding "what a touch of grossness in our race . . . is shown by the natural growth amongst us of such hideous names—Higginbottom, Stiggins, Bugg! . . . by the Ilissus there was no Wragg, poor thing!"[10] (When recently I defended Nat Hentoff against the charges of David Holbrook, the latter sneered, in *The Use of English* for Spring 1967, "I did not realize that Americans are all 'Nat,' 'Nance,' 'Mike' and 'Barb' etc.") Fixed symbols of this nature are better called what Schopenhauer termed them—*emblems*. They comprise a sort of crude armorial bearings we are forced to tote around life with us, combining the sign and the thing signified in a decorative manner. Schopenhauer cites the laurel of fame, the Cross of Christianity and so on—precisely the kind of automatic attribution Robbe-Grillet is fighting.[11]

[9]Professors Wellek and Warren give also: Fielding's Allworthy and Thwackum; Dickens' Pecksniff, Rosa Dartle (=dart + startle), and Murdstone (where we hear murder + stony heart). They add a useful bibliographical footnote, as always, but do not go into the particularly British continuation of this Renaissance trait. (René Wellek and Austin Warren, *Theory of Literature,* New York: Harcourt, Brace & World, 1956, pp. 208–209, 297). This sort of self-designatory name causes all sorts of difficulties for translators, of course. In Bode's German *Tom Jones* Squire Allworthy can easily become Herr Alwerth, but when Schlegel turned Sir Andrew Aguecheek into the Junker von Bleichenwang he created a German entity, rather like the translator who set a modern novel about Yorkshire in Germany by calling "fish and chips" *Wurst und Brot* on the understandable grounds that fish and chips is not a cheap workman's meal outside England.

[10]May one be so sure? Romance and other language names with musical rings to Anglo-Saxon ears often turn out to be of the most pedestrian nature imaginable. There are French equivalents of Bugg. Arnold is here ignoring allophones. Richard Stiggins, spoken by a Frenchman with no English, could sound quite musical. It might be mentioned, however, that Jewish appraisive names—Morgenstern, Lichtenstein and the like—do deliberately involve poetic affects.

[11]Arthur Schopenhauer, *The World as Will and Idea,* trans. R. B. Haldane and J. Kemp, New York: Doubleday & Company, 1961, pp. 250–251.

Sound-naming

Names invite listing. H. L. Mencken compiled one of his Teutonically elaborate chapters of *The American Language* on "Proper Names in America," and a British writer has recently traced the origin of twelve hundred surnames in his country.[12] A comparison shows that in America the principles of second- and middle-naming have been different, thanks, largely, to minority customs less evident in England.

Thus the American Negro has a marvelous thesaurus of "armorial-bearing" names, like Sunday-Night-Supper Jones or Are-You-Ready-for-the-Judgment-Day? Brown. British Caribbean dialects, heavily compounded of course with French, reflect much of the same—I particularly like the descriptive Barbadian term for a fussy, effeminate fellow, an *auntie-man,* or (patois) *mamapoule.*[13] According to Mencken, Hebrew given names were apparently often translated into German and made into surnames with the various additives for -son.[14] America also varies from England in the habit of a woman converting her surname, or even her first married, into the middle name of her current marital status.

Mythological nomenclature is no less curious, however, than functional naming by physical trait (or would-be or hoped-for trait). Oedipus presses the word for his name into the future in a parable of language. Boccaccio was presumably named for his ugly or foul mouth (the *-acciù* suffix being the quickest way to make anything and everything pejorative in current Corse). I assume that Cincinnatus grew curly. Fortune-telling by words in this way has by no means vanished, nor been wholly sidelined to the comic.

To avoid using proper names, indeed, with a potential of descriptive connotation, and therefore a reduction of individuation, the Californian Yurok developed a system of residence-names, thus: a village or house, plus suffixes expressive of gender, marital status and so on, all rather reminiscent of some contemporary

[12]James Pennethorne Hughes, *Is They Name Wart?* London: Phoenix Books, 1966. (Title spelt *sic.*)

[13]Frank A. Collymore, "A Few More Words and Phrases of Barbadian Dialect," *Bim,* IX:13 (July-December 1961), p. 67. More recently Collymore has collected his observations of such dialect into a delightful volume: *Barbadian Dialect,* 3rd ed., revised and enlarged: Bridgetown, Barbados: Advocate Co., 1965.

[14]H. L. Mencken, *The American Language, Supplement II,* New York: Alfred A. Knopf, 1956, p. 417.

passport entry. Similarly, Australian tribes had a series of names applicable to those living in certain age-groups, or who had not had any teeth extracted, or been circumcized, or the like. In Borneo an individual evidently has an "umbilical" name.

In this way, Lévi-Strauss suggests, the conflict between classification and individuation is demonstrated in the binominal nature of our naming—e.g. John (= the individual) Robinson (= the class, or family). In Corsica, I have observed, Toussaint Mattei is still addressed on his envelopes as if he were in the Army—Mattei, Toussaint (viz., from the class to the individual). "At one extreme, the name is an identifying mark which, by the application of a rule, establishes that the individual who is *named* is a member of a preordained class. . . . At the other extreme, the name is a free creation on the part of an individual who *gives the name* and expresses a transitory and subjective state of his own by means of the person he names."[15]

Euphonic stage names are nearly always sought, and in a typical playback the star then finds herself retailored to the personality bought by the sound, or allophones. (Tuesday Weld, it was complained, looked too like Saturday Night.) Allophonic confusions seem to grow annually more fantastic, one such lately concerning the similarity in sound between the Boys Club of America and the currently blacklisted Du Bois Club. "Radio and television announcers and reporters in reading the news during the past several days have tended to say Doo-BOYS. Many listeners have apparently misunderstood this as 'the Boys,' rather than Du Bois" *(New York Times)*. James Wechsler ran this item as a joke in the New York *Post* (March 9, 1966), but Richard M. Nixon was evidently serious in decrying the similarity in sound, and its repronunciation became the subject of a CBS/ABC/NBC interoffice directive.[16] It appeared that members of the wholesome Boys Club were getting beaten up by superpatriots on the West Coast, following Attorney General Katzenbach's decree against the Du Bois Club.

In the recent naming of missiles and space shots Greek myths have been pillaged for the grandiose ring of good sound. Thus

[15]Claude Lévi-Strauss, *The Savage Mind,* Chicago: University of Chicago Press, 1966, p. 181. Lévi-Strauss' main argument here is to disallow Russell's idea that there is a continuous passage from the act of signifying to that of pointing.

[16]This confidential directive, worthy of Terry Southern, can be seen in full in *The Realist,* no. 67 (May 1966), p. 24.

"The Thersites shot at Venus today was aborted for a centrifuge" sounds classier than, say, "Irving failed today." Women's groups repeatedly protest the naming of hurricanes as feminine. On one West Indian island, 1958 is known not by its numerals but by the fact that Janet came that year.[17]

Perhaps the lower levels of show biz reveal this logo-cathection at its best, or worst. The names taken by wrestlers are highly indicative of the roles they are likely to play. Hans Schmidt, Ivan the Terrible, Karl Van Hess and Skull Murphy would all be expected to be villains, while names recalling the Indian past are usually staged as heroes—e.g. Chief Big Heart. Britain has seen the same: in one corner the Hairy Man, the Giraffe Kid; in the other, Professor Frank Numps, Lord Harris, Tip Top Smith.

Similarly, the semantics of strippers has never had its due. Even Mencken did not get around to this. Here we find the usual barefaced puns: Ana Mation, Candy Barr, Iva G. String, Simma Down, Fanny Shaker and the like. But is such predictive or toponymic naming different in *kind* from calling your son Junior or, as if he were some foreign King, the Third? There are also ecdysiast zeugmas trying to ride herd on the coattails (or G-strings) of other names, such as Norma Vincent Peel, Georgia Raft, Samya Davis, Jr. Other methods include what one might call function—the Bazoom Girl (with relevant, and reverent, statistics), Legs Diamond, Ding Dong Bell (the moniker of the magnificent Virginia Bell), Hope Chest, and Miss Cleanhead (a Negress with a bald head who danced chiefly around Chicago and billed herself as "the female Yul Brynner"). Even more in line with language incantation, and future-controlling magic, are such burly queens as Stormy Knight, Shady Lane and Tempest Storm (whose colossal "hope chest" can be seen in a plate of my *Parade of Pleasure*). Then there is the kids' game with names of books, like *Into the Jungle,* by Hugo First.

Functional naming was obviously one of primitive man's easiest methods of controlling the reality about him, as in the criteria for

---

[17]An island nearby, known for its rough waters adjacent, is called Kick'em Jenny. This is a good example of sound-sense collaboration since it derives from the French Cay Qui Gêne (isle that gives you trouble). Of course, a nickname can vary in meaning, depending on the intention of the speaker: "In consequence of Dobbin's victory, his character rose prodigiously in the estimation of all his schoolfellows, and the name of Figs, which had been a byword of reproach, became as respectable and popular a nickname as any other in use in the school" (Thackeray, *Vanity Fair*).

animals Noah Jacobs specifies: place of origin (Great Dane, Pekingese, tarantula—from Taranto); size (horsefly, bumblebee); means of sustenance (anteater); method of locomotion (grasshopper); mode of excretion (the butterfly's feces evidently resemble butter). Professor Jacobs lists altogether eleven such categories, and one can think of others.[18]

It is when we imagine we are using functional naming, which is designative, but are in fact employing prescriptive naming, which is horoscopy, that a kind of semantic optical illusion occurs. Calling someone Baron, Duke, Earl, King (or even Dean) guarantees no such degree of eminence for the named one. And often you can guess a person's age, or generation, by the star after whom he or, usually, she was named. The Marilyns in America and the Brigittes in France are coming of age.

There is nothing "wrong" with this. It is even endearingly human. Jack London's story "Samuel" tells of a woman who names a series of children Samuel despite the fact that all of them die violently. A certain Pavlovian reaction is involved; I am reminded of the night I watched Pancho Gonzales playing tennis at Madison Square Garden. He grew more and more irritated—justifiably so—with the flashes of strobe lights from the rows of spectators. At a dinner for the players that evening one of the bulbs in the chandelier over the table popped. Gonzales yelled, "Get that photographer!"

Detroit wants us to salivate automatically as they reel off their car names under our noses—Wildcat, Tempest, Fury, Mustang, the vocabulary of the panting adolescent. Gogol's *The Overcoat* contains that charming moment when Akaky, the elder, has to name his son. Various ideas are offered to the simpleminded mother but " 'No,' thought the poor lady, 'they are all such names!' " Still more are suggested. " 'What an infliction!' said the mother. 'What names they all are!' " Finally, after another batch has been discarded, she retorts grimly, "Since that is how it is, he had better be called after

[18]Noah Jacobs, *Naming-Day in Eden,* New York: Macmillan, 1958, pp. 15–16. In fact, the fecal theory for butterflies is considered fairly farfetched. There are many others, one that the name derives from the color of an early English species. I far prefer the more physically trembly *papillon, farfalla, mariposa* and *Schmetterling.* For Lewis Carroll, if you can have a butterfly you can also have a "bread-and-butter fly, whose wings are thin slices of bread and butter, and whose body is the crust." Similarly, he proposes a rocking-horse fly.

his father, his father is Akaky, let the son be Akaky, too." And this imitative, uncreative moment forms the man's life, for he is destined to turn into a humble copyist.[19]

I have selected naming, then, as the last rung on the ladder of "apparent" language since, in Ryle's words, "Saying is not naming." In the course of the first part of this book my principal business has been to illustrate transformations of experience prior to, or unavailable in, the notations of discursive language. Of course, "apparent" does not stand to "transparent" word-wisdom in the emphasis I have placed on it in this book; the reason for more space on the former here is that it is, on the whole, less studied. The vagaries of "transparent" language are by now matters of libraries in themselves, and I only propose to select some salient problems of immediate use to Mr. Mits. One cannot advance on such a broad front at all points at once.

"The cat," writes Susanne Langer, "does not act humanly *because he does not need to.* This difference in fundamental needs, I believe, determines the difference of function which sets man so far apart from all his zoölogical brethren."[20]

It was for this reason, then, that I took naming last. Here is no language barrier, properly speaking, at all. We are involved in a fine relation between signs. Like a number to a mathematician, a name has no inherent connotation in it. Yet the persistence in attaching such "meanings" to names shows, I think, discontent with the scientific discourse of our times. "When I like people immensely," says Wilde's Lord Henry, ignorant of Freud, "I never tell their names to anyone. It is like surrendering a part of them." Precisely because it is not symbolic, the name frees the object from its surroundings and creates an identity—in the manner of the old midwife who presided over childbirth, uttering one name after another, until the child came out, and into being, at the utterance of the "right" one. It is not for nothing that the Yogi and mystic are so esteemed in Western intellectual circles today, nor that Hollywood —in the worst of both worlds—has thrown up theosophic cults. It is well known that astrological journals have a huge sale in scientific America. We need a sense of delusion to live. Socrates put it

[19]Vladimir Nabokov, *Nikolai Gogol,* Norfolk, Conn.: New Directions, 1944, pp. 84–85, discusses Gogol's names, but oddly fails to mention this incident.
[20]Langer, *Philosophy in a New Key,* pp. 43–44.

better, bridging the gap between the first and second parts of this book, by being given to say, in the *Theaetetus:*

> the primeval elements out of which you and I and all other things are compounded have no reason or explanation; you can only name them. . . . None of these primeval elements can be defined, they can only be named for they have nothing but a name, and the things which are compounded of them, as they are all complexes, are expressed by a combination of names, for the combination of names is the essence of a definition.

The reader may thus find the time has come to cross the bridge from a principally physiological (or "superstitious") aspect of words to "the combination of names," mentioned by Plato. "John Charley Dog Peter" means nothing—to anyone other than a ham radio operator. But "John gave Charley a dog called Peter" does.

A communication must be with someone. "Transparent" language is the passing of messages, rather than meanings. "Communication does not consist of the transmission of meaning," writes David Berlo. "Meanings are not transmittable, nor transferable. Only messages are transmittable, and meanings are not in the message, they are in the message-users."[21] Messages are passed by propositions, by what we roughly think of as sentences, questions. As Aldous Huxley summarized in *The Perennial Philosophy,* "Thanks to his reasoning powers and to the instrument of reason, language, man (in his merely human condition) lives nostalgically, apprehensively and hopefully in the past and future as well as in the present. . . ." Benjamin Lee Whorf claimed that "linguistics, like the physical sciences, confers the power of prediction."

Naming does give actual power. Captain W. L. Guthrie, a pilot with twenty-five spotless years with Eastern behind him, recently began a one-man crusade against the semantics of airport weather observation stations. Guthrie maintained that what is called *haze* is nearly always *smoke,* and "once they name it, they can do something about it." In the same way, the American press on the spot, or "territory," in Vietnam did not believe the "map" or *name* of Ngo Dinh Diem's optimistic and simplistic communiqués, and,

[21] Berlo, *The Process of Communication,* p. 175.

when Ambassador Nolting and General Harkins insisted these were true, still resolutely went on believing in reality. The word exacted its revenge, or playback, for such misuse, however; Diem was overthrown and American officialdom held up to public ignominy. Lenny Bruce was arrested for obscenity in a nightclub act which was, in fact, a re-enactment of a previous arrest elsewhere. The hideous thing about confusion is its order.

"The essential act of thought," writes A. D. Ritchie, "is symbolization." When I got out of bed this morning I put on my clothes. Perhaps each item of apparel I donned could be seen as symbolic of something, and so interpreted, as we shall see, by Sherlock Holmes, the master of the manic syllogism. But I could not put on my complete set of clothes at once, and my finished appearance would have to qualify Holmes' deductions concerning its items. If time is a limitation, we know ourselves better by recognizing such. The predicative sentence has, we shall see, very definite limitations as a language act, but that does not invalidate the wisdom of words.

Before turning to such activities of "transparent" language, however, it must be emphasized again that the purpose of this study has not been to laugh at the follies of "apparent" language, as though the latter were something unenlightened. Far from it. Monroe Beardsley has actually suggested that the greatness of our word-wisdom today lies in precisely this area, in our ability to manipulate signs:

> If it is not too extravagant to say, it is as though Western Civilization in our day has broken through to a new level of consciousness, or self-consciousness—has learned to think easily in terms of the distinction of sign from significatum (or referent) and characteristically approaches problems in awareness of their semiotic dimension. No previous age has quite achieved this. . . . This combination of fascination with meanings and at-homeness with the manipulation of signs is a pervasive characteristic of the most advanced intellectual activity of our age, and marks an important advance in human thought.

PART TWO:
TRANSPARENT LANGUAGE

Words are fortresses of thought. They enable us to realize our dominion over what we have already overrun in thought; to make every intellectual conquest the base of operations for others still beyond.

SIR WILLIAM HAMILTON

SIX

Serious written English may be regarded
as a rather artificial dialect of our language.
Harold Whitehall,
Structural Essentials of English

MEANING: THE CASE OF
THE MISSING SNUFFBOX

How Not to Learn a Language

It is a truism of semantic study that words do not mean, people
mean. "There can be no true word," wrote Samuel Butler, "without
its actually or potentially conveying an idea." Meaning is an intrinsic of the dramatic character of language as a whole. Words
cannot be held still, in the hope that they will always mean the
same thing in separate circumstances. As T. S. Eliot put it:

> Words strain,
> Crack and sometimes break, under the burden,
> Under the tension, slip, slide, perish,
> Decay with imprecision, will not stay in place,
> Will not stay still.

When you learn a foreign tongue, you are uncommitted. You are
in the position of a child, searching for meaning and wanting to
convey a message. Technical problems of grammar and accent are
subsidiary to this desire. Imagine yourself sitting on a restaurant
bench at the top of one of the Harz mountains, unbearably thirsty
after the sunny ascent. *"Bier,"* you demand. *"Ein Glas Bier?"* asks
the waiter. Your friend, knowing German a bit better, replies,
"Nein. Eine Flasche Bier." The waiter is puzzled, he has to know
which of you wants the glass, which wants the bottle. Finally, your
friend develops his German a little further and says, *"Geben Sie
mir zwei Flaschen Bier."*

In fact, no theory of the genesis of language seems so binding on the sacred nature of words as that which sees the speech development of humanity typically coterminous with that contained within an individual's life history. Margaret Schlauch's theory of the multiple interrelationships of language, of "parent" tongues and language "families," seems to fortify this principle, though Schlauch drew back, finally, from the monogenesis argument (as propounded by Alfredo Trombetti)—that there was a single origin for the many tongues of Babel.[1]

Some sort of antithetical influence was to be discerned behind the manner of learning foreign, or "modern," languages in even the relatively recent England of my youth. Of course, the trouble here was that the typically tripartite system of education—prep school, public or grammar school, university—had to be delegated from above. The schools wanted to get boys into the universities and so did what the universities did; in the same way they passed on higher attitudes below, in their emphasis in scholarship, exhibition, or common entrance examinations.

Language study at the universities of England half a century ago was textual. The idea that meaning might come from sources other than *lettera scripta* was heretical. I studied, or rather I "read" (the term is significant) Modern Languages. The usual Latin or Greek preliminaries were required, of course. This "school" bifurcated out of Greats, or the classics, sometime around the turn of the century, I gather. I also gather there was a pretty reluctant condescension about the occurrence and indeed, when I was "up," there were no courses at all given post-1830. In French literature this was patently ridiculous; Enid Starkie, who was adventurous enough to get a set of lectures going on such improbable characters as Baudelaire, Flaubert and Rimbaud was considered fairly eccentric by the powers-that-were. But as recently as 1965 Professor Alistair Campbell, who has the Chair of Anglo-Saxon at Oxford, could still say, "English literature proper stops at 1830—after then, it is only books"!

[1] See Margaret Schlauch, *The Gift of Tongues,* New York: Viking Press, 1942, a slightly expanded version of which is now called *The Gift of Language*. Schlauch's Communist sympathies no doubt forced many such reluctancies on her, and certainly pushed her to savage General Semantics (in "The Cult of the Proper Word," *New Masses,* April 15, 1947). Indeed, how she remained such a sensitive philologist and determined Marxist at once is a word-world contradiction in itself.

The point propagated was that your relationship to language should properly be that to nonspoken classics, or "dead" languages, such as Latin and ancient Greek. Anyone could learn to speak a "modern" language. Such instruction was the function of Berlitz Schools (at which "underbred" characters—*q.v.* Virginia Woolf—like James Joyce taught). The product of such textual emphasis was able to give subtle explications of *Faust*, but found himself at a loss in the Speisewagen of his first train to Berlin. Textual analysis paid minimal attention to the relationships of tune and cadence to meaning; for this reason most German dons at Oxford in my day could be English.

The American academy, developing in answer to needs, reversed this trend, and I shall not soon forget my impressed surprise at the ease with which US soldiery in the war got their meaning across to foreigners, despite grammatical inaccuracies I had been persuaded to regard as worthy of the garotte in the Oxford Modern Language School. The Englishman of this ilk was taught to get out accurate sentences, full (if possible) of outmoded subjunctives and literary inflections. The American is taught to transmit meaning. A century or more of nationalist expansion, when other countries had to learn your tongue, together with a hierarchy of absurd social requirements, lay behind the language study of my youth. Word play was all turned inward, to noting ridiculous velleities of social class, via dropped letters and mispronounced vowel sounds.

It is by now evident that this attitude dogged other forms of symbolic study in England, J. Bronowski lately complaining:

> Mathematics is the language in which we discuss those parts of the real world which can be described by numbers or by similar relations of order. This is a simple statement of what mathematics is, but it becomes profound when we understand that the nub of it lies in the word "language." For mathematics is a language in the most literal sense. Like every language, it has three branches: a grammar, a vocabulary for translating from and back into the real world—and, odd though that may seem, a poetry. . . .
>
> The tragedy of mathematical teaching is that, by tradition, it is modelled on the teaching of the dead languages. Just as children are taught, not to speak Latin, but to avoid grammatical mistakes in it, so children are taught, not to speak

the language of mathematics, but to obey its grammatical rules. . . . What is needed, then, is a deep change in the aim of mathematical teaching: the change of method will follow. The aim should be to speak the language, that is, to express naturally those aspects of the real world which can be described by number and order. It follows of itself that the right way to teach mathematics is, in essence, the direct method of teaching a living language.

The purpose of this introduction to "transparent" language is to cast suspicion on the nature of any authority, or holy rectitude, in the study of language at all. It is generally the most authoritative who claim least authority here. The best scholars are satisfied with Puttenham's distinction of 1589 that language is simply speech "fashioned to the common understanding and accepted by consent." To follow the policemen of the old language schools, you might as well argue that all Italians (including professors) are speaking corrupt Latin.

No doubt someone like Boyd at Oxford, sweating over three lines of *Faust* per lecture hour or gloating over nine preterite verbs in a page of Schiller, would have been far happier with an even more highly inflected language even than German, in fact, he was known to lament that Latin was no longer the *lingua franca* of the learned West.[2] Positive that precision of meaning was conveyed by intrinsic elements of the sort, a man like this found the glory of the "dead" languages to be, of course, that they couldn't change, as modern tongues did in such ghastly word-events as slang. The whole social orientation of a man of this nature was revealed by his attitude to language.

Predication, or English as She Is Spoke

In order to pass meaning, anywhere other than in the Academy of Lagado, we form physical sounds or signs into units. On the page you are now reading a printer has marked off such units by fullstops (UK) or periods (US) The artificiality of punctuation in general has been briefly mentioned. Man is thought to have been speaking for over 700,000 years. He has practiced alphabetic script for perhaps 3,500 years. He has punctuated for but a fraction

[2]About one word in four in an average English sentence is inflected.

of that time—in the sense in which this is understood by English teachers today, for less than 300 years. Ancient Greeks did not always "separate" their thoughts or messages into sentences, and they ran words together in their manuscripts. Indeed, the one claim that cannot be made for the late e. e. cummings is that he was in any way inventive, or "experimental." Children who talk about a nelephant would not raise a neyebrow in the household of a linguist, whose wife wears a protective cloth in front of her dress that was originally a napron.

For the Greeks letters were gestures, a feature of written communication somewhat retained by the medieval manuscript illuminator and engraver *(celator)*. So what is correct? Is the sentence a set of words followed by a pause and revealing an intelligible purpose (Gardiner)? Is it "the linguistic expression of a proposition" (Sapir)? Is it, rather, a set of words which expresses a completed thought (a common lexical definition and the one almost universally discredited)? What, then, is a thought? Well, is a sentence something even vaguer—a set of words which makes sense (Sonnenschein)? Or simply a matter of sound, a "wordless song," so many auditory signs used in a whole (Jespersen)? All such authorities agree that the goal of this group of words is the conveyance of meaning. And within this conveyance of meaning it is usually considered that, so far as English goes, a sentence must contain the equipment of subject and predicate, for "thinking and predication seem to go hand in hand" (Ballard).

In the sense of a time structure predication was for Kant the most characteristic mode of our existence. Unlike animal behavior, human behavior is intrinsically consistent since it is a summary of time formulations. As an index of selfhood, succession belongs to the deepest data of the human and, indeed, by denigrating lineal perception McLuhan seems once more characteristically antihuman. The sentence becomes thus a common basis of discourse and, in Richard Ohmann's words, "the primary unit of understanding" (structurally, Ohmann likens it to the equation in algebra). The sentence is a linguistic form, and forms transmit meanings; different types of grammatical sequence and texture are accordingly a function of content (what I roughly call the world), and at the level of sentences represent options. Our confrontation with these options brings us into association with metaphor, and style. Grammar will not generate deviations of itself, but when content calls for them a grammar can be arranged or fixed to allow highly eccentric deviations, such as those of Hopkins and Dylan Thomas, so often studied.[3]

Depending upon what part of the globe you happened to have been born in, you may read from left to right or right to left, or vertically. You still predicate. In *Our Language* (London: Penguin Books, 1950) Simeon Potter puts it: "Word order has become more significant than hitherto, far more important than in Old, Middle or Tudor English, and yet it has retained enough of its elasticity to give to the skilful speaker all the scope and power he needs." The present book is called *On the Wisdom of Words,* not *On the Words of Wisdom.*

Signals of the Jabberwock

What is certain is that the sentence, as a message, is not a lexical grouping. Twain toyed with this by translating, or traducing, his jumping frog story back from French ("clawed back from the French into a civilized language") via a one-for-one swap of dictionary definitions: "Eh bien! I no saw not that that frog has nothing of better than each frog." He fooled around with German in the same manner.

This shows all sorts of pertinent "transparent" fallacies, incidentally pointing up the weakness of insisting that the double negative is illiterate or "wrong." Because some thick individuals in the seventeenth century saw that Cicero and Caesar didn't multiply negatives, *I ain't done nothing* is supposed to be grammatical error; school texts tend to follow the eighteenth-century grammarian, Bishop Lowth, in maintaining that two negatives make an affirmative (I have done something). But Twain puts in three negatives, which, by the canons of this logic, should bring us back to a negative again. Romance languages, of course, stream in negatives in an intensive and qualitative rather than numerative and quantitative manner. So did educated Elizabethans. "I will not budge for no man's pleasure," declares Mercutio in *Romeo and Juliet.*

Here the reader may object that the lexical meaning of a word,

[3]Theories of syntax and of linguistic descriptions must remain rigorously outside this study; excruciatingly subtle linguistic distinctions, on the fringes of literary criticism, have been made in the past decade by men like the Hunter Professor Samuel R. Levin (in particular, in a famous analysis of e. e. cummings' "he danced his did"), by Sol Saporta, Thomas A. Sebeok, Richard Ohmann, Noam Chomsky and others.

or of most words in a sentence, must be known. We cannot converse in sets of sound-units, outside an insane asylum. Were we to do so, we would be talking Jabberwocky. As a matter of fact, Carroll suggested by this famous rhyme what we now call structural or immediate-constituent grammar. This outcome of American linguistics of the thirties and forties is only now getting any sort of secure foothold in the schools, although it has already been usefully supplemented, and at times corrected, by transformational and/or generative grammar.

The reader, and more particularly the reader-parent, must not be put off by the long and technical-sounding names for these "new" grammars. The father of structural grammar, Charles Carpenter Fries, was a Michigan professor who recorded fifty hours of telephone conversations and in 1952 came up with a book called *The Structure of English* that made a permanent contribution to linguistics and to teaching tenets. Its influence, in a modified form, is being felt in British secondary schools now.

Fries understood the signaling significance of Lewis Carroll's nonsense words. The lexical meanings were purposely unnecessary. As Alice herself said of the rhyme, "Somehow, it seems to fill my head with ideas—only I don't exactly know what they are!"

Why we feel the same is a process so intrinsically human only its failures attract attention. It is, Fries puts it, like "the muscular adjustments of balancing when we walk." The framework, the structure, is what stimulates the signals. *"The grammar of a language consists of the devices that signal structural meanings."* In *Language, Thought, and Reality* Benjamin Lee Whorf said the same: "the patterns of sentence structure that guide words are more important than the words." What Carroll is doing in the Jabberwocky poem is giving us a series of structural meanings sans lexical meanings:

> 'Twas brillig, and the slithy toves
>   Did gyre and gimble in the wabe:
> All mimsy were the borogoves,
>   And the mome raths outgrabe. . . .

Note how easy Carroll made it to define the parts of speech with our Latin-based grammar; *toves* and *wabe* have to be nouns, they are formally marked off as such by the rules of the game.[4] It is like trying to explain cricket to a foreigner.

The cricketer has agreed, like the English language user, that certain acts fall into certain patterns. Men like Bloomfield, Fries and Roberts (of Cornell) can be said—however they vary one from another—to study these patterns, rather than a Latin dictionary or grammar. *The boy milked the cow* is not the same utterance as *The cow milked the boy,* or *Fresh fruit is good* the same as *Fruit fresh is good.* On the other hand, *Puella amat agricolam* is lexically the same as *Puella agricolam amat.* Unlike Chinese, and despite Marshall McLuhan, our language is enumerative. This example, taken from an absurd "Correct the following sentences" test for British children (and really no more than mistyping), is fairly good Jabberwock: *"Gretty swam bacefully to the toat. Ge are woing for our tolidays homorrow. Flave your wags."*[5] *Toat* and *wags* are nouns. They belong to that "form-class" of language. Fries concludes: *"An English sentence then is not a group of words as words but rather a structure made up of form-classes or parts of speech."*[6]

In this connection the Barzun/Follett *Modern American Usage* strikes a thin-red-line note, citing sentence inversions in English and claiming, "At this point, again, a grammatical rule is a means of rescue and reassurance."[7] But to instance inverted word order (such as *Silver and gold have I none*) hardly detracts from the importance of word order!

[4]For Carroll's own interpretations of this looking-glass poem, see Martin Gardner's excellent *The Annotated Alice* (New York: Clarkson N. Potter, 1960). Meanwhile, I found *mimsy* used as an adjective, to describe the work of e. e. cummings, in *TLS* for July 7, 1966, p. 596.

Daniel Kirk's *Charles Dodgson Semeiotician* (Gainesville: University of Florida Press, 1962) is a full-length study of this aspect of the creator of Alice. Balancing when we walk (as Fries suggests above) is incidentally a feedback oscillation common to thermostats and automatic gundirectors.

[5]R. J. Harris, "The Present Day Debasement of the Language," *The Use of English,* XI:2 (Winter 1959), p. 90. Mr. Harris is a Chartesey Secondary School Teacher. I discuss spoonerisms below. Logan Pearsall Smith's example for transpositions of predication is "The wolf ate the lamb" (Logan Pearsall Smith, *The English Language,* London: Oxford University Press, 1912, p. 5).

[6]The best bibliography of this subject I have seen comes from the excellent Denver, Colo., Public School system, where the "new" grammars (really the old grammars) are used to advantage. See their "Bibliography for K-12 English Program Committee" (Division of Instructional Services, Department of General Curriculum Services).

[7]Wilson Follett, *Modern American Usage,* edited and completed by Jacques Barzun, New York: Hill and Wang, 1966, p. 23.

Tongue Fun

Personally I wish someone had told me this in my youth. I wish someone had told me that language is primarily speech and only secondarily writing. I wish someone had also told me that most grammar texts are so many etiquette books, and accepted usage a dialect of middle-class residents of a capital city. Instead of cramming Latin down my throat every day, in senseless imitation of eighteenth-century grammarians, someone might have shown me basic sentence patterns, thus suggesting that syntactical exactitude is not exactly communicating. I wish, finally, I could have had as much sheer fun as Denver third-graders today seem to get with rhythmic patterns, with the grasp and sense of function, and with "transforming" kernel sentences into dozens of exciting and individual differences.[8]

Instead, of course, I had it hammered into me that there were eight parts of speech and to distinguish these was to result in communication. The tail-chasing ineptitude of this attitude is crystallized by the girl, a high school senior, who recently wrote:

> "I have always felt that grammar was an unnecessary and evil thing. That it didn't make sense when someone told me to take a sentence apart, just to see what made it tick. The difference between a noun or a verb, a phrase or a clause. This all seemed quite useless to me. . . . But I tried to understand grammar, and where did it get me? Right back where I started from. Lower grades, still scared to enter a classroom when we have grammar, and that attitude that I'll never get grammar.[9]

She failed to distinguish noun from verb and therefore failed to "get" grammar and therefore failed to distinguish . . . etc.

[8]A Denver teacher writes to me: "Think it will be fun, and probably work, to try to teach this structural grammar to third-graders next year. While third grade seems, on the surface, a rather barren field for planting the new seeds, if the teaching were done by someone who really knew his stuff, every darn bit of grammar that needs to be learnt could be taught . . . tried last spring to get across the idea of 'kernel sentences' and was pleasantly surprised at the way several youngsters developed the 'kernels' into colorful stories. After all, in reading stories, poetry, plays, and newspapers the third-grader comes in contact with all basic types of writing, and of course punctuation."

[9]Quoted in John R. Searles, *Structural and Traditional Grammar: Some Uses and Limitations,* Oshkosh, Wisc.: Wisconsin Council of Teachers of English, Inc., 1965, pp. 8–9.

Grammatical virtue, like semantic meaning, resides not in words
This girl was taught that sentences were sets of rules, and a preposition a bad word to end a sentence up with.[10] Defective in rules,
a sentence failed to communicate. Frustrated by this negative ap
proach, she gave up trying; doubtless she had heard, in some form
or another, the words of that neo-Latin Luddite, Ernest Weekley—
"If the first duty of the writer is to make himself clear, the second
is to avoid unpleasing clumsiness." The poor girl then wondered
why on earth she was getting so much enjoyment out of the prose
of, say, Defoe and Nashe. New language behavior is inculcated
more readily by rewards than by avoiding punishments.

For notice Weekley's insistence on *avoidance*. Latin grammar
teaches the psychology of avoiding error. "He is a demon on your
shoulder," yips Margaret Nicholson of Fowler, "teaching you how
not to write. . . ." It is not for nothing that Fowler's discipular re-
viser, Sir Ernest Gowers, listed himself in *Who's Who* as a member
of the commission on foot-and-mouth disease.

Sparts of Peech and Amphiboly

For the average child today the parts-of-speech system, as au
thority for excellence, has been shot to ribbons. You cannot live in
the world of Ernest Weekley and the world of newspaper head
lines at the same time. Joyce hinted this in his "Aeolus" section of
Ulysses and went on, in *Finnegans Wake,* to explore the heresies
of ambiguity with delight (Baudelaire—body lair—bawdy lair—
boudeloire).

Written on a blackboard the word *fast* can suggest to sensitive
children several things: speed (adjective or adverb); abstinence,
probably that of Lent (noun or verb); fixity (adjective or adverb
again, usually the latter). The matter of varying speech parts modifying nouns has already been mentioned (e.g. the headline before
me, "MINE FAMILIES QUIT CONGO BORDER TOWN"). For
it is of course the contemporary newspaper, that cubistic crosscut,
which must principally riddle all Teach's rules about parts of
speech with the grapeshot of healthy ridicule.[11] "SUSPECT SHOT

[10]Cf. Churchill's famous, "This is the sort of English up with which I will
not put." Gowers gets four prepositions at the end of a sentence, as follows:
"What did you choose that book to be read to out of for?" Actually, *out of*
is surely one preposition here. The Bible teems with final prepositions.

[11]The newspapers themselves, of course, often fail to acknowledge the direction of their grammatical influence, falling back on such defenses of the
so-called formal as the following:

AFTER HOLDUP" . . . "RULE BOOK NOT OBSCENE." The *New Yorker* enjoys culling such puns of misplacement, e.g. their "FRENCH DAM SITE BETTER OFF WITH U.S. AID FUNDS."[12]

This sort of thing, sometimes known as amphiboly, cannot be ironed out by simple resort to parts-of-speech rules. In instances like *Your answers were all right* or *She didn't care for the pigeons* intonation enters in, rhythm patterns, or the substitution of such via punctuation. Speech is thus with us once more, like it or not, and despite all the guff currently coming down from Toronto I happen to hear one sound in a sequence after another.

In modern English, word order has strong structural meaning; the signaling significance of sequence is high. Writing from San Jose State College, in the *English Journal* ("Structured Structuralism: Composition and Modern Linguistics"), Michael Grady describes a method he used to put the "new" grammar across to children. One would go to the board (the world), another would select cards from a deck (the word). The one at the blackboard would write down, in sequence, the words called out by the child with the word-cards:

> The demonstration, of course, developed the concept that English is a word-order language, and that unless words are arranged in a relatively strict order, members of form classes placed in a particular syntactical "slot," one simply does not have an English sentence.

This "pattern" is so important that Alice could think she was get-

---

Your best bet as regards helping your youngster to develop his reading abilities is to encourage (not force) him to read THE NEWS, daily and Sunday, year in and year out.

He'll enjoy reading this newspaper. . . . Also, he'll be reading a paper which flatly refuses to print long, involved sentences, and to use fuzzy, unfamiliar words such as 'imponderables,' 'viable,' 'miniscule,' or 'geopolitics' without explaining what the word means when no simpler term will do the job.

As time goes by, daily reading of THE NEWS will make your boy or girl a sharper, faster, more understanding reader.

(From an editorial—not an advertisement—in the New York *Daily News*)
[12]"GRACE TO FACE KNIFE THIS WEEK" I found to cover a story that a Swiss surgeon might operate on the Princess of Monaco. *MAD Magazine* gave us "TELEPHONE OPERATOR NAILS RED" (survey of nail-varnish habits of phone operators) and "STRIKE CALLED THOUSANDS WALK OUT" (a baseball story).

ting messages by it alone. In the sentence *The man killed the bear* the word *killed* is established as a verb not because an English monk so determined nine hundred years ago, from the Latin *verbum* (the word), but by its word order alone. "Genuine poetry," wrote T. S. Eliot, "can communicate before it is understood."

Nor need this be limiting. Fries' theory of "form-classes" leaves the sentence pleasantly free and, indeed, only distributes patterns always found in any human communication. No one could call Henry Sweet a structural linguist, yet he wrote:

> Grammar satisfies a rational curiosity about the structure and origin of our own and other languages, and teaches us to take an interest in what we hear and utter every day of our lives. . . . Language and grammar are concerned not with form and meaning separately, but *with the connexions between them, these being the real phenomena of language* [italics added].

We are in the presence here of that paradox of word-wisdom, that those who know most about language are least exacting of it.[13] If you want to sneer at them, you call them "permissive." But it is the journalists, the Bernsteins, who are so concerned with departure from rules and "the unclear, imprecise, and often vulgar voice of the masses." Ahem.

One lady editor recently went through a novel of mine and substituted, for the compositor, *around* for my *round* every time that word appeared to her to be an adverb: thus I was not allowed to say, *It went round and round,* but rather, *It went around and around.* It was useless to show her that *round* can appear as five different parts of speech in an English sentence. You will notice her Latin-oriented notion that to inflect this word by the prefix *a-* axiomatically established it as a certain part of speech, in ignorance of the devices of word order and function. It was equally useless to

---

[13]I might mention that the footnotes alone in Charles C. Fries' *American English Grammar* of 1940 substantiate this over and over, as they do much else I maintain in this chapter. Of course, the very nature of a convention loads the dice against language neologism; when nouns move to verbs (e.g. the prevalent *winds gusting*), it is unlikely to sound pleasant at first. The *New York Times* now uses *cost* as an ex-Yiddish transitive—"it has cost him in Washington" (April 2, 1967). I have seen a sign in a bar that read, "WE DON'T SELL MINORS"!

quote Russell to her—"it is clear that anything that can be said in an inflected language can be said in an uninflected language." A well-known linguist, H. A. Gleason, writes, "Almost any sort of noise that the human vocal apparatus can produce is used in some way in some language."

The truth is that "rules" never existed. "Say It Right," "Speak Correctly"—these are chapter headings of Norman Lewis' *Thirty Days to Better English;* they have little to do with language. They were superimposed on organic word-wisdom by a set of largely clerical-minded inkhorns, standing around with a lot of egg on their faces, and introducing a bogus *b* into *det* from France in order to try to show its supposed derivation from Latin *debitum*. Such men were manics of what Bacon called "the science of grammar," as opposed to "the art of grammar." One of the most famous instances of inadvertent transposition in English is Spenser's successful use of *derring-do* as a noun, probably misunderstood from Chaucer, where it is a verbal phrase; another well-known one is Macbeth's use of *incarnadine* as a verb.

In *From Script to Print* (Cambridge: Heffer, 1945) H. J. Chaytor tells us that in the medieval period "grammatical accuracy was not highly esteemed." Nor, of course, was individual authorship of such very vital importance, a trend that is perhaps returning today, though for other reasons. In our literary market place books are sold, rather than authors; when Marquand's *Sincerely, Willis Wayde* was high on best-seller charts, a woman walked into Brentano's in New York and asked for *Sincerely,* by Willis Wayde. When Truman Capote went to a Kansas town to research his famous study of two murderers, he found, so he told us, that far from his name being an asset in acquiring interviews, no one had so much as heard of him there.[14]

Even by Shakespeare's day grammar was still popular, with a healthy word-world relationship in what rules, or rather customs, there were. What Professor Lloyd calls our "mania for correctness" altered this emphasis in the direction of a set syntax; it did so owing to a basic difference in the harmony between speech and writing

[14]See my articles: "The Non-Fiction Novel," *The Critic*, xviii:5 (April/May 1960), pp. 19–20, 86, 88; "Sociology and Fiction," *Twentieth Century,* 167:996 (February 1960), pp. 108–114; "Blockbuster Publishing," *Trace,* 46 (Summer 1962), pp. 189–195 (the last article, reprinted in *Atlas,* resulted in a particularly vicious attack by Jack Fischer, from the warmth of *Harper's* editorial chair).

(mentioned in connection with Johnson's dictionary), and it did so thanks to repressive social prejudices. Directly this happened, words began losing their magic. There is something certain, fixed, about written words ("I'd like to see that written down") Grammar, in Sweet's phrase, tended to study "form and meaning separately." Correct English ceased to be native English. The rules of logic started to stifle sentence patterns and subdivide "form-classes," thus altering the whole psychology of written communication. What concerns us here is that this integrally affected predication. In Philip Ballard's words, "thinking and predication seem to go hand in hand." This is the first problem of "transparent" language.

Reh-Pi . . . the Light Flashed

Benjamin Lee Whorf was keen on pointing out that languages like Hopi Indian were more suggestive, if not richer, than ours since they could express events nonpredicatively. What modern physics calls the *field* could be better expressed in Hopi than in English or, for that matter, Greek.

So in Hopi *reh-pi* meant flash in space and time. Other examples could be furnished, Kluckhohn writing of the Navahos that they "are perfectly satisfied with what seem to Europeans rather imprecise discriminations in the realm of time sequences." Thus Navaho reports distinctions in happenings which the English time-based predication neglects. Indian languages had the calculus built into them. Evidently the verb *to go*, used by us principally to suggest going somewhere, was more attached by the Navaho to qualifications of that travel—by mule, foot or boat.

Old English had at least thirty words for *sea*, and even contemporary Polish has a number of verbs for *to work*, depending on the kind of work under discussion. The sense of *work* even in English is varied: it has a specialized referent in Physics; and students do not *work* in the way yeast *works* in bread. Gabelentz, in his *Sprachwissenschaft*, tells us that Araucanian Indian "distinguishes nicely between a great many shades of hunger." Russell would seem to side against the supposedly constricting nature of predication here:

> To express this by a language closely reproducing the structure of the fact, we should have to say simply: "lightning, thunder," where the fact that the first word precedes the sec-

ond means that what the first word means precedes what the second word means. But even if we adopted this method for temporal order, we should still need words for all other relations, because we could not without intolerable ambiguity symbolize them by the order of our words.

I am neither clear on nor convinced of the morphology of this. Surely Russell here requires too representational a task of our tongue: as Langer puts it, "If relations such as temporal order are symbolized at all, let the symbols not be those same relations themselves."[15] The predicate *precedes* the subject in Modern Welsh. So it does in many questions (as it did in the old jussive). I could equally say, *Thunder follows lightning.* I am reversing the physical order of the events, but if I do so it is for a certain emphasis, one not present in, say, *Lightning precedes thunder.* You could argue that *amo* is a predication. Greenlandic *I hear* is literally expressed by *me-sound-is.* In Melanesian Pidgin the expression for dust is *smoke belong ground,* hair is *grass belong head. I am shaving my beard* comes out, in this tongue, *Me razor-im grass belong face.* In French *il me manque* means *I miss him.* I would throw in here the southern *you-all.*

It would be tempting to argue down the line, but I am forced to restrict my focus. Word order is a primary signal. This does not mean that words have to be in a special order to form word order. There was a word order in Old English, to transliterate which would get us in as much difficulty as Twain's attempt to claw his story back from the French. When Twain amused himself with the signal system of German, he transliterated (in *A Tramp Abroad*) a newspaper item as follows: "In the daybeforeyesterdayshortly-aftereleveno'clock Night, the inthistownstandingtavern called 'The Wagoner' was downburnt." There are certain English sentences you simply cannot say in even contemporary Chinese. Kenneth Burke describes the subject-predicate pattern as a path worn across a field by use. Psychological emphasis will decide the proper place for a word before logic. Yet there must *be* a place. A symbol cannot be a symbol unless it is such to someone. A message is bipartite.

If we look at predication as a social relationship, rather than as

[15] Langer, *Philosophy in a New Key,* p. 77 ("A structure cannot include as *part of a symbol* something that should properly be *part of the meaning*").

a problem of bookish study, we will see once more how damaging the arbiter-of-elegance approach is to healthy communication. If I step hard on your toe and apologize, the message is not the same as if I had apologized first, and then stepped on your toe. The business of the accusative case is too large to enter into here, but essentially a transitive verb demands to be followed by an accusative. The classic ungrammatical accusative *whom* is in *Matt.* 16: 15: "But whom say ye that I am?" I have noticed that Americans, picking up a telephone, preserve the nominative complement of the verb *to be* in such locutions as "This is she." I very much doubt, though, whether the lady who thus replied would disagree with Otto Jespersen's acceptance of Shelley's "Be thou *me*, impetuous one!" Actually, "This is she" seems a modern echo of Chaucer's *It am I,* in which the subject is *I* (in OE, *Hit eom ic*). Still, no one shown a photograph would gabble, "Oh which is I? Is this I? . . ." Anita Loos deliberately titled her recent best seller *A Girl Like I.*

Similarly, precisians all over the schools and colleges of America are blue-penciling at this moment the marking FRAG (for fragmentary, or "incomplete," sentence) in the margins of English essays. Which is a bad thing.

The last paragraph is concluded with what is called, then, a fragment, of a kind employed in sophisticated journalese, such as that of the *New Yorker.* To the overworked English instructor this example is a relative clause, dangling on its own and referring within its "pause" to no direct antecedent; further, I have phrased the offense so that the antecedent is a whole thought. Which is doubly dire.

Varietal indices of usage, like the best-selling guide of Porter G. Perrin, now struggle manfully to allow for the fragmentary sentence. But unless you can come to terms with some new system, like that of Fries, the battle is always going to be a losing one. Our language is our way of understanding our world. Logic does not sit lightly on sentences, for logic is a means of establishing rules from which conclusions can, and indeed must, be drawn. A sentence is not this watertight. "How can we know the dancer from the dance?" If I turn to my wife and say, "Good Lord, lightning!" I am to an extent including thunder in that statement, or exclamation.

In his new, umpteenth edition Perrin has an elaborate and utterly point-missing chart which claims to characterize varieties of usage, or social locutions. His Nonstandard English is thus "not appropriate for public affairs or for use by educated people." Informal English, which forms a third of his Standard English, is "speaking and writing of educated people in informal situations; often includes shoptalk or slang and some localisms." How depressing it is to think of this stuff being churned into our high schools and colleges. Why does it make one wince? It is all so wrong, as well as very horrible. No wonder the incoming freshman calls English One a "crap course." Yet other "educated people" in the field prove little livelier than Porter Perrin. Theodore Bernstein lumbers on: "There are, of course, gradations of casualisms: *falsies* is low and unacceptable in most contexts." This is typical of a managing editor of the *New York Times;* the word described is not only "unacceptable," it was nonexistent years ago.

The errand of a sentence is normally to convey meaning. Meaning can be intimated by patterns, or forms, and one of these is predication. The addition of a predicate to a subject is typical of our arrangement of sense-data. Mallarmé claimed that the poet writes with words, not thoughts. Predication does not carry the "linear, sequential" etc. ratio with which it has been aspersed, as a mark of opprobrium. At the head of a story in the New York *Herald Tribune* in front of me I find: *"Gets Only a Ripple/*HUMPHREY TRIES FOR A SPLASH." Here the second element, for Messrs. Bernstein, Perrin *et al.*, requires to come before the first. But it did not do so, and was presumably understood by the "low" and "undereducated" who actually read daily newspapers, and incidentally maintain men like Mr. Bernstein in office.[16]

Without entering into the minute distinctions of a Littré in the matter, I would emphasize that our experience is not static, neither does it move backward. We don't grow younger. Communication is *with* someone or *to* someone (the former in informal America, the latter in overcrowded England). The whole vocabulary and

[16]The mendacity, or predicative looseness, of newspaper headlines was pointed up in the celebrated coverage of Napoleon's escape from Elba:

THE MONSTER HAS ESCAPED
THE BEAST LANDS
THE ANIMAL IS IN MARSEILLES
NAPOLEON GATHERS AN ARMY
OUR EMPEROR CONQUERS THE MIDI
OUR GREAT AND BELOVED LEADER ENTERS PARIS
    TOMORROW.

arrangement of prepositions alone carry forward suggestions, and show us in this way our world.[17]

What is awkward about the predicative arrangement of experience is that it presupposes some consensus on the part of the recipient of the message. But that the word is a predication, that it contains this magic unity, is partly attested by the fact that textbooks as standard as those of Perrin will now accept *Yes* and *No* as sentences. For *No* contains within itself past and future relationships, since it replies to a meaning behind it and initiates a meaning ahead of it. It is at least as much a unit of discourse as Mrs. Bentley's snuffbox. In the article already mentioned, Michael Grady puts it best:

> Merely marking a particular fragment as "Frag" does not aid the student in realizing the abstract idea of "completeness" which most expository sentences demand. I found, after teaching both traditional and structural syntax, that a structural approach to sentence completeness appealed to the students as being both more logical and more easily understandable.

Contrary to much popular belief, structural grammar is *more* exacting, as well as more enjoyable, than what is erroneously called the traditional. Lacking time, the teacher turns too often into proof reader, margining papers with useless signals like *Frag., Sp., Agr* A Madison, Wisc., teacher, John Searles, shows us a student theme in which there are no "mechanical errors" at all, but which he failed all the same.[18] Alas, the steely gleam of Sherwin Cody con-

[17]See Weller Embler, "Metaphor in Everyday Speech," *ETC.,* xvi:3 (Spring 1959), pp. 323–342. Embler discusses this vocabulary, with its pejorative uses for *down* and meliorative for *up*. It seems we treasure uniqueness more than we know or care to admit. Milton's Puritan Adam, I was reminded, leapt *up* (erect) after his creation. Consider the margarine ads referring to butter as "the high-priced spread," while National Dairy Association ads call margarine "the low-priced substitute." One travels *up* to London, from any point in England.

[18]Searles, *Structural and Traditional Grammar,* p. 8. The gap between usage and textbooks on usage was well studied by Jean Malmstrom in the *English Journal* for April 1959: thus, "an overwhelming majority of all informants in all areas say *it's me.*" But of 205 textbooks published between 1940 and 1955, 180 refused to concede the practice. My friend Andrew Schiller comments on this in his "The Coming Revolution in Teaching English," *Harper's Magazine,* October 1964.

fronts our children out of ceaseless ads—"Do YOU make these mistakes in English?" Do you, that is, say *None are* with twice the number of people than those who say *None is?* Do you conclude your sentences with prepositions, like Shakespeare, Milton, Tennyson and Scott? Or do you, with (presumably) Mr. Cody, say *She sings as a bird?*

This kind of "correct usage" drill, treating us all as erring children, reminds me strongly of those Soviet representatives referring to political positions as *correct* or *incorrect*. They mean *our view* and *your view*. The trouble is that the major part of a contemporary student's life is spent in a climate of objective criteria. His Physics, Math and Chemistry answers were either correct or incorrect. Hence he responds more readily to "rules" in grammar. It takes longer to show him that a syntactically accurate essay is a failure.

I happen to be writing these words in a railway carriage, moving from Lyons to Paris. Opposite me sits a man wearing a blue blazer, with the ribbon of the *Légion d'honneur* in his left buttonhole. I submit that he is already a predication, or little parable. His word is his world. His past is present in the buttonholed honor, as well as in his selection of the blazer, too. It is not every Frenchman who wears blazers. Yet he did not put on this picture of himself that is himself at once. And what am I to say about the lady beside him, perhaps his wife, from the lobes of whose ears dangle whole sets of sentences, in the shapes of interlaced Chinese characters, apparently white ivory? Those who know words best require least rules of them. As Thomas Hardy pointed out, "Language was made before grammar, not grammar before language."

Grammar or Glamour?

In fact, there is no more vivid testimonial to the vitality of words than their ability over the past century to withstand the confinements, or "little-ease," of book grammar. Within this period standards of uniformity have increased as printing's busy minions have grown, for the existence of secretaries, proofreaders, typesetters is a dependency of standardization.

We know that in fourteenth-century England scribes varied their spellings within single texts, like so many Joyces playing on the harpsichord of words. We know that they did not regard our kind of orthographic uniformity as an ideal to strive for as a method of communication. A variant spelling was not an error, and the whole manuscript, like a perfumed *billet doux,* appealed to several senses. It was richly tactile. How the hand instinctively reaches out to caress the glorious Piccolomini manuscripts at Siena, say. So much so that fine-binding clubs, like that of Claude Tchou in Paris, actually advertise their wares in this way.[19] Thus, full of drawings, doodles and word-jugglings the Notebooks of Gerard Manley Hopkins seem like those of some ardent *celator—après le jour—*with constant little curiosities as to how better to recreate the word for its world, how to represent reality or the reality of a perception.[20]

Scholars have carried off tricks like kennings and homophones from Hopkins' poetry to show him a grammar nut; out of about eighteen recent books the poet emerges as a supersubtle grammarian, bolstering all the practices in English One. He is seen as a study scholar juggling with syntax and punctuation within accepted norms, and picking the sonnet form because of its Pythagorean premises.[21] This is understandable since such books are the products of clerks paid to genuflect to book grammar. The emphasis is still mistaken. Indeed, Hopkins' reluctance to publish may basically have been the anti-Latin emphasis of his poetic usage, with its throwback to Anglo-Saxon. A quick glance at his charming, and largely unanthologized, sonnet on Andromeda, will tell any alert language-lover how sensitively this seer foresaw the evils attendant on fissures within the complex of perception today.

Hopkins makes a reversal not easy to read from within the book-grammar establishment itself. ("Only the dumbest calves," as the saying goes, "select their own butchers.") I have suggested that grammar rules are repressive, the silt of a certain system of education. Hopkins' "grammar" was, rather, expansive; he was a medieval manuscript illuminator. To adduce certain of his letters to the con-

[19]"Depuis quinze jours que j'ai sur mon bureau les douze titres de cette collection nouvelle, il n'est pas un visiteur, homme ou femme, qui n'ait eu le même réflexe. Chacun tend la main, prend avec délicatesse un exemplaire. Et la séduction opère." Of another offering we read: "Vous pourrez prendre, tourner et retourner entre vos doigts ces véritables témoins du passé . . ." (from publicity letters from the *Cercle du livre précieux*).

[20]See the diary entries under September 24, 1863—"In fact I think the onomatopoetic [*sic*] theory has not had a fair chance" (*Poems and Prose of Gerard Manley Hopkins,* Selected with an Introduction and Notes, by W. H. Gardner, London: Penguin Books, 1961, pp. 91–92).

[21]For an extreme, but not unrepresentative, example in the case of Hopkins, see Chapter 13 ("Number, Metre and Music") in Alan Heuser, *The Shaping Vision of Gerard Manley Hopkins,* New York: Oxford University Press, 1958, pp. 82–87.

trary does not help too much, I believe, since such references were usually the conscious priest's self-rescue operations, at one with his masochistic Catholicism, efforts to show that his designed disorder was, in truth, quite within the logic of his times.

The medieval illuminator's work was to extend the literary act into other sense-media, deriving from both painting and music. Hopkins loved to draw and he also tried to write music. It is significant that our illustrated books are more and more confined to literature for children; and when Dylan Thomas tried his hand at technopaegnia—configurational shaping of poems—he was regarded as eccentric. In a book on modern manuscripts Wallace Hildick writes, "Virginia Woolf, it becomes clear, used the manuscript page as a painter uses a palette."[22]

But, most important, the illuminator assumed a level of equivalence, rather than perspective, which is entirely Hopkinsian. Thus the illustrator of a capital letter could find a cow, a castle, and a cat all of the same height. Laws of proportion could become homiletic, as when Christ was presented taller than his disciples, and the latter taller than ordinary people. Hopkins used this method in rummaging the world for words, in searching out disparate images, or emblems, to illuminate an "inscape." Read his little fragment on a moonrise in this regard.

To play with grammar is to destroy book grammar. Often it is to write poetry as well. We note Hopkins' passionate interest in Welsh, which tends to reverse the usual English habits of predication (in a manner that might have interested Heidegger). McLuhan suggests that had Hopkins had access to the typewriter he would have composed like e. e. cummings.[23] While hoping not, one gets the point.

The briefest garnering of grammatical idiosyncrasies in Hopkins and Thomas shows both to operate against book grammar. The fre-

[22]Wallace Hildick, *Word for Word; A Study of Author's Alterations with Exercises,* London: Faber and Faber, 1965, p. 177.
[23]McLuhan, *Understanding Media,* p. 261. The discussion of the typewriter in this chapter is characteristically uncritical. It is assumed that the typewriter is a boon, capable of "Njinsky [*sic*] leaps or Chaplin-like shuffles and wiggles," but any real consideration of the effect of typewriting on literature, let alone literacy, is avoided. Yet this has been considerable. Just as certain inventions of paper and ink produced "their own" literature, the typewriter produced and is producing its own prose. The reduction of "three-decker" fiction to single novels sold on stalls may well have been responsible for some of Conrad's ellipses.

quent omission of the relative pronoun (usually nominative) in Hopkins, or of the hyphen in Thomas, is not a counterpoint-like fiddling in the margin of accepted convention. Such omissions unusually involve the reader, who is compelled to supply his own syntax. Both poets were fascinated by devices that would disrupt normal grammatical habits, the price for which was occasional self-parody. The acrobat looks suddenly ludicrous as he topples from his tightrope, and Hopkins could write to his watch, "Mortal my mate, bearing my rock-a-heart," just as Thomas could open a sonnet with the alexical and virtually Jabberwock line, "Altarwise by owl light in the half-way house."[24] The fact remains that a study grammarian does not look at language this way.

> I muse at how its being puts blissful back
> With yellowy moisture mild night's blear-all black. . . .

So writes Hopkins of a candle indoors. The lines are loaded with contraventions of Mr. Cody's code. Is *blissful* an adjective being used for an adverb (blissfully)? It can't be a noun, the object of *puts*, since the verb would seem to govern *black*, which asks to be an adjective used as a noun (blackness). Or can it?

Elsewhere, is the famous phrase "shining from shook foil" meant to mean foil (of multiple connotations) shining from having been shaken? Observe the damage deliberately done to conventional predication by the following:

> Yet God (that hews mountain and continent,
> Earth, all, out: who, with trickling increment,
> Veins violets and tall trees makes more and more)
> Could crowd career with conquest while there went
> Those years and years by of world without event
> That in Majorca Alfonso watched the door.
>
> *(In Honour of St. Alphonsus Rodriguez)*

---

[24]Both self-parodies have of course been reparodied. Roy Campbell's hilarious Hopkins spoof is little enough known to cite (*v.* Roy Campbell, "Homage to G. M. Hopkins," *Nine,* III:3 (April 1952), p. 272). Kingsley Amis probably embedded parody of Thomas in his novel *That Uncertain Feeling,* New York: Harcourt, Brace and Company, 1955, pp. 103–104; e.g. "Words like 'death' and 'life' and 'love' and 'man' cropped up every few lines, but were never attached to anything concrete or specific").

Finally, we observe how this dislike of formal grammar spills over into Hopkins' prose: his letters are haunted by Freshman English heresies (like "more than equal"). To be involved in a form reversal, as Hopkins was, surprises the truth out of language. It *is* possible to be more than equal (or more equal than, as Orwell had it of his pigs), if language is to remain language rather than algebra. An alternative is now frequently used between three and four, as well as two.

The point of fastening on an eccentric late nineteenth-century poet here has been to try to illustrate the crisis in book grammar. These matters, Mr. Mits may feel, are so many baubles for silverlip scholars. But language teaching is at a crossroads, between the professional and the amateur. Our children learn their language from the latter—their parents—and other tongues from the former —their teachers, most of whom today are accredited by certification.

The paradox then obtains that the disruption of grammar rules is seen as another rescission of discipline. Parents search out schools where English teachers *hold the line*. Yet structural, transformational and generative grammars may be no more "permissive," and are certainly more traditional, than what we have at present.

"Today," writes Jacques Barzun, "it is the educated who lead the way in destruction. . . . Our lax democratic manners tolerate everything, while literature of every grade uses by preference the language of the gutter." Like Shakespeare. What a terrible world, indeed, it must be for the Barzuns of this world—lax manners, democratic dissent, the language of the gutter, color television, instant wine, music at meals and the MBE for the Beatles. The Rot creeping in everywhere. Even capital punishment being thrown out the window.[25]

It is possible that a conventional system operating to uphold a social code so strict as to be nearly logical (as in ruling-class U English) will carry forward proper communication for a while. But the imposition of conventions on language proposes also that language can die. To fix a system of communication at an arbitrary stage of its existence is to deny it a future, and this we have seen

[25]See Barzun's article, not in defense of capital punishment, but "In Favor of Capital Punishment," *The American Scholar,* xxxi:2 (Spring 1962), pp. 181–191.

exposed in the muddle and mess over Webster's Third.[26] "Purism," Hardy wrote, "whether in grammar or vocabulary, almost always means ignorance."

The Verbal Shape of Thought

While castigating any attempt to arrest language development by conventions, the great mathematical philosopher Friedrich Waismann wrote: "It is hardly going too far to say that a whole world picture is wedded to the use of the transitive verb and the actor-action scheme that goes with it—that if we spoke a different language we would perceive a different world." By now this, too, has become a truism of semantic study. Benjamin Lee Whorf believed that the structure of a language strongly affected the thought available in that language ("users of markedly different grammars are pointed by their grammars toward different types of observations").[27]

Following in Whorf's footsteps, Stuart Chase has suggested several examples of this semantic in action:

> Chinese thought has been traditionally tolerant, not given to the fanatical ideologies of the West. . . . This happy lack of two-valued thinking raises an interesting question. Communism, as formulated by Marx and developed by Lenin, is rigidly two-valued. The heroic worker stands against the wicked capitalist and one or the other must go down. There is no place for shades of gray or for innocent bystanders.
>
> Russian is an Indo-European language, and the two-sided choice is readily accepted by its speakers. The choice is accepted, too, by top leaders of the Chinese Communists today, for they went to Moscow to be indoctrinated, and to learn the Russian language. But four hundred million Chinese have not been to Moscow or learned Russian, or any other Indo-European language, and there is small prospect of their doing so. How, then, can the Chinese people become good ideological Communists, since it is difficult if not impossible for them to take seriously the central dialectic of

[26]See Dwight Macdonald, "The String Untuned," *New Yorker,* 38:3 (March 10, 1962), pp. 130–160.

[27]For a convenient digest of Whorf's thought see *Language, Thought, and Reality: Selected Writings of Benjamin Lee Whorf,* ed. John B. Carroll, New York: John Wiley, 1956.

214

Marxism? *The structure of their language seems to forbid the idea* [my italics].

To this theory, that Chinese cannot swallow Marxism, one is tempted to reply that it is doing pretty well so far. The Chinese semantic is being everywhere modified in the direction of that bi-valued Western which is contemporary world politics, with the *correct* gunman awaiting his ineluctable confrontation with his *incorrect* adversary. One wonders, too, if Chase is right about the lack of "fanatical ideologies" in Old China.[28]

Thanks to the work of Fries and others, it now seems safe to say that word order is an important signal, or pattern of perception, in English. It is so also in Latin, to be sure, where an alteration in the order of words alters the emphasis of those words. This is what is sometimes called an "epistemic" difference between languages, and between language families. There are doubtless many such differences between our language and that of majority China. But in *Interpretation in Teaching* I. A. Richards reminds us that even we can "put one thought form into many different word patterns." He himself has entitled a rather pleasant poem "Harvard Yard in April/April in Harvard Yard" (we note he did not, however, give the second half of the distich, as he might have in Latin, "April in Yard Harvard").

The structure of that verbal screen through which we receive experience enables us to increase our perceptive ability; it enables us to predict, it reduces the nightmare of our uncertainty. As has been suggested, reiterative language is close to physiological processes: the pattern of our perception is thus built into language. You might normally say of a girl *I like her*. If you went to Spain the congruent feeling might most commonly be predicated *Elle me gusta* (She pleases me). To alter the active element, or make other analogous changes, is not to challenge the structure of language. The patterning of the experience changes from tongue to tongue, and one mode of receiving sense data cannot be required to be logically equivalent to another. But it is surely obvious that

[28]The day I read the passage from Chase cited I saw in the Frankfurt *Handelsblatt* the following: "The Red Guards have made themselves clear with a cry which echoed through the streets of Peking—'Out with the foreign devils!' Thus it becomes apparent what all this commotion is all about—a wave of xenophobia which has rolled over China periodically for hundreds of years."

the difference between saying *I like her* or *She pleases me* (or a Chinese equivalent) is a choice of emphasis; and such choice constitutes style.

Word order is hardly a mathematical concept, right or wrong. "Epistemic" differences run through the human race. Yet, as Richard Ohmann put it in a recent English Institute address, within a given language family "the similarities are more noticeable than the differences." Ohmann attacks the Whorf-Korzybski hypothesis that certain language systems carry built-in artificialities of experience. By Whorf's argument (reiterated by Chase above) he wonders why, if certain Indian tribes were so close to the realities of the cosmos as Whorf imagined, they failed to throw up an Einstein. (Whorf might have replied that they did not need one, already having an Einsteinian relationship to experience.) It may well be that general semanticists have been "utopian" in this respect. Chase has exaggerated Whorf to the point of indicting language structure with bias. Nonetheless, a consensus of choice within a given cultural group tends to limit the members of that group to receiving experience in a certain way. As Ohmann himself admits, "any language persuades its speakers to see the universe in certain set ways, to the exclusion of other ways." Such could well be called its *style*.

At least one linguist, Bernard Karlgren, believes that when the Chinese abandon their script they will abandon their culture. Ideograms and phonograms carry a depth relationship to language; the Chinese character for *good* is made up of the characters for *woman* and *son*, and has therefore solidified family unity, and ancestor worship. Values have been easily perpetuated in a country which can still understand its linguistic medium of over two thousand years ago, whereas even Middle English, of a few hundred years back, causes us to pause. It is said that science, and mathematics, are forcing romanized or alphabetic script on the Chinese, but when this happens it will be—as Karlgren suggests—like flipping a coin, a form of severance from the past that we have not known, and which might well result in a fanaticism beyond all imaginable bounds.[29]

It is more than probable, then, it is almost certain, that a language transmits certain thoughts more easily than others. The word

[29]See Margaret Coughlin, "Good is Woman and Son," *Columbia University Forum,* ix:3 (Summer 1966), pp. 47–49.

relates its world. There is a convincing theory, first expounded by Dolf Sternberger in his *Aus dem Wörterbuch des Unmenschen* of 1945, and enlarged by Cornelia Berning's 1965 *Von "Abstammung-snachweis" zum "Zuchtwart,"* that German grammar was such at the time that Nazi policies lodged very easily within the language. Words like *Judenfrage* and *Entjudung* were current in the 1880's; habits of inflected epithets, of abstract inflections and generally tormented syntax are said to have been ready to house the "thought" of Hitler, Goebbels, and even Streicher. If so, Whorf's hypothesis finds shocking corroboration in Fräulein Berning's book. This taught me, incidentally, wherefrom Joyce must have got his otherwise inexplicably prophetic references to "concentration camps" in *Ulysses*.[30] Evidently German propaganda had used the term *Konzentrationslager* about the British cages for Boers. Even so, Joyce's application of it to a Jew is prescient. It says that if we make a hate-absolute like Jew, we make a verbal concentration camp; and a verbal concentration camp forms a literal one. Today optimists learn Russian, pessimists Chinese.

The age of electricity seems to some to have torn predication off its rails. The world in which you can reach Borneo by the roll of a thumb on the radio dial, or live visually in the past by movies, such appeared to writers like Eliot and Pound a kind of concertina-ing of past, present and future, an ideogram of civilizations and modes. But if predication is seen as I have tried to see it here, it is far from fractured.

Communication is bipartite; someone speaks and someone listens. Without this relationship the message cannot exist. Books on semantics and speech are clogged with contorted charts showing this rather elementary principle.[31] These semiological diagrams—

---

[30]Nor does everyone, I think, know that *commandos* was copied from a term used in the Boer War; interestingly, the initial Second World War cross-Channel raids were made by British *Storm Troops* (i.e. against German Storm Troops).

[31]Wendell Johnson uses a fantastically elaborate schema on the endpapers of *Your Most Enchanted Listener*. Roman Jakobson's is much more sensible: "All these factors inalienably involved in verbal communication may be schematized as follows:

CONTEXT
MESSAGE
ADDRESSER . . . . ADDRESSEE
CONTACT
CODE."

with their light waves and nerve impulses—for a very ordinary daily happening testify how often the relationship goes wrong. It does so, I have suggested, owing to the degree of agreement needed for the predication to be effected. Before concluding this chapter, it would be as well to look further into the nature of this agreement.

What Do You Mean, "What Does It Mean?"

The following occurrence is reported from an analytic session:

> They met after work one evening and turned into a lounge for a drink. When they entered, the husband, Bob, turned to his wife, Marian, and asked her what she would have. Marian said "Anything." Bob, feeling rather gay, turned to the bartender and said, "I'll have a bourbon, and give the lady anything." To him, this was funny, it was light, it was gay, it was just what she had said. However, Marian, on the receiving end, heard Bob say, "give the lady anything," which meant to her that she was not worth very much, that almost anything that the bartender picked up and threw in her general direction would be good enough for her, that here was evidence of the low esteem in which Bob held her.[32]

The word exchanged here was *anything*. There is nothing intrinsic in that word to precondition it. Yet it caused unhappiness to Marian, and confirmed her in her fears that her husband was leaving her. It did so owing to her inner feelings and emotional conflicts. When "agreement" is not present, words can wound. No amount of training in rhetoric would have altered the above situation. And on this predicative principle—of the precedence of inner demands over external concepts (that we are, in short, our own enchanted listeners)—one teacher, at least, has based an approach for helping children to read: "the printed word acts as the trigger that releases its oral counterpart, which, in turn, releases a meaning we already possess."[33]

[32]Norman Locke, "Semantic Psychotherapy: An Exchange of Views," *ETC.*, xv:1 (Autumn 1957), p. 34. The block would have been made even clearer if Bob had said, "Give the lady anything she fancies."

[33]James P. Soffietti, "Why Children Fail to Read: A Linguistic Analysis," *Harvard Educational Review*, Spring 1955, pp. 63–84.

For to find speech is, as Coleridge's Mariner learnt, to enter into the covenant, or predication, of "transparent" language. To express thought we have to go beyond or through. In doing so, we find that the instrument of intelligence is itself the sense of significance. Langer instances the cross as having *the physical attributes of a good symbol.* In a Christian culture we walk through this sign to a sense of holiness, but it is also, when tilted, a sign meaning plus or addition, it can be a marker on ballot sheets and so forth. Within this range Marian and Bob will choose as dictated by inner directions.

Although the meaning of meaning is itself a meaning, it would be true to say that if we lived in the world of Robbe-Grillet's automata we should regard the recurrence of the two words *Wall Street,* in any context, as indicating a single street down which it is possible to walk, buy a paper, summon a cab and so forth. We would cease to go through the words to our world, cease to let *Wall Street* stand for finance, stocks and shares and the rest. As Langer puts it, "Every object that emerges into the focus of attention has meaning beyond the 'fact' in which it figures."

This dilemma of circularity haunts our use of metaphor. Figurative language forms a subject too large in itself to be discussed in these pages, but it should be touched on here since it is vitally predicative. The effort of junction involved in seeing something in terms of something else represents an activity of full perception by the human mind, and was considered true word-wisdom by Aristotle. ("The greatest thing by far is to be a master of metaphor. It is the one thing that cannot be learned from others.") "Language is vitally metaphorical," wrote Shelley; "that is, it marks the before unapprehended relations of things and perpetuates their apprehension. . . ." Our metaphoric store is an indication of our language life. Eliot called the whole of the *Divine Comedy* one vast metaphor.

In Back of Squeedunk

In any discussion of the transmission of meaning the easiest thing to say about metaphor is that it is a semantic bridge, a linking device, borrowing one activity to exemplify or enlighten another (the snow *blanketed* the countryside). It is generally associated with poetry, and literary critics have taken it largely in hand.

Actually, nearly all language is figurative. The only strictly "factual" language we can find is in the sciences, where "The world divides into facts" (Wittgenstein, *Tractatus*, 1. 2). Our hallucinatory regard for these alleged facts is being illustrated, as I write, by the spectacle of an American President wandering around the White House and pulling sheafs of statistics out of his pyjama pockets.[34] Total objectivity is virtually impossible with words—"For all of us, grave or light," wrote George Eliot, "get our thoughts entangled in metaphors, and act fatally on the strength of them." Here is a Detective-Superintendent, Deputy Head of the Essex CID at the time, giving evidence in court: "He had a gunshot wound in the chest. I was present at the postmortem and at 10:40 this morning I saw the accused at Saffron Walden police station. I told him the deceased had died of gunshot wounds which I understand he had inflicted" *(Daily Telegraph,* June 23, 1966, p. 32).

This is, correctly enough, colorless language, but it is not devoid of a degree of judgment. To say someone is *accused* is to put him into a metaphoric situation; this may be justified, but it cannot be said to be neutral in overtone. The following is an ad from a Sears, Roebuck catalog: "Rough-grained Split Leather Brief Case; artificial leather gussets. 3 position lock with key. 16 × 11 in. Color: black or brown. Shpg. wt. 2 lbs. Price, $4.86."

Sears, Roebuck is largely a mail-order company which has built up its reputation on informational integrity of this sort (matched by that of the colossal Army and Navy Store's catalogs in England before the war). The brief case either weighs two pounds, or it does not. It is sixteen inches by eleven or not. Yet the words *with key* are not without inference; the prepositional phrase is suggestive of something given, an addition. In actual fact, a lock would be pretty useless if it did not have a key.

Similarly, the stock market prices give the appearance of being wholly factual, denotative. Again, it is true that they are bald—after all, they are figures. But they are *accompanied* by a connotation. Their placing in, say, the *Wall Street Journal* (or *The Financial Times*) gives a higher estimate of their importance than their placing, often attenuated, in the New York *Post*.

In *What Is History?* Edward Hallett Carr denies the possibility of an historical fact. Far from "speaking for themselves" facts, he

[34]See Darrell Huff and Irving Geis, *How to Lie with Statistics,* New York: Norton, 1954.

says, "speak only when the historian calls on them." We are interested in the Battle of Hastings because "historians regard it as a major historical event." Russian historians might not regard it as such. One can extend Carr's point: for an historian the "facts" in Napoleon's life were, first and foremost, a series of battles. But to a psychologist those battles were presumably subsidiary to the "facts" of the Emperor's life as an infant. In law, too, libel cases often turn out to be so many Marian-Bob tussles. In short, reality is nearly always, in Robbe-Grillet's term, "contaminated" by the human. His term is not unjustified. Metaphor is a falsification. The snow is not a blanket. Since many birds eat one hundred times their own weight in a year, to *eat like a bird* would mean sitting down to about forty-five pounds of meat, vegetables, fruit, milk etc. every day.

Of such expressive ability Dr. Johnson wrote, "It gives you two ideas for one." A subsequent chapter will inspect this proclivity of language to unite and connect. The harmony is quite obviously an ordering or control activity, the mind's tool for emphasis, clarity and consistency. For this reason figurative imagery is a basic function of "transparent" language. Intelligence is strongly related to this ability. The schizophrene finds it difficult to distinguish between figurative and factual.[35]

Rather naturally, this activity gets distorted. Zeugma, or very remote verbal connection of this sort, is a distortion or stretching that is indicative enough to be considered below. In passing, one might instance here the way in which American sports reporting is notoriously bedizened by metaphors out of Krafft-Ebbing or Stekel —*lash, flay, whip,* for what in England would probably be *defeat,* or at best *trounce,* though British sports writing is now starting to follow this trend too. The reverse, to be found less and less in British sports reporting, is equally irritating, however. Alan Ross, of *The Observer,* used to specialize in cricket reports so fogged with pseudopoetry—about clouds, grass, thatched pavilions, linseed oil and the like—it was sometimes hard to find out what had happened in the actual match.

[35]See Gregory Bateson, "A Theory of Play and Fantasy," *Psychological Research Reports 2,* New York: American Psychiatric Association, 1955. The same difficulty is defined by Jacob Wyrsch, "Der Geisteskranke und die Sprache," in the 1955 volume of *Semantica* published by the Archivio di Filosofia, Rome.

A boxer in America is a *bearcat*, he is (or was) a *bozo*, a *biffer*, and sometimes an *assassin;* this last term contains in this connection an inadvertent pun. It comes from a sect of Moslems dedicated to killing Christians, but the source word *hashshashin* means "eater of hashish," i.e. those who have taken a drug. It is a plural noun like *Bedouin,* another Crusader capture. Violence is thus made verbally foreign, it is distanced, as in *harakiri,* literally a belly-slitting. In baseball, *in back of squeedunk* means to be of extremely low rating. Meanwhile, the synecdoche, taking the part for the whole (*sail* for *ship,* say), may prove of service to art, but gets monstrously misused—and misuses us—in politics. To talk about "Jackie Kennedy, the Cleopatra of the Potomac," as did one journalist recently, may sound gracious but is eventually disfiguring; it is saying that Mrs. Kennedy is to the Potomac what Cleopatra was to the Nile, and it is not inviting a very careful analysis of the latter half of that metaphor.

In *A Grammar of Metaphor* Christine Brooke-Rose distinguishes "five main types of noun metaphor." Synecdoche would seem to fall under her category of *Simple Replacement* ("the proper term is replaced altogether by the metaphor. The metaphor is assumed to be clear from the context or from the reader's intelligence"). She cites the telling ambiguity of Browning abbreviating his sense of expressive language to *the harp.* Yet, as she observes, "there was a time when poets really did play the harp." Advertising synecdoche is not based like this on an image or imagined scene. Jackie was never Cleopatra to the Potomac. Indeed, more often than not, the reality is mutilated by the linking device.

Similarly, whenever we get excited, we try to overextend language. To say, with the Revlon ad, that a lipstick is *like a cannon* is fetching the articles from afar, but not making meaning, since nothing is really added to either end of the comparison. Hyperbole is metaphor carried to the impossible. All truly creative cursing is of this order ("He's so low he could crawl under the crack of a door with his top-hat on; what's more, he's so crooked he has to screw his socks on in the morning"). Shelley's "Blind with thine hair the eyes of Day" is a synesthesic hyperbole, but when Hamlet gets alarmingly excited, after fighting with Laertes in Ophelia's grave, he challenges him to "eat a crocodile," continuing:

> And if thou prate of mountains, let them throw
> Millions of acres on us, till our ground,

Singeing his pate against the burning zone,
Make Ossa like a wart! Nay, an thou'lt mouth,
I'll rant as well as thou.

Equally, those who cried recently of Adolf Eichmann, "Killing him once isn't enough, you gotta hang him six million times," were re-echoing Othello's:

O, that the slave had forty thousand lives,—
One is too poor, too weak for my revenge![36]

The "dramatic" nature of language is not factual. According to the tests made recently by the University of Manchester psychologist, Professor John Cohen, *certain* to a child means *sure to be;* to an adult there is only about 70 percent possibility accorded the "certainty" of this word. The nature of language is not to *be* life. Such is, rather, the new Alexandrianism of McLuhan and his minions, as it is the topical fad of fashionable artistic circles. By this notion words are seen as a stimulus to some other sense state. In fact, it is always the least sophisticated readers who say, halfway through a novel, "I can just *see* that character" (or put down a book because they cannot perfectly picture an event in it). As I. A. Richards had it, in an incisive lecture given at Bryn Mawr in 1936, "visualization is a mere distraction and of no service. . . . They think the image fills in the meaning of the word; it is rather

---

[36]The metaphoric activity itself is not compromised by its misuse. Compare the following passages:

A fire had been lighted out of whose flames in time to come a sword was bound to arise that should win again the freedom of the Germanic Siegfried and the life of the German Nation.
And beside the coming upheaval I felt strode the goddess of inexorable revenge for the act of perjury of November 9, 1918.

But Herr Hitler is not thinking only of stealing other people's territories or flinging gobbets of them to his little confederate. I tell you truly what you must believe when I say this evil man, this monstrous abortion of hatred and deceit, is resolved on nothing less than the complete wiping out of the French nation and the disintegration of its whole life and future. . . . All Europe, if he has his way, will be reduced to one uniform Bocheland, to be exploited, pillaged, and bullied by his Nazi gangsters.

The first passage, from Hitler's famous speech of February 24, 1920, comes from a megalomaniac; the second, to be found in Churchill's *Blood, Sweat, and Tears* of 1941, is from the future winner of the Nobel Prize for literature.

the other way about and it is the word which brings in the meaning which the image and its original perception lack."

Words are not inferior substitutes for the world. They offer a discipline which is its own wisdom. Predication is not some lesser version of sensory perception. Properly understood, and handled, it is a careful definition of our condition. Baudelaire's correspondences, Eliot's objective correlative, these were metaphoric attempts to comprehend; they united two subjects, what Richards called in his talk "a tenor and a vehicle," in an inclusive meaning. But they were not so uniting them in the same terms as other senses. These were little models for ideas. Richards' golden words sum up the problem best:

> For words cannot, and should not attempt to "hand over sensations bodily"; they have very much more important work to do . . . language, well used, is a *completion* and does what the intuitions of sensation by themselves cannot do. Words are the meeting points at which regions of experience which can never combine in sensation or intuition, come together. They are the occasion and means of that growth which is the mind's endless endeavour to order itself. That is why we have language. It is no mere signaling system. It is the instrument of all our distinctively human development, of everything in which we go beyond the other animals.

SEVEN

The glory of God is to conceal a thing,
but the glory of the king is to find it out.

Francis Bacon

THE PRIVATE EYES OF INFERENCE

"God's Playfellows"

As we have it in the opening words of the Gospel of St. John, man is a symbol-using animal. Kenneth Burke writes: "to say that man is a symbol-using animal is by the same token to say that he is a 'transcending animal.'" The symbolic process depends, Burke emphasizes, on a single motive force, operating both in man's words and in his world.

Symbol-chasing in literature simply parodies this reality.[1] Mary McCarthy wrote up a true account of a real event, concerning a train journey with a racist Colonel in *Harper's Magazine*. After it had been published, she received letters from students enrolled in what are called Creative Writing schools. Why had she given herself a green sweater? Did this symbolize attachment to Ireland?

Similarly, when Robert Conquest led a spoof symbol-chase through *Lucky Jim* he was deluged with letters from students, seriously contesting his "findings." In the suicidal cult of modern literary symbol-hunting the student is set before the "pudding" of

---

[1] "For the sake of variety, let us consider his dogs. Thomas was as much taken by the fact that *dog* spelt backwards is *god* as he was by what *live* spells backwards. The dog-god identity is reinforced by the authority of Thoth, the dog-headed Egyptian god who invented speech and writing and became the demiurge of the Hermeticists. Thomas, who was a sly dog, a lazy dog, a gay dog, and a dog in the manger, was also, as poet, an inventor and a creator. *Dog*, then, can be, and is, used to mean dog, Thomas, creator, God. But *God* in these poems often includes Satan, whom Thomas sometimes celebrates as God's creative partner; the word may also mean libidinous energy, nature, the force that through the green fuse drives, the process of living toward death" (George Stade, Review of William York Tindall, *A Reader's Guide to Dylan Thomas*, in *The Morningsider* [a Morningside Heights, N. Y., local paper]).

Wimsatt's poem, and told that the best boy will find the most number of charms within it.[2]

In an early story by James Joyce a character goes into a bar and orders some ginger beer. With it he orders a plate of peas. A literary critic, interpreting this story as parallel to the Esau-Isaac legend, tells us that the peas stand for a "mess of pottage." They do not stand for a mess of pottage; they stand for a state of internal compulsions and elements of social sequence. Did or did not the character order a plate of peas? Joyce's first observation is that he did so, in common with other drinkers of his day, and he embeds in this observation a deal of social history. You could not order peas in a Dublin pub of the kind today, and that you could do so then is evocative commentary. At the beginning of the century most Dublin pubs were also grocers (the publican's assistants often known as "curates"), and a plate of peas was a cheap dish to fill a belly with. Joyce was extremely careful and telling about such details; he has one drinker order a caraway seed, for instance, again available in the grocery section and used to hide the smell of drink. That such a drinker may make a pun with Esau, or Isaac, or Nebuchadnezzar, is secondary, or unnatural symbolism, so much often rather charming ornamentation grafted on reality.

The mode of transcendence is present here in the primary symbolic act, but absent in the secondary; if this rhetoric were reversed, it would not matter what a character did. The structure of his actions might be that of a madman, with delusions that he was Esau. (Every time wine appears in these early stories by Joyce it is automatically, for the same critic, Eucharistic.) One is reminded of the story of the voice from the insane asylum cell crying, "I'm King. God told me so." To which the answer from the next cell was returned—"I never told you anything of the sort." We are not far here from the British Colonial officer of former times who dressed for dinner, as though he were in England, when in fact he was in the stifling heat of the jungle. That action is good secondary symbolism.

For it is in clothes that we find elementary examples of natural group symbolism. Lacking an organic relationship with our uni-

[2]For some excellent criticism of these excesses, see Harry Levin, "Symbolism and Fiction," in *Contexts of Criticism,* Cambridge, Mass.: Harvard University Press, 1957. I. A. Richards gives some hilarious examples of symbolhunting in his "Poetic Process and Literary Analysis," available in *Style in Language,* ed. T. A. Sebeok.

verse, we express our transcendence by the cult of commodities. By such, as popular journalism has it, we seek status. We still have to wear clothes, and so clothes are the man, little models we make of totemic rites. And that there is more to observation than meets the eye can be checked by watching the passing of a pretty girl with one's wife, or her husband. The point of view will emphasize diametrically different matters. "O what a miracle to man is man," wrote Edward Young, in *Night Thoughts*. My Frenchman in his blazer was symbolizing himself, just as was the Englishman who that same morning donned his old school tie. A woman can be induced to buy a dress by being told, "It's just you." For, after all, clothes are an organic part of a way of life; it is only today, as Camus suggested in an early essay on Algiers, that we are reverting to Greek ideals of body exposure, recognizing, that is, how expressive the unclothed human body can be, instead of seeing such as an automatic relapse into the beast.

This natural process is predicative. Wedding, military and academic dress are all "transparent," if not transparent. An excellent instance would be mourning, which requires white in China. Nathanael West begins *The Day of the Locust* on a Hollywood boulevard where nobody is wearing anything that identifies his real job.[3]

In the last century Thorstein Veblen studied the symbolic restriction of freedom in women's clothing, via items like corsets and hobble skirts (at one time British bucks used to wear nailguards as evidence of appropriate idleness); and Rom Landau was easily able to complement Veblen by showing feminine emancipation in dress.[4] The subject indeed invites almost daily elaboration, with textured stockings currently carrying implications of the dance into a chick's daily chores and contemporary corner boys looking considerably less masculine, if more Renaissance, than their corner girls.

[3]"A great many of the people wore sports clothes which were not really sports clothes. Their sweaters, knickers, slacks, blue flannel jackets with brass buttons were fancy dress. The fat lady in the yachting cap was going shopping, not boating; the man in the Norfolk jacket and Tyrolean hat was returning, not from a mountain, but an insurance office. . . ."

[4]Rom Landau, *Sex, Life and Faith, a Modern Philosophy of Sex,* London: Faber and Faber, 1946. See also in this connection: Marianne Ostier, *Jewels and the Woman,* New York: Horizon Press, 1958; the many excellent books on the history of women's clothing by C. Willett Cunningham; Harriet T. McJimsey, *Art in Clothing Selection,* New York: Harper & Row, 1963 (especially here "Clothes to Flatter Your Personality").

Even though we may see ourselves as wearing what we like, and the carrying around of feathers and teeth and shells as amusingly "savage," we still have our own such Schopenhauerian emblems. How rich in pins and rings we are! The wearing of dark glasses is by now far from functional in modern cities; it is less so in winter, less so in dark subways in winter, and least of all by vision-high Negroes in dark subways in winter. (One functional wearing of such must be excepted, namely as a disguise of the eyes by those who take drugs.) A young model I took round the Metropolitan Museum retained her dark glasses throughout, even in front of long uncleaned old masters.

The Clothes of Office

These adornments are our quaint tribute to the symbolic process. Today the acquisition of a tanned skin as a symbol of leisure reverses skin symbolism of less than a century ago. We know that Byron took medicaments to retain his Napoleonic pallor, but even much later we have only to count the parasols and wide hats in Impressionist paintings, or the veils worn by the swells round their "toppers" in Frith's *Derby Day,* to see how strongly white skin remained a requirement of class. When I was sent out to North Africa in the last war, the British solar topee was still being issued to all ranks.[5] It was the German Afrikakorps, trained in Bavarian hothouses, who first found these unnecessary, and we soon "dumped" ours.

According to Ernest Dichter, taking off gloves is a socially permitted striptease. Sherlock Holmes knew that a man had sailed the China seas by the nature of his tattoo. Tuaregs paint themselves blue, veil their heads, and wear face masks and penile ornaments. A glance at either photographs or fiction of the early twenties reveals that women all over fashionable Europe were binding their breasts in order to produce the desired "shallow" effect.

The conditions of symbolism via clothing have been summarized many times, Pascal suggesting that magistrates were clad in ceremonial robes so that the essential emptiness of their pretensions might be hidden. In much the same spirit Carlyle, in *On Heroes, Hero-Worship and the Heroic in History,* protests the slanted pred-

[5]The spelling, or rather misspelling, here forms a nice language feedback; actually the hat was first named after the pithy *sola* shrub from which it was made.

ication of judge "in fine Red" and prisoner at the bar "in coarse threadbare Blue:"

> Has not your Red hanging-individual a horsehair wig, squirrel-skins, and a plush gown—whereby all mortals know that he is a JUDGE?—Society, which the more I think of it astonishes me the more, is founded upon Cloth.

But the false symbolic hierarchy attacked in this famous statement is with us still; only the other day Lord Goodman reiterated Carlyle's criticism on this score, writing:

> I do feel that it is no longer appropriate and indeed fairly ridiculous that grown members of a learned profession should wear period costumes. This is particularly so since they adopt the convention of our undergraduate days, that the honorable nature of a garment is reflected by its age and tatters. But I also believe that there is a more important aspect of the wig and gown than the question of maintaining tradition or discarding it. I think it reflects an attitude on the part of the people who wear it which is no longer a relevant or a contemporary one.

In my day at Oxford one went to great pains to assure a properly ragged aspect to one's gown. In the Brigade of Guards young officers envied an aged and fraying set of "blues" in the mess and even exposed the shiny braid of their new forage caps to the sun to acquire, as quickly as possible, a suitably dingy look. New clothes, like new residences, were equated with the nouveaux riches. Khrushchev showed himself a victim, rather than a master, of such niceties when he refused to wear a tuxedo at formal dinners in America.

Today students seem to have turned their backs on the semantic of clothing symbolism, shrugging at the petty tyrannies of such stratification by their choice of clothes for comfort. Almost anything can be worn. Sherlock Holmes would have had a hard time with them. For it was Holmes, above all, who professed to use a man's garments "transparently," as enigmatic identities of something else. In this way he played cheap-jack magician to a parvenu age, a Caligari-cum-psychologist investigating such puzzles much in the manner of Carlyle's comment, "Happy he who can look through the Clothes of a Man . . . into the Man himself."

The "Tec" as Ape of God

With Holmesian "inference" we arrive at meaning-transmission by logic. Or, rather, what presumes to be logic. Its distortions are here its attractions. "Every inference," wrote John Dewey, "just because it goes beyond ascertained and known facts . . . involves *a jump from the known to the unknown.*"[6] This, of course, is "how we think," in Dewey's phrase for the title of his book in which this often-used assertion appears. We generalize from the particular. It is sometimes called learning from experience.

Repression of this activity can lead to neurosis. We need to infer, just as we need to classify. A doctor infers, and a botanist classifies. Lack of ability in either activity can be as damaging as excessive abuse of both. "The aphasic adult with whom I worked," writes a well-known speech therapist, investigating a case of brain damage, "had great difficulty in making inferences about a picture I showed."[7] We would have no philosophy without induction, and no science without deduction. Unfortunately Holmes confused the two.

In doing so he stood for a habit of mind, or culture, and therein lay his appeal, one so durable that a room has been set up in his honor in Baker Street and more than one book written on his "life."[8] Posterity is insisting that Holmes existed in a kind of back formation of Doyle's own spiritualist beliefs. The nature of this appeal is interesting. In *A Scandal in Bohemia* Doyle wrote of his creation, "He was, I take it, the most perfect reasoning and observing machine the world has seen."

[6]John Dewey, *How We Think,* New York: D. C. Heath & Company, 1933, p. 96. Cf. "When we make inferences, we are constructing sentences that talk about unknown events, based on other events that are known" (Berlo, *The Process of Communication,* p. 237).

[7]Laura L. Lee, "Brain Damage and the Process of Abstracting: A Problem in Language Learning," *ETC.,* xvi:2 (Winter 1959), pp. 154–162.

[8]William S. Baring-Gould, *Sherlock Holmes of Baker Street,* New York: Clarkson N. Potter, 1962. See also: Pierre Nordon, *Conan Doyle,* trans. Frances Partridge, London: John Murray, 1966; Kingsley Amis, "My Favorite Sleuths," *Playboy,* 13:12 (December 1966), pp. 145, 343–349; Gavin Brend, *My Dear Holmes; A Study in Sherlock,* London: George Allen & Unwin, 1951. Holmes incidentally, and significantly, despised Dupin as a "ratiocinator."

At first glance Holmes looks like a highly British development of someone out of Gaboriau, a typical product of late nineteenth-century science and its attendant fascinations. With Watson we watch the wizard puffing at his pipe as Jabez Wilson rushes into the room (in *The Case of the Red-Headed League*) and gets summarized in an instant; John Hector McFarlane (in *The Case of the Norwood Builder*) is similarly simultaneously told, "I assure you that, beyond the obvious facts that you are a bachelor, a solicitor, a Freemason, and an asthmatic, I know nothing whatever about you." The facts are "obvious." A shiny sleeve will indicate a writer, a watch-charm Freemasonry, short breathing asthma. All bachelors, of course, are untidy in the era of The Great Family.

Here Holmes is inductive; he looks at the evidence and infers an idea. What's more, his knowledge is worldwide. Presumably, for instance, he would know that in Cuba an engagement ring is a wedding ring, and vice versa. He would have known that the smooth-skinned Malay who used to sweep so elegantly (if inefficiently) round my father's office in Kuala Lumpur did not know how to write at all; the pen he wore clipped into his sarong was no more than a pen *top*, to indicate that he was of bureaucratic status. So, as Professor Wolfgang Kayser puts it, when discussing Poe and E. T.A. Hoffmann, "The ominous has thus been transformed into a puzzle capable of being solved by a sharp-witted individual. . . . But by turning the crime into a puzzle that can be solved, and by letting an ingenious detective find the solution, Poe originated the genre of the detective story."[9] How well the Goncourt brothers sniffed out the whole Holmesian pretensions in advance. Even by 1856 they were noting:

> Reading Edgar Allen Poe is a revelation of something that criticism does not seem to suspect the existence of. Poe, a new literature, the literature of the twentieth century: the scientific miracle, the creation of fable by $a + b$; a literature at once monomaniacal and mathematical. Imagination the product of analysis; Zadig become an examining magistrate. . . .

Scientific analysis produces surprises, which are in turn taken for "fable." And as if surprising Robbe-Grillet in his very study, the

[9] Wolfgang Kayser, *The Grotesque in Art and Literature,* New York: McGraw-Hill, 1966, p. 80.

Goncourts added—"Things here play a greater part than beings." Zadig was arrested by the emperor's minions because of his extremes of inference . . . which is to say that, given another twist of fate, he might well have been a magistrate.

Watson's reverence, then, is that accorded by our society to the plumber, who diagnoses what is wrong with our backed-up drain by a few empirical tests, to the mechanic, who discovers why our jalopy won't start, to the doctor, who attributes the stab of pain in our knee to a slipped cartilage rather than rheumatism, to the legal eagle expertly sifting evidence, to the Weather Man, and so forth. We are on the road to that genuflection before science invited by much contemporary advertising—*Most dentists agree . . . Research proves*, accompanied, of course, by pictures of white coats and gleaming laboratories.[10] Here is Holmes at work on Wilson:

> "How, in the name of good fortune, did you know all that, Mr. Holmes?" he asked. "How did you know, for example, that I did manual labor? It's true as gospel, for I began as a ship's carpenter."
>
> "Your hands, my dear sir. Your right hand is quite a size larger than your left. You have worked with it and the muscles are more developed."
>
> "Well, the snuff, then, and the Freemasonry?"
>
> "I won't insult your intelligence by telling you how I read that, especially as, rather against the strict rules of your order, you use an arc and compass breast pin."
>
> "Ah, of course, I forgot that. But the writing?"
>
> "What else can be indicated by that right cuff so very shiny for five inches, and the left one with the smooth patch near the elbow, where you rest it upon the desk?"

It is fairly easy to show—logic texts frequently like to—that these observations are so many sets of false syllogisms. Twain gives us a

[10] 'Shampoo Plus Egg the only Shampoo made with fresh whole egg . . . Nature's own amazing hair conditioner! 2%,' when viewed in its setting and promotion, including the color of the contents of the article, was false and misleading since the label, setting, promotion and color represented and suggested and created the impression that the article contained a significant amount of egg and was an egg shampoo, whereas it contained an insignificant amount of egg, namely, approximately 1/150 of an egg per shampoo, and it was not an egg shampoo" (Notices of Judgment under the Federal Food, Drug, and Cosmetic Act, U.S. Department of Health, Education and Welfare [Food and Drug Administration]).

glorious sequence of these, as demonstration of popular prejudice, in his story "Disgraceful Persecution of a Boy."

To some extent this explains the Holmesian appeal. The legerdemain between events and objects becomes mesmerizing, and to sum up a man's history via objective reality about him mirrors our times—I write not long after J. Edgar Hoover made his stirring appeal that every living American should be fingerprinted. Holmes simply exaggerated the clarity of significance available here; he "mugs" us in the manner of bureaucracy.

Aristotle, defining the enthymeme as syllogism,[11] suggested that inferential wisdom of this type would always have wide appeal since "the uneducated argue from their everyday knowledge, and base their conclusions upon immediate facts" (*Rhetoric*, II, 22). *Particulare sentitur.* . . . Holmes conflated this collaboration with reality into science worship, and made the human being who was not a human engine look ridiculous. To this ape of God, lipreading his victims like so many specimens or imbeciles, the human being was an automaton, totally predictable.

"There's Money in This Case, Watson, if There Is Nothing Else."

Total predictability is godlike, ahuman. The modern state plays Holmes to its masses, perpetrating—to their applause—acts of inferential diagnosis illicit on the individual level. I am far from denying that Holmes was another safety valve, of the Mike Hammer-James Bond variety, for like Bond he achieved his effects with the instruments of science (e.g. the celebrated magnifying glass).[12] Like Bond he attached his reader, via the safety valve, to a culture.

[11]To understand a syllogism properly you really have to live it. I did so once, working on a book out of a left-bank hotel room in Paris. The room was so small that when I was in the room I was in the bed: thus when I was in the bed, there being no other area in the room, I was in the room. See Manuel Bilsky's excellent section on "Ordinary Language and the Syllogism" in his *Logic and Effective Argument,* New York: Holt, Rinehart and Winston, 1956.

[12]"AMAZING REFLECTING MICROSCOPE—Lights Up Like a T.V. Screen!

"*Projects pictures with 50X and 100X magnification on illuminated screen.

"*Amazing precision unit allows study from ten feet away. Fabulous news for doctors, students, researchers, etc. A revolutionary advance in Microscopes."

This ad was given the following analysis by *Consumer Bulletin* of April 1962: "The 'lighting up' is not much like the screen of a TV in working order, and the unit isn't either 'amazing' or 'precision' in any proper use of those terms. The last two lines are not applicable either. We hope your doctor and researcher friends do not use this sort of microscope."

But I would refer again to Trilling's remark about any excessive concentration on objects; Holmes' mode of thinking was paranoiac. To elevate the state into an idol, freed from moral sense of the individual kind, to claim for politics the internal infallibility of logic, such is the insanity of our days and ways.

A great deal of advertising bases its appeal on a technological race of aheadofness, the latest being *per se* the best (it often is); to this get tied the connotations of Americanism, with the inference that you must be a Communist or traitor if you don't buy the product. Insurance and floral and automotive associations are forever writing new Gettysburg Addresses on their own behalf, based on such inferences ("Can't you see Ivan's eyes popping if he walked into Smitty's dealer's showroom? Here's a man, now, who has built his business on the solid rock of fine products. . . . This dealer and John Smith have been friends for a long time. See each other at the PTA and the lodge, the town council and the Little League practice sessions. . . ."). A full-page ad before me, clipped from the *New York Times* (January 11, 1966), consists entirely of text. Under the banner headline "I AM THE NATION" we read, "I was born on July 4, 1776, and the Declaration of Independence is my birth certificate . . . I am Nathan Hale, and Paul Revere. I stood at Lexington and fired," etc. In tiny print at the foot of this patriotic gore run the words, "Published in the public interest by Norfolk & Western Railway, Roanoke, Va." Like that of consumer products Holmes' patriotism is never in doubt.

When all is said and done, this comes down to an issue of sanity. As President Kennedy is reputed to have said, to a reactionary Senator suggesting that the Russians might drop the atom bomb the next day, "Yes, everything is possible." Exactly, but we do not act that way. The explosion under my window a few minutes ago did not cause me to run out into the street looking for a dead body; I assumed it was the backfire of a car. Indeed, I may drop dead before I type to the end of this page, my wife may set fire to the house, and my dog drown.

If one is sane one lives by what is likely—"A certain faith in life, in oneself and in others is necessary in order to operate. In the twilight of our probationership here on earth—to use Locke's phrase—we learn to depend on probabilities."[13] But Holmes does not have

[13]James R. Newman, *The Rule of Folly,* New York: Simon and Schuster, 1962, p. 29.

234

this "faith in life." For him the height of human activity is to be a reasoning instrument. In the passage first cited, Doyle went on:

> as a lover, he would have placed himself in a false position. He never spoke of the softer passions save with a gibe and a sneer. . . . Grit in a sensitive instrument, or a crack in one of his own high-power lenses, would not be more disturbing than a strong emotion in a nature such as his.

The world is *not* predictable in the Holmesian sense. Science would have made proles of us all by now if it were. Science itself rests on the probable. Writing on "Energy Transformation in the Cell" (*Scientific American*), Albert L. Lehinger reminds us: "From the standpoint of thermodynamics the very existence of living things, with their marvelous diversity and complexity of structure and function, is improbable." We should not get too far if we confined our reactions to those of the logician who, when his friend showed him a flock of sheep with the remark "Those sheep seem to have been sheared," replied cautiously, "On this side, at least."

Holmes set himself up as irrefutable umpire, and because he was dealing with automata, rather than human beings, he never failed —at any rate, virtually speaking not, the few miscalculations being inserted in order to show the basic infallibility of the method. So he is the ballistic or fingerprint or handwriting expert, called into court today. Note that it was years before authors' associations could get expert literary testimony introduced into cases concerning books, although medical testimony was always admitted; and the judge's comments about Bernadine Wall in the British *Chatterley* trial showed with what contempt literary activity was (is?) held by the law.

True human beings, however, make errors of perception. They are not perfect reasoning machines, nor should they be. Deer hunters (I am happy to report) are always knocking off a few other deer hunters every season. Doyle claims that since Holmes has no emotions, he must therefore be icily accurate, impartial as his magnifying glass (or the FBI). And then we come across Holmes' exclamation—"It's attempted murder at the least. Nothing less will hold the London message-boy. There's a deed of violence indicated in that fellow's round shoulders and outstretched neck." It was Hitler's round shoulders which Dali claims to have seen as an indication of Fascist horrors to come.

This sort of reasoning runs, then:

> Men with round shoulders are violent men.
> This man has round shoulders.
> This man is a violent man.

On the principle, presumed equally unquestionable:

> Wheaties make champions.
> You eat Wheaties.
> You become a champion.[14]

The thought process which a syllogism expresses is here patently wrong on a number of scores. The basic premise, from which the conclusion is derived, is far from any universal truth, and the middle term is "undistributed," leading us to assume that to have one characteristic in common is automatically to have other characteristics in common. But of all the many and various forms of fractured syllogism, Holmes, it seems to me, expresses once more the most popular, a habit of thinking of an age to come.

For Holmes typically confuses philosophy and science. His inductive reasoning is constantly compromised, in a fashion characteristic of our age, by deductive methods. John C. Sherwood, a University of Oregon professor of English and logic, summarizes the twin processes: "Where induction puts facts together to get ideas or *generalizations,* deduction puts ideas together to discover what other ideas can be inferred from them."[15]

We have seen such an enthymemic syllogism above. Another is Holmes' belief that all men who dress untidily (like John Hector McFarlane) are bachelors. Thus, on the one hand, Holmes is supposed to operate on reality like some precision instrument, con-

---

[14] So much is it the case that ads utilize false syllogisms, I was actually able recently to clip one that parodied this principle:

> Orlon has chic;
> Knits have chic:
> It follows: knits of orlon have chic to spare!

This advertiser deserves to win, there are so many false arrangements in this enthymeme (or syllogism with one proposition missing). What is being said is that some zebras are striped, and some toothpaste is striped, therefore some zebras are toothpaste. It is as much use as saying: Here is a mane, here is a yak, here is a maniac.

[15] John C. Sherwood, *Discourse of Reason,* New York: Harper & Brothers, 1960, p. 42.

cluding from irrefutable evidence, in the manner of Crusoe finding Friday's footprint on the shore and inducing the presence of another human being thereby.

On the other hand, he can be observed deducing wildly, working down, like some seventeenth-century biographer, from a central ruling passion, or "humour," and anticipating a character's action according to that humour. But again, as Ben Jonson showed, this Theophrastian principle threatens to treat men as automatic. This kind of "inductive leap" reminds me of Mark Twain's Buck Fanshaw, who, "in the delirium of a wasting typhoid fever, had taken arsenic, shot himself through the body, cut his throat, and jumped out of a four-story window and broken his neck—and after due deliberation, the jury, sad and tearful, but with intelligence unblinded by its sorrow, brought in a verdict of death 'by the visitation of God.'" Here is Doyle offering us this two-in-one circularity of our times, neatly turning generalizations into evidence:

> With a resigned air and a somewhat weary smile, Holmes begged the beautiful intruder to take a seat, and to inform us what it was that was troubling her.
>
> "At least it cannot be your health," said he, as his keen eyes darted over her; "so ardent a bicyclist must be full of energy."
>
> She glanced down in surprise at her own feet, and I observed the slight roughening of the side of the sole caused by the friction of the edge of the pedal.
>
> "Yes, I bicycle a good deal, Mr. Holmes, and that has something to do with my visit to you to-day."
>
> My friend took the lady's ungloved hand, and examined it with as close an attention and as little sentiment as a scientist would show to a specimen.
>
> "You will excuse me, I am sure. It is my business," said he, as he dropped it. "I nearly fell into the error of supposing that you were typewriting. Of course, it is obvious that it is music. You observe the spatulate finger-ends, Watson, which is common to both professions? There is a spirituality about the face, however"—she gently turned it towards the light—"which the typewriter does not generate. The lady is a musician."
>
> "Yes, Mr. Holmes, I teach music."
>
> "In the country, I presume, from your complexion."
>
> "Yes, sir, near Farnham, on the borders of Surrey."

This is pretty fine. Either the sole of the girl's shoe is roughened, or it is not. Her fingers can be said, approximately enough, to be spatulate or not. In this manner, elsewhere, Holmes supposed that the owner of a certain pair of pince-nez was "a person of refinement and well-dressed" since the glasses were "handsomely mounted in solid gold, and it is inconceivable that anyone who wore such glasses could be slatternly in other respects." Here the scientist is working on his specimen.

But he then proceeds to offer us a wild hypothesis about something called "spirituality" and does so *on the same terms as* the induction. This is like a doctor finding, from laboratory tests, that a man has an excess of alcohol in his blood and is therefore likely to be drunk, and then moving quickly to a host of generalizations about drunks. We notice that Holmes' "beautiful intruder" is hardly the pre-Raphaelite type; her complexion is ruddy, and bicycling was in those days an energetic pastime. It is the Doyle-Betjeman axis that finds the hockey-playing head girl "spiritual."

Spirituality cannot be tested, least of all in the manner of worn shoe soles. It is not a statement of anything approaching fact, and unless we want to spend a lifetime setting up a system like that of Kant's Antinomies, we will call it a vague and hasty generalization and leave it at that. But we must be allowed our sleuthing, too. We notice that Holmes uses it as logically equipollent with the shoe sole and the spatulate fingerends. He offers the spirituality as evidence on the same basis of potential predictability. (Actually, the girl's typing might have been that of her own manuscripts, and the typist hypothesis might then have supported rather than ruled out the spirituality.) All this is sensibly artificial, and what I mean by his confusion of inductive and deductive logic. It is frankly impossible, and probably undesirable, to found a general principle for spirituality. What is a spiritual look to one may resemble a sick-dog look to another. Before he died Mencken invited his friends to "wink your eye at some homely girl" in remembrance of him. How to arrive at homeliness (or Holmesian spirituality) he did not define.

The Detective as Dictator

For this is an "appraisive term." It is "internally complex." It is "variously describable." And, finally, it is " 'open' in character," being able to be used both "aggressively and defensively" (the con-

notations of spirituality, or of homeliness, are largely in the user).
I pick here the criteria given for an "essentially contested concept"
evolved by Walter Gallie, Professor of Logic and Metaphysics at
the Queen's University of Belfast, in a paper on the subject (*Proceedings of the Aristotelian Society*, vol. 56, 1955–56).

The point for my purpose is this: Holmes is here assuming an
illegitimate assent in the communicatory process. He is camouflaging his tactics by first provoking assent where it can, and more or
less does, exist—worn shoe soles, spatulate fingerends. This is the
tactic of the dictator, or of the dictator's successor, the technocratic
elite; that is why Holmes hits close to home. He tricks us, ruthlessly
enough, into a confusion of "apparent" and "transparent" language,
into taking symbol for sign. In this way he says more about himself—about the psychological state of his times—than about the bicycling pianist. In fact, Holmes often seems to me a kind of manic
pre-McLuhan, graveling the groundlings as personified by Watson.

The word *spirituality* is useless for deductive purposes. It has no
intrinsic predictive power, and yet all words are in some manner
anticipatory. Holmes hopes we won't notice, as he pushes the retrodictive value of his concept into the future, into an appraisal. This
method, or mismethod, of thinking is a contemporary language
abuse, the technique of witch-hunting, and racism—to have a
spiritual look gets converted into having an *Oriental* look, a *Jewish* look and so on. The crops fail, the mage has lost his power;
equally, the mage has a sick look, the crops are bound to fail. A recent study of the McCarthy era finds no argument possible against
the credibility of the testimony of Whittaker Chambers and Elizabeth Bentley; but, as Alan Barth remarked, "one could with equal
fairness put it differently and say that much of their testimony has
not yet received the corroboration that enables us to accept it."[16]

John Sherwood cites "the case of the unhappy victim of a Congressional investigation who was told that his repeated public denunciations of Communism did not save him from the suspicion of
being a Communist agent, since the public utterance might simply
have been intended to distract attention from secret subversive
activities."[17]

[16]See Earl Latham, *The Communist Controversy in Washington: From the
New Deal to McCarthy,* Cambridge, Mass.: Harvard University Press, 1966.
Barth's comment was made in a review of this book which I read in the Paris
edition of the New York *Herald Tribune* (August 13–14, 1966).
[17]Sherwood, *Discourse of Reason,* p. 67.

A New York paper before me reports the arrest of a suspect in a *slaying* (a specialization descent out of German *schlagen*); the summary of the accused's appearance concludes as follows—"and every inch of him is criminal." Like Joë Bousquet's complaint that once you tell a girl you'll take her in your arms there's nothing more to do, so there is really little point in putting such an individual on trial, least of all if the reporter who penned that legend gets called for jury duty at the time. It is like saying a man is a *latent* homosexual.

Doyle's case was one of slightly colossal psychic chiasmus. For the fallibilities of the infallible Sherlock remind me that in my youth boy's reading in the private-eye or superman-hero field in England was of the order: Buchan's Hannay, Charteris' Saint, Haggard's Quartermaine, Wallace's Sanders, a bit of Berry, "Sapper" 's Drummond. I never read Conan Doyle as a boy, nor did any of my friends. It was one's parents who provided his large and faithful readership. Unlike Raffles or even Bulldog Drummond, Holmes supported authority.

In my own case this seemed odd since for a while I lived in a house in Sussex quite near the Doyles. The strange split was there, evidenced by Doyle's interest in mechanics and provision to his sons of powerful sports cars (called, respectively, *Chutabangbang* and *The Grey Ghost*), and in his weird spiritualism. The latter resulted, after his death, in the maid being made to serve an empty place at table each night, as if the master were still present.

I am, finally, reminded of Friedrich Duerrenmatt's detective "hero," Barlach.[18] It is necessary to qualify the term *hero* in this instance since Barlach is weak, elderly, and physically inefficient—the most he will do is pad an arm against a dog. Here, of course, the whole private-eye mystique is reversed, and well parodied: the often unrendered subtitle of the original edition of *The Pledge* is *Requiem auf den Kriminalroman,* and in *The Quarry* Barlach conducts his investigation from a bed!

Barlach's power is purely moral, as Holmes' was amoral. Barlach makes killers kill themselves, or other killers. Final justice is more than a mere squaring of accounts, in which it is appropriate that only the victim can execute the hangman. That is why Duerrenmatt has the Jew Gulliver eradicate "the evil dragon" Emmen-

[18]See my article "Duerrenmatt and the Kriminalroman," *Commonweal,* LXXVI: 13 (June 22, 1962), pp. 324–326.

berger in *The Quarry,* and why Barlach destroys Gastmann in *The Judge and His Hangman.* In the latter work a character called Tschanz sees Barlach as follows:

> The old man stretched out on the couch and pulled the cover over him. He was lying there, frail and helpless, and all of a sudden he looked terribly old and withered. . . . Then Tschanz looked into Barlach's eyes. They were calm, clear and inscrutable, and they returned his gaze without flinching.

If it is true that Poe created the contemporary detective story, he did so by making the solver of the puzzle element inhumanly sharp-witted. The criminal minister of *The Purloined Letter* is a wizard mathematician and only matched by the famous Dupin, who has the same superhuman faculty for combination.[19] The murder chamber in *The Murders in the Rue Morgue* is explicitly described as "absolutely alien from humanity." This initiates the least pleasant side of the murder-mystery since it assumes a pattern of thinking wherein nonhuman status can be accorded to humans. From here it is but a step to the concentration camps—Duerrenmatt implies as much in *The Quarry.* His victim is seldom the convenient Other. In *Traps* it is explicitly—you.

In the Holmesian rhetoric the enemy was another social class, never your own. Just as in the "spaghetti Westerns" mentioned, Italian-made copies of Hollywood originals, it is not unusual for the bad guy to win out, so in Duerrenmatt's detective fiction, and theater, the enemy is a way of life—conventional bourgeois existence, symbolized, for this Swiss author, in immaculate sanitoria and lots of chocolates. Moreover, Duerrenmatt flagrantly violates the repayment code, the villains of both *The Pledge* and *The Judge and His Hangman* dying in "accidents," while in *The Quarry* the retribution is well outside the law. In this book we note the comfortable, cheese-sounding name of the ex-Fascist surgeon, an end-product of the technocrat as dictator.

Iconographical violence is relative, or contextual. Barlach is non-violent in a violent time. But the inept writing of Holmes' struggles

---

[19]The late Wolfgang Kayser most pertinently compared Poe and E.T.A. Hoffmann in this respect; he showed that in similar stories the German writer always pitched a poetic, and therefore human, intelligence against the sinister and criminal elements (Kayser, *The Grotesque in Art and Literature,* pp. 76–81).

with, say, Jack the Ripper or the infamous Professor Moriarty were undoubtedly violent fare for their readership, and should not blind us to Sherlock's training in boxing at Christ Church, resulting in his later love of loosening the front teeth of adversaries, as he himself put it. The huge Siger Holmes wanted his son to be an engineer! "I'll make a bruiser of him yet, Violet," he told his shuddering spouse.

The errand of this exercise in detection has been to identify another imbalance of word-wisdom. Today inference has swung into a type of willful social symbolism. Everything technological must be good. Our reverence for the Holmeses of this world was best summarized, perhaps, by Virginia Woolf's antirational use of the name in *Mrs. Dalloway* or by Henry James at the outset of *Washington Square,* when he discussed the medical profession in America:

> In a country in which, to play a social part, you must either earn your income or make believe that you earn it, the healing art has appeared in a high degree to combine two recognized sources of credit. It belongs to the realm of the practical, which in the United States is a great recommendation; and it is touched by the light of science—a merit appreciated in a community in which the love of knowledge has not always been accompanied by leisure and opportunity

EIGHT

Words are wise men's counters—they do
but reckon with them, but they are the
money of fools.[1]

Thomas Hobbes

THE CHIMERAS OF CONTEXT

The Next Time You Say That, Smile

In early 1966 Federal narcotics agents raided a meeting in a
Greenwich Village hotel, allegedly a benefit for a man picked up
on a marijuana charge. The agents stated that the raid was
prompted by a threat made against a government witness (an
individual used also against Dr. Timothy Leary). The words had
been, "Man, you're dead." The witness took this as a threat on his
life. But the hipster who'd uttered the words explained in court
that *dead* was locally the equivalent of "finished in this town." It
had not at that time reached the dictionary. Similarly, you can
murder someone in sports, make a *killing* on the market, but—
watch your language with the fuzz.

It is in this spirit that Socrates reminds Phaedrus that words
can't be moved from place to place and still retain their same
meanings. A definition delimits. It is, roughly speaking, the verbal
equivalent of a pointing activity. Dictionary criteria point to evidence of usage. A sound, or a series of sounds, is not related to
an aspect of our world by intrinsic characteristics.[2]

"Take the word 'rot,'" writes Anatol Rapoport. "To a German
it means 'red,' to a Russian 'mouth,' and to us you know what. How

---

[1]Cf. Bacon's similar sentiment that words are "tokens current and accepted
for conceits as moneys are for values."

[2]I except, of course, phonetic intensives and other forms of sound symbolism, briefly touched on above under onomatopoeia. Thus Jespersen thought
the English word *roll* contained intrinsically the ideas that it stood for more
satisfactorily than Russian *katat*. Swift's unspellable *Houyhnhnms* derived
from the whinny of the horses that they were.

good a philosopher do you have to be to discover the 'real' mean
ing of 'rot'?" I hope Anatol also knows that to a Frenchman the
word could vary between roast meat and a belch after the meal.
Thus the idea, or necessity, of context for conveyance of meaning
gets pushed back whenever you remain your own enchanted listener. The various examples one can cite from time to time of
Greeks feeling *democracy* to be intrinsically theirs is evidence of
this self-hypnosis. It is saying that democracy resides within
Greeks. Thus any other context for the word is factitious. I suppose the same would apply to *hyena,* a Greek word in English
guise beloved of Marxist rhetors, or even to *tyranny.*

The dictionary becomes a vast operation in popularity. It
samples insistent illisions, or comings-together, of word and world.
Children learn to talk by such pairings—as in that instructive text
used in many US schools, the *Junior Vocabulary Builder* (published by Manter Hall, Mass.). No. 8 in this series matches up
words with contexts for eighth-graders as follows:

> "Absolute": the power of dictators in totalitarian states like
> Communist Russia.
> "Barren": the fields on Russian cooperative farms.

The pupil is marked wrong should he fail to feel that *barren* here
describes much more than the state of mind of his invigilator.
Transformational grammar helps children build up further pairings, for definitions make definitions. Two standard American dictionaries define the word *bear:* one subdefines *teddy bear* without
doing the same for *polar bear,* and vice versa. They base their
choices on popularity of usage, like polls.

But is it necessary for meaning that such illisions exist? Can
they, in fact, do so for "transparent," unobservable entities like
democracy or *justice?* Must someone else, in short, have the same
meaning as I have for these collaborations of letters in order that
there should be a meaning within them? We have seen that proper
names have no meanings as such. Some semanticists like to say
that no word can ever mean the same thing twice. Nor was public
sharing, for either Locke or Hume, a precondition of meaning.

The contemporary dictionary-maker might answer that all a
definition is saying is that it is *possible* for that word (*democracy*
or *justice*) to have that meaning. The Webster employee, let's

suppose, who culled that single meaning for *democracy* is expressing, in so doing, the principle of relationship, or what I call the word-world harmony. The private language of a maniac still has meaning to him, in the relationship that the letter-unit *gun* or *tree* has to a certain observable reality for me. You can apply this to Rapoport's *rot*. It means different things, but it means.

Meaning is not naming something, but saying something. Was not this brought home by a certain legal case in England a few years ago? Here the compiler of one publication giving railway timetables alleged that another publication was copying those tables, after they'd appeared, and publishing them in its own compilations. This was extremely hard to prove, since the trains ran at certain hours or at other hours. A timetable was naming, not saying. Actually, in this case, a subterfuge was resorted to, and errors fed purposely into the first publication's listings. When these errors were repeated, i.e. copied, the impasse was broken.

Russell cleared this up nicely by distinguishing between reference and meaning. Sir Walter Scott was the author of *Waverley* but did not *mean* the same as the author of *Waverley*. As the housemaids crowded into a hallway to watch Scott pass, it would not have *meant* anything to say, "There goes the author of *Waverley*." Scott's authorship was initially unknown.

But even if it had been known, it would not have mattered. Russell's point is good. If your housemaid had never seen Scott, yet had read *Waverley,* and you then took her to a police lineup of the time comprising twenty men, one of whom was Scott, she would have had to guess to get him. In the same way, Ryle observes that "the third man to stand on the top of Mt. Everest" doesn't refer to anyone. But it carries meaning (could be translated, etc.). To illustrate the same point, William Alston links in this manner "the President of the U.S.A. in 1962" and "the U.S. President assassinated in Dallas." He writes: "Such examples show that it cannot simply be the fact that an expression refers to a certain object that gives it the particular meaning it has."[3] Beside which can be put Wittgenstein's "Don't ask for the meaning, ask for the use."

[3]William P. Alston, *Philosophy of Language,* Englewood Cliffs, N.J.: Prentice-Hall, 1964, p. 13. Russell first made his famous equative relation, or appositional construction, in an essay "On Denoting" in *Mind* for 1905, one subsequently much reprinted—"One and only one entity wrote *Waverley,* and Scott was identical with that one."

Vocabulary shifts more than other features of language, and words vary with speakers and with what is around them. "CONTEXT, in its widest sense, is the relation between linguistic form and everything which is not language, the 'world at large.' "[4] The US Food and Drug Administration judges against the claims of a product by what is around it in advertising—its context. Hunter Diack has pointed out that if you put the word LITTER on a wire basket, it immediately means something, and something unambiguous.

I have risked this elementary exposition of an important topic since it is sometimes a matter of life and death. At the outset of this study I gave some examples—*appeasement* and so forth—showing how meaning must be largely in the user. The housemaid above confronted the lineup with only an inner picture in her mind of the kind of man she would imagine writing *Waverley*. In 1933 the *Oxford English Dictionary* showed very little interest in the word *Right* as a political noun; in six and a half columns, all it could find to say was "In continental legislative chambers the party or parties of conservative principles." So, prewar, the Right was thought of as "continental." Now the unifying agent has shifted to opposition to Communism, with, in France, *la droite* (the right wing) finding a shadow of semantic support from *le droit* (the law). In 1622 Pope Gregory's *Congregatio de propaganda fide* was an attempt to spread a certain view. The word *propaganda* has been consistently poisoned since, until *New World* now lists it as often used "in a derogatory sense, connoting deception or distortion."

But that the words around a word can be a matter of life and death was nowhere better illustrated than in 1898, when Massachusetts replaced hanging by electrocution. The first man to be sentenced to death appealed, claiming that the United States Constitution disallowed "cruel and unusual punishments." Chief Justice Holmes of the State Supreme Court could hardly deny that electrocution was locally *unusual,* but concluded that "the word *unusual* must be construed with the word *cruel,*" and thus since the hot squat was not cruel (?) it was not unusual—or not cruel-unusual. The individual in question fried. Since the death penalty has recently declined in the United States (one execution in 1966), liberal organizations like the American Civil Liberties Union hope

[4] Leech, *English in Advertising,* p. 8.

to abolish it altogether by the same appeal to the Eighth Amendment. After all, if it occurs infrequently, it becomes "unusual."

Less forensic niceties were observed, incidentally, in the Yemen in 1966, over another celebrated "first." A court in San'aa established the precedent of sentencing a sixty-year-old to death for homosexuality. The method of extermination was debated. Islamic law demanded that such an offender be thrown from the highest point in the city, and respecters of tradition urged defenestration from a plane. But in order for the punishment to be properly *public* the court permitted beheading, instead. However, the official executioner failed to show and, on being asked if he would like to be shot, the condemned consented. He was shot.

It is a principle of law that meaning relies on context and that context includes everything around the word, even to the gestures and actions with which it is accompanied, if spoken. Again, this has meant life and death for many.

In *Language and the Law* F. A. Philbrick recounts how a 1900 British murder case "hung" on the way in which the accused, a mother who had overlaid her child, had pronounced certain remarks. This distraught woman, who had been seduced and abandoned by a married man, was said to have made the statement to another, on the night of the infant's death, "How can anyone get rid of a little baby like this!" Cross-examination revealed that the bewildered parent had been lovingly fondling her infant at the time, and put her stress on the word *can*. She was not, in other words, asking how best to kill it. Later, too, she told the police, "I killed it—I did not know what to do with it—I put it in a box." This admission was wholly alleviated by punctuation, which turned the second sentence into a causal dependency of the third, i.e. hasty shorthand for "Because I did not know what to do with it, I put it in a box," rather than "I killed it because I did not know what to do with it." The woman was acquitted.

Similarly, one astute high school girl revised the International Paper Co.'s slogan from "Send me a man who reads" to "Send me a man. Who reads?" Searching for a sentence to contextualize without any amphiboly the word *passionate*, one dictionary editor, Clarence Barnhart, decided on, "The fathers of our country were passionate believers in freedom." But by placing a comma after *passionate* a reader changed his sense.

Often, however, mere punctuation will not a meaning make. It will not do so in Chinese, where the pitch pattern of an utterance can considerably vary its meanings. The difference between a smoking room, as part of a gentlemen's club, and a smoking room, as a room on fire, is subtle but distinct; few sensitive speakers would fail to convey it. The White House is a white house. We are on the fringes of pun.

Spoken context can extend the word into the world. Happiness is walking in the grass in your bare feet, and so on. But even when we come to written language I. A. Richards' statement stands up, that the meaning of a word is the missing part of its context. A child who does not know the meaning of the word *crest* may hear the sentence, "John climbed to the crest of the mountain." If he knows the other words in this sentence he is already on his way; perhaps John climbed to the middle of the mountain, but he certainly did not climb to the bottom. His father then says, "Just look at the crests of those waves." And so forth. Later, he will find that a family can have a crest.

These hidden lives outside words sustain them for us. Advertising, we know, thrives off missing contexts and deliberately organizes misconstructions of this order. The trick of the incomplete comparative can be employed in many ways: *More Americans drink orange juice for breakfast* is an unrelated statement since the "more" demands completion (more Americans than mice?). Alternatively the ad can be phrased: *Americans drink more orange juice for breakfast,* insinuating, no doubt correctly, that they drink more orange juice than gun oil.

The incomplete or unrelated or "unqualified" comparative, also termed by the *New Yorker* the "agency comparative," has been the cause of considerable comment.[5] In his famous essay on Sunkist oranges the late Leo Spitzer classed it as an "advertising elative" similar to *different*. Since advertisers are not allowed directly to disparage competitors' goods, their language is often forced into a vagueness extremely harmful to communication. Does *different* mean different from, or does it really mean *better, superior* (as an absolute)? Laws of proportion cannot pertain if standards of comparison are wholly illusory like this. On African safari your wash could be called *whiter* (than it was when dirty) yet *inferior* (to

[5]See E. K. Sheldon, "The Rise of the Incomplete Comparative," *American Speech,* xx, 1945, pp. 161–167; Randolph Quirk, *The Use of English,* London: Longmans, Green, 1962, p. 223; Leech, *English in Advertising,* pp. 160–161.

norms of brilliance of your society at home). To have a comparative without comparison is, in essence, to dress and perfume a girl up for a place she will never get to. "If people were careful thinkers," writes Jules Henry, "it would be difficult to sell anything." This is not so. But it would be more difficult to pass off false promises as real. Context-consciousness is a verbal dynamic that furthers environmental control.

In the second instance, Richards' observation makes particular sense in the matter of translating. Everyone knows that there are dozens of foreign words which are unamenable to direct transfer by an English word. Are we to translate *quatre-vingt* four twenty, or *dans le Nord* in the north (when the department of that name is intended)? German *leise* has no exact, extra-contextual equivalence in English, while *bitte* can be made into dozens of German senses. *Un homme d'un certain âge* means a well-aged man (cf. Sagan's untranslated title *Un Certain Sourire*). Everyone could add his favorite. And this is not to touch on the matter of inflections, nor on the famous English lack of a *thou* today.[6]

Like a pun, translation shows that words are clusters, connections. In *Explorations in Awareness* (1957) J. Samuel Bois writes:

> I wanted to have the correct English word for "fleuve". . . . "River" means "rivière," and anyone who has sense knows that a "rivière" and "fleuve" are two entirely different things. . . . I looked into my dictionary. To my great surprise, "fleuve" was translated by "river". . . . Only one English word, "river," to translate both "rivière" and "fleuve." What a discovery! I had a vague suspicion that English was a very poor language compared to French. . . .
>
> A little later I had to translate English into French. The word "giggle" was in the sentence. . . . The French term was "ricaner." You see, for every English word, we have at least one French word—clear, precise, picturesque. Further down came "titter". . . . "Titter" and "giggle" had one translation in French: "ricaner". . . . In another context was the word "chuckle". . . .How do we say that in French? Well, well! I

[6]So emphatic is this lack that when an English dialect still contains a second person singular, as does D. H. Lawrence's Derbyshire, it becomes virtually a falsification, or at least an artificiality, to translate it by *tu* or *Du*. This can be seen in French and German translations of *Lady Chatterley's Lover*.

could hardly believe it: "ricaner" is the only word we have. The score was turning against us. I was disturbed.

This is to exhume the hoary head of lexical translation, interred by Friedrich Schleiermacher at the beginning of the last century and by Valery Larbaud at the end of it. It is like looking up *put* in the dictionary, then *up*, then *with*, and subsequently complaining that there is a single word for all these—*endure*. Bois is searching for synonyms, not meanings. (When Gérard de Nerval translated the first part of *Faust* he hardly bothered about dictionary equivalents at all; yet his work delighted Goethe and was used by Berlioz.) By Bois' book *ça va sans dire* would come out "he walks without talking," or some such. It would be to assert that French only has one word, *louer*, for to rent and to praise, so that you could say, as Margaret Schlauch suggested, *"Je loue votre maison parceque je la loue."* It would be to allege that there is only one French word, *hôte*, for guest and host. In the latter instance, you could go still further in Spanish and cite the idiomatic *Te voy a dar una hostia* (I'm going to knock you down).[7]

Translation is not a matter of swapping referents as unequivocally as possible. If it were, a German translator of a novel about Yorkshire working-class life, in which *lunch* is unused, would, as one has, invariantly translate *dinner* by *Abendessen* even though the context showed the occasion as occurring at midday. English could be further indicted for having no single-word equivalent for *Geschwister* (brothers and sisters) or *Essbesteck* (table setting— knife, fork and spoon). *Rivière* and *fleuve* carry what I can only call instant contexts with them, and *ricaner* is varied adverbially, to gain countless distinctions; *Il ricana doucement* is a cluster. The adverb "declines" the verb. You would be unlikely to translate this, "He sneered softly"—though dictionaries give sneer for *ricaner*. This is incidentally Dr. Johnson's charm; his celebrated description of *network* as "anything reticulated or decussated, at equal distances, with interstices between the intersections" can only be termed thoroughly *nettish* (as well as highly prophetic of the TV screen).

For it is, of course, the context that is principally operative in

[7]Compare lexical equivalence for *por* in the following sentence: *Iba por los campos, por las montañas, por los puentes, por las curvas, y por las quebradas* (It went *through* the fields, *over* the mountains, *over* the bridges, *around* the curves, and *across* the ravines).

translation, a feature of language Joyce played with in the poly-phonic sections of *Finnegans Wake*. No Frenchman has difficulty discerning whether he is to be guest or host when *hôte* is used. A novel of mine had for its title *Rage on the Bar*, a pun on the Carib-bean idiom meaning a storm on a reef; it was published in Italian by the Rizzoli translator as *Anime Bianche e Nere* (and all cricket references within properly expunged). "Some literal translations mean practically nothing," writes Eugene Nida, Secretary of Trans-lations of the American Bible Society. "They are incongruous words —nothing more." He cites a translation of the Holy Spirit which came over in one Sudanese tongue as *clean breath*. The German translator of Melville, Dr. Fritz Güttinger, instances a similarly lexical transposition in a German version of *Erewhon*, where "a nice point of etiquette" turns into "*eine hübsche Frage der Eti-quette*." Here the word "nice" means tricky (*knifflige*, perhaps?) rather than pretty, or good-looking.[8] The Duke of Wellington called the Battle of Waterloo "a damn nice thing."

Needless to say, in passing, sound is often the most secure con-text of all. An actor at Stanislavski's Moscow Theater told Roman Jakobson that he was once called on "to make forty different mes-sages from the phrase *Segodnja večerom*, 'This evening,' by diver-sifying its expressive tint." In fact, the actor made fifty such mes-sages for Jakobson on tape, the majority of which were correctly understood by Russian listeners. One story has it that synonym-hunting of Bois' kind virtually resulted in the dropping of the atom bomb. After the Allied ultimatum demanding unconditional surrender, the Japanese premier used the term *mokusatsu* to char-acterize his country's reply. It was understood by both the cabinet and himself as meaning "taking no action at present." A news agency translated it as a rejection. Indeed, as Lowell wrote, there is at times death in the dictionary.

Happiness Is Dumping the Dictionary

An unabridged dictionary today contains about half a million entries. How many of them are worth reading? Etymology is an-other contextual extension, this time backward in time. It gives you

---

[8]Güttinger, *Zielsprache*, pp. 78–81, 116–117; *Erewhon* poses, of course, almost insoluble problems for the translator. Larbaud left the title the same in French. But to get the reversal effect unavailable in *nirgends*, or *nirgendwo*, the German translator tried *Aipotu*, Utopia backwards. Ydgrun (alias Mrs. Grundy) was turned into *Komil Fo*. Dr. Güttinger praises these ingenious substitutions which are literal to the meaning rather than to the lexicon.

the history of a word's use. The term itself derives from Greek *etymos,* true or genuine, and conveys the connotation that the dictionary is a Divine Book.

Look it up in the dictionary, one is directed on all sides. "HOLD THE ENGLISH LANGUAGE IN YOUR TWO HANDS" reads the appeal across the advertising brochure for Webster's Third. "Never has our language been so understandable," runs the claim in a handout for the same, circulated to college and high school teachers, "for in this dictionary every definition is given in a single, flashing phrase of precise meaning." *Are You Misunderstood?* asks the title of a recent work from another dictionary publisher, Wilfred Funk, Inc., offering successful communication "through word lists and vocabulary tests." The *Random House Dictionary* is "a dictionary of today's English . . . with every meaning and every usage made crystal-clear."

An interesting instance of this dictionary adoration occurred in an American jury trial of early 1963. The action concerned *negligence* in operating a motor vehicle, and after long deliberation the jury requested a dictionary. The court rejected this request—presumably on the basis of its being introduction of an outside source. For a long while the jury was unable to reach a decision, but finally did so the following day—only to have their verdict subsequently set aside. Why?

It transpired that the jury foreman had come back the next day with a dictionary definition of the word—interpreting the judge to deny them access to a dictionary in the jury room, but not to forbid them looking at one. This he had done overnight, and a jury, which upon evening recess had stood seven to five for one party (mainly on the court's definition), reversed itself on the morrow on hearing "a single, flashing phrase of precise meaning" from the dictionary.

Here, as so often, a jury was asked to make a determination on a level of abstraction that is not finally determinable without considerable contextual extension. You are simply not going to find "a single, flashing phrase" that will define *negligence,* or *wisdom—* for failing to teach him which an American student recently sued his alma mater. Similarly, David Berlo asks what is *intelligence.* We can reply by giving the results of our boy's IQ test, how it was administered and scored and so forth. But this is relative to a context. "All we have," as Berlo writes, "is a set of operations, for a given situation, that produce a result. We label this result and call it intelligence."

Erich Fromm has suggested the sad state of affairs that might ensue if we tried to reduce all the many abstractions we fight for to sets of operations: "The only people who take the Russian Communist ideology about world revolution seriously are the Americans. The Russians don't believe a word of it themselves. Similarly, Americans talk about God and the rights of man—while everything in our society moves toward the dehumanization of man and the neglect of religious precepts of brotherhood." (Thou shalt not kill—except when in uniform.) Of course, as I have said, we can find approximate synonyms for *negligence,* and *wisdom,* and *democracy,* but this is simply shuffling counters across at each other. In a passage of Bacon's *Novum Organum* of 1620, later paralleled by Hobbes, he wrote: "Yet even definitions cannot cure this evil in dealing with natural and material things; since the definitions themselves consist of words, and those words beget others; so that it is necessary to recur to individual instances. . . ." Yet, as Richard Falk puts it, our legal system is a mass of high abstraction, based on "individual instances," to be sure, but often arbitrarily employed: "On closer examination, we discover that legal technicalities are devices used to permit high-level abstraction and therefore to cloak the manipulative and self-manipulative forces imbedded deeply in the language of law."[9]

Dictionaries do seem to have a bemusing effect, similar to that felt by Wells' Mr. Polly—"New words had terror and fascination for him. He could not avoid them, and so he plunged into them." The British would appear to have a corner in this hypnosis, the many best-selling books of Ivor Brown collecting idiosyncrasies and etymologies, and idiosyncrasies of etymology, but not telling us too much about language. John Moore's *You English Words* (three impressions in three years) is a characteristic case of this interest, an odd, highly personal admixture of scholarly citings and nonagenarian scuttlebutt out of authorities like Skeat, Partridge and the *OED*—where etymology is seen at its liveliest. It must be a kind of crossword-puzzle satisfaction people get out of reading these recurrent collections. And they should not be scorned, for they are often charming, as any amateurism is likely to be in our

[9]Richard A. Falk, "Legal Language as Semantic Fog," *ETC.,* xvii:2 (Winter 1960), p. 228.

age.[10] If most of these books are hobbyists' manuscripts, a hobby is nonetheless motivated by affection. An *amateur* in French remains a *lover of*.

Still, this verbal philately does not take us very deep. Neither Skeat nor Partridge presumed to set up language laws. For such we have to go to (Henry) Bradley and Bréal, as well as to the pedants of the academies. It was Bréal who said that the shifting of meanings over the ages testified to the virtual impossibility of defining. Bradley was of course an *OED* editor. He anything but ossified. Partridge quotes against himself (out of William Cowper), at the front of his *Origins:*

> Philologists who chase
> A panting syllable through time and space,
> Start it at home, and hunt it in the dark,
> To Gaul, to Greece, and into Noah's Ark.

This was in the spirit of Johnson's definition of *lexicographer* as "a harmless drudge." To be sure, it is of use to know that *lewd* once meant unlearned. One is told that it is essential to do so when reading Chaucer. But this is largely a matter of translation, or transliteration. The French Academy tells me that the adjective *plain* (as in *plain-chant*) is not a synonym for *plein,* but is, rather, linked to *plan* (fem. *plane*). This has enabled me to say, doubtless to the delight of the kind of body who taught me "modern" languages at Oxford, *Une religion de* plain-pied *qui* aplanit *toutes hauteurs.* But it does not help me with context. It does not tell me, for instance, that when an hotel is full it is *complet* rather than *plein,* and that for a woman to say she is *pleine* after a meal is highly indecorous since to be full in this sense is to be pregnant, and only used of animals. That a dictionary definition of *semantics* is a contradiction in terms can be seen by the way in which it is shuffled back and forth with *semasiology.*

Scarcity lends interest and value, like the case of the miswater-marked stamp that came out in America a few years back and was

[10]At the start of his book Moore calls it "an amateur's book, and a personal one" (John Moore, *You English Words,* London: Collins, 1961, p. 11); but it shows considerably more insight than that available to most popular novelists: cf. in this connection—"sometimes there is no need to involve the dictionaries: a word encountered by chance may set off a whole train of personal mnemonics" (p. 30).

hailed as a gold mine by the few who got the first pulls. But postal authorities quickly "reclassified" this rarity by issuing a long run of purposely incorrect copies. It is nice to know that *treacle* comes from Greek *therion* (meaning wild beast), and *alcohol* from Arabic *kohl*. *Swastika* in Sanskrit meant good luck. Even in English a *smirk* was once a smile and *resentment* gratitude (as in the country's formal thanks to Milton). *Barter* once meant to deceive. Milton's Satan "winnow'd the buxom air," which we cannot do today. As recently as in the nineteenth century *grateful* and *disinterested* and *brilliant* (cf. Henry James) were used with refractions of meaning lost to these words today. Yet a sensitive reader catches these refractions, just as he does Coleridge's special use of the word *romantic* in *Kubla Khan*. He does so thanks to context. To comprehend in French is to hear—*entendre*. The sensitive reader hears.

Nor is either the drudge, or the judge, always quite so harmless after all. There comes a time when the most impartial of monitors must direct. A clock face would seem objective to the point of inscrutability—a perfect Robbe-Grillet *thing*, and often used by him as such—and yet what we call *half-past five* the Germans refer to as *halb sechs*. In the old Met in New York seats whence view was obscured by columns were known as *half-seats:* they were not sold at half-price, however. The Atlantic City Weather Bureau now likes to call a sky *partly sunny* that they used to define as *partly cloudy*.

Someone is called on to arbitrate. It's a little like the Carlsberg Beer ad showing a *half empty* glass of beer—or is it, in fact, *half full?* The Carlsberg people themselves answer by asking, "Are you an optimist or a pessimist?" But it illustrates again that meaning is the missing part of its context.[11] Professor Cohen of Manchester University found that the word *some* varies considerably with context; to most people *some* friends means about five or six, while *some* trees suggests at least twenty.

Well, *some* years ago a US judge tossed out a politician's petition as "saturated" with fraud, since *some* signatures on it were found to be false. But a higher court ruled against him, deciding that the false signatures were in the minority and should be ignored. Leo

[11]My wife, an unbearably refined cook, refers me, from her gastronomic library, to the French cookery instruction, *désosser* (bone): you are supposed to remove the bones and leave the shape. But to do this with tiny birds like *merles, grives* (or even the lovely *bécasse* I shoot in Corsica) means the reverse—to deflesh.

Hamalian sometimes shows the "missing meaning" idea to a class by printing it upside down under a declarative, "out of context" statement, thus:

He looks at me blankly when I speak to him.
I therefore assume he is still unconscious from the blow.

Best of all, however, was Bacon's reasonable skepticism, in exemplifying this point: "It was a good answer that was made by the man who was shown hanging in a temple a picture of those who had paid their vows as having escaped shipwreck. They would have him say whether he did not now acknowledge the power of the gods.—'Aye,' asked he again, 'but where are they painted that were drowned after their vows?' "

Inevitably, if indirectly, the dictionary has to decide on missing meaning, on whether the glass of beer is half empty or half full. This was entertainingly brought home in the February 1966 issue of *Playboy,* in which a Merriam editor replied to charges that his dictionary was still euphemizing, or fudging over, the terms for well-known sexual practices. The editor answered gracefully enough, disclaiming the blue stocking and pointing out that verbal contexts for these practices barely existed. In short, in matters of *cunnilinctus, soixante-neuf* . . . it was damn difficult up there at Springfield, Mass., to find out just who was springing on whom, or who. Still, these terms exist. They are part of discourse. One is a euphemism in itself.

If we were all etymology addicts, we should be able to push one button with the name of a word on it, push another button with a date in history on it, and come up with a set of given reactions. This is not the prejudice of a Partridge. Secretary of Labor W. Willard Wirtz, as quoted in the *Hat Worker* (October 15, 1962), said, "the discourse and the dialog of public affairs is dominated by an approach in which somebody pushes a button, and that is all the thinking that goes into it." As such push-button terms in labor relations today he instanced: *featherbedding, right-to-work* and *compulsory arbitration.* I myself particularly enjoyed the jazzing given the etymology experts in a recent issue of *Down Beat,* in the course of an article showing that the origin of *jazz* was *jass.* This word, according to Charles Edward Smith, "went back to a time when the Romans put *rocks* on British roads and the Druids *rolled* stones at Stonehenge. (They somehow couldn't get the two words together until the kettle drum from Africa was introduced.)"[12]

Preconditioned Conscience: The Contextual Fallacy

There is one last area in which the extensions of context affect us intimately. As Robert Smith's lighthearted, but by no means lightheaded, *Translations from the English* showed, a kid's context can be something else again. "I love you, Daddy," may principally mean that he wants a jackknife, "My stomach hurts" that he doesn't want to go to school, while "I want to go to the bathroom," said in bed, generally expresses a desire to sneak a last look at a television program.

Parents spend a good deal of time building up the conditioned responses known as conscience in a child. When they are faced with today's media, their task is even harder. The mentally mature make acts of identification in works of fantasy which are psychologically allaying, or pacifying. But this identification is not necessarily with a hero or other strong character. Men like Kris, Fraiberg, Sachs and Lesser have built up an impressive literature, the burden of which reveals that identification with a hero figure, far from acting as a defense against anxiety (as in Tarzan or Bond fiction), often causes the reverse effect. Such identification becomes a cause of fear, not relief, since the great hero (Hamlet, Othello or, to change gender, Anna Karenina) stirs up destructive forces.

Now the child is not mature, and in watching television material he does not automatically accept that happenings are consequences. His is still the world, very largely, of what psychologists call "shallow affects." The context here is still fairly physical, "apparent" rather than symbolic. Professor H. J. Eysenck, of the University of London's Institute of Psychiatry, early recognized that it scarcely matters if virtue triumphs in a TV drama, or a comic book, for a kid. It may be that the child will recognize the moral (CRIME *does not pay*); but essentially he is inhabiting a comfortable context, sitting in a soft chair or on a warm rug with a cup of cocoa in one hand, while human beings get macerated in front of him. If frequently repeated, this may be damaging to conscience, which is a questioning faculty. In actuality, there is nothing particularly

[12]Charles Edward Smith, "The Origin of a Term. Or, Jass Me for a Donkey," *Down Beat*, February 10, 1966, p. 24.

new about this observation; Lucretius made it in the first thirty lines or so of Book II of *De Rerum Naturae*. It's like watching a shipwreck from a distance.

When dictionaries break down the habit of context, they hurt human conscience. Three thousand new words are coined each year, and more in times of scientific invention; by now radio alone is said to have poured over five thousand words into popular use. Who has the context for these words? Mr. Mits can scarcely handle such dated discoveries as watts and ohms and amperes. There is a necessary terseness about these dictionary offerings which conflicts with the severity of their usage by our courts and government departments. If the whole myth-making structure of context gets lost we cannot see the form for the content. And it is of course form which winds back and holds at bay and informs with pattern the darkest and most threatening and taxing tragedies of the imagination.

It is by now a truism that the happy ending sidesteps reality, and falsifies issues. But it is not always remembered that context occasions this. Two pages of retribution at the close of forty-eight of successful violence in a comic book will achieve little more for the conscience of a child than the happy ending will for the wish-fulfillment reader under her hair-dryer. Parents are always being worried by their children's interest in the violent and/or morbid aspects of TV fare. They should not be. It is simple enough to identify yourself with Prince or Princess Charming, or Tarzan, or Sheena; this is subjective, it is looking in the verbal mirror. It is the ogres and demons threatening Prince Charming who must be of principal fascination since they exist outside the word—they are the world. (Notice a child's interest in gore when you next drive past an accident.) It is partly a question of context, that which Langer defines as the break between fairy tale and myth. The former is individual and personal (thus, "the fairytale is irresponsible"[13]). The latter (myth), even when treating similar material, is normally tragic. It takes life seriously, for life, alas, comes to an end. But, as any children's book editor will confess, fairy tales no longer sell. Only tales by fairies do.

The exhilaration one feels at the end of a great tragedy is the consequence of recognition, until we can feel in our bones Lear's "Pour on; I will endure." Richards is of great help in reminding us

[13]Langer, *Philosophy in a New Key*, p. 151.

of the whole "dramatic" human context. Imitative acts prove little. A mother kills her child after hearing on the BBC that a murderer has been executed. In America Frederic Wertham advances the case of a boy who killed his grandmother with a poison recipe printed in a comic book (Wertham's findings were hotly challenged partly because they were supposed to concern *children;* they would have been accepted more readily if that term had been changed to *deranged adults*). The British Moors murderers read de Sade. The imitative theory was "established" by the "Blazing Car" crimes, a German being executed in 1929 for murder by car arson, which was then copied by an Englishman in 1931, and by many others subsequently. Researching homicide in England, Louis Blom-Cooper writes:

> This theory of imitative crime gave way in recent years to the view that the reporting of crime was a "healthy outlet," and a "safety-valve." Far from wishing to imitate, the reader sat back in comfort, secure in the knowledge that it was others and not he who indulged in criminal activities.[14]

Surely Falstaff put to sleep forever the wish-fulfillment theory, in his self-identification with both the victim of a theft and the perpetrator of that theft at one and the same time. To steal a purse was, he assured us, to have a purse. Children, and deranged adults, naturally put a premium on those who excite rather than soothe them. It has been shown again and again that children's play is *not* imitative, it is only superficially so. From the earliest stages it is intrinsically symbolic. It is, parenthetically, for this reason that the regular repetition of the television commercial comes to the child as a relief; it provides a framework, and form, to contain the fantastic content. Early readers of both *Madame Bovary* and *Ulysses* complained that these masterpieces of construction were formless. Such is the contextual fallacy. The child is not amending his world, he is creating it, gazing with that wonder which made Ruskin write, in *Of King's Treasuries:* "There are masked words abroad, I say, which nobody understands, but which everybody uses, and most people will also fight for, live for, or even die for, fancying they mean this, or that, or the other, of things dear to them."

[14]Louis Blom-Cooper, "Murder: How Much Should Be Reported?" *The Observer,* May 1, 1966.

NINE

In short, society regards as 'true' those
systems of classification that produce the desired results.

S. I. Hayakawa,
Language in Thought and Action

TRIBAL TYPING:
THE CODE OF CLASSES

The Hierarchic Psychosis

Not long ago an unidentified object arrived at an American port
and came up for Customs examination. It was duly taxed on the
basis of the materials of which it was composed. The recipient of
this object, an American museum, complained that it had been incorrectly classified by Customs officials, since it was in fact a *work
of art*. And so the Supreme Court eventually decided. This repeat
of the Brancusi *Bird in Space* controversy of 1928 showed that Customs inspectors are not interested in art, only in what the courts
decide is art; that section of the US Tariff Act devoted to antiques,
for instance, classifies on existence prior to 1830, regardless of
whether the object might be art or a mundane household effect.

At about the time the Brancusi affair was creaking with
wasteful expense through the tax-supported courts, a young Oxford University undergraduate was trundling the large bass viol
he liked to play along the sidewalk outside his college. It was too
big to put in taxis and too heavy to carry, so he had affixed a wheel
at the bottom. The local police identified this item as a *vehicle*, and
the offending undergrad had to keep it off the pavement and affix a
taillight to it for use by night. In fact, when a New York lady inventor patented "motorized suitcases" in 1967, specifications called
for headlights and license plates.

Finally, again at roughly the same stage in the advancement of
our hypercommunicatory civilization, a lady of my acquaintance
was involved in a lengthy suit, initiated by New York's Finest, to

260

deny her custody of her pet puma. The cops complained that this was a *wild animal,* and thus illegally kept. They won their case, and killed the puma, despite my friend's attempt to convert her pet into a pet by clipping back its claws, filing its teeth, muzzling its mouth. This case anticipated one even more extreme, involving the attempted suicide of a Bronx barmaid who owned a pet jaguar. This distressed lady took an overdose of sleeping pills, collapsed and cut her forehead as she fell; the police found the jaguar overcome with grief and tenderly licking his mistress' blood from her face. Again, the jaguar was adjudged a *wild animal* by the law (and duly shot) although it was demonstrably less dangerous than the *pet* boxer in Wisconsin which had just nearly bitten a mailman to death. There was recently a case of a monkey getting itself unionized in Australia.

As with induction, the ability to build categories out of our complex environment is a form of harmony. For it is, of course, to see similarity in dissimilars. Like metaphor, it originates in a type of affection, or at least affectionate recognition. Such can be seen when kids are collecting things. Classifying lends consistency and relevance. As another control activity, it is built into our language. Our words show a constant specialization. Although there is a language change toward generalization, as in *butcher* (originally the slaughterer of only one kind of animal), or *pawn* (formerly a foot soldier), the narrowing of meaning from some generic class has been a prevalent development. Centuries ago both *harlot* and *girl* could be applied to either sex, while the word *wench* was so inclusive as to be applied to Christ in the thirteenth century. *Bitch* could also be used of men until quite recently ("The Landlord is a vast comical bitch," *Tom Jones*); the eight-year-old Marjory Fleming, whose diary was bowdlerized in 1864, "called John [her brother] an Impudent Bitch." *Liquor* and *corn* have both become specialized, as have *deer* (German *Tier,* originally for all animals) and *fowl* (as in Chaucer's *Parlement of Foules*). Another celebrated example of a class term being robbed of its original unity is shown by *virtue* and *virtuous;* as Stuart Robinson points out, it is particularly curious that these should be applied principally to women and their chastity when the original sense was closer to *manliness.*[1]

[1]Stuart Robertson, *The Development of Modern English,* 2nd ed., revised by Frederic G. Cassidy, Englewood Cliffs, N.J.: Prentice-Hall, 1954, pp. 234–245.

These collective terms were the results of cognitive acts, and cognition lends consistency; whereupon the classification becomes available for future use. Like Lou LaBrant's kid playing on his grandfather's lap, we learn to use this recognition of likeness in order to group buttons, and then bows, scarfpins and so on. You could tell my setter bitch that of the three posts visible from the window one is a lamp post and two are telegraph poles. For the dog, however, they are from here three virtually identical items. Rudimentary classification might take place in my setter's sensory system when at night one of the posts emits light, and the others do not. But for a human being the equivalents and dissimilars in the poles have already been collected into certain functional gatherings. I will not expect light to be emitted from the telegraph pole.

When we invent a class we assume a *quidditas* of equivalence, some special presence making two or more objects similar. This not only forms a function here and now, but makes possible future acts. Furthermore, the classifying technique is typically reflexive; for we can, of course, collect classes into classes. The Navaho evidently sorted everyone into a brace of basic typologies—witches and nonwitches. Both classes were collectable under the category *human being;* but in practice, for the majority of Navaho, the classification *witch* subsumed that of *human being,* rather than vice versa. In this way the labeled category tended to include itself, and formed thereby a logical contradiction, one which doubtless assisted in putting the tribe out of existence.[2]

It is particularly easy to see this at work in racial bias. One does not have to be a Russell or Frege to catch the cant in the incantations of our current vocabulary of race. When I first came to America I spelt Negro with a small *n.* In common with most Englishmen, I imagine, I had to be reminded by the exigencies of a different social situation that the term is a racial cognate, parallel with Caucasian. Asked my *race* on my first immigration forms, I am afraid I was somewhat at sea. I simply put British and hoped for the best. But would the Immigration and Naturalization authorities interrogating me have been able to tell me how many races there are? Or why all people with dark hair should not be considered a race? I understand the capital for Negro has now led to capitalizing the

[2]See Ralph D. Norman and Katherine L. Midkiff, "Navaho Children on Raven Progressive Matrices and Goodenough Draw-a-Man Tests," *Southwestern Journal of Anthropology,* xi:2 (1959).

euphemism *Coloured Gentleman* on official forms in England, where no less a personage than Denis Brogan made a craven public apology, in 1967, for writing Negroes without a capital. Will he now, one wonders, use a capital letter for Whitey?

The word is its world. We torture words by calling people frogs, wops, krauts, spicks, spades, chinks, hebes, greasers and the rest, and then torture the people concerned because they are frogs, wops, krauts etc. That words mean what we want them to mean is summarized in the headline from the San Francisco *Nichi Bei Times* (October 1, 1963) cited: "JAPANESE IN MOSCOW COMPLAIN, MISTAKEN FOR CHINESE, ABUSED."

There was a time in the southern states of America when Negro was used as cognate with white, or yellow, or what-have-you. But to say that someone is a black man, or a yellow man, or even a white man, let alone an egghead, is to muddle the category with the defining attribute of the category, in the disastrous manner mentioned. Much semantic capital was made out of this by Malcolm X. Nietzsche, so unrepresentatively represented in the minds of the young, was thoroughly aware of the pressure of these labels. In discussing the class aspects of vocabulary, Nietzsche wrote:

> The origin of the opposites *good* and *bad* is to be found in the pathos of nobility and distance, representing the dominant temper of a higher, ruling class in relation to a lower, dependent one. (The lordly right of bestowing names is such that one would almost be justified in seeing the origin of language itself as an expression of the rulers' power . . .).[3]

In short, is the human being I see in front of me a singer, a lawyer, a Communist, a ball player—or a Negro? At one time Paul Robeson would have fitted all these categories. To test the semantic potency of racial classes you could list a raftful of qualifications of a candidate for your company—married man, churchgoer, college graduate, house-owner, investor—and then toss in *Negro*, and watch the effect on executive responses. The denial of vote to south-

---

[3]This quotation is taken from *The Genealogy of Morals;* but Nietzsche's work is everywhere penetrated by a prescience of modern communications. There is an Abhandlung at the end of *Beyond Good and Evil* where we read, "To use the same words is not a sufficient guarantee of understanding; one must use the same words for the same genus of inward experience. . . ." A little later on he writes, "each word is a mask."

ern Negroes, and the formal deceit used to implement this denial, lay in this inconsistency. To cry "Are Negroes citizens?" as a tool for opening the polls was a logical fallacy, since in America *voters* and *citizens* are self-containing classes. To realize this identifies the true nature of the prejudice at issue, which could be briefly rephrased "Are Negroes *human beings?*"

An evidently careful article in front of me claims that Mao Tse-tung is sick. The writer suggests or reports that his successor will be Lin Piao, China's Defense Minister. Lin Piao had at this time just supplanted China's Head of State, Liu Shao-chi, as top-ranking party member after Mao. Lin Piao was rewarded for having foiled a succession coup by the now purged members, Peng Chen, Lu Ting-yi and Lo Jui-ching. On the other hand, perhaps yet other leaders are using Lin Piao as a "straw man" to ensure Mao's succession for themselves. In which case, the man to watch is Ten Hsiao-ping.

Now I can pronounce none of these names, and I suspect that to the average Anglo-Saxon politician they are all roughly *Chinese*. Reciprocally, a Cantonese paddy-field worker cannot be expected to differentiate between Johnson and Goldwater and Reagan, any more than between Wilson and Brown and Heath and Stewart. They are all vaguely *enemies*.

In brief, fiat classes reflect us to ourselves. As a technique, classification is a necessary response to the world about us. Even in its distortions it therefore shows the nature of our culture. The mirror image here is really this: on one side, the ability to single out similar intrinsic attributes; on the other, the use of these attributes as diacritica in our culture. It was put pleasantly by Coleridge when he wrote: "There are three classes into which all the women past seventy that ever I knew were to be divided: 1. That dear old soul; 2. That old woman; 3. That old witch."[4]

In common with inference, then, classification occupies a stratum of definition in our minds, and unless you can label, and infer, you cannot live a mature life. A part of your response to your environment will be blocked. Both are "transparent" activities.

---

[4]This is surely the source of Bertrand Russell's famous "irregular verb" conjugation, on a BBC "Brains Trust" program of 1948—"I am firm, you are obstinate, he is pig-headed." The *New Statesman* ran one of its self-consciously ingenious competitions based on this model, but in fact politicians surpass it daily.

Yet, in even the few examples I have given so far, classifying compels or persuades us by its nature to ignore the dissimilarities in equivalents. Politicians love rolling a couple of juicy generalizations into one. "Pornography," said Enrique Green, brother-in-law of Brazil's President, in August 1966, "is the real basis of Communist infiltration," thus agreeing with Congresswoman Kathryn O'Hay Granahan, Chair"man" of the subcommittee of Post Office operations, and instrumental in the conviction of Ralph Ginzburg, that obscenity is "part of an international Communist plot." Or again, "What's good for General Motors is good for America." Whenever a class winds up meaning more than it generalizes, it becomes another word about words, rather than a word about the world. Communists are all pornographers, we conclude, and Americans should all invest in General Motors, if they haven't already.

Such clinging to classes as themselves, as hierarchies, can be damaging to both personality and social fabric. Two therapists recount the case history of a neurotic boy, "Larry," enslaved by classification habits,[5] while the following cameo from the Chicago *Sun-Times* shows how our social semantic contrives to make damn fools of us in public:

> WASHINGTON: (UP)—The House voted Monday to make the word "wife" mean "husband" too—sometimes. It passed and sent to the Senate a bill extending to dependent husbands of women veterans the same pay and privileges given to dependent wives of men veterans. It was done by defining the word wife to mean husband, too, when that's necessary.[6]

Similar classificatory problems were raised in the 1963 Supreme Court *Empresa* case, a matter of international commerce. Should ships flying what are often called "flags of convenience" (e.g. Hon-

[5]Salvatore Russo and Howard Jacques, "Semantic Play Therapy," *ETC.*, XIII:4 (Summer 1956), pp. 265–271. Play therapy here, of course, included sorting into categories: birds and nonbirds, for instance. At one point the therapist had to reclassify himself as friend.

[6]Similarly the cow became a horse in India a few years ago, when an animal of the antelope family started causing widespread damage to crops. Farmers would not touch it because it was named *nehil gae,* or blue cow, and the cow is sacred to the Hindu. The government thereupon declared that the animal's real name was *nehil goa,* or blue horse, and so could be destroyed.

duras, Liberia, Panama) be subject to US labor relations when their crews were 100 percent American? If the vessel concerned had only the remotest connection with the flag nation, scarcely ever seeing its home port, was it in fact under the sovereignty of that nation? Here, in an application of Occam's razor, the law of the flag was nonetheless called on to prevail. But it was estimated, in March 1967, that the United States had more shipping tonnage flying foreign flags than flying its own merchant marine pennant.

The Constitution of "Things"

Unless we use it properly, then, a classification can turn into another fictitious entity—rather like Alice's flamingo. You will recall that Alice tried to use a flamingo as a croquet mallet and that every time she got the bird's neck set it would turn and look at her before she could hit the ball.[7]

So classifications twist in our grip since a category gives rise to a universal and human beings are genetically dissimilar. The short way of saying this would be that you can't really generalize about human beings. The long way would be that of medieval debate, which was occupied with the relationships between a class and its members as to whether, for instance, the former truly existed in the latter, or whether it was merely the sum of its component parts. Jules Romains' theory of *unanimisme* (now forgotten except as utilized by Sartre) was an attempt to show, chiefly through fiction, that a class had an independence of its own, that a pair of shoes, say, has aspects other than a collection of two shoes, one right-foot, one left.

We know that Berkeley challenged the triangle *in general,* not a drawn example. If I ask to see the landscape, you will show me trees, grass and perhaps a lake; but you have not shown me the landscape *an sich.* You can similarly show me various colleges and libraries and dining halls at Oxford, but you cannot show me the *university.* This is another way of saying that you have to be really profound to talk about nothing. Or as Jane Austen had a character in *Northanger Abbey* declare, "I cannot speak well enough to be unintelligible." To which the reply was returned—"Bravo! an excellent satire on language."

[7]The whole complex of classificatory systems as primitive perceptions of patterns is brilliantly evoked in Claude Lévi-Strauss' *La Pensée Sauvage,* now available as *The Savage Mind* (University of Chicago Press, 1966).

This path, of course, follows Platonic methodology and Christian inclination. The absolute is always superior to the individual. All chairs, that is, are replicas of the perfect Chair existing in the noetic place, or heaven. They may possess somewhat differing attributes, but they fit the major requirements of their class and reflect, therefore, some pure form of chairishness "up there." Christianity, taking God as cause, continued this metaphysic. We are all imperfect models of our "form."

Unfortunately this sense meets rebuff after rebuff at the hands of reality. The predictive power of language is annulled. Things . . . objects . . . may have an essential constitution, so that a twentieth-century Chinese peasant would just recognize an eighteenth-century French *chaise longue* as a "chair," i.e. as something on which to rest the body. Most of the chairs I have sat in during my lifetime have contained this requirement, however individually and/or eccentrically shaped. They have supported my sit-upon. But this trait is not really ancestral, inherited or derivative. It simply *is*. Things you regularly sit on are chairs. Chairs are not things you sit on. Robeson was a singing Communist lawyer. The reverse was not necessarily the case.

This is pretty crude, I confess, but to return to the poor lad wheeling his viol along that Oxford street. His musical instrument was not inherently changed by being called a *vehicle*. Nor did the addition of a wheel and rear light alter its ability to render Mozart. However, we should note that the man himself was changed. From being a musician he turned into a *driver,* and was doubtless subject to the usual penalties incurred by drivers for faulty lights and the like. But the norms of difference between a viol and a trumpet would be different for a musician than for a policeman, or an antique-dealer. Perception is based largely on difference, but difference is particularity, and the love of equivalence is spurred by the mind's appetite for particularity.

Coffee houses in Greenwich Village have been persecuted recently as *cabarets,* which have to take out licenses; and there have been threats of litigation as to where inner space ends and *outer space* begins. When the San Francisco Police Department Bagpipe Band wanted to give a public performance, they became *warriors;* local logic made it conveniently unnecessary for the cops to join the Musicians Union since the bagpipe was declared an *instrument of war.* (As Herb Caen put it in the SF *Chronicle,* "Has there ever been any doubt?") Here we see the indiscriminate, invidious and bureaucratic nature of that class inclusion to which our language is unfortunately predisposed, or perhaps into which it is forced. You can call a thing a different name, you can say that a tomato is a *fruit* rather than a *vegetable* when you want it to be that way, or that a *shampoo* has more of the characteristics of *soap* (and is thus exempt from taxation) than of a *cosmetic;* all these are so many social diacritica. You cannot create another *kind of being.*

In England the Inland Revenue differentiates, for the purposes of taxation, between *earned* and *unearned* income. It has frequently been pointed out that the item called *unearned* (e.g. dividends and the like) is often the result of savings from income earned by the sweat of one's brow, and converted into capital. Taxation classes form an area in which the canons of identification become altogether corrupted, and the class is quite arbitrarily institutionalized. The semantic of revenue services is very close to psychotic. The recent cases of Edmund Wilson, Joan Baez and others in this connection illustrate human resentment to being made into a fictitious entity. To be as efficient as a modern state strives to be is to be *in*human.

Blowing Verbal Bubbles

To continue to draw on musical misclassifications will perhaps most cogently show how we burlesque this language tool, or word wisdom, today. Until 1948 the American Federation of Musicians ruled that the harmonica was a *toy* (thus making Larry Adler a toy-player rather than a musician); by the same token, and by the bagpipe analogy above, S. I. Hayakawa has suggested that a comedy drummer who beats time on someone's head may be said to have reclassified the head as a *musical instrument*—as Alice tried to reclassify her flamingo a croquet mallet. Hayakawa's example is no more exaggerated than much modern reality.

In West Germany, as I write, classical music concerts can claim certain tax exemptions. In 1966 four judges attended an opening performance by the Beatles to decide whether Leonard Bernstein was right, that Beatles' music was "as pure and elemental as a Bach fugue." Similarly, more than one prizefighter has been denied the right to sing his national anthem in Madison Square Garden because he wished to accompany himself on a guitar—a famous case of a Buenos Aires heavyweight comes to mind, from late 1966. The Musicians Union successfully objected to his doing so.

This is fracturing the "word." It is saying what I have tried to show is impossible, or heretical, namely that a sentence is an inventory of names. It is claiming that Man + Guitar = Musician. In short, if you want a national anthem, hie ye to the proper local. When harmonica players became popular in the late forties, they were seen as a threat by the AFM, who suddenly decided that they were *musicians* after all.

In New York it is still obligatory to join a plasterer's local in order to practice the trade of set designer for the theater. This reminds me that, in his *The Folklore of Capitalism,* Thurman Arnold reported the instance of plasterers being held to be *miners* in a suit that had to go to a State Supreme Court, since one side in this quarrel maintained that scraping gypsum from the ground constituted the act of *mining.* Meanwhile, a tragi-comedy of self-inclusive classes is daily instanced in New York's huge municipal housing "projects." Here underprivileged families are allowed to have city housing, at controlled rents, provided that their incomes are under certain levels; but many of these tenants are employed as city workers—"sanitation engineers," and the like. Thus, when the city as *employer* raises their salary the city as *landlord* kicks them out of their apartment. Alice's Uncles could do no better.

All this is to claim that a collection of words, strung together, equals or has only the meaning of its own ingredients. It is like putting flour, yeast, cheese, anchovies, tomato paste into an oven and saying that the result will be a dish tasting of heated flour, yeast, cheese, anchovies and tomato paste—rather than a pizza. The point about word-wisdom is that combinations of words are harmonies, and jointly result in a meaning beyond what is severally accomplished by an addition, or putting together, of their component parts.

To say that the introduction of a guitar, or musical instrument, into any set of ingredients including a man infringes the rights (or category) of *musician*—this is pulling language about at will. More whirling words, or verbal bubbles. It might be argued that in practice this protects musicians. Such has nothing to do with my analysis. So might a blackjack. I am out to protect language. Boxer plus Guitar does not *equal* Musician. It equals something like boxer-musician, or perhaps some new and unnamable class. Or possibly no "class" at all. You cannot derive for the nature of man.

The *Soviet Military Encyclopedia* classifies the same basic operation—let's call it *spying*—under two heads; when they do it, the result is *military intelligence*, but when anyone else does it, the proper term is *espionage*. The techniques of simultaneous translation get strangely stretched at times.

Singing Heavyweights

The instance of the singing heavyweight disallows the classification of classes . . . that three or eight boxers can all be musicians, that there are such people as boxer-musicians. In this way classificatory recognition is held up, language is arrested as a tool of experience; we are told that there are only musicians, and only boxers. This lag is ridiculed in Swift's division of Lilliput into those who cracked eggs at the top (Big-Endians) and those who cracked them at the bottom (Little-Endians). But the lampoon appears as daily reality in our midst. The case of the monkey who, for "technical" reasons, had to be admitted to a union in Australia is to point; many of Camus' last stories (in particular, one about a union) were attempts to illustrate and arraign these stiffnesses of our semantic.

In their *How to Lie with Statistics* Darrell Huff and Irving Geis show how easy it is today to fall into fallacies of correlation, initiated by classing people. Thus, "milk-drinking English women get some kinds of cancer eighteen times as frequently as Japanese women who seldom drink milk." But further factors show that cancer strikes in middle age or after and, at the time of this study, English women were living twelve years longer than Japanese women. The tie-up between sexual indulgence and education, largely provoked by the researches of Dr. Kinsey, would be another case of the kind; in the New Hebrides it was once believed that body lice produce good health since "observation over the centuries had taught them that people in good health usually had lice and sick people very often did not." Lest the fallacies of such reasoning should seem too "primitive" to be with us still, let me cite the following case of overlapping classes that I turned up the other day in David A. Embury's excellent bar book, *The Fine Art of Mixing Drinks:*

It is true that more drinkers than non-drinkers suffer from cirrhosis, but that is merely because there are more drinkers than non-drinkers. By the same token there is more cirrhosis among right-handed people than among left-handed; more among people who eat three meals a day than among those who eat only one.

A man who can argue like this can surely, in the words of Miss Phyllis Diller, make radio taste like television.

With wearying persistence it has been remarked that two plus two does not equal four. Two peaches do not *equal* two lemons. One carrot and one turnip do not *equal* two college professors. The two-ness of the items either side of the equal sign is all that agrees, and all that mathematics asks us to agree as agreeing. Four of anything is a formal result of two two's, not an entity. It has been said that the sane man is he who says that two plus two equals four; the psychotic, or insane man, that two plus two equals five; and the psychoneurotic that two plus two equals four—*but I hate it!* "Bah, gentlemen," says Dostoevski's underground man, "what sort of free will is left when we come to tables and arithmetic, when it will all be a case of two times two makes four? Two times two makes four even without my will." Business is business, after all.[8]

Some semanticists try to help out here by using the terms *cognitive* and *noncognitive* as guides to our classificatory habits. Thus the only reliable classes are those that serve some cognitive purpose (or are "operational," in Anatol Rapoport's formulation); in this way words teach us perception. I have mentioned that numerous different words cover what for us is a single entity, in other languages: the favorite instance given is that Eskimos have some twenty different words for *snow*. (Lévi-Bruhl tells us that Lapps

[8]Cf.: " 'Businesses are organized and operated for the purpose of making profits. People organize, join and operate cooperatives to provide themselves with specific services without profit.' Exactly! Why then associate the word *business* with co-ops, and then be compelled to explain, to modify, to apologize, almost? Why not simply substitute *service* for *business* and eliminate the latter word from our vocabulary, just as *carrying charges* have replaced *rent,* and *cooperator* the term *tenant* in the lexicon of cooperative housing?" (from the Bulletin, or house organ, of a New York co-operative housing project).

have forty-one.) When the Bible was translated for Eskimos, it was found that they had no word for *sheep*.

On the other hand, Aztecs subsumed cold, snow and ice under a single word-stem. There are six thousand different Arabic words for camel, its parts and equipment. In Bassa, a Liberian language, there are varied terms for specific colors but only two for classes of colors. This in the face of the fact that there are evidently more than seven million discriminable colors ("the eye has none of the delicacy of the ear").[9] The Roman grammarian Varro discerned 228 meanings for the word *good*. The lack of generic classification here is far from being a symptom of semantic inability, it is a response to environmental needs.

After all, most of us think of snakes generically and, as in Lawrence's poem, we react with illogical hyperclassification to the sight of one.[10] More snakes are nonpoisonous than are poisonous, but you would not know this from city-bred classificatory habits. There is a snake in my Corsican garden, and when I was drawing water a week ago it slid across my ankle. It was not in the slightest degree *slimy*. Such habits, then, make us their victims, directly a class, arranged on a higher level of abstraction than any part whereof it is composed, is seen to carry more meaning than the individual unit, or the grouping of such individual units. *Snake-poisonous* goes our signal reaction. *Grass-snake-gentle-ecologically useful* might read the reaction of a cognitive classifier, such as an Indian.

In this connection, what one might call the "concretion" theory of classification seems to have been adequately put to rest by Claude Lévi-Strauss. The popular view (shared by McLuhan, among others) seems long ago to have been that "primitives" found difficulty in abstracting knowledge and thus were closely governed by immediate economic needs. Most semantic texts cite the Eskimos and their many words for snow as an example of a community verbally bound to organic necessity.

[9]McLuhan, *Gutenberg Galaxy*, p. 27.
[10]In fact, Lawrence seemed only half to understand the psychology of this phobia, attacking chiefly the Christian matrix for verbal *snake*. Yet the snake is an archetypal fear-symbol (one to be found in children all over the world); this fear is probably of man frightened by the specter of himself—that is, of his presymbolic self—the serpent being sensed as a hangover from another kind of being (see Ramona and Desmond Morris, *Men and Snakes,* London: Hutchinson, 1965).

In the first part of *La Pensée Sauvage* (literally, though inadequately, translated as *The Savage Mind*) Lévi-Strauss rebukes Malinowski on this score, and adduces much evidence to show that such tribes accumulated wisdom of a metaphoric or classificatory nature for intellectual requirements rather than simply for satisfying needs. "Classifying, as opposed to not classifying, has a value of its own, whatever form the classification may take."[11] Magic, Lévi-Strauss here reminds us once more, is far from being a stage in technical evolution, a rather charming curio of thought designed for organizing phenomena. It is, rather, "a sense complete in itself."[12] In its essential curiosity it is probably more balanced a procedure than so-called scientific method today.

To some extent, however, the cognitive/noncognitive approach is helpful, certainly in illustrating our idiocies in this respect. The methods for typing human beings on the documents that plague them so today are thought to be cognitive: age, sex, marital status, country of origin or residence, hair color and so on. Such are supposed to serve purely denotative purposes.

Yet profession has been dropped from the listings on US passports in the past years, though it is still required on the somewhat similar French *fiches* handed tourists in hotels. (The age listing has evidently also been considered for eradication since so many women falsify this in their applications: next to *Born* on all applications I now enter the word *Yes*.) Thanks to the ease of dyeing, hair color has become a fairly useless physical description, while even sex can be altered today. Sex tests for women athletes, officially initiated in 1966, provoked one British doctor to declare, "there is no definite line between male and female." Women can be found with testes concealed in the *labia major*, or outer vaginal lips. Are such women female? Medical panels, or juries, are now asked to make a "general semantics" decision here.

For age it would be more cognitive to give some description of the state of the jaw, which guides autopsy surgeons in the case of decomposing corpses. And it would be as cognitively irrelevant to ask a man his religion for an insurance policy as it would be to inquire his police record when putting him up for Boodle's or White's.

[11]Lévi-Strauss, *The Savage Mind*, p. 9.
[12]*Ibid.*, p. 13.

That is the limit of this approach. When I was admitted to a New York hospital a few years ago I was asked my religion. I realized now that I need not have answered, but I was not in a mood for philosophic debate at the time and duly mumbled something to speed the process. A priest popped into my room almost as soon as I came round from the anesthetic. Cognitively—my surgeon would have agreed—religion was inessential to my cure. We have seen case after case lumber through the courts in America, in order to maintain what is obvious to any semanticist, namely that classing devices of this nature are noncognitive and biased.

She is twenty-four is open to empirical testing. *She is spiritual* is not. We have watched Holmes' misuse of the latter. Sociological studies of the quality of GI's as students in college after World War II broke down because the category *GI* told you nothing cognitively except that the individual concerned had suffered a period of service. Again, the generalization had to include both sexes. Indeed, owing to such prejudices, women's organizations all over America have been working for the elimination of sex from car insurance papers and applications. They are saying that a qualification is being made over into an evaluation: namely, that *Mrs. Jones is a woman* (cognitive) is being surreptitiously converted into *Women make untrustworthy drivers* (noncognitive). In 1967 the Association of Assistant Mistresses met in London to decide, among other things, whether they still wanted to be called "mistresses." They decided not to change the term, even though some of the mistresses might have been *mistresses.* It is a fact that Army psychiatrists have found that soldiers whose fear attained neurosis were helped if they could change their emotionally noncognitive *I was a coward* to the cognitive *I ran away on such-and-such an occasion.* Stephen Crane's *The Red Badge of Courage* is an application of this.

But the insight is limited. You are still left with this social excretion, the fictitious entity. Suicide is suicide . . . only it isn't. The stock retort to the success of socialism in Sweden is that everyone is committing suicide there. In fact, the allegedly high "suicide rate" in Sweden is largely due to the honesty with which doctors there classify self-killings, and to the inclusion of euthanasic deaths as suicide in some cases. For emotional reasons, problems of stigma and so on, these would be put under other heads elsewhere.

An intern friend at a New York hospital explained to me how statistics there are shuffled to bring out a high percentage of hospital deaths when certain emphases are needed (for funds and the like), and to show a low percentage (as a demonstration of efficiency etc.); in the latter case, those who have died shortly after admission, or by accident or gunshot and so forth, are known as *ME deaths*—deaths that have to be investigated by the city Medical Examiner. Such deaths are not deaths. In the same way, venereal disease can be artificially increased—when the police want to crack down on prostitution, say—by resort to widening the classification of V.D. Mayor Lindsay rationalized a New York crime wave as "an increase in the number of crimes resulting from improved statistical techniques for assessing crime rate."

And a Plea for Tea

As Hayakawa pointedly puts it, society gets the classification that it wants. Or deserves. Words create their world. If you want to haul in a lot of hookers, you create them by definition, or diagnosis. Murder by warfare, remember, is an act of heroism. Unless, of course, like one pair of celebratedly unfortunate Americans, you bumped off a brace of men behind the lines in the sincere belief that such were your country's foes, only to find out later you had simply been used as private hatchet-men for some overpartisan "partisans," and to be had up for murder as a consequence. Moravia's *The Conformist* centers on this dilemma of political killing by misclassification. Compare also the following typical attempt to anesthetize by classifying:

> A peace rally turned into a violent clash between the police and demonstrators in Times Square yesterday. Forty-two persons were arrested. Several were injured. . . .
> The Times Square demonstrators began to gather about 3 P.M. They had printed instructions ordering them to maintain order and avoid violence. . . . A few of the marchers wore beards and were described by the police as beatniks.
> *(New York Times)*

In short—more pinko bleeding hearts.

The Swedish reformer Lars Ullerstam maintains that our classification *sexual deviates* is responsible for . . . sexual deviates. Animal experiments have shown that sexual "deviation" can be artificially provoked merely by overcrowded conditions—as in our cities. I would suggest that the same wordfact, or reflex, operates in the matter of adoption procedures, of abortion (or "removal of intra-uterine wart," as it has been called),[13] of gambling, atheism and youth drinking laws.

A murder case appealed to the House of Lords in 1961 rested almost wholly on a medical definition of the meaning of *drunkenness*. This case, which was fully reported in issues of *The Lancet*, is far too complex to condense here, but it concerned the question of diminished responsibility and the sense of the famous McNaughten rules. A drunk man killed his wife and it was a problem of deciding whether he was drunk, purely and simply, or insane at the time, due to the liberation of a quiescent psychopathic condition by the alcohol. In England you are arrested for being *drunk and disorderly*, the sense of which is that you are a danger to your fellow citizens, which you are not when *drunk* (e.g. in front of your fireplace at home); recently a pacific drunk was judged *drunk and disorderly* in private because he had a car key on him. Similarly, we now try to reclassify alcoholism as a *disease*.

The *Kinsey Report* demonstrated that New York State still classified *divorce* out of the statements of Jesus Christ, thereby creating all sorts of unreal situations as well as stepping up the traffic to Las Vegas. To contrive adultery artificially in order to square with purely Christian tenets for dissolution of a marriage is to atrophy the New Testament itself. Not so long ago students at Columbia petitioned the university to recognize certain Jewish holidays; their request was reviewed, but rejected on the grounds that Columbia was first and foremost an American university and America was a Christian country. How the latter view can be maintained in any meaningful manner is hard to discern. Even in England, a far more fully Christian country, less than one in five adults attend church regularly. Finally, there was that nice case involving Helen Hayes, who retired from a show because she was going to have a baby. The producer closed the play and met the

---

[13]"There is no such thing as a 'good' abortionist. All of them are in business strictly for money" (*Look Magazine,* August 14, 1962). Including the gynecologist who terminated the pregnancy of the Crown Princess of Japan a few years ago? Note the Churchillian use of the term *abortion* in the passage of invective cited. And see "An Impolite Interview with an Abortionist," *The Realist,* no. 35 (June 1962), pp. 14–20. There was a similar interview with an abortionist with a CCNY degree in *The Village Voice* at this time.

objections of Actors' Equity Association by claiming that mother-hood was *an act of God,* and thus let him out of the contract.

This sort of tautology has been brought abruptly into the fore-front of the public imagination in the matter of drug addiction. Presumably, by definition, everything is a drug in a drugstore. In-cluding the packets of peanuts and light bulbs and babies' diapers you can buy there. Of course, when supermarkets and delicates-sens want to sell aspirin, pharmacist associations wail and the result is that in several states aspirin is classed as a *drug.* In Eng-land *The Lancet* has called repeatedly for the removal of mari-juana from the list of dangerous drugs, asking that it be given the same status as alcohol, than which it is demonstrably less harmful, as shown by Mayor La Guardia's investigating commis-sion years ago.

As long as the Narcotics Bureau, however, keeps up its alarmist vested interest in all *drugs,* just so long will vaguely ancillary crime and sickness be roped into the classification concerned. If you treat heroin addicts like the most dangerous of criminals, the organized underworld is obviously going to create itself around the issue. And if you treat a user of marijuana as identical with a user of heroin, the two will begin to act alike. This is a law of language. It is for this reason that a more relaxed classification will probably come only if and when control is shifted from the Treasury Department's Bureau of Narcotics to the Department of Health, Education and Welfare, who would supervise pot under its Food and Drug Administration. Meanwhile, in England at any rate, they can still ask you across the counter, "Do you want tea or tea?" Since marijuana is, in fact, sometimes brewed in real tea, it may become *pot-in-the-pot,* or even *T 'n' T.*

Gentlemen, Players and Citizens

The Aristotelian *genus* can be said to be operational, in Rapo-port's sense of that term. It helps us to recognize, remember and live. Science proceeds by overthrowing accepted categories and deducing new ones. Paracelsan medicine rejected the suspicion that the sick were sick because they were wicked. According to one eminent scientist the wheel was invented by dissociation of mechanical structure from animal form, i.e. by classing the two separately. The unified field theory in physics was a very satis-factory generalization, indeed. Freud forged a measure of control over psychoses by redirecting them to differing origins, rather than lumping them together under a single snake-pit class called *madness*.

J. Z. Young writes: "The word atom or electron is not used as the name of a piece. It is used as part of the description of the observations of physicists. It has no meaning except as used by people who know the experiments by which it is revealed." Alfred North Whitehead put it another way: "The greatest invention of the nineteenth century was the invention of the method of invention." It is here that General Semantics can be of definite service in the teaching of science, in insisting on the human capacity to clothe present classes in future classes or mount to, as it is sometimes called, a "higher" level of abstraction. All too often the Chemistry lesson simply teaches one that a hydrogen atom is made up of one electron and one proton as so much information to feed back in a quiz. As Anthony Standen suggested in *Science Is a Sacred Cow:*

> an official pronouncement may be made in some form of words that *sounds* as if it had a meaning, such as "The cell is the fundamental unit of all life." Anyone can learn and remember this statement, and if ever you undergo a quiz in biology, that is *the answer*, it is what you are supposed to write down. And yet what does it mean? If the cell is a unit, in the sense that bigger things are made up of it, this only means, all over again, that living organisms are made up of cells (except those that aren't). But if the cell is a *fundamental* unit, what does "fundamental" mean?[14]

The Platonic notion of universals reflected a desire for certainty and permanence in a changing and often hostile environment. The human being affronts this tribal typing on a variety of levels. The technicalities involved in classifying an object as *boat* or *ship* are singularly other than those involved in determining whether a certain cricket player was a *gentleman* or a *player*; for until 1962 British cricket so discriminated, classing an amateur as the former and a professional as the latter. The two had an annual match at Lord's. Both sides played. "Shamateurism" in sports is, of course,

---

[14]Anthony Standen, *Science Is a Sacred Cow*, New York: Dutton, 1958, pp. 96–97 See in this connection Wilfred F. Croft, "General Semantics and the Teaching of Science," *ETC.*, xvii:4 (December 1960), pp. 440–448.

quite famous now. The compensation given to amateurs in certain sports is far above that given most professionals a few years ago. The average Russian athlete could not begin to qualify as an *amateur* by most Western distinctions. Indeed, the West has had to retaliate in kind in order to compete on an even keel, the 1960 US Olympic team being documented under various heads (shot-putter Davis being classed as a writer), though of course this clash came up years ago over Jim Thorpe.

As a principle of identity, classification is nearly always likely to become generalization in the human domain. The similars and dissimilars here are too equivocal, and often indissociable. As Kenneth Burke well put it, "correlation depends upon the place at which our concepts draw the line between merger and division." As you step up generalization, you blur this line. A man is born a man, finds himself a member of a certain race, a citizen of a certain country. But what does *citizenship* mean? Thomas Mann tried several in his lifetime, including Czech, but it did not alter his sustaining characteristics, it merely showed man's inhumanity to Mann. These days *statelessness* is a synonym for inexistence.

In 1966 a Wisconsin woman learnt that she had been Irish most of her life. For in 1919 she had married an Irish alien living in the United States and, under a law in effect from 1907 to 1922, any American woman married to a foreigner took on her husband's nationality. The lady divorced, and supposed her citizenship restored when the law was repealed. But the State Department saw otherwise. As I have said above, *citizen* and *voter* are cognate classes, yet this Irishwoman had voted continuously in America since 1922, since local election officials also assumed her status to be what she herself assumed it to be.

Thus all human labelings are likely to be unsatisfactory, and labels which have arisen in recent years, like *egghead, exurbanite, beatnik*, are hasty blanket terms that reveal more about the state of feet of the labeler than anything. Tight shoes were responsible for *beatnik*, as probably much abstract expressionism. New York firemen came under fire recently since it was found that many of them were making more than double their salary in other, out-of-hours occupations. One student I know drives a cab all night. Is he a *student* or a *taxi driver*? Or a *student taxi driver*? Or a *taxi-driving student*?

The class of *models* took on somewhat suspect overtones, largely owing to the nature of the publicity given the Pat Ward/Mickey Jelke case, and in England the term *model* has been even further abused—so that a *New Statesman* cartoon could depict a prostitute undressing in front of her client and saying wearily, "My dream was to be a model, but I didn't make it, so I had to be a model."

In America a pregnant woman cannot collect unemployment insurance benefits, because to do so she has to be able to work. It would seem, then, that such a woman could logically pick up unemployment disability insurance. But again, to be *pregnant* is not to be *disabled*, although officialdom has just effectively said that it is! The courts have here stated that a woman who is *not able* is not a woman who is *disabled*. (They kick out Bertrand Russell yet!) And so it goes. The defense attorney for a famous sexual felon in Boston in 1967 suggested that his client was not a human being at all but a "completely uncontrollable vegetable." Am I a *teacher* or a *writer*?

The revenue "services" decide such matters annually. The Peter Cheyney case in England, involving among other things the ability of an author to *retire* (something Maugham was constantly trying to do), was only one of many that illustrated how bureaucracy is by its nature destined to defeat logic when dealing with human beings. Taxation, treasury, postal, customs, "welfare," immigration—such departments are more likely to be consistently inconsistent than otherwise in their attempts to pigeonhole us all.

An hilarious, albeit chastening, article by a friend of mine, John Rosenberg of Columbia's graduate English staff, well illustrated such idiocies, in reciting the auditing of a *teacher* who was also a writer.[15] John filed claims for educational expenses incurred in the acquisition of the Ph.D., which degree was necessary for tenure rank. After three years of prevarication Internal Revenue decided that he was a temporary employee taking courses in order to get a job he didn't have. This made his expenses an at-

[15]John D. Rosenberg, "A Matter of Motive," *Harper's Magazine*, 223:1335 (August 1961), pp. 71–73. Veblen saw how subject to classification-phobias even teachers (who should know better) were, when he observed in 1918, "Professors refuse to join unions or engage in collective bargaining because of a feeling among them that their salaries are not of the nature of wages and that there would be a species of moral obliquity implied in overtly so dealing with the matter."

tempt to get a *new* post, and thus disallowable, and disallowed. He maintained that he already had the job and would long ago have lost it if he hadn't taken the courses, which he was asking the government to deduct. He was, however, informed that in the eye of Internal Revenue he was not yet employed and, after wavering in the classification of *unincorporated charity* (thanks to unpaid learned articles) for half an hour, he was saved by the bell of financial motive. He had written some articles for possible renumeration and so could be considered a *professional writer*.

Dickens' Office of Circumlocution, in *Little Dorrit*, or Gogol's Person of Consequence, pales beside such Kafkaesque semantic. Its tergiversations are self-generative, and Parkinson's Law becomes a fact. There are officials in our official departments being given time off to fight their own departments. (That's how fair they are.) This is the very mesmerism of word-wisdom. It creates a climate in which the individual cannot live. The words themselves have power over the dice. Witness this gem, from the British National Insurance Act of 1964 (1st Schedule, Part II):

> For the purposes of this Part of this Schedule a person over pensionable age, not being an insured person, shall be treated as an employed person if he would be an insured person were he under pensionable age and would be an employed person were he an insured person.

"You Savvy Disfela Man?"

A few years ago a Chinese gentleman left Communist China on a ferry for Hong Kong. In Hong Kong he was detained on account of some irregularity in his papers. He was shipped back to the Communist mainland. But by this time he had incurred sufficient residence on British territory to make him ineligible for "repatriation," and he was accordingly bundled back on the ferryboat again. Here he was forced to stay for many months, now in Classification No. 3, that of ship's passenger, neither country accepting him and the boat going nowhere else. Finally, after his many fares to and fro, his money gave out and the irate skipper tossed him over the side where, being unable to swim, he joined his fourth classification, that of the dead.

This true fairy story also pales beside the persecutions suffered by groups of luckless individuals (with us often "Oriental") whom bureaucracy finds it can abuse by means of classification. Quite recently that tireless liberal Pearl Buck discovered some five hundred Chinese who had overstayed the terms of their admission into the United States, and who were being shipped back— not to China (who would not take them), but to Holland. The basis of this crazy classification was that they had entered the country from Dutch ships, thus had to be removed on Dutch ships, to Dutch territory, though none of them had ever been to Holland in their lives and had no desire to repair the omission. (One is reminded that Joseph Conrad built up his requirements for British citizenship largely by service on British ships, viz. British territory.)

As Miss Buck here pointed out, "The situation is analogous to a Chinese seaman on an American vessel which he deserts in another country. Would the United States at the request of that country agree to the deportation of such a Chinese seaman to the United States?" You can bet your life it wouldn't. In truth, the ruse seems to have been little short of old-fashioned press-ganging, a method of finding cheap labor for the Holland-America Line, since the five hundred Chinese were offered the alternative of an Amsterdam prison or a ship's galley. The case of the nine tailors was no less cruel an abuse of classification.

In 1942 the US State Department imported from Peru nine Japanese tailors, to be followed by other South American Japanese, in the hopes of exchanging them at the time for valuable Americans interned in countries then occupied by Japan. Actually, the nine tailors remained in the United States, moving from one "Nisei" camp to another, and when their use expired after the war, so did the Federal Government's interest in them. They were told they were to be deported to Japan on account of having entered the country without proper papers. An ACLU lawyer in San Francisco won reclassification for them, however. After much delay, and official cynicism, he got Washington to consent to their deportation to Peru. But by now Peru refused to permit their re-entry. It was only in 1954, after more than a decade of constant litigation, that the tailors were permitted to apply for permanent residence in the United States.

Such Alice-in-Wonderland injustices bring home how low on the social scale, in America at least, the Far Eastern races have been classified. The vicious Fu Manchu stereotype has done its work and we are reaping the harvest of what Harold Isaacs, in an impressive study of American images of China and India, calls "scratches on our minds"—hate-fakes of another world, in movie, comic strip, fiction.[16] For much of the past two years the widely syndicated *Buz Sawyer* strip has been set in Vietnam, with our hero happily making "napalm strikes" here, there and everywhere: the *Sergeant Rock* comic book was rather worse—and if it is true that the napalm for American operations in Vietnam was partly made in Japan, reality itself becomes a horror-comic.

Built into the contempt for "Orientals" of such media—and perhaps responsible for it—is a ridicule of their verbal habits, usually via pidgin English. It is sobering to reflect that Chinese is today spoken by more people as a native language than any other, and it is likely, now that the Latin alphabet has apparently been preferred to the Cyrillic for eventual alphabetization in China, that this majority will increase. Forty percent of the Chinese population is under eighteen. (In passing, I might mention that pidgin English is authentic Business English, the term being taken from the difficulty Chinese had in pronouncing the word *business*.[17]) You could also argue that the "Oriental mind" is one of the last in our time not to see the acquisition of money as the solution to the problem of identity or, rather, to fail to see freedom in financial terms. Alas, there is relatively so little travel to these maligned and suffering countries that the world is wrenched off its word, and the equivalents by means of which a classification is honestly built up cannot be discerned. The "yellow devil" mentality is called crudely into the service of American idealism, and even General Semantics has been vilified as an Oriental cult. As Hayakawa has put it, "Since Buddha, Confucius, General Tojo, Mao Tse-tung, Pandit Nehru, Syngman Rhee, and the proprietor of the Golden Pheasant Chop Suey House all have 'Oriental minds,' it is difficult to know whether to feel complimented or insulted."

[16]Harold Isaacs, *Scratches on Our Minds,* New York: John Day, 1958. During the Korean war comic books became hysterical in this xenophobia (see the illustrated section dealing with the same in my *Parade of Pleasure*).
[17]The expert on pidgin is Professor Robert A. Hall, Jr. See his *Pidgin and Creole Languages* (Ithaca, N.Y.: Cornell University Press, 1965). John J. Murphy's *The Book of Pidgin English* (Brisbane, Australia: W. R. Smith and Paterson, 1962) contains some delightful pidgin Shakespeare.

Yet it is no good pooh-poohing this issue. Such classifications determine our destinies. As I write, *lawlessness* in the South means civil rights demonstrations, while in some circles defending the Constitution equals disagreeing with the Supreme Court. Is HUAC fighting *un-American* activities or supposed *Communist* activities?

In a particularly incisive article written before the Middle East hostilities of 1967, Leo Hamalian showed how useless the racial class *Arab* is today. When Damascus Radio and Cairo's "Arab Voice" scream about "Arab unity," they are doing little more than stirring the shifting sands of local prejudice. The only Arab unity in this sense, or non-sense, seems to mean something like *anti-Israel unity*. The appeal is to a mentality that classes all Jews as Zionists (i.e. that cannot class).[18] When Mike Wallace interviewed Hussein Fahmy, supposedly no ignoramus but a leading Egyptian Minister, part of the exchange went as follows:

Fahmy: ... How is it all the key posts filled by the head of your Supreme Court are filled by Jews only?

Wallace: What jobs are you talking about?

Fahmy: All the jobs filled by the head of the Supreme Court, a Jew.

Wallace: The Chief Justice of the United States is Earl Warren, former Governor of California, who is not a Jew. There is one Jew on the Supreme Court today, Justice Frankfurter.

Fahmy: Well, I spoke—I am told ... but there have been studies ... I can send you some references. There are several judges who have written literature about it. There are several army officers, navy officers, who have written. You have one of your Undersecretaries of State for War who is a Jew and Zionist. I think she and her brother or her husband were condemned to death as spies.

Wallace: No, no, no. Anna Rosenberg was Assistant Secretary of Defense in the Truman Administration. But

[18]A hate-absolute of this nature can veer at will. During the 1967 hostilities Cairo's "Arab Voice" broadcast: "The United States is the enemy ... Israel is the United States, and the United States is Israel. . . . Here, Arabs, dig graves everywhere; dig them for every U.S. existence. . . . And so the pirates, the blood-suckers of peoples, the criminals of the 20th century, have joined the bands of outcasts, the scum of the earth, against the Arab people."

the Rosenbergs who were convicted were other
people, no relations.
Fahmy: No relation?

(New York Post)

No, but their names ended in -berg. And the attitude in war.

In fact, as Leo showed before reality did in 1967, the "Arabs" hate each other almost as much as, if not more than, the Israelis, with the Iraqi and UAR despising the Syrians, Syrian Baathists in turn loathing the Iraqi, and more or less everyone using the word Lebanese as an insult. The British were undoubtedly mesmerized by their own classification, or misclassification, Arab, suggesting as it did a largely inexistent national identity among eighty million people of neurotic dissimilarity. Indeed, their one supposed equivalent—religion—breaks down on inspection, Lebanon's Christian community being as high as 48 percent and that of Syria 25 percent. These communities themselves subdivide into Greek Orthodox, Roman Catholic, Syriac, Armenian and so forth.[19] Their one actual equivalent, language, also breaks down since if anyone who speaks Arabic as his native tongue is an Arab, then such are a large number of citizens of Israel. Sixty-five percent of the faculty of the American University of Beirut are "Arab."

In cases like these the distortion is once more caused by political convenience. We want Arabs to be . . . well, Arabs. Chinamen, chinks, are some fictitious entity out there. Statutory definitions of a Negro in some southern states made this classification apply to anyone with one-eighth of African blood. This is practically classifying by a dissimilar, since the other seven-eighths might be totally disparate. In 1966 Sandra Laing, a dark-skinned South African girl, was classed as coloured (i.e. of mixed-race descent); in July 1967 she was reclassed as white. In filling forms legally requiring such discriminations one might enter C. This can stand for Colored or Caucasian.

It is like calling someone a spick. The term is usually reserved for Latins, South Americans and the like; it derives from the pidgin, I no spik English. The laws of language make it equally applicable

<hr>

[19]Leo Hamalian, "The Muddle East," Issues, xix:3 (Autumn 1965), pp. 24–31. I would myself venture to observe that the current phrase Arab-Israel conflict is illogical: the terms are not cognates. Israel is a substantive surface of soil. Arab is an epithet with extremely blurred connotations.

to the banana businessmen who *no spik* Spanish, or Portuguese, in South America. By the same token we are all *dagoes*, or Jimmies, since the word comes from the Spanish Diego. Despite John Huston's casting choices ("I'm shooting it as if I were in the presence of God"), Adam and Eve were almost certainly black, since the human species is believed to have originated in an African area of high sunlight. Genesis makes no reference to race and is as ignorant of melanin skin content as children in playgrounds. Guys are chaps and spicks are greasers.

It might be emphasized, too, that the word *white* did not carry *primary* skin-color connotations, or any particular racial theory, in the minds of many British colonial administrators. Orwell noted that Gandhi "did not think of people in terms of race," though today Gandhi is largely lauded as a racial liberator. E. M. Forster's character Fielding, a teacher in India, "did not realize that 'white' has no more to do with a colour than 'God Save the King' with a god." At the end of *A Passage to India* Aziz and Fielding, Indian and Englishman, are enjoying a friendly discussion, when "something racial intruded—not bitterly, but inevitably, like the colour of their skins." Forster's parenthesizing adverbs are all-important here —*not* bitterly, but inevitably. Forster is simply remarking that skin color is an inevitable, something we are born with, one of several determining agents (or what he calls "rhythms"), such as sex and age, which are part of our world.

In the same way, the man Conrad's Marlow last sees "white from head to foot" is not a racial digit. Lord Jim is a man discovering a quality. There is, in fact, a chasm between Hindu and Moslem in the Indians of *A Passage to India* (as in India of the time) as wide as that between Indian and Englishman, or among Leo's Arabs. Forster's Aziz, for instance, keeps on wishing that Hindus didn't remind him of cow dung. Note, too, the emphasis placed on the native foster mother in Kipling's *Kim.* "These be the sort to oversee justice," says the old woman accompanying Kim and the lama (of future local administrators). "The others, all new from Europe, suckled by white women . . . are worse than the pestilence." Orwell observed that "the phrase 'lesser breeds' [in Kipling's *Recessional*] refers almost certainly to the Germans, and especially the pan-German writers." Current British movements like CARD (Campaign Against Racial Discrimination) and RAAS (Racial Action Adjustment Society), largely led by Michael de Freitas, or Michael X (or Abdul Malik), would seem to be lodging a grievance, no doubt a legitimate one, against the world rather than a word.

The Labels of Prejudice: Ethnophaulism

Racial bias is a pathological symptom, and language can be forced into its service. It was Wittgenstein's greatness to direct us to a proper understanding of our language, and thereby the relation of word to world. Pathological manifestations have a mesmerizing effect, and all sorts of silly saws are embedded in our metaphoric vocabulary as a result of xenophobia.

Thus an *Indian giver,* in America, is someone who retracts his gift; to play a dirty trick in French can be *faire une chinoiserie,* in Polish *oszwabic* (to do a Swabian), and so on. On a *Dutch treat* you pay for yourself. In baseball a *Chinese homerun* is a foul behind the plate, while in cricket a *Chinaman* is a googly, or "wrong 'un." French leave, in English, turns roughly into *filer à l'anglaise* across the Channel, while another example of Anglo-French rivalry is found in the famous *French letter,* which in Paris and elsewhere in France becomes *une capote anglaise* (or just *une capote*).[20] Sicilian for prostitute is an *Englishwoman. To put English on the ball* is similarly loaded with national mistrust, and Noah Jacobs, who supplies a list of antinational epithets and phrases,[21] remarks that a *Dutch wife* is "a poor bed companion." In the Malaya (FMS) of my youth a Dutch wife was a bolster that planters and others in very hot areas placed between their legs at night in order to reduce perspiration. Currently in New York to be *on c.p. time* is to be idle, since c.p. stands for *colored people* here and presupposes them lazy.[22] Calling people frogs or krauts has been dubbed ethnophaul-

[20]In *Ulysses* Bloom makes several references to French letters, or contraceptives. The sleeve of the Caedmon recording of part of Bloom's Nausicaa soliloquy suggests that Bloom is here referring to continental correspondence!
[21]Jacobs, *Naming-Day in Eden,* pp. 60–68.
[22]Of course, Negro itself is ineluctably ethnophaulic; although arriving from Spain it has become a distinctly American word carrying with it an accumulation of inferiority; for this reason recent groups have found *Afro-American* more positive in connotation, thus initiating a style for supposedly African-like accessories (pierced ears, and the like). Actually, the word *Negro* simply means black, whereas Africa may carry more derogatory connatations—*a fero* = from a wild place (Partridge). One has to know a little bit more about language than most politicians, white or Negro, before one indicts the English language as a carrier of racism. One of Langston Hughes' Simple stories, "That Word Black," shows how odium is attached to a word rather than existing in the language system ("When it came down to the unlucky ball on the pool table, the eight-rock, they made it the *black* ball. So no wonder there ain't no equal rights for the *black* man")

ism, and is nowhere more delightfully kidded than in the conversation Twain stages between Huck and Jim, when the latter learns that the French talk another language:

> "Looky here, Jim; does a cat talk like we do?"
> "No, a cat don't."
> "Well, does a cow?"
> "No, a cow don't, nuther."
> "Does a cat talk like a cow, or a cow talk like a cat?"
> "No, dey don't."
> "It's natural and right for 'em to talk different from each other, ain't it?"
> "Course."
> "And ain't it natural and right for a cat and a cow to talk different from *us*?"
> "Why, mos' sholy it is."
> "Well, then, why ain't it natural and right for a *Frenchman* to talk different from us? You answer me that."
> "Is a cat a man, Huck?"
> "No."
> "Well, den, dey ain't no sense in a cat talkin' like a man. Is a cow a man?—er is a cow a cat?"
> "No, she ain't either of them."
> "Well, den, she ain' got no business to talk like either one er the yuther of 'em. Is a Frenchman a man?"
> "Yes."
> "*Well*, den! Dad blame it, why doan' he *talk* like a man? You answer me *dat!*"
>
> (*Huckleberry Finn*, Ch. xiv)

Much the same ribbing is given this prejudice by Gogol, whose Zhevakin is asked to describe Sicily. He replies that oddly enough they never heard a single word of Russian there: "Just take the common man there, some filthy fellow that carries about all kinds of stuff on his neck and just say to him: 'Give me some bread, good man,' and he won't understand you—I swear to you, he won't. But tell him in French! 'Dateci del pane' or 'Portate vino' and he'll get it for you, sure enough." We are not far here from the contemporary tourist shouting his own language in the belief that to do so will make it more intelligible.

A new edition of a British dictionary is said to be omitting any ethnophaulism from the definition *Jew* (having previously included, as a verb, *to cheat, to outwit*). In fact, if *Dutch courage* and *French leave* are left in, this condescension should properly be opposed by Jews. But the religious classification is one of the most noncognitive of all, nearly a contradiction in terms. The true horror of the Orwellian National Data Center proposed in Washington, with its computerized bank of dossiers on every living American, is that at a flick of a switch it will regurgitate petrified classifications—grades, military service, prevous convictions, religion, race —*on the same level* of cognition. The exposure of personal details is one thing; riding roughshod over word-wisdom is another.[23]

The Wondering Jew

In summary, then, we have seen that classification is a name for a relationship, an equivalence. This projection or attribution is a necessary sophistication of consciousness. There is a satisfaction in classifying. It is an integrative act. We have only to watch a child adding to its collection to see this. A native of Zambia, we are told, cannot readily understand a film about Senegal, since he cannot sufficiently generalize his experiences to do so. Thus by classifying we are exercising a properly human faculty. In *Art and Illusion* E. H. Gombrich stresses the appeal made by a painting on the basis of what I would call its pictorial zeugma—that it is at once what it depicts and also the brush strokes that depict it.

The discovery of these patterns is the learning of significance, but this word-wisdom becomes a mere hallucination unless it is grafted securely on the world. We hypnotize ourselves with absolutes—Arab, Negro, Jew, Democrat, Tory—and have repeatedly to remind ourselves that these are often "invisible men." After all, we are all *natives;* yet in 1964 Hardy's *The Return of the Native* was temporarily banned in South Africa because of verbal connotations in the title. As a matter of fact, Hayakawa has suggested that one way to avoid anti-Negro prejudice is to act as if it didn't exist, until there is firm evidence that it does.[24] Living in an inter- and

[23]"The truth is, of course," editorialized the New York *Daily News* only a few years ago, "that it's a toss-up whether Hitler, Roosevelt or Stalin was the most to blame for the present upset and hate-filled state of the world." This might be called assassination by classification.
[24]S. I. Hayakawa, "How to Be Sane Though Negro," *Contact I*, 1959, pp. 5–20.

multi-racial co-operative, I can endorse his view. Actually, Haya-kawa's thesis here is not dissimilar from the evidence given in Bruno Bettelheim's *The Informed Heart,* already mentioned. Bettelheim shows SS extermination as enforced suicide. Saul Bellow puts the shift of classification very beautifully, I think, in one of those touching early works of his, *Dangling Man:*

> meanwhile I had the confirmation of people like Mrs. Harscha for my suspicion that I was not like others but (and I now know that it is an old belief and at the heart of what we call "Romantic") that I concealed something rotten. And perhaps it is world-wide, such a conviction, and arises because we know ourselves too well to accept the good but, rather, embrace the bad opinions others have of us.

The classification of someone by religious faith, then, presents peculiar problems. There are more than two hundred and fifty separate and autonomous religious cults in America, so that the celebrated separation of church and state celebrates in fact a dissimilar, the right to be different. Here the common association (the national classification) is the security of the differing. This is our premise. "We do not think that individuals should be alike," wrote Russell in *New Hopes in a Changing World.* "We conceive society as like an orchestra in which the different performers have different parts to play."

Such a state *must* be secular. The national association must be an entity apart from its component parts, for the very equivalence here—the sought similarity on which the class is based—is itself a dissimilar. (Or, if you like, a similarity of dissimilars.) Thus the introduction of special privilege—by, say, the Catholic hierarchy—will distort and destroy this equivalence of dissimilars. Russell's theory of *orchestration* has in fact been found to be a broad unifying principle in such classes, since this kind of *Zusammengehörigkeit* preserves differences rather than liquidating them by some process of osmosis. This was brought home a few years ago in the celebrated case of Brother Daniel.

Teaching in a predominantly Jewish college (to the life of which both Russell and Ayer have, incidentally, made notable contributions), I found this case to have a boringly familiar ring in student ears. The subject was well worn, and could not be calculated to set the Bronx on fire. There is no *official* penalty for being Jewish in the United States, as there was in Nazi Germany, with the result that the semantic of prejudice comes to be analyzed very closely, even expertly, when it appears. As Russell wrote at the conclusion of the passage just cited, "The State is, for us, a convenience, not an object of worship."

Born Oswald Rufeisen in Poland, Brother Daniel was a Jewish war hero in Nazi-occupied Poland and fled to a Catholic convent when betrayed within the Polish underground (allegedly by another Jew). After the war he entered a Carmelite friary near Haifa, and eventually petitioned the Israeli government for citizenship, under the Law of Return giving every Jew the right to migrate to Israel. The Israeli High Court denied his claim. It did so, deciding that the Law of Return is secular and that a Jew is not simply classified as such by a religion, race or ethnic stock, but rather on the basis of a common historical experience, or *Zusammengehörigkeit.* Togetherness. In the words of Judge Moshe Silberg, "we do not sever ourselves from the historic past and we do not deny the heritage of our forefathers." This symbolic bond was, then, to be considered the equivalence factor.[25] Daniel, an apostate, had broken this bond. "Jew and Christian," said Judge Silberg, "are two titles that cannot be combined into a common subject."

But of course they are—in America. So are Jew and skeptic, in such famous instances as Jews Louis Brandeis or Albert Einstein. What, moreover, of the fanatical Neturai Karta sect, of the congregation of the Lubavitcher, who live in Jerusalem but fail to recognize Israel? In fact, in the very case of our wondering Jew, Brother Daniel, Judge Silberg stated that the priest well might have been considered a Jew in Rabbinical courts! What of the case of Israeli Justice Haim Cohn, whose resignation was all but forced from his country's Supreme Court a few years ago when he married (in Manhattan) a divorcee, and by doing so violated the nature of his name? Cohns or Cohens are considered by the pious as descendants of Moses' brother Aaron and the first hereditary priests, or *kohanim,* of Israel. They are forbidden to marry either harlots or di-

[25]This factor is almost the only one *not* found as within the "characteristic features of religion," in the list prepared by William Alston, a Michigan professor, to show that "When a cultural entity exhibits all these features to a marked degree, we have an ideally clear case of religion, as with Roman Catholicism, Orthodox Judaism, Orphism" (Alston, *Philosophy of Language,* p. 88).

vorcees (or, presumably, any combination of both). What's in a name, indeed?

In truth, the Brother Daniel affair hashed over old ground. B'nai B'rith had put out a pamphlet series with the title *What Is a Jew?* years before it, while some claim that the classification *Judaist* was coined to take care of just such difficult cases as those I have instanced, notably by permitting skeptical Jews to be Jews, if not Judaists.[26]

Once again we see that the labeled category cannot contain itself, and the inclusion of dynamic human relations in religious ossifications often gives rise to an identity that simply isn't there. Leo Hamalian, a great teacher, will start a class on classes by drawing a circle, or a square or a series of dots on the blackboard, saying, "That's a Jew," or "That's an Arab." He is recently confirmed by a French Jew, Georges Friedmann—"Where anti-Semitism fades, Jewish specificity tends to disappear. . . . Where it survives, it expresses itself and desires to express itself only in religious forms." The rider to this approach might be the persuasion of writers like Leslie Fiedler and Bernard Malamud that we are all Jews.

This notion has also become pretty clichéfied by now, but it was convincingly suggested—in the selection of heroes by Joyce, Kafka and others—that the intellectual community of the West was heading for an alienation which the Jew already knew on the racial level. The equivalence factor was there. More, Leopold Bloom's warm bed and cozy kitchen contrasted with the cold prejudice and hostility of the outside world in a widely symbolic way. The ghetto was virtually preindustrial (as Albert Memmi has dramatized it), and the goy world "outside" was sensed as tough, cold, sequential and technocratic.

The religious class cannot by its nature obey the logic of social relations in America. It must remain a fictitious entity, for a similarity is no more than a quality of other qualities and—as the Israeli High Court hinted—other courts . . . other findings. A Chinese Jew might be held to be more Jewish than a Jewish Jew, were the diacritica to be set up appropriately. In *The Black Jews of Harlem*

---

[26]See Horace M. Kallen, " 'Jew' and 'Judaist,' " *The Jewish Spectator*, November 1962, pp. 7–8. The American Council for Judaism appears to balance the proponents of that classification which would make of all Jews, presumably even of Arabic Jews, automatic supporters of Israel.

(Glencoe, Ill.: Free Press, 1964), Howard Brotz shows the use of the classification for social purposes alone. He argues that Negro converts to Judaism are basically manifesting intraspecific revolt, that of separating from other Negroes.[27] Whether this is the motive or not, the real test for such fallacies of class comes when you introduce atheism into the debate. Here all the agreed dissimilars—chaplets and synagogues, swinging incense and broken glasses—have to give way. The self-consuming nature of a religious classification is shown up for what it is, the whole paraphernalia repudiated. At this point the tolerant authorities break down. You will not find officialdom conceding atheism as an answer to religious category on government forms; but if you are allowed to believe, you should be allowed to disbelieve. In fact, the Constitution so suggests.

Prejudice literature is bound to thrive when the cognitive nature of the classification is low. Pound, Wyndham Lewis and Eliot all exploited the fictitious nature of this enemy-entity. Writers are especially sensitive to words and England has never really had a large enough Jewish community to threaten the conventional stereotype of their presence. For a poet, Pound was singularly uninventive in his anti-Semitism, merely continuing continental bias and coining a few phobia symbols like his well-known *Jewspapers*.[28] Céline was altogether sharper.

In *From Shylock to Svengali: Jewish Stereotypes in English Fiction* Edgar Rosenberg discriminates between the British heritage of traditional imagery, with the Jew as Christian enemy or villain, and a consciously evaluated attitude. Thus he would refer to Lawrence, Wyndham Lewis and Ezra Pound as "conscious anti-Semites." But Evelyn Waugh and Graham Greene ("who publicly defends the Jews in his radio broadcasts while peopling his novels

[27]See also: Carey McWilliams, *A Mask for Privilege: Anti-Semitism in America*, Boston, Mass.: Little, Brown, 1948; John P. Dean, "Patterns of Socialization and Association between Jews and Non-Jews," *Jewish Social Studies*, xvii:3 (July 1955), pp. 247–268 (replete with tables); Geoffrey Wagner, "The Classical Revival: A Dossier of Anti-Semitism," *Chicago Jewish Forum*, 12:4 (Summer 1954), pp. 207–212.

[28]This stale ideogram—that all major Western newspapers are in the hands of Jews—has a long history; it was featured in particularly emphatic form by Alphonse Toussenel over a century ago. Despite the fact that no Jew serves on the board of more than one British paper, the *canard* dies hard. It is resurrected again in John Beaty's 1951 *The Iron Curtain over America.*

with odious Jewish characters") are not necessarily anti-Semitic. For Waugh and Greene—one could surely add C. S. Lewis' fantasies—the Jewish villain is conventional, a cultural inheritance.

This seems to me specious. Greene's Colleoni, in *Brighton Rock*, is a consciously imagined character in an evaluated social situation. You cannot make words lightly. After all, François Mauriac's novels are not peopled with anti-Semitic grotesques and, stereotype or evaluation, such alignments usually add up to the same gas chamber in the end.

The religious class, then, is now so overspread with content as to function more as an adjective than as a noun. I have suggested that a *white man* is not a man who is white so much as a "white" man, a man with certain qualities called "white"—cf. the term *yellow peril*.[29] This can be seen when we try to inflect certain of such attributions—e.g. the feminine Jewess, Negress. In *The Nature of Prejudice* Gordon Allport remarks that we do not say *Protestantess*. We have seen that for a leading Egyptian the suffix *-berg* acts as instant disqualification. When language is used as laxly as this, you can pour any ingredient into the well of the bias modifier at will.

For this is the formalized madness of dividing the animal kingdom into *Aryan* and *non-Aryan;* Krum Heller, German Ambassador to Mexico in the last war, hoped to seduce the Mexicans by telling them they were really Nordics, having migrated south by way of

[29]See L. L. Brown, "Words and White Chauvinism," *Masses and Mainstream*, 3, 1950, pp. 3–11.
Compare, also, for cross-classifications: "The WHITE man's present insane refusal to recognize the basic importance of RACE can only result in his own extinction. He is being exploited and his TAX money is used to support and encourage a NEGRO WELFARE STATE, for the benefit of that race, which is rapidly OUT-breeding the WHITES, largely at the Whites' expense . . .
HELP!
Our American Birthright,
Christian Heritage and our American
Way of Life need your active DEFENSE.
USE AND DISTRIBUTE
FIGHT COMMUNISM
Stamps
200 for $1;   1000 for $2
"The use of these stamps is an easy and inexpensive way to STAND UP AND BE COUNTED. Their use injures or embarrasses no other than tools of those of evil influence, communists, anti-anti-communists, traitors, dual loyalists, fellow travelers, one-worlders, gullible stooges (including educators and churchmen, male and female) . . ." (American Birthright Committee, Los Angeles, Calif.).

the Bering Straits. This is the lunacy of Robert Welch of the John Birch Society calling Dwight Eisenhower "a dedicated and conscious agent of the Communist conspiracy." Xenophobia turns into moral duty, patriotism into bigotry, and in *The Scourge of the Swastika* Lord Russell of Liverpool can show a plate of an SS thumbscrew, on which is proudly stamped the name of its maker.

A side-effect of this semantic, unbelievable outside any insane asylum unless it had actually happened, was the blanket inclusion of Protestantism in Jewishness; this was evinced on a number of occasions but at no time more shrilly, perhaps, than by Alphonse Toussenel in his *Les Juifs, rois de l'époque: histoire de la féodalité financière* of just over a century ago. Both Protestantism and Jewish aspiration being revolutionary, "*Qui dit Juif,*" screamed this "thinker," "*dit protestant.*" Charles Maurras said the same, and Wyndham Lewis seemed perfectly happy with this paroxysm-as-classification. We meet, finally, the sometime Mayor of Vienna, the well-named Karl Luger, who used to declare, "I myself decide who is a Jew."

In 1922 the British actor-manager Seymour Hicks published a book that became extremely popular, called *Difficulties.* Among the "difficulties" was the question of how a "gentleman" should deal with a Jew. Classification came to the rescue. Scared for a second that he might be considered a pro-Semite, Hicks warned his public: "I am not going to discuss with you the Polish or Russian Jews. I know nothing of them and don't particularly want to: all of them are ugly and most of them smell. You and I are only concerned with the Jews of the British Empire." The Protestant-Jew syndrome was another case of such semantic misrecognition: among the Indians of the southwest United States an animal was man's rival when its behavior was like his own, his enemy when it was the reverse.

In fact, the term *Puritan* in early seventeenth-century England was evidently, to a considerable extent, another hate-absolute, something not altogether unlike our *red.* One can certainly substantiate that it was used this way, while there is a case for supposing that in Shylock Shakespeare was expressing the ethos of minority Puritanism of the time, of the busyness type mentioned above.[30]

[30]"The money-lender appeared an arrant individualist, disrupting for his own selfish purposes the traditional relationships of a hierarchical society founded upon the laws of man's nature. Shylock . . . is the spirit of that economic self-seeking which is indifferent to the welfare of others, stultifying

Shakespeare showed his knowledge of the role of cognates in classification, in Shylock's famous speech:

> I am a Jew. Hath not a Jew eyes? hath not a Jew hands, organs, dimensions, senses, affections, passions? fed with the same food, hurt with the same weapons, subject to the same diseases, healed by the same means, warmed and cooled by the same winter and summer, as a Christian is? If you prick us, do we not bleed?

Finally, one is reminded of Harry Golden's Jew who, visiting the South, swung on a crowd of urchins staring at his long black coat and curly earlocks—"Vot's de mattah? Hevn't you ever seen a Yenkee?"

The semantic of prejudice deserves, and has had, a library to itself. I have treated it here as one aspect of classification, of man mocking his own ability to generalize.

But if meaning is a function of use and the status of classification depends on what people do with it, then language itself will burlesque its burlesque. Indeed, it does so here, in a figure I have mentioned briefly, namely the zeugma.

Zeugmas and Spoonerisms

A zeugma is the bringing together of disparates in grammatical unity. You could call it a clash of classifications. One frequently cited in dictionaries is: *I took my hat, my coat and my leave.* "What meal do we have in the morning?" the teacher asks Johnny. "Oatmeal," he answers. If someone is hit over the head and comes out of hospital *two weeks and seven stitches* later, you have a zeugma. Blondie calls to Dagwood, "How much longer are you going to stay in the tub?" Dagwood answers, "About five chapters." Asked to an orgy by a dissolute group of Parisians, Voltaire is said to have given such a good account of himself that they invited him again the following night. But Voltaire declined. "Ah no, my good friends," he said with a smile. "Once a philosopher; twice, a pervert."

Of course, metaphor itself is a pun. Our language is constantly

those whom it possesses and oppressing the rest of humanity. Jewishness, Puritanism, usury are only incidental; this spirit is what is universal in him" (Paul N. Siegel, "Shylock the Puritan," *Columbia University Forum,* Fall 1962, pp. 15, 17).

getting stretched out of true in odd shapes of this nature. A *shot* is a shot, but also a measure of liquid at a bar. A *reefer* (deriving, acc. Mencken, from Mexican Spanish *grifa*) is a double-breasted sailor's coat as well as a marijuana cigarette. A *fin* is a five-dollar bill, a *pony* twenty pounds in England (and a small glass for liquor in America). *Eighty-six* means sold out in the restaurant business (*thirty-four* is the same in the shoe business). Apart from the use mentioned, *skinning* is sometimes applied to sorting mail in a special way. *Goat* and *passenger* are yank and limey poor players respectively. In physics *power* is the product of the voltage and the current and the angle between these two; in chemistry *reduction* describes a lowering of valence of a radical. One could continue indefinitely. All language infringements of this sort will naturally arouse attention and, as a critic of British advertising writes, "a reader has to find some mode of interpretation which will reconcile a seeming incompatibility of meaning" (e.g. a recent English ad, "In the best circles washing machine is pronounced Parnall").[31]

Inclusion of disparates under the same modification is the word's criticism of its world. A burlesque producer protested that all of his strippers were *covered*—by insurance. When asked to what *family* the whale belongs, Johnny answers, "No family on our block has one." A drunk stumbles after a screeching fire engine, hits a lamp post and shakes his fist at the departing vehicle—"All right, keep your damn peanuts." Another emerges from the subway and says to his friend, "Gee! I was in some guy's cellar. And did he have a set of electric trains!" Tommy is found talking to his pet rabbit. "Two and two?" he keeps asking. When invited to explain by his mother he replies, "Teacher told us that rabbits *multiply* rapidly, but this dumb bunny can't even *add!*" "I'm sorry," says the dentist to the waiting patient. "I can't give you an appointment today. I have eighteen *cavities* to fill." And he reaches for his golf bag. A cartoon shows husband and wife emerging from either side of their car, one with golf clubs, the other with a shotgun—"Bet I get more birdies than you do." DRAFT BEER NOT STUDENTS is a zeugma.

Meanwhile, the infinite wife jokes, most of them a last legacy from medieval antifeminism, are based on this double modification which presupposes that you classify a wife as a "wife." "Friend of

[31]Leech, *English in Advertising*, p. 179

the groom?" asks the usher. "Don't be ridiculous," comes the answer. "I'm the bride." "There goes that woman Bill Pearson is in love with," says the husband from the window. "Where?" His wife drops everything to take a peek. "Idiot! That's his wife." A warning sign on an overcrowded golf course reads: *The wife you shave may be your own*—but this is really a spoonerism already. I well remember the numerous Flanagan and Allen variations on the old wife chestnuts:

> *Slim:* Who was that lady I seen you eating with last night?
> *Jim:* That was no lady. That was my knife.

These widely disparate juxtapositions are imported into advertising in an effort to startle. The dissimilarity must be as farfetched as possible, to provoke the necessary paranoia. Paradox, said Wilde's Mr. Erskine, is truth "on the tight rope," truth turned upside down. The Wildean epigram contrived to reverse utility, the sacred cow of the time, in order to reveal what really went on— "Punctuality is the thief of time," "Nothing succeeds like excess," "I can believe anything, provided that it is quite incredible," "The tragedy of old age is not that one is old, but that one is young," "The only way to get rid of a temptation is to yield to it," and the famous "Nowadays people know the price of everything and the value of nothing." Wilde certainly showed himself a semanticist when he wrote, "The man who could call a spade a spade should be compelled to use one."

Unfortunately Wilde created a cliché out of this inversion itself, so that the audience tends to await the classificatory strategy. Yet these are replicas of serious social situations; the classification *mother* is frequently used to arouse emotion and condemn criticism, though it presumably includes murderers, like the late Elizabeth Duncan, who hired assassins to bump off her pregnant daughter-in-law.

Sensitively used, this contradicting of usual habits of linking can say a lot about both society and the state of man's soul. T. S. Eliot's so-called spatial form,[32] the concatenation of periods and places in

---

[32] See Joseph Frank, "Spatial Form in Modern Literature, Part I," *The Sewanee Review*, 53:2 (Spring 1945), p. 225. Eliot's most famous zeugma, perhaps, was to spread the evening out against the sky "Like a patient etherized upon a table."

head-on collision throughout *The Waste Land,* is one telling example of this sort of zeugma, and highly reminiscent of the same in Pope. When Belinda plays flippant cards in *The Rape of the Lock* and we read, " 'Let Spades be trumps!' she said, and trumps they were," we get both parallel and parody of God's creation of light in Genesis. Byron generally handled this kind of comic echo more crudely:

> But ah! he died; and buried with him lay
> The public feeling and the lawyers' fees.
> (*Don Juan,* i, 34)

The same sublime-to-ridiculous pratfall is effected over and over by Flaubert, as reality's corrosive corrective to romance. When Léon is enslaved by his passion for Emma, in the latter portions of the masterpiece, we read that he admired "the exaltation of her soul and the lace on her petticoat."

It was on such contradictory contexts that Kant, Nicole and (to some extent) Bergson based their theories of humor. Kantian "incongruity" was a zeugma. The man runs for the bus and falls flat on his face in the gutter. This makes us laugh in that we contrast two modifications in one: (a) man sitting warm and comfortable in friendly surface transit system, (b) man lying in gutter and swearing at banana peel. Saul Bellow's Henderson is described as having a face like Grand Central. It was really for this reason—a mixture of serious and silly—that Dr. Johnson found some of Shakespeare's puns so shocking.

The zeugma was thus the basis of Dada. Here the inverse of utility which produced humor for Wilde was taken to extremes. "To compare two objects, as remote from one another in character as possible, or by any other method put them together in a sudden and striking fashion, this remains the highest task to which poetry can aspire." So wrote André Breton, and, though the doctrines of surrealism and Dada vary, nevertheless a fur-lined teacup was the putting together "in a sudden and striking fashion" of two disparates. Further, the result defeats or contradicts the function for which a teacup was formed, and in which it is classed. What it is is no longer what it does. The same was true of the upside-down urinal, a favorite at Dada exhibits and usually placed over the entrance, of the spiked flatiron, and of limp watches (the inverse of mechanical precision). The extent of its shock was Dada's only criticism of reality. For it arose at the end of and after World War I and, as André Gide put it in a knowing analysis:

What! While our fields, our villages, our cathedrals have suffered so much, our language is to remain untouched! It is important that the mind should not lag behind matter; it has a right, too, to some ruins. Dada will see to it.[33]

In *The Philosophy of Rhetoric* I. A. Richards demonstrates that actual distance of fetching conveys no especial merit to the metaphor. It is perhaps true that remoter things, when joined, create a greater tension than nearer things; but that does not guarantee a finer ordering action in the metaphor. Richards makes a comparison with the bow, whose string is the source of energy for the shot and which we can stretch very tightly. We can still miss the target. Dada was not art. And today, the soft washbasins and sculptural sight gags of Robert Rauschenberg and Claes Oldenburg are mild fare indeed, all set for eulogy in *Life*, rather than ridiculing life. They have to do, rather, with fashion and some of them are not far removed from the excremental joke shops along Broadway, or in Soho. As Irving Babbitt put it, "Nothing is more tiresome than stale eccentricity."[34]

As a matter of fact, misclassification in such matters was made into a focal (if fecal) scene in Miller's *Tropic of Cancer*, when an Indian boy misclassifies a bidet.[35]

[33]Dada did see to it, of course, not only by drawing the letters of a poem out of a hat, but by sensitive techniques for punning on sound and sense by writers like Raymond Roussel, whose metagrammatism united phonetically similar and lexically disparate elements to produce weird effects, in the manner of *Geschichtsklitterung* mentioned.
[34]The following story is not bad Dada, more especially since it actually happened:
At the height of the Christmas rush in New York a befuddled matron wandered into Womrath's bookstore.
"Is this Scribner's?" she enquired of a clerk.
"No, madam," was the reply. "This is Womrath's."
"Oh," said the lady. "I saw the sign Womrath's on the window, but I thought it might be Scribner's."
[35]"There is nothing like a debate over a bidet to bring all the hidden creatures of the libido dancing nakedly forward into the open" (Donovan Bess, "Miller's 'Tropic' on Trial," *Evergreen Review,* no. 23 [June 1962], p. 12). This article provided a curious case of literary schizophrenia, since the same author dismissed the same book exactly a year before in a *San Francisco Chronicle* review which concluded: "It does not merit the inches of newsprint spent on it here."

The Indian didn't get the "pun." One boy introduced to his first bidet imagined it just made for sailing toy boats on. Similarly, the button craze that swept America in the sixties contrived to criticize hypocrisy by reliance on zeugma ("CURE VIRGINITY"). Subway graffiti in our cities have long parodied ads in order to ridicule shibboleths ("You Don't Have to Be Jewish to Oppose the Vietnam War" and "Where's Oswald Now We Need Him?" were two I saw on the Columbia University station walls in 1967). Buttons became personal graffiti, protesting from lapels and shirt pockets that "GOD IS ALIVE in the White House" or "AMERICA has gone to POT." Reactionary attitudes were killed by context, banana highs kidded. In this way students wore sarcasm as part of their person. "We don't serve niggers here," said the racist southern restaurant-owner. "We wouldn't eat 'em if you did," was the reply he received.

Indeed, paradox, irony and the like—particularly of the New Critical persuasion—can largely be regarded as potent antisyzygy, sudden shifts of context. Antisyzygy derives from Greek *union of opposites*, and thus belongs more to oxymoron, but the expression "Caledonian antisyzygy" (to express the varied Scottish *Geist*) has been employed, by those ranging from Professor Denis Saurat to Hugh MacDiarmid, as a kind of mental Dada. There is an agreement to regard a symbol as covenanted to one set of ideas, or level of abstraction (in *The Waste Land* Cleopatra or Dido equals Heroic Love); then by verbal sleight it is associated with another (in the same poem, the sordid love of a contemporary typist). This gets vulgarized into the zeugma—"I'm sorry, Boss, I need a raise; my wife's voice and the food prices are rising." Dr. Johnson was offended by eccentric and recondite coincidence of images in the metaphoric vocabulary of the metaphysical poets and, though to-day's taste inclines us to consider Dr. Johnson wrong in this case, he was, I think, right in keeping his eye on the whole target, on word-wisdom.

From zeugma one moves naturally into inventions and inversions depending on some similar misclassification, often simply verbal. Ogden Nash, famous for modern macaronic verse, made a lot of money out of developing the so-called clerihew. This was named after Edmund Clerihew Bentley, who only died in 1956 and who specialized in rhyming biographies, so:

> Alfred de Musset
> Used to call his cat Pusset.

Puns, which are obvious biclassifications, arouse little more enthusiasm in me than this sort of thing, though Bennett Cerf is indefatigable in his affection for them. (If for every pun I said, I should be pun-i-shed, where can I find a puny shed, in which to hide my pun-ished head?) The celebrated "Cerfboard" is an unpleasantly present compendium of classification crossword puzzles, in which the alert reader is he or she who switches the tracks of categories most quickly. In advertising, too, puns are all too with us—"You Auto Buy!" came out during a Detroit slump, "Garters—All Thigh-zes" not long after, while the triviality of much contemporary church wisdom was evident in one pastor's advice to his flock, "Be the soul support of your children."

One subvariant of the shifted classification joke is the spoonerism, named after a Dean of Oxford's New College, William Spooner (1844–1930). *Shook a tower* is a spoonerism for took a shower, a *blushing crow* for a crushing blow. The true spoonerism has to form other words. And this kind of pun is perhaps more interesting because more oral. After all, you have to *see* "sole" in the "soul" of the example above. *May I sew you to another sheet?* does more than a mere malapropism, then, for it spoonerizes inebriation.

The Girls' *Bum and Droogle* Corps, inadvertently announced at one college, made another telling instance since it described the reality in uneuphemized terms—I am taking it that *bum* is here heard in the British sense. Julian Huxley quotes his choicest spoonerism as coming from the good doctor himself, when suddenly losing his clerical headgear in a windy Oxford street—*Will nobody pat my hiccup?* I well recall Gilbert Ryle delivering a withering *reductio* of such absurdities at a meeting of the Christ Church Twenty Club in my rooms at Oxford, during the course of which he accused his opponent in debate, Hugh Trevor-Roper, a fox-hunting buff, of *Tally-Ho'sis*.

My own favorite, however, is the famous moral appended to the story of the African potentate who hid his valuable throne in the thatching of the roof of his kraal, only to be kay-ohed by it when one day it fell through—*People in grass houses shouldn't stow thrones.* Inventing spoonerisms ought to be much more fun for children than parsing Latin syntax, and would teach them principles of word-wisdom, too. For within the spoonerism Noah Jacobs well distinguishes the *chiasmus;*[36] and this word inversion—

---

[36]Jacobs, *Naming-Day in Eden*, p. 135. This gets produced by misprint. A British Forces paper in the last war wanted to refer to a famous senior officer

some coeds pursue learning, others learn pursuing—is a little model, or maquette, of language reflex.

One can add a final footnote to the spoonerism by alluding briefly to the classificatory nomenclature for animals—a *pride* of lions, a *muster* of plover, a *covey* of partridge and the like. Some of these get particularly fancy, and practically produce their own self-spoonerisms, e.g. a *watch* of nightingales, a *wisp* of snipe, a *cete* of badger, a *plump* of duck. The stress is on formation of another entity, or class.

A director of laboratories in Santa Clara, Calif., has come up with some excellent coinings in this rank: a *joint* of osteopaths, a *nursery* of obstetricians, a *stream* of urologists and a *plague* of administrators. His best work, however, concerned the classification of a group of streetwalkers (euphemism! euphemism!), thus: a *flourish* of strumpets, a *peal* of Jezebels, a *jam* of tarts, an *expanse* of broads, an *anthology* of pros and the very nice a *pride* of loins.[37] I confess I myself once inadvertently introduced Pamela Hansford Johnson to an undergraduate audience as a "female Trollope."

The much-derided *Time*style is really not more than an extension, or exacerbation, of British donnish humor of this nature. Although the anonymous pens of *The Times Literary Supplement* regularly sneer at such semantic acrostics, I have lately seen in that journal "Eliot-wise and Pound-foolish" as well as "sophomoriac" (in review of a work by Mauriac), and "Nothing to Lose But Your Keynes" (May 11, 1967).[38] There was also "Up Hill, Tell Tale" (December 23, 1965), reminiscent of the similar spoonerism of Hugh Trevor-Roper when reviewing, for the *Sunday Times*, a book co-authored by the Oxford Marxists Christopher Hill and Edmund Dell—" up Hill and down Dell."

---

in England as *a battle-scarred veteran*. It came out as *a bottle-scarred veteran*. In apology they tried once again, but the Italian printer once more confounded them, publishing *a battle-scared veteran*. Truth is, indeed, stranger (stronger?) than reality.

[37]Seth L. Haber, "A Plethora of Words," *Medical World News*, December 3, 1965, pp. 158–159. Haber also gives: a *stand* of salmon, and a *mekhaya* of lox, the latter term Yiddish for what can roughly be translated, with loss, as pleasure. But I am not convinced of the originality of all his examples; his *anthology* of pros, for instance, is attributed by John Moore to "a well-known Divine" (Moore, *You English Words*, p. 263).

[38]One cannot overgeneralize about *TLS* notices. McLuhan's reviews there are fairly easy to spot partly because he seems to think this irritatingly know-all *Time*style is the proper "medium" for his "message."

These are fringe benefits of our habits of classification. In forming a class we summon at least one characteristic that is the same for all members. All birds grow feathers. This rests on a probability factor (a bird may be born that does not grow feathers). I have attempted to show that empty classes inhibit our word-wisdom, and result in "intensional orientation," or talking to ourselves.

So we have examined in this chapter cases of classificatory rigidity. And perhaps the most fascinating and compelling finding in the long and brilliant survey of "primitive" classifying habits, given in Lévi-Strauss' *The Savage Mind*, is that "*the principle underlying a classification can never be postulated in advance.*"[39] For "the savage mind," or way of thinking, that is, "nature is so constituted that it is more advantageous if thought and action proceed as though this aesthetically satisfying equivalence also corresponded to objective reality."[40] In a way, you create your reality by classifying it. Such is the mode of mythical thought. When tax and customs and police inspectors employ classifications, however, they do so in the reverse intention—by postulating *in advance* what the class is, and then claiming that you fall into it.

Finally, before passing on to the wider class of the forbidden as a last "transparent" activity, it would be as well to bear in mind the words of Justice Holmes on the subject—"the chief end of man is to frame general propositions, and no general proposition is worth a damn."

[39]Lévi-Strauss, *The Savage Mind*, p. 58 (original italics).
[40]*Ibid.*, pp. 15–16.

TEN

"Denis, I do love you. I've never felt like
this. Don't tremble so. You're not frightened,
are you? Denis. tell me, how many girls have
you had?"

He withdrew his lips from her cheek but
did not otherwise move. "How many—how
do you mean?"

"How many girls have you made love to,
been to bed with?"

"None."

Iris Murdoch, *The Unicorn*[1]

TABOO: THE FORBIDDEN TREE

Sacred and Obscene

A few years ago an enterprising West German marketed a toilet
paper, rather appropriately called *Adios*. For a while the product
sold pretty well. Then (as reported in *Der Spiegel* for March 14,
1962) it was brought to the attention of the Bishop of Munich, who
protested violently. A less sacrilegious name had to be, and was in
fact, selected. I confess I found his protest paradoxical at first, but,
generically, what the Bishop said about the sacred and the fecal in
his objection was that they are both exceptional. And exceptionally
exceptionable, i.e. nonutterable.

Not to say something "transparent" is a stage before the litotes
or ellipsis touched on in my first part, since here it is intrinsically
assumed that what you don't say is a message tacitly known (take
the reluctance expressed by writing *G-d*). A fairly simple instance
might suffice.

The so-called lavatory or toilet is a euphemism taken from
French *toile*, and so used, knowingly, by Pope. It has never been

[1]Cf. "Yossarian was in love with the maid in the lime-colored panties because she seemed to be the only woman left he could make love to without
falling in love with" (Joseph Heller, *Catch-22*).

verbalized in polite discourse as the place where men and women excrete. In recent US TV it has been called the *bath bowl*. Rolls Royce had to rename their Silver Mist model in Germany because German *Mist* is shit.

At first thought there is nothing overcomplicated about this. One's privacy is involved and a lady driver would hardly be expected to use either medical or street corner language to a filling-station attendant when requiring to relieve herself. Yet need the degree of avoidance here be as intense as it is? It is not so long ago that the appellation LADIES ROOM over a door in a movie rush resulted in the reshooting of an entire sequence, with the offending sign changed to POWDER ROOM (though it was unlikely any powdering went on there, in this case, and *rest* room describes a place where ladies jostle actively for places in front of the mirror). Such cost the company concerned some thirty thousand dollars. Similarly, "Let me show you the geography of the house" was a parallel British get-out of Professor Ross' youth. "I'm going to take a leak" (to members of the same sex), "I want to spend a penny" (non-U), and the more fanciful "I'm going to give a Chinaman a music lesson" are other examples of the kind. The assortment is no doubt legion. Cloacal taboos reach some kind of self-parodistic apogee in the numerous (and mostly American) books on toilet training. A book before me called *The Bathroom* has, for its Figure 34, a solemn "Plan View of Sitting Position on a Conventional Water Closet." We read, "Point support of this sort also, however, necessarily involves a greater concentration of force than is normally the case. Some preliminary experiments on normal seating and buttock loads conducted by Hertzberg at the Wright Air Development Center . . ." etc.

It was, of course, Puritan culture that particularly vetoed reference to the fecal, and gave impetus to such inventions;[2] Puritanism was the age of busyness, and subsequent repression of the mention of money ("May we look forward to an early remittance?") is tied into this privacy taboo. WC—for water closet—is today everywhere adopted in France as a satiric denial, although the terms for which the letters stand might well be meaningless to many French

[2] See: Peter Fryer, *Mrs. Grundy: Studies in English Prudery,* London: Dobson, 1963; Edward Sagarin, *The Anatomy of Dirty Words,* New York: Lyle Stuart, 1963; Norman L. Farberow, *Taboo Topics,* New York: Atherton Press, 1966. More generalized still is Armand Denis, *Taboo,* London: W. H. Allen, 1966.

who use the "facility." It is said, however, that French hotels developed their own euphemisms, or solecisms, for such places, one such being *Numéro Cent* (the door being marked with a neutral-looking 100). The British U euphemism, the *loo*, is presumed to have come out of franker French slang, the *lunettes* or spectacles replying visually to the seat-up position of a WC *(Concise Oxford)*.

British culture is, or was, especially rich in the forbidden. Upper-class education was founded on a set of prohibitions. As Henry James remarked, in his brilliant reply to Sir Walter Besant, Anglo-Saxon fiction was ringed with a host of prohibitory inscriptions, of *Don't* signs . . . "It is forbidden to walk on the grass, it is forbidden to touch the flowers. . . ."[3] English excremental taboos are still such that an hotelier friend of mine, who runs a small *camping* by the sea in Corsica, discovered that his English clientele was leaving him largely because the latrines were hard to find in the pinewoods, so that such guests were forced to ask the way. The following year he installed signs with arrows indicating the route to the WC's. If anything, this made matters worse. The British could then be *seen* going to the lavatory.

In Swift's "Voyage to Brobdingnag" Gulliver ridicules the seat of government thus:

> I desired the Queen's woman to save for me the combings of her Majesty's hair, whereof in time I got a good quantity, and consulting with my friend the cabinet-maker, who had received general orders to do little jobs for me, I directed him to make two chair frames, no larger than those I had in my box, and then to bore little holes with a fine awl round those parts where I designed the backs and seats; through these holes I wove the strongest hairs I could pick out, just after the manner of cane chairs in England. When they were finished, I made a present of them to her Majesty, who kept them in her cabinet, and used to show them for curiosities, as indeed they were the wonder of every one that beheld

[3]This is the famous essay in which James says that Zola "reasons less powerfully than he represents." Later in his argument, however, James borrows broadly from Zola, e.g. "Questions of art are questions (in the widest sense) of execution, questions of morality are quite another affair. . . ." Zola had said the same, in a comment to be vulgarized by Oscar Wilde—"For me there are no obscene works; there are only poorly conceived and poorly executed ones."

them. The Queen would have me sit upon one of these chairs, but I absolutely refused to obey her, protesting I would rather die a thousand deaths than place a dishonorable part of my body on those precious hairs that once adorned her Majesty's head.

Here Swift perfectly exemplifies what Freud·was to investigate in *Totem and Taboo,* namely how "scatology and eschatology overlap." This phrase is from Kenneth Burke, who cites Marx's suggestion that Egyptian pyramidal tombs closely resembled their dung piles, and that the Dalai Lamas "would like to persuade themselves that the world from which they derive their subsistence could not continue without their holy excrement." One does not have to have studied in Vienna to recognize that once again the word is its world, the organs of sex being those of excretion. Such has been called God's final joke on man. Swift's ridicule was enacted in fact in a recent blasphemy case in Holland, where an author, Gerard-Kornelis Van het Reve, was prosecuted under Article 147 of the Dutch Penal Code concerning blasphemy, when it was considered likely he might get off on the score of obscenity.[4]

Yet it is not always remembered that the basis of this nonsaying parables or burlesques an external social situation. Freud assumed that, when you came to his comments on taboo, you realized that to the savages studied the dead were *literally* unclean. Dead bodies stank. Their putrefaction was a menace. They were thus cast out, "untouchable."

Needless to say, echoes of such fear are with us still, in Californian mortuary customs which spawn exaggerated death-euphemisms, like *passed on, given up the ghost, no longer with us;* these, in turn, are mocked in vulgate—*croaked* or *kicked the bucket* (this last providing Quiller-Couch with the mixed metaphor of all time, when an Indian student reported to him the death of his mother— "Beg to inform you, the hand that rocked the cradle has kicked the bucket"). S. I. Hayakawa relates that the Japanese word for death, *shi,* has the same pronunciation as their word for four; this makes

[4]V. Ton Neelissen, "Dutch Trial," *Censorship,* no. 9, (Winter 1967), III:1, pp. 28–30. In the Spring 1967 issue of *Sewanee Review* I examined recent French attitudes as regards literary censorship; early that year France's famous Article XIV was stiffened to give the Ministère de l'Intérieur power to stop the sale and/or publicity of any work supposedly carrying a "caractère licencieux."

it actually difficult to calculate with *shi*, so much so that another word, *yon*, is used instead. In Mexico male genitals are *eggs*, so that you have to watch your language in the *supermercado*.

Forbidding Forbids

Taboo, or tabu, is a Polynesian Janus-term. It is a Tongan word, reputedly brought back by Captain Cook, and most people, I fear, know it now by the perfume of that name showing, in the famous Kreisler Sonata ad, the longest kiss on record. Freud, however, assures us of the double, or "ambivalent," meaning of taboo: (a) sacred, (b) forbidden-unclean. Thus his study of taboo once more instances word-wisdom, since the sacred/unclean polarity is another self-complementary antithesis—"so that," as he writes, "the objects of veneration become objects of aversion." If this human dynamic were properly understood, we would not be supporting by our taxes small armies of official snoopers all trying to detect something called obscenity, and world statesmen would not be making damn fools of themselves in public by saying that pornography is the origin of Communism. To date most fully Communist states have proved exceptionally puritanical.

Indeed, the irrational nature of the fear we repress here is evident in what might briefly be termed the obscenity grammar. (We smile at taboos on eating cattle, but the same taboo exists in our culture over dogs.) For a feature of obscenity prosecutions in the arts has traditionally been—at any rate until new laws in the last decade—a combination of juridical uncertainty (notably in jury trials) coupled with a rigor of correction. In 1966 the publisher of the relatively mild *Eros* magazine, Ralph Ginzburg, was sentenced by the juryless Judge Body [sic] to five years' imprisonment; appeals were carried to the Supreme Court, which denied so much as a reduction of the sentence, and this case lies particularly to point since semantics *outside* the offending work—as that Ginzburg sought to mail his publications from such places as Intercourse, Pa.—were taken into account in the decision.[5]

The US postal authorities, who retain inspectors dedicated to this field, will—must—allow through the mails books found to be nonobscene by the courts, yet set their own exacting standards over

⁵The Ginzburg affair was full of semantic implications. See my (untitled) article in *The Realist*, no. 67 (May 1966), pp. 1, 16–18. Were *other* mailings from Intercourse, Pa. (or Middlesex) suggestive?

personal correspondence. An "obscene" letter can ruin a career, of course, and at present writing it would seem perfectly possible to send a sexually stimulating book through the mails one day with impunity, and the next copy the same text, head it "Dear Bob," sign and send it as a personal letter and receive a whopping sentence!

The power of restriction here has always been very strong, and not least so because taboo is an integral aspect of our semantic structure. If we freed ourselves from all taboo, there would be—amongst other things—an entirely new relationship in our word-world. That is why there is a certain pubic puritanism in the nudist magazines, and a pedantry about such apostles of free speech as Wayland Young. Pleasure is hardly pleasure if you have to be clobbered into it by the successors of D. H. Lawrence.

The abstinence of Eden was a "word." It associated knowledge with punishment and told us much about our nature. We can hardly continue to survive without "unclean" thoughts and deeds, and even the US postal authorities admit sexually stimulating material through the mails in the form of perfume. The late, and lamented, Judge Jerome Frank hit this particular nail on the head, in a dissenting opinion in the US Court of Appeals, October 1955:

> Suppose we assume, *arguendo,* that sexual thoughts or feelings, stirred by the "obscene," probably will often issue into overt conduct. Still it does not at all follow that that conduct will be antisocial. For no sane person can believe it socially harmful if sexual desires lead to normal sexual behavior since without such behavior the human race would soon disappear. . . . Suppose it argued that whatever excites sexual longings might *possibly* produce sexual misconduct. That cannot suffice: Notoriously, perfumes sometimes act as aphrodisiacs, yet no one will suggest that therefore Congress may constitutionally legislate punishment for mailing perfumes.

In the context of General Semantics Freud's contribution to this problem was to show that taboo was not so much the prerogative of a theism as the code of a common human heritage. Secondly, by the nature of the dilemma, it was self-generative; it demonstrated the recoil mechanism inherent in language. For a prohibition makes its own prohibitions, until you come to the Kabyles, who forbid all reference not merely to sexuality, but even to eating (another form of self-preservation, after all). I have long felt that one of my own college's customs at Oxford, that of the *sconce,* was a lighthearted application of a similar taboo group. If an undergraduate talked sex unduly at dinner, or told "suggestive" stories (in the dismayingly degenerated sense of that word, one shared today by *candid*), then he was *sconced* by common consent and had to buy his table beer, usually the best Audit too.

Ambivalence in this instance merely means a veto on a forbidden action, toward which there is strong unconscious motive. With us today the resultant circumlocutions generate intensional meanings. If you don't talk about something, you talk but whirling words, mostly about yourself. It would not be going too far to point to menstrual ads (Tampax, Kotex, Pursettes, Modess, Meds, Confidets), rife throughout the republic, where this whole grammar can be identified weekly, and scarcely needs detailing here. Menstruation is "unclean," yet a vital body rhythm, resisting decay. Advertising copy falls over its feet to come to terms with these contradictories, resorting to and building up odor taboos. There is a natural drive toward something, which is then disallowed. Entropy is accelerated. The libido recoils. And of course this is simply history's "aside," an anagram of the technology. Illicit impulses have to be aroused in order to sell many goods—My Sin, Extase, Temptation—while the death fear is legalized in insurance ads ("Have you told your wife the things a widow should know?"), and the subway-riding *Backfisch* can read that stirring appeal, "Did you remember your Wunderbriefs today?" But after the impulse-buying comes the reckoning. You get nothing free from the social ego.

"Holy Tchee!"

Perhaps the desecration of the divinity is nowadays one aspect of taboo that can be more impartially regarded than most, and surely more calmly discussed than those still surrounding sex or death, though Canon Montefiore's suggestion (made by de Sade) that Christ may have been homosexual certainly aroused ire in England in 1967. This was due not only to implicit disparagement of the homosexual's conventionally inadequate father, but to laws of taboo in general. England's Mr. Mits was made to realize, what any teacher of the Bible as literature knows, that you cannot discuss Christ as a biographical character, and ask whether he suffered from piles, or corns on his knees, or whatever.

Yet even if you will not allow that religion has lost its authority symbolism, you are compelled, I believe, to concede a God of "absence," in the sense of an invariant. In conducting space-travel experiments, let us say, Cape Kennedy scientists are hardly allowing for something called God. Indeed, the very fact that some of these same scientists and technicians may return home each night and pray to G-d (pray, too, for the success of their shot) merely underscores the point.

Totemism was the preservation of taboo, and originally involved *not seeing*. To write G-d is to escape the visually identifiable blasphemy of which Faust was guilty. Yahveh was a protective tetragrammaton meaning *I am who shall be* (i.e., the Eternal). "Thou shalt not take the name of the Lord thy God in vain." Moses was rebuked for wanting to know God's name. Elizabethan drama was full of such avoidances, which today come through, of course, in *Gee, Holy Tchee, Jeepers* and so forth. We express a similar reticence over naming the d-vil, allotting him the *deuce*, the *dickens* and *heck* (for hell). One of the theories for the origin of British *bloody*, which Shaw picked to pillory an England filled with people smiling at each other's accents, is that it was a protective contraction of *By Our Lady*.[6]

Tchee (or *bloody*) thus fulfills the taboo for the ear, while making no verbal infringement. This is the basis of much comedy. In 1966 Bantam Books issued *This Is the Nice (and Naughty) Book*, which consisted of a series of rhymed illustrations of how the meaning of a word becomes taboo by implicit context:

> And is nice . . .
> But is naughty!

> Bell is nice . . .
> Knocker is naughty!

The point was that a number of these couplets made their point by a shift of sound alone:

[6] The term is seen by Partridge as "resulting naturally from violence and viscosity of blood." But who said blood is viscous, and why is viscosity "appalling"?

Voltaire is nice . . .
Balzac is naughty!

Saturn is nice . . .
Uranus is naughty!

The comedian Shelley Berman published a tract called *Cleans and Dirties* at the same time, designed to illustrate that the substitution of "clean" words for "dirty" words only sharpens our interest in the latter. Thus, *proposition* is a "dirty" word and *proposal* a "clean" one. (Who wants to listen to proposals except in Congress?) *Balls* is "dirty," *spheres* clean. "Spheres to you" would hardly be considered rude.

You could also say that, by this system, *come* is "clean" and come is "dirty," rather like the seventeenth-century use of *die* or *dye* (or Biblical *know*). It is sometimes maintained that the spelling *dye* represented for Donne the sexual ecstasy rather than the physical death such ecstasy parodies, but one would really have to know a great deal more about printers' habits of the time, before rushing into such a conclusion as excitably as does Miss Marjorie Nicolson, the Beatrice, for so many years, of Columbia's Graduate English school.

Sexual Trespass

A lot has been written lately about the literature of sexual trespass, and to any semanticist the nature of the euphemizing generated by this problem has been socially indicative. Censorship involves the misevaluation, or fear-fetichism, observed among savages by Emile Durkheim when he wrote that *"images of the totem-creature are more sacred than the totem-creature itself."* The very word *syphilis,* we have seen argued, should be expunged for its intrinsic contaminatory character. Although I have mentioned that *bitch* covered both sexes until a century and a half ago, Victorianism did its work so well that we meet this passage in Arnold Bennett's *The Old Wives' Tale:*

"You are fond of dogs?" asked Mr. Povey. . . .
"I have a fox-terrier bitch," said Mr. Scales, "that took a first at Knutsford; but she's getting old now."

The sexual epithet fell queerly on the room. Mr. Povey, being a man of the world, behaved as if nothing had happened; but Mrs. Baines's curls protested against this unnecessary coarseness. Constance pretended not to hear. Sophia did not understandingly hear. Mr. Scales had no suspicion that he was transgressing a convention by virtue of which dogs have no sex.

Not long after this passage was written, Lawrence was getting hauled over the coals for using the word *stallion* in his first novel. By the close of his career Lawrence had written twenty or thirty pages into a novel, in the course of which a celebrated four-letter word was used a number of times. He could not publish these pages in his lifetime, though his was an obvious effort to redeem the word by usage, and context, as Helen Gardner observed in her semantically aware testimony during the *Chatterley* trial.

At roughly the same time, once again, Hemingway was ridiculing the obligatory avoidances of being faithful to speech by substituting the term *obscenity* itself in long passages of dialog. This parody resulted in further parody, one recent sample giving us:

> "It was wonderful," she granted. "But it is even better when thee joins thy obscenity to my obscenity and we obscenity and obscenity and obscenity."
> "You're fucking-ay-right it is!" I agreed.[7]

That we smile at such scruples of censorship now gives us the impression of a sliding scale of liberation in the field. The sheer accumulation and objectification of sex today is a sort of definition, it seems. In America, at least, we can read more or less what we like, with all Burroughs, Miller, Frank Harris on sale, with Genet sainted, an aphrodisiac book club thudding its wares into our mailboxes alongside the brochures from the redundant League for Sexual Freedom. *Lolita, Naked Lunch, Candy, My Life and Loves, Fanny Hill, Venus in Furs,* the *Kama Sutra* (not to mention the *Koka Shastra,* or even the *Ananga Ranga)*—the Times Square racks begin to look pretty Book-of-the-Month Club by now.

[7]Ted Mark, *The Real Gone Girls,* New York: Lancer Books, 1966, p. 139. An American detergent called Delete has also mocked the obscenity grammar in its ads (e.g., "Oh (*delete*) it! Isn't there anything that will take the (*delete*) rust stains off this (*delete*) (*delete*) bathroom tile?").

314

The Formentor award is given to a novel replete with pony-girl fantasies, a Guggenheim is handed to a playwright whose latest piece allegedly contains "sodomy performed on stage," the intelligentsia applauds a Swedish movie showing a woman copulating with a dog, and the celebrated St. Louis sex researchers, Dr. William Masters and Mrs. Virginia Johnson, get a grant from the US Public Health service, no less, to photograph intercourse. No wonder that when an "artist" showed sculptured excrement in a New York gallery not long ago, the *New York Times* critic merely yawned ("These aggregations of colonic calligraphy contain many formal excellences . . ."). On March 1, 1965, Justice Douglas—roughly anticipating the literary state of Denmark today—could say: "I would put an end to all forms and types of censorship and give full literal meaning to the command of the First Amendment." The development is "capsulized" by Harry Golden in his *For 2¢ Plain:*

ONE HUNDRED YEARS OF THE AMERICAN NOVEL.
1856—"She has cancelled all her social engagements."
1880—"She is in an interesting condition."
1895—"She is in a delicate condition."
1910—"She is knitting little booties."
1920—"She is in a family way."
1935—"She is expecting."
1956—"She is pregnant."

All the same, any conscientious semanticist must feel uneasy at the sliding-scale conception of literary liberty. Advertising lives off an anxiety about sex and fosters its maladjustment, either by obvious cathections like narcissism or simply by attempts to organize a woman's sexual psychology into a man's, and vice versa, so that both will be subsumed under a general desire, or irritation, for allure and thus make reciprocal or complementary consumer demands. We unman ourselves in a new way, that is all (there is a high incidence of impotence in recent American fiction). The limits of literature are far from tested yet, since in the demonic sense sexuality is not here at stake at all.

Our view of sex is romantic. The damage that a capitalist economy has done by extending this bias into metaphoric behavior of all kinds is probably immeasurable, and almost certainly responsible for wars. It was Napoleon Bonaparte who remarked, "We are a machine made to live. . . ." The metaphoric vocabulary of our advertising, as of our commercial fiction in general, gives woman an almost wholly erotic role, which robs her of stability and surrounds her with anxieties. The inexorable demands of the industrial system, with its "mandate" for unbridled competition, commercializes sex and does so by trading off the ambiguities introduced into love; to make a fetichistic ideal out of allure, or glamour, is to introduce a sense of increasing inadequacy into intersexual relations. This cannot be emphasized enough: the debasement of the very word *glamour* (an old term for magic) over the past quarter of a century alone testifies to this fetichism. The metaphoric vocabulary of sex in America is insistently associated with deception: in the Preface to his *Dictionary of American Slang* Stuart Berg Flexner writes, "As expressed in slang, sex is a trick somehow, a deception, a way to cheat and deceive us. To curse someone we can say *screw you*, which expresses a wish to deprive him of his good luck, his success, perhaps even his potency as a man." Equivalents to *screw you* exist in other languages, of course, but Flexner substantiates the sexually revealing nature of our vocabulary of failure in America. I do not think it is paralleled in England.

In a clever attack on this driven ethic, called *Culture Against Man,* Jules Henry writes: "Advertising is an expression of an irrational economy that has depended for survival on a fantastically high standard of living incorporated into the American mind as a moral imperative." When the Caribbean island of Anguilla struck out for some sort of independence in 1967, the *New York Times* pontificated that "Its people subsist on agriculture and fishing and lack such modern amenities as telephones." The scathing tone of the technology is its own self-criticism. We note that Anguillans *subsist* on agriculture, while the lack of telephones may seem a dreadful indictment in the august eyes of a *New York Times* editorialist, but might prove of less consequence in an island of thirty-five square miles where you "telephone" by strolling up the road and talking to someone. I have lived for years now in Corsica without electricity, let alone a telephone. Needless to say, the pressure of this industrial ethic is felt increasingly in England. One learns that approximately a quarter of the British population now take sleeping pills at night.

Psychologists have not had to go far to demonstrate that in our so-called normality there is, in fact, frantic fetishism—of breast, buttock, whatever. The nakedness totem does not exist (yet) among the Japanese, and to promulgate it mythically, in the manner of contemporary consumer advertising, is to slice the human personality into different psychic parts, in order to manipulate the whole more malleably. *Divide et impera* has long been Madison Avenue's psychic motto. "One is permitted to think that the glut of sex in our prose and verse fictions," writes the ever-wise Jacques Barzun (*Montreal Star*, October 1, 1966), "will remain as the special mark of our work, the brand of the times on our genius." The brand, in short, of our world on our words. "I know sex is a taboo subject," as one father is said to have said to his so contemporary child, "I just don't feel like discussing it all the time, that's all." The liberating sliding-scale idea becomes suspect, since it in fact urges us to accept our urban culture.

After all, it was in 1962 that the word *bellies* had to be expunged from a Rodgers and Hammerstein musical before it could be shown to the Royal Family. Swift is not so far off; filled bellies, as the lyric originally went, might result in what Blue Cross calls *unmarried maternity* (no cover). *Belly dancers* have sometimes been renamed, by theatrical agents dodging local laws, *Anatolian folklore dancers*. The term *love child* or *natural child* says a lot about the society that popularized such; for by implication love does not exist in marriage, any more than in "nature."

The true issue is that the inhibition has not been altered by allowing the printing of—say—*fuck*. Doubtless it is healthy that this word can be printed here without penalty, and without the asterisks of Partridge's *Origins*, but what is often glibly dubbed "the communications process" has hardly been clarified thereby.

As a matter of fact, Lawrence's effort to reintegrate this word was hardly enlightened. Dr. Albert Ellis has continued Lawrence's debate, arguing that since *fuck* connotes on nearly every occasion a pleasurable activity, it should not be employed for negative purposes.[8] Ellis suggests *unfuck*. This shows no knowledge of language. It is the hearing of these words which primarily offends us; a *u* sound has been shown to be dominantly unpleasant—as in *ugly*, or that British U term for anything nasty, *ugg* (cf. Norse *ugga*, to

[8]See Paul Krassner, *Impolite Interviews*, New York: Lyle Stuart, 1961. Ray Russell has suggested substituting the "spiky, barbed, forbidding" asterisk in Partridge's *F**k* with some sign less repellent—e.g. *F!!k*.

fear). This is not imagination, but the result of serious study in phonetic intensives, or, as they are also called, phonesthemes. Examining over six hundred English monosyllables, Professor Householder found the vowel sound in *mud* to have generally "undesirable" connotations.[9]

Still, by using *fuck* at all we are somewhat further forward. For Professor H. J. Eysenck, Freud's true importance lay in his gift for words, in formulating and popularizing a language which contained ideas people could use, so that what was previously taboo could be legitimately discussed.[10] *To sleep with* or *go to bed with* has been shown up as a seriously inadequate deputy for the sexual act. There are many other such, from *having relations* to the faintly legal *sexual congress* and, in a literary spectrum, from Elizabethan *tupping* to Dr. Johnson's *palliardise*. Partridge found a virtual dictionary of such in *Shakespeare's Bawdy*. In *Take a Girl Like You* Kingsley Amis refers to "it" as *The Old Hoo-Ha*, John Barth in *Giles Goat-Boy* as *swiving*. In Oxford of my day the verb *to do* was equivalent to contemporary American *to score* (a *done* girl was one with whom you had *scored*). We know that Dr. Bowdler's friend, the timid Plumtre, revised Shakespeare's song

> Under the greenwood tree,
> Who loves to lie with me. . . .

to,

> Under the greenwood tree,
> Who loves to work with me.

Ozark women used to *lay down* for the same activity. A few years ago a British lawyer put a prostitute on the stand and asked her if she had *slept with* the accused. She replied that she had not. This considerably disconcerted counsel, since she had previously admitted that she had indeed had sexual intercourse with the man named. The question had to be rephrased in franker terms so that she would understand that *sleeping with* meant "sleeping with," not sleeping with. The case brought to mind a chestnut of British colonial days. An administrator of the pukka sahib type had for

[9]F. W. Householder, "On the Problem of Sound Meaning, an English Phonestheme," *Word,* 2 (1946), 83–84.

[10]"He [Freud] was a very great writer—he would have made a great novelist. In fact I think he *did* make a great novelist" ("The Mind Explorer,"*Penthouse,* II:7 (May 1967), p. 44).

years enjoyed the sexual services of a native concubine; but when asked by his friends, who knew of this, whether he had ever *gone to bed with* the woman, he fervently denied having done so. On being pressed, over cups, to come clean, he got out sterterously the three words, "On the mat!"

Such stories are locker-room shorthand for serious problems. You talk better, you convey a message more truly, about human activities when talking about humans, rather than birds and bees. To walk along the halls of academe and hear some Hygiene Professor's voice booming complacently away about menopause and menstruation is not such a very great liberty.[11] Some might be willing to forego it. The substitution of technical terms for sex is merely, in a manner, re-euphemizing, as when the chairman of a faculty committee at Cornell declared the college against "overnight unchaperoned mixed company," or when we read in a book called *Human Sexual Response*, by the Masters-Johnson team, that "This maculo-papular type of erythematous rash first appears over the epigastrium." I learn in *The Lancet* that "sexual desire for young girls," a rather common affliction, I'd imagine, is really *neanirosis*.[12]

To talk about sex like this to city students can get pretty hilarious. To euphemize rape, in the manner of current police reports, as *criminal assault* resulted recently in a knowledgeable high school principal's remark: "We used to have the three R's at this school, but now we've got four: readin', 'ritin', 'rithmetic and criminal assault." One wonders whether his English Two studies *pari passu* that well-known poem by Pope, *The Criminal Assault of the Lock*. In passing, I might refer to the British *foul play*. Again, the euphemism is socially indicative, demonstrating the common reverence for its reverse, *fair play*. Foul play may even mean that a girl has been *interfered with*. It is in this spirit that many school systems in America now expel a pregnant girl for what is termed (to her parents) *glandular imbalance*.

Even quite lately, however, regional groups around America have reported the damaging lack of any real vocabulary with which

[11]The ads and literature concerning Ovulen birth-control pills, or "tablets," are full of this pseudoscience. Pregnancy is "ovulation," and a current ad shows a bangled hand holding out the "unforgettable" Compack dispenser, "error-proof and jam-proof, with no moving parts," the days of the week inscribed on the side. The Puralin ads against B.O. (another euphemism) equally attempt to anesthetize the instinctual.

[12]"The Doctor's English," *The Lancet*, August 19, 1961, p. 420.

to talk about such matters. The result is the girl who obeys her mother's injunction not to let her date kiss her, yet is later found pregnant. As Kipling put it in his poem about euphemistic fiction, *The Three-Decker,* "We never talked obstetrics when the Little Stranger came."

Saying What You Don't Mean

We seem, then, to have reached a point—unless we turn back from it—when most any word can be used in print. Including *fuck, cock, shit, prick* and the rest of the so-called four- or five-letter words, complete with the unpleasantly harsh consonants in which we have wrapped such terms. Today sexually titillative books are seldom attacked for an excess of four-letter words alone. There was not one such in *Lolita,* yet only a decade ago it received this damagingly hands-off and libelously up-tight preview from the Virginia Kirkus Service:

> That a book like this could be written, published, sold, presumably over the counters, leaves one questioning the moral and ethical standards. . . . Any librarian would surely question this for anything but the closed shelves. Any bookseller should be sure in advance that he knows he is selling pornography.

We have agreed that in literature and art generally we must allow what Babbitt called "the ethical or generalizing imagination." This is a quick way of saying what James had said in his reply to Besant, that to be moral we must be whole. (James' fictions are generally about some sexual/moral deficiency; if you have an inadequate knowledge in James, you're vulnerable.) In James' own words—"the essence of moral energy is to survey the whole field."

To a considerable extent, then, we seem to have closed the gap between what we know and what we admit we know. The man who defended *Lady Chatterley's Lover* for Penguin Books soon after became Lord Chancellor of England. While James was answering Besant, suburban England was clothing its table legs, to hinder physical analogy therefrom, and there is even record of legs themselves, in an anticipation of the mechano-morphism of our day, being called *benders.* Ramsbottoms and Higginbottoms were, needless to say, altering their suffixes to *-botham.*

It would be tempting to expatiate on the virtual monopoly of embarrassment about the *bottom* possessed by the British, but there is no space for this "basic" subject, which is in any case more the preserve of sociologists. It seems to have a considerable history —or *ars longa*—however. Boswell tells us that when Johnson said, of an errand-girl who had just married, "the woman had a bottom of good sense," there was universal consternation in the company, only the Bishop of Lillaloe keeping countenance. Johnson looked round sternly—"Where's the merriment?"

> Then collecting himself, and looking aweful, to make us feel how he could impose restraint, and as it were searching his mind for a still more ludicrous word, he slowly pronounced "I say the *woman* was *fundamentally* sensible"; as if he had said, hear this now, and laugh if you dare.

When *Lolita* came out, Gilbert Highet, Anthon Professor of Latin Language and Literature at Columbia University, called it "a wicked book" because it showed an evil practice in an alluring guise. This is on a par with the confusion I have mentioned elsewhere, that of supposing a reader so primitive he will accept the symbolic as the actual—"The story he tells," as the noble Lord protested of Lawrence, "is pure invention; it never actually happened." Nor has it been shown that *Lolita* stepped up *neanirosis*, by turning red-blooded American males into Humbert Humberts. Anyway, Lolita-ism was a normal libidinal state in the Renaissance. But more to my point, Highet went on to protest that if a novel showing arson as attractive were written, it would surely be outrageous to welcome its appearance. "The principal effect of *Lolita* is the enjoyment of wickedness." This, as I say, assumes a reader unable to distinguish between what is symbolic and what is extensional, an African native fleeing at the sight of someone chasing him on the movie screen. In all the fuss over the 1966 Moors murders in England it was seldom remarked that alcohol undoubtedly led to violence before, and more directly than, the literature of de Sade; in fact, Dr. Lars Ullerstam claims of such killings, "Everything seems to indicate that sadism rarely plays a part in these murders."[13] But sadism is so misunderstood, and utterly taboo, that it is shelved as

[13]Lars Ullerstam, *The Erotic Minorities*, New York: Grove Press, 1966, p. 91.

the *perversion* responsible for Fascism, when in fact it has been the preserve of the democracies *(le vice anglais).*

James would have insisted that we both could and should show desirable arson, if necessary ("the province of art is all life"). For unless we know arson from within the mind of a convinced arsonist, we do not know what it is. It may be said that such confessions belong more to the clinics; but literature is our collective clinic *in advance.* You do not learn what Marxism means, and menaces, from William Buckley, Jr., nor even from Professor Hugh Trevor-Roper. "Three-quarters of the universe," wrote de Sade, "may find the rose's scent delicious without that serving either as evidence upon which to condemn the remaining quarter which might find the smell offensive, or as proof that this odor is truly agreeable." In Africa the Siwa tribe still consider it abnormal not to be bisexual. Unless we are whole we cannot be moral. The word is its world. As that confused character Maurice Girodias well put it, "We cannot send our astronauts into outer space, and still forbid them to read *Fanny Hill.*"

So while France is turning itself into a cultural Ireland the English-speaking countries have allowed fantasy the scope of most emotions. As Lionel Trilling put it in his perceptive review of *Lolita,* "It is one of the effects, perhaps one of the functions, of literature to arouse desire, and I can discover no ground for saying that sexual pleasure should not be among the objects of desire which literature presents to us, along with heroism, virtue, peace, death, food, wisdom, God, etc." This was almost to rephrase Sir Kenneth Clark's remarks on nude art:

> The human body . . . is ourselves and arouses memories of all the things we wish to do with ourselves; and first of all we wish to perpetuate ourselves. . . . No nude, however abstract, should fail to arouse in the spectator some vestige of erotic feeling, even though it be only the faintest shadow—and if it does not do so, it is bad art and false morals.

Human personality is integral and we cannot arbitrarily redistribute libidinal power, as advertising would. "To accept animate life as good," writes John Wilson, in *Logic and Sexual Morality* (1965), "is to accept the satisfaction of desire as good."

This shift in emphasis from word to world, or situation, as a matter of offense, has been crystallized by literary prosecutions in England of late. In 1954 the Director of Public Prosecutions brought actions there for "obscene libel" (note the term) against five reputable publishers, nearly all on the grounds of four-letter words. Three were acquitted, one convicted, and one pleaded guilty to save the bother and costs involved. Even after the passing of the 1959 Obscenity Act, *Lady Chatterley's Lover* was very largely hammered by the Crown prosecutor, in Regina *versus* Penguin Books, for its confident reiteration of a taboo term. Some four years passed between this acquittal and the arraignment of John Cleland's *Fanny Hill*. Although we here find the same prosecutor, Mr. Mervyn Griffith-Jones (now Judge Griffith-Jones), the emphasis has perforce shifted to situation. In 1967 the Calder issue of *Last Exit to Brooklyn*, which might well have been attacked for four-letterisms, was assailed (successfully) mainly for situation.

What is at issue here is the dirty book, rather than the pornography. There was no charge that I know, in either England or America, against Wallace's *The Prize*, say, or Robbins' *The Carpetbaggers* (known in the American trade as *The Garbagebaggers*). Yet in each fiction there were fanciful sexual situations as extreme as in any Olympia Press *porno*. The latter kind of publication, after all, simply iterated what the dirty books of the time left unstated, elliptical; and in this way they served the literary community at large, making Anglo-Saxon censorship look the anachronism it then was. There was no serious charge against *The Prize* at all because the situation was not *whole;* similarly, the titillation of the old tough thriller was an ellipsis, filled in, and thus mocked, in the recent line of "man from O.R.G.Y." spoofs, by Ted Mark.

The dirty book—the *Peyton Place*, or *No Orchids for Miss Blandish*—is really so much literary *coitus interruptus*. The scene is imagined, started on its route, then derailed, forbidden, frustrated, like a cut in the cinema, unsaid, incomplete, both uncreated and uncreative—unwhole. Traditionally this used to be effected by a series of ellipses, or some such device as, "Later, John turned to Mary. . . ." As Balzac put it in a charming early story, "Only those who have known such happiness themselves can imagine the delight they shared." There are other methods for the same suspension now.

But the fissure between sexual world and word is clearly there, and clearly unhealthy, since it suggests that one can exist without the other. It is a feature which besets a work of imagination the more publicly it is performed, and it heavily invests pictorial representation. In 1957 a reproduction of Goya's *Naked Maja* (unclothed version) was printed by the *New York Times*, but rejected two years later by the same newspaper in an ad for Alitalia showing European "art treasures." The United Artists ad for its movie based on Goya's life was similarly shunned, postal authorities seized 2,000 postcards advertising the film, and Spain annulled a stamp showing the nude. In this connection, too, I wonder how many readers of the *New Yorker* and *Cue* have noticed that Aubrey Beardsley's drawing of Salome, borrowed to advertise the Cattleman restaurant ("Dine in the plush intimacy of a candlelit Victorian alcove"), has been touched up. Sharing the fate of Michelangelo's lovingly painted male genitalia, Salome's breasts and navel have here succumbed to inking-out. The penalties of public domain are sere, indeed.

In cases like these public exhibition qualifies fantasy, involving it in the impurity of persuasion. Beardsley never drew Salome to draw New Yorkers into a restaurant (in fact, she has here been taken out of her context, which was, in the original, a tête-à-tête with another well-known character). Alliance of sexual suggestion with commercial motive compromises art, until it turns in vengeance into its opposite. Although, as Sir Kenneth Clark suggests, the *Naked Maja* should properly arouse erotic feelings, the painting is not a lure. Semantic extremes collide, and what Mill meant by connotation is forced into—usurped for—the role of denotation.[14] When this occurs, you get such a contrast between the unspeakable, or disallowed, and the elegant that the result is itself "suggestive." The cover-up token of euphemism looks so absurdly hyperelegant that it really mocks itself.

Your Derriere's Darling When You're Two!

Thus in the last century ladies of refinement would talk about the *lower back* for the buttocks, *limbs* for legs (even of pianos),

[14]"When pictures of nude colored figures are shown, people call it ethnography; when they are white, it's called pornography," commented Knut Henrik Lindquist, Vice-President of the Swedish Film Institute, when informed that the Quebec Board of Censors had turned down an entry made from a Stig Dagerman novel.

and one's *birthday suit* for nudity.[15] In actual fact, *nude* was not called on to substitute for *unclothed* until about the middle of the nineteenth century, when it was itself a euphemism (and so used by Swinburne). There is the story of the Victorian model who, when asked if she posed naked, replied that she only did so in the nude.

That is one thing. To use these terms today, or similar avoidances like *derriere*, as in girdle ads, spoofs taboo itself.[16] The artificiality of the situation, in this case women's fashion, is what here gets publicly derided. The primitive fear of the unclean was attached to the bowels and organs of excretion. As observed, excretion is so euphemized that you reach the comically self-parodistic "toilet paper" ads of today, in which some impossibly elegant beauty drifts in evening gown through a mistily photographed bedroom, presumably on her way to the *loo*, and use therein of Scottissue, or some such.

Originally, obscenity meant that which violated the excremental taboos, and modern cosmetic activities cannot, by their nature, come to terms with such taboos. They must, that is, allude to and stir up our fear of the unclean at the same time as denying that same fear in their word-world. It is perhaps for this reason that the feminine backside (largely uneuphemized in Italy) becomes more taboo than the breasts in an urban culture. *Tail, rear, fanny, tambo, tushy, butt, end, can* are our multiple echoes of British *b.t.m.* (a desecration avoidance), French *bas-reliefs* or, slangier, *batteries,* German *Popo, Popochen, Sitzplatz. Hindquarters, rump, nates, cubs, stern, sit-upon, south-south-west, lower deck* and the like— there are far more of such euphemisms current than for the humble

[15]The kind of elegance acquired by disused euphemisms is itself soothingly old-fashioned; cf. "Year after year, the nicest Birthday Suits stay wrinkle-resistant with Tender Touch, the bath oil priced to use every day" (Helen Curtis Tender Touch).

[16] 'There are no ugly women,' say the ads for Manhattan's Diedre line, 'only lazy ones.' Says Steve Mayham of the Toilet Goods Association: 'This is an industry of ideas and imagination, and what we are selling is hope.'

"The industry encourages hope by surrounding itself with the most enticing come-ons since Eve described the apple. It glamorizes its products with names suggestive of romance, adventure, passion: such foundation powders as Pond's Angel Face, Revlon's Love-Pat, and Max Factor's Creme Puff; such lipsticks as Rubinstein's Red Hellion, Revlon's Fire and Ice, Helen Neushaefer's Torrid and Pink Passion" (*Time Magazine*).

female breast. As I write, advertising is in fact acquiring some charge out of bucking this very trend, and mocking the euphemisms involved; I am thinking of the explicitly punning nature of the Barbasol *can* ads, or something like Nutrament's copy under a buxom girl, "This Little Round Can Turns Corners Into Curves."

The famous "cleavage" fuss over women's breasts, as shown in the Hays and then Johnston cinema codes, resulted in a battle which biology won easily many years ago. It is dead as a doornail now. Yet it is only in the past few years that fashion has accepted the twin nature of the so-called behind.

For cleavage or division emphasizes biological function and calls down on its head, or seat, the fury of taboo. Only a decade ago Maidenform ran its ultrasuccessful "YOUR DERRIERE'S DARLING WHEN YOU'RE TWO" by-line of a naked moppet heading for the surf, seen from the south. The implications were plain. Only as babies did American women show the double nature of their lower backs, not as big babes. *Time* crowed over the "monobuttock" girdle, while French ads (as for Gaine Barbara) were advertising the reverse, in all senses, as a come-on, or go-away: *"son dos double indépendant."*

Unmentionables

As I have tried to show elsewhere,[17] the created taboo could be traded on, and girlie magazines poured out pictures of twin-featured fannies, or *natural curves*, as they came to be called in subsequent fashion language. One such, American Art Agency's *Tip Top*, specialized in rear shots, printing some indescribably affecting gluteal tributes to Venus Callipyge Americana; nor do these magazines sell to paupers. When I was researching for *Parade of Pleasure* a decade ago, the average pinup magazine, of the kind from which Marilyn Monroe surfaced, sold for 25 cents. *Tip Top, Thigh High* and the like sell for two dollars each. Such offerings may not go entirely unread by account executives.

For gradually these emphases fed back into fashion, and at the time synchronized with ease and increase of European travel. Frankly, the US corset-style swimsuit of not so very yore looked

---

[17]Geoffrey Wagner, "The Buttock Books," *The Realist,* 57 (March 1965), pp. 27–29. *Callipygean* is another euphemism for beautifully buttocked, deriving from a classical Miss Superior Posterior contest (*Athenaeus,* XII, 80). Still another is *pygophiliac.*

plain peculiar on bikini-frequented Riviera beaches, while the monobuttock girdle was quite impractical under the new toreador tights and stretch pants coming in. American women began to yearn for a girdle of lycra or spandex that "makes you round where a woman should be round" (Gossard's Answerette); today's teeners have rejected the flatiron effect in back and squeeze into their levis until the rear pocket couldn't accommodate so much as a razorblade—rumor has it that coeds have to lie on their backs to manipulate the new button flies! Herrick's "brave vibration each way free" is a must, and Youthcraft's The Shift [sic] girdle calls to the buyer for "derrière shaping." Poirette's Princess girdle is "a new nude experience." "Don't look now," coos Corde de Parie's similar come-on, "but lovely things are happening behind you." The desirable outline below the waist emphasizes a supple, whiplike grace, with arrogantly brisk legs, the eight-way panty girdle "a whisper-light wisp of spandex elastic with a lickety-split hipline, proportioned to match the body length from waist on down (everyone's is different)." If today bulges are assets rather than liabilities, one recalls James Laver's theory that pelvic emphasis in fashion goes hand in hand with cultural confidence—"wide hips mean that women have sufficient confidence in the future to produce large families."

Reluctantly enough, then, fashion yielded, and Vogue, which had fought the bikini as bitterly as any Grundy, began to admit the need for an "easy-going roundness that moves right with you." The body-stocking made woman "all leg," instead of. arresting the eye at that "ugly line," or artificial sulcus. With short skirts the legs are compelled to continue their line upward; the word had once more fed back its world.[18]

When I published Parade of Pleasure, the girlie magazines, appealing principally to a truck-driver public, were involved in an undressing race. Barer was more daring, and the book in fact contains one charming shot of an unknown pinup starlet of the time called Marilyn Monroe. Secondly, the breast battle was in full fling, with fashion photographers airbrushing out all visible nipples (and

[18]Society pursues desirable symbols. It was said that far from "realists," like Dickens, giving us a true photograph of the wasp-waisted, sloping-shouldered Victorian miss, the reverse obtained; the girls of the day copied fictional heroines. Contemporary American breast fetishism seemed to increase actual statistics.

navels). I showed photos of fantastic "upper decks," the master-pieces perhaps of mammaplasticians, like those of "Irish" McCalla (42″), Tempest Storm (44″), and Eve Meyer (39″), the lovely wife of West Coast photographer Russ, later to make the *Mr. Teas* nude movie, or "nudie." Today Carol Doda—not to mention her colleague who beats a drum with her breasts on the Coast—is ex-ceptional, an "exotic."

Breast taboo could be bucked first because industial civilization had deprived women's breasts of their biological function. Breast fetichism received its death kiss in *Lolita*, where, in the logical conclusion of such cathection, the pornographer offers the esthete a girl with three breasts as bait. *Lolita* was a parody of the *porno*, the guilty Quilty representing lust, the bumbling Humbert repre-senting love. Euphemistic fashion too, the world of *unmentionables* and *lingerie*, got its ration of parody in this book, since the "hero-ine," a perfect consumer patsy, dies in childbirth, unable to re-produce.

For fashion has bred its race of enchanted inverts, listening to their own words and loving only themselves. In the pages of *Vogue* and *Harper's Bazaar* women adore women, in a sort of semantic parody of Pentagonese. The vocabulary of such narcissus-neuter-ism has been ridiculed often enough by now, of course, and it threw up its own criticism in the creation of the male-magazine market. The *Playboy* phenomenon was healthy at first, since it ap-pealed to an audience in some touch with ideas, in the colleges, and thus eroticism could be envisaged as a source of taste. But this development, with its many impersonations, seems by now to have lost its nerve.

If fashion magazines can be seen, semantically, as the word with-out a world, the ultimate of "intensional" thinking and therefore the very enemy of art, the reverse operation bedevils the literature of sexual excess. There is little space to discuss this here, but since the sexual activity is crescendic, sexual literature replies in kind. In common with *Candide*, classic pornographies began with the cor-ruption of the innocent and ended with the initiate corrupting. Nabokov realized that this pattern penalized the early acceptance of *Lolita*, as he explained in his Epilogue to that work.

The editors who first read and rejected the book were allegedly obeying bodily rhythms, somewhat like the reader in the salacious store thumbing through a *porno* for titillative, or turning-on, passages. This is not esthetic. Yet advertising responds to aphrodisiac rhythm, as in the famous 1966 Noxzema Medicated Shave Cream ad.

In this way a culture often throws up self-protection, issuing a stream of semantic parodies of its own taboo situations. A final clincher of such might be instanced, in illustration of the excrementally obscene. Some years ago a gentleman called Mr. Prout organized SINA, Society for Indecency to Naked Animals. The New York *Post* reported:

> School children, he said, are subjected to the sight of dogs scouting trees and hydrants or in the throes of unabashed necking. The morals of cats are equally uncertain and disturbing. Diapers for cats, shorts for dogs and horses and eventually a working agreement with zoo authorities—these are the aims of Prout's organization. . . . Prout has also advocated the widespread use of comfort stations for animals.

The parable in Prout's campaign is that it started as a joke, but got taken seriously by the world.

First Steps to Heaven

Behind all taboo lies the fear of the unclean. Since the unclean were infectious, they were a threat, and savage societies had a high incidence of taboo in connection with the dead.

But what I have written could equally be said of contemporary American society. Apart from some common psychic universals, what makes this comparison possible? There is such a love of cleanliness in America that bathing has become synonymous with progress, and there are certainly US tourists who proceed through Europe via an itinerary of plumbing fixtures.

No one wants to die. And stink. No one enjoys putting words to the death of a friend, who is accordingly described as having *passed on, passed away,* or (British) *shoved off,* etc. Yet again it can be seen that the reluctance is far in excess of these rather mild verbal needs. It is one thing to call a cemetery a *memorial park,* or to refer in officialese to shipment of a stiff back home as *horizontal repatriation;* the whole Forest Lawn semantic, with its cosmeticians, "beautiful memory pictures," symphonic music, artificial bird songs, Resthavens and Babyland ("shaped like a mother's heart") is quite another, and has by now received the ridicule it merits. The "leave-taking" in Forest Lawn of millionaire mortician Hubert Eaton seems to have been little short of a Fascist ceremony.

As a matter of fact, such criticism was singularly stale some time ago. The whole construct got a going-over in Mencken's chapter on "Euphemisms" in *The American Language*. Here Mencken tells us that *mortician* was proposed by a writer in *Embalmers' Monthly* for as long ago as February 1895. Actually, *mortician* supplanted what was simply another euphemism, since *undertaker* used to cover the undertaking of any job (German *Unternehmer*), another specialization history. But Mencken well illustrates the way in which taboo spawns itself through language, citing such progeny as *beautician* (which has remained) and *bootician* (for bootlegger —which hasn't).

Rather naturally death gets pushed from sight in big cities today, with our friends and relatives hustled out of their apartments into elevators, strapped on "funeral-parlor" wheelbarrows under black leather; this happens because death is itself taboo in the sense that it directly criticizes and defeats our civilization. We can fly to the moon but we can't stop that old limping sickle-bearer. (The most extreme attempt to do so to date has perhaps been the refrigeration joke.) While death is hushed up in cities, then, it is still indulged in throughout rural cultures, such as those I have watched in Corsica, Ireland, Sicily, Mexico—though, of course, as the West gets industrialized, it increasingly shares those semantic phobias. In 1966 the village of Camposanto, in central Italy, changed its name because of the (hitherto ignored) connotations of cemetery.

In areas still vitally rural the mourner prolongs the reminder that death is a change into another state, a view inherently disallowed by a technocracy. When the Sicilian bandit Giuliano Salvatore was finally killed, and his body tossed ignominiously into the courtyard of his former home, his mother licked his blood off the cobblestones there. When she could no longer do so she was replaced, and her grief prolonged, by a woman of the village.

Although it is said that this further licking (even when no blood was visibly left) was done somewhat for the benefit of the contemporary press, the woman concerned was still an authentic *voceratrice*. Corsican tombs are taken for hotels by some tourists, and Ajaccio's cementery, on the Route des Sanguinaires outside it, was bombed by the Germans in the last war in mistake for the town itself. The difference between Forest Lawn and Corsican "memorial parks," like that at Ajaccio, is that in the Imperial City there is no need for euphemisms in this connection. On the contrary. But when varieties of pressure are exerted to forbid the expression of extensional reality, you are forced into a substitution. You utter something to conceal the truth. Such is euphemism.

Gilding the Lily

In a recent TV broadcast of *Hamlet* the sponsor insisted on the deletion of Polonius' words, "Neither a borrower nor a lender be." The sponsor was, you see, a savings bank, which feared that such counsel might come over to viewers as a guide for conduct. Not long ago a *Dennis the Menace* cartoon showed Mother serving a disgruntled Dennis with a steaming plateful of spuds: the caption ran, "The expression is 'leftover' potatoes, not 'USED'!" In the same spirit used-car lots will refer to their offerings as *owner-tested*. A trash lot turns into a *sanitary landfill*. The diamond firm of De Beers likes to refer to installment buying as *divided payments*—possibly anticipated years ago by Twain, when he wrote, "Let us not be too particular. It is better to have old second-hand diamonds than none at all." To every reader his favorite euphemism. The gangster Anastasia used to have a member of his organization whom he styled his *social adviser*.

Properly, a euphemism is a piece of self-protection. When one's verbal skin turns too sensitive to a reality, that reality must be softened to be assimilable. Unpleasant realities, as I have already suggested, are clouded in this merciful manner. The language, indeed the appelation, of hospitals is euphemized in order literally and physically to assist.

Just as savages would not at first enter brick and concrete clinics near their thatched kraals, so the International Society for the Welfare of Cripples was repellent enough a name to need a change, in 1960, to the International Society for the Rehabilitation of the Disabled. Nebraska's Hospital for the Crippled and Deformed is now the Nebraska Orthopedic Hospital, while artificial limbs are termed *prosthetic devices*. This naming evidently helps. To tell someone he is *crippled*, or *deformed*, is clearly more brutal than to suggest he is *handicapped*. True, both are exceptional situations, but a sports player in the best of health can be severely "handicapped."

To be blind could be said, as a consequence, to be *visually handi-*

capped, in the sense that the expert typist or concert pianist may lack the sight of eyes. Reciprocally, it has been said that *culturally deprived* is a guilty middle class's euphemism for a reality they cannot bear to face. The *strategic withdrawal* that I recall Cairo BBC announcing we had made, in the last war, may have been more effective than we cynically assumed at the time;[19] certainly, retreating Japanese had their spirits maintained by being told they were drawing the enemy closer. It is in such ways that euphemism becomes an index. Don't forget that it was the creators of fallout who rechristened it *atmospheric inversion.*

But lately the habit has grown out of all control. It invades almost every area of our lives, from the concealments of supermarkets where goods are never cheap (always *budget, economy* or *thrifty*), glasses are known as *stemware* and watches as *horological creations,* to the *motor inns* (as motels are now renamed) with their *Holiday Girls* for waitresses (supposedly conjuring away the servant implications thereby), concluding in Pete's *Cocktail Lounge,* which is little more than a sawdust bar where a bunch of *intemperate* (rather than drunk) *senior citizens* and other sundry *underachievers* are standing around in their *custom-made* shoes, *expectorating* rather than spitting, and making an *aroma,* instead of a stench, with their *family-size* cigars.[20]

You decide to stay, and after Pete has found you the smallest glass manufactured on the American continent and poured Scotch all round it, you settle to your paper. Here you find an article on something called *hereditary subjection* in South America, when you had, in your ignorance, always thought of this as feudalism, and another on a *Higher Horizons* educational program for the *underadvantaged.* In thumbing through the small ads in back, you chance on landlordese; apartments are offered with *sweeping, scenic view,* meaning that on clear days you can see the fire escape next door, while *terr.* means you can sit on your fire escape; *grdn.* is a sight of sumac in the well of the air shaft. The area I live in

---

[19]Many military euphemisms were simply protective. Early in the last war British tanks were referred to, in this spirit, as *steel assemblages.*
[20]Frank's, a Harlem restaurant I go to occasionally, has this advice hung over its bar area:

In Consideration of Our Diners
We Would Appreciate a Lower Tone of
Social Amenities
From our bar patrons.

is euphemized by landlords as *Col. Univ. vic.*: it could equally be called South Harlem.[21]

Anyone can make his own random anthology of daily euphemisms. One day the Arizona Lath and Plaster Institute objects to *plastered* as a synonym for drunk,[22] the next a Congressman suggests that *petty* officers be given a new name. The chefs of America declare against *cook*, while education jargon gets going early in its euphemizing. In his popular *Translations from the English* Robert Paul Smith retranslated the following educationese, "To be perfectly truthful, he does seem to have developed late in large-muscle control," as *He falls on his head frequently*. Similarly, *He cries easily* becomes educationesque "He's rather slow in group integration and reacts negatively to aggressive stimulus." Meanwhile, librarian jargon—from the code of Cataloguing Research—now includes: *syndetic references, information retrieval systems*, and *generalia classes*.

As a matter of fact, book salesmen are now sometimes called *educational counselors*, and we hear a lot about *driver education*. A barber becomes a *hair stylist*, with fees to match. Nor is this tendency confined to America. In England bookies have long been termed *turf accountants*, though some may never go near the turf, while recently it is reported that a chimney-sweeper there has turned into a *flueologist*.

Occasionally you get a backlash to the habit. The term *juvenile delinquent* has had a history rather like the case of *budget-bougette* cited. First coined many years ago to disguise a repellent reality, it came round to be an outright pejorative—*j.d.*—for which further euphemisms had to be hunted up. In the same way, manure was euphemized into *fertilizer;* however, this term also began to be too closely associated with its stink (or *perfume*, or *bouquet*), so that *plant food* was substituted. Similarly, *face-lifting* became *cosmetic*

[21]The vicinity reminds me that some years ago Columbia students objected to being taught by *preceptors*, rather than by professors. President Grayson Kirk had to explain that the university had long employed preceptors, though under another name. Similarly, a midwestern Department of Architecture was found to be teaching one course under two names—*Planning* in one part of the college, *Design* in another. Queens College unhelpfully revamps its Department of Speech to Department of Communication Arts and Sciences.
[22]Perhaps because of Prohibition, and the consequent myth of the lovable drunk, American substitutes for inebriation include a considerable percentage of meliorative terms—*happy, high, flying*, etc. Actually the N.Y. Plasterers Union ad, as I write, runs, "Get Yourself Plastered!"

surgery, which then became too close to face-lifting and was turned into *skin sculpture.*

By this stage it can be seen that the euphemism is no longer performing any protective role. Lewis Carroll, whose Humpty Dumpty tells Alice that words mean just what he chooses them to mean— "neither more nor less," and who wrote a book on *Symbolic Logic,* knew that as a technology recedes from the extensional world, it can do more or less what it likes with the vocabulary at its disposal. Naming things without imagining them is semantic perversion. As Orwell put it years ago, "Defenceless villages are bombarded from the air, the inhabitants driven out into the countryside, the cattle machine-gunned, the huts set on fire with incendiary bullets: this is called *pacification.*" He might well have been writing yesterday. And in fact he was—"One village [in Vietnam] so persistently resisted pacification that finally it was destroyed" (*Baltimore Sun,* November 6, 1966, AP).[23] We now have *damage limitation* (a device to blunt total attacks with ABM systems), *rippled attacks* (missiles sent in salvos), *preferential defense* (for military or manufacturing centers), *penaid* (= penetration aids, such as decoy warheads), and acronyms like ICM (the Improved Capability Missile, which can maneuver in the atmosphere and destroy practically anything). Doubtless, the next few years will throw up others.

Don't Say It!

Oxford Universal defines the euphemism as a rhetorical figure "by which a less distasteful word or expression is substituted for one more exactly descriptive of what is intended." It cites Froude as nicely substituting "a shorn crown" for decapitation. And who is to object? I should prefer having my crown shorn any day rather than my head cut off. However, the end result is that I am executed, phrase it as Humpty Dumpty may.

The euphemism tells the reader, or listener, nothing about the reality except that it is unwelcome to the user of the euphemism. To call a janitor a *superintendent,* a cabdriver a *metered fare chauffeur,* or slums *substandard dwellings,* this alters nothing in the reality, and advances no argument about it; the new usage simply

[23]In April 1967 Washington tried to get our journalists to use another term for *escalation;* when asked if an obviously aggressive move to step up the war constituted *escalation,* a government spokesman said he preferred the term *supplementary bombing.* Yet *escalation,* so common now, was called a "fancy new term" in *The Nation* as recently as 1961.

334

reveals the speaker. As a matter of fact, the term *senior citizen* deprives the old of much of their dignity, according to at least one critic (Inez Robb in the New York *World-Telegram and Sun*). Feiffer did a delightful cartoon of a derelict who is told he is no longer poor, he is *needy,* then *deprived,* then *underprivileged, disadvantaged* and so forth. As he puts it at the end, "I still don't have a dime. But I have a great vocabulary."[24]

Now, since the *sanitation engineer* still shifts as much trash as the old garbage collector, nothing much has happened but the exchange of our by now familiar counters. Yet the user is revealed, and the identification of the obscurantism involved is what gives index to our social trends. So students wisely reverse this semantic, retitling Scholastic Aptitude Tests *college boards,* which is what they are. For the way in which officialdom lies is important. And the way in which it does so shows another genuflection to the technocratic status quo, i.e. itself. More and more the errand of our social euphemisms is to make everything grandiose in resonance via some form of technical jargon. Here again science admires itself in a mirror.

Mencken caught a bit of this in his pages on the use of *engineer* as an automatic meliorative. He found a bedding manufacturer calling himself a *sleep-engineer,* and he also turned up an *exterminator-engineer.* Evidently the objections he reported from real engineers, protesting against such pseudoengineers, did not last long (in 1935 the National Society of Professional Engineers tried to get American railroads to call their locomotive engineers *enginemen*).

For today everyone is an engineer. The plumber is a Household Engineer and the ditch-digger is a Construction Engineer and a salesman is a Sales Engineer, and presumably I am a Word Engineer. There are Social Engineers. This reverence says a lot about our society, as once more it bows to its golden calf. Even when the actual term *engineer* is not used, something like *technician* will act as mask in the same exaltation of technology.

The neologisms of technology, which artificially swell our dictionaries, are generally libido-poor, and thus depriving in effect.

---

[24]There is a slightly different kind of euphemism, or subsaying, when the reality *has* changed: e.g., a paperback reprint novel with the "junk" removed but the sex left in gets emblazoned *Uncensored Abridgment* in drugstore racks. I have not gone into this prevalent practice here.

"The smatterer in science," Melville has a character say in *White Jacket*, "thinks that by mouthing hard words he proves that he understands hard things." Thirdly, the effect of continual technological euphemism—since such provide hard words, less well understood than the terms for which they stand—is to make everything rather foggily similar, and in the end to work against eccentricity and individuality. *Agrypnia, cephalalgia, cholelithiasis, pyrexia* surely do not convey to the layman the variety of complaints they actually stand for (insomnia, headache, gallstones, fever), any more than the convenient officialese term *nuke,* with its homely sound, really suggests the death-dealing nature of the nuclear weapon so euphemized (e.g. *tactical nukes*). The AMA wants to reclassify all GP's (or family doctors) as *specialists.* The attempt seems to be to get as neutral as possible (cf. *OED*'s definition of *bosom* as "the enclosure formed by the breast and the arms"). Words like *polyunsaturates, quasars* and *rhochrematics* occur daily in our breakfast-table journalism, but mean little. We end up less whole than before the coming of these Humpty Dumpties.

Strained Jaw Relations

To conclude on a lighter note, one could take dentistry as evidence of the above. Dental communication—euphemism!—has been the subject of much study of late. Quite a number of books come out on how dentists ought to speak to their patients, which in some cases boil down to primers on how to misuse plain English. For instance, if the recent *Interviewing, Counseling, and Managing Dental Patients* by S. Joseph Bregstein is a fair sample of this trend, which I am given to understand it is, we shall soon need new dictionaries for our dentists.

Dr. Bregstein divides dental patients into three groups, attentive, marginal and projective. The last group is the best. The marginal patient "daydreams" while in the chair, a state of mind probably itself a euphemism for being bamboozled by the new rhetoric buzzing about his head. The first is, however, the bad boy of the bunch—"The patient who listens carefully to what the dentist says, but whose interpretations do not necessarily coincide with the doctor's." The fact that the patient understands anything the new dentist says at all—outside details of the fee, which are uneuphemizable—would score him high in the use of English by my book.

For the current dental Webster lists so many normal and unobscure terms *Obj.* (objectionable) and substitutes for them so many scientifically obfuscating and recondite euphemisms, you will be lucky to come out of it with any teeth—that is, organs of mastication—left in your mandible at all. If you are successful in protecting your masticatory apparatus (*Obj.*—"See *stomatognatic system*") intact, then I congratulate you—you are dentulous.

The document to which I refer is the Second Edition of the *Glossary of Prosthodontic Terms* compiled by the Nomenclature Committee of the Academy of Denture Prosthetics (St. Louis, Miss.: C. V. Mosby Co.). Now naturally this glossary is principally concerned with useful clarification of technical jargon; thus it explains that "mandibular retraction," which I used to think was growing longer in the tooth, is simply "a type of facial anomaly in which the gnathion lies posterior to the orbital plane," and similarly helps out by defining the "pterygomaxillary or hamular notch" as "The notch or fissure formed at the junction of the maxilla and the hamular or pterygoid process of the sphenoid bone."

It is this sort of thing that swells Webster, giving an impression that our vocabulary is increasing and, along with that impression, somehow causing Mr. Mits to imagine that the invention of new words steps up actual communication. Nothing could be further from the truth. The new edition of this glossary, "the result of suggestions made by dentists everywhere" and boasting "a gradual improvement . . . in the clarity of the literature of prosthetic dentistry," is a genuine tribute to technological obfuscation.

For it everywhere attempts to cover disturbing or repellent references—as to dentures, bridges and the like—with a heavy cream of scientific neologism, which is invariably considered wonderful whenever it appears. Why? The Hospital for Special Surgery was *simpler* as well as less repellent than what it previously stood for. It helped everyone out by being *less* technical. In "prosthodontics" the reverse is afoot.

Prosthodontics should not be confused with orthodontics, which deals with jaw relationships—or rather, *malocclusion.* Bands, wires, braces (highly *Obj.*) and so on. Prosthodontics is defined as "That branch of dental art and science pertaining to the restoration and maintenance of oral function by the replacement of missing teeth and structures by artificial devices"—and you certainly need all your organs of mastication to say that one.

A prosthodontist is "A dentist engaged in the practice of prosthodontics." Since his substitutions are also semantic, I suggest he is yet another Humpty Dumpty.

For even a brief glance through the glossary reveals that any short, direct term, understandable at all, is resented by the prosthetic lexicographers. Bite, for example, is particularly *Obj.* and nearly always replaced by *occlusion*, or its variant. Gums are *gingiva*. Free-way space (whatever that may have been, but at least it was simple) is now *Obj.*, and emerges as *"interocclusal distance."*

So you could not, it seems to me, buttonhole an honest-to-God prosthodontist and say, "Care for a bite to eat?" Instead, you would have to get out—articulate—something of this nature: "Would you care to deflect your occlusal surfaces and stimulate your swallowing threshold with an act of deglutition?" Chewing gum would be impossible to translate, at least in anything under two lines. You smile? My sagittal outline sinks in contemplation of the mandibular movements necessary in jaw separation for you to be able to demonstrate the *Pleasure Curve*. But I err. The last is now *Obj.*, too. No longer "an occlusal curve described by Pleasure," it has been downgraded to a mere "reverse curve." How traumatogenic or even temporomandibular can you get?

At this point we come full circle and are back once more with Durkheim's warning, in *Les formes élémentaires de la vie religieuse*, "One comes to the remarkable conclusion that *images of the totem-creature are more sacred than the totem-creature itself.*" Science is not religion. It is distortive when language is made to treat it as such. Science is a leap of the human mind, requiring considerable imagination, between reality and "reality." Its unity is clarity, not the fudging-over we have seen above.

The most impressive activity of the human mind is its generous attempt to form a form, to conceive the world in terms of unity. As I stated at the start of this study, the human being is not himself a representation. Confronted with the marvelous maze of language, the human being is in a sense his own design—the only sign which is not the sign of something else. Thus man is a kind of quintessence. He has been called "the unwritten poem of his own existence." He alone exists, while everything around him can be "transparent," a "porous pretext for many other meanings; what was happening became the symbol of something that was perhaps

not happening but was felt through the medium of the first."[25]
To be "condemned to meaning" like this was, for Sartre's Roquentin, the most terrifying of all human responsibilities. Emily Dick-
inson cleverly suggested this way in which words take life when
she wrote:

> A word is dead
> When it is said,
> Some say.
> I say it just
> Begins to live
> That day.

[25]Robert Musil, *The Man Without Qualities*, New York: Capricorn Books,
1965, p. 298.

ELEVEN

Words are like men.

Aristotle, *Rhetoric*

ESCALATION OF RHETORIC:
THE POWER OF NEGATIVE THINKING

Condemned to Meaning

"The end of a philosophical epoch," writes Susanne Langer, "comes with the exhaustion of its motive concepts."[1] When all the questions are in, there is little more to formulate, and the intellectuals play with ideas. Contrary to common assumption, intellectual acrobatics—of the little-magazine variety—are not too taxing an activity. It is the engagement of the word with its world that takes energy. "Communication is hard work."[2]

We have studied here some engagements of word with world. Our world is a technology. A technology's reversed symbology accelerates the urban ethic to the point of paranoia. One authority predicts that in fifteen years the United States will have less than 10 percent of the world's population, but will be consuming 83 percent of all the available raw materials and resources. The irrationality of this situation steadily approaches that of *grand guignol* and, as Shirley Temple runs for Congress, we are reminded of Robert Morley's remark that the only people who really understand the Vietnam war today are the resident comedians. A parody of the machine civilization destroying itself, in Jean Tinguely's self-consuming engine, or as in the "computers" devised by the British cartoonist Emmett, were long anticipated by Chaplin in *Modern Times*. The fate is not uniquely American. That England is hardly a much happier society in this respect was surely testified by a late 1967 Gallup poll there, showing half of a sample of British youth between the ages of eighteen and twenty wanting to emigrate.

[1]Langer, *Philosophy In a New Key*, p. 20.
[2]Berlo, *The Process of Communication*, p. 199.

"The semanticists often say," writes Anatol Rapoport, "that our language does our thinking for us. This is true, of course, of the language of science." We have examined the advertising of a technology in the spirit of that great comparatist, Leo Spitzer, who wrote: "The present writer must confess that it was by applying *explication de texte* to American advertising that he was given the first avenue (a 'philological' avenue) leading toward the understanding of the unwritten text of the American way of life."

American optimism is undoubtedly concealed, perhaps syphoned off, in the language of advertising, in the technological neologism examined, and in such devices as the incomplete comparative. The neologism conveys a sense of flux, one seen in the fast turnover of meaning codified in the Wentworth/Flexner *Dictionary of American Slang* mentioned, while the incomparable comparative dangles an open-ended future in front of the panting millions. "The difference between the American and the German concepts of the word," Professor Spitzer added, writing just after the last war, "can be seen in the absence of free speech in Germany: freedom of speech involves a concept of non-finality of speech. In America the human word is thought of only as having a provisionary value. One word can be undone, and outdone, by another."

We have glanced at the strange power of names, and seen their connotative abilities active even in a scientific civilization, so that when General Pershing coined *Sammies* for American troops in France in the First World War (to partner British *Tommies*), his men protested that it was too "sissy." Throughout we have tried to establish and insist on the bipartite nature of communication, the blocking of which means no less than lives lost daily on the battlefields of the world—"To the people on the receiving end, a U.S. *commitment* is what you hope the Americans will do to help your side. An American *intervention* is what they do to help the other side."[3]

Nietzsche identified the *accidie* of the intellectual at the close of Greek civilization, which, like ours, seemed to him to have exhausted its symbols and become merely "Apollonian." In such a phase the intelligentsia is no longer, in Barzun's terminology, "intellectual." It may still be intelligent.

[3]Flora Lewis, "The Many Meanings of Commitment," International *Herald Tribune*, August 18, 1967, p. 4 (italics added).

The real danger in this tendency is the danger of unsensed authoritarianism. The essence of the word-world system is what I have here rather unsatisfactorily called *feedback*. Feedback implies a reciprocity of message-bearing, that there should be a listener as well as speaker. Proudhon has been called a great communication analyst; and if so, it is in the sense of a cyberneticist before his time, realizing that agreements were two-way affairs. The more word-wisdom is impaired by technology, the more easily and unnoticeably can authority pass out fiats; these can be creamed over with democratic sentiments, but if they lack the potential of feedback they are no more than commands. And perhaps I have failed in this book to face up to the uglier implications of its findings, namely that our technocracy *is* a dictatorship. At least, if that term is found uncongenial, it is the technological autocracy predicted in Wells' *When the Sleeper Wakes*, of 1899, in which we have high-speed elevators, television, moving sidewalks, and Boeing 747's; a third of the population of Wells' science-"fiction" here is in technological slavery, one partially maintained by propagation of "the yellow peril."

In this climate there is a tendency for human beings to turn into specimens, and it has been against the automatizing effect of excessive Apollonianism that this book has been partly directed. Our new eclecticism has resulted in some of the most vicious newspeak imaginable. It is ultimately degrading, repulsive, to have to continue in the same world as such double-talk. Socrates, in fact, died so that he would not have to concede his humanity in this respect. In a now famous formulation the French philosopher Merleau-Ponty put it, "Because we are in the world, we are condemned to meaning, and we cannot do or say anything without its acquiring a name in history."

If Margaret Mead is right about this being a supremely vital moment in such history, it is all the more important for the young to ask questions, and formulate problems. It is extremely encouraging that they are doing so; young Americans seem to be able to boast of more negative thinking than most young Frenchmen. General Semantics forms a free-running channel for these questions, and this doubt. Indeed, if Don Hayakawa wants to call General Semantics "how not to make a damn fool of yourself," I might venture my own definition, namely—

Telling It Like It Is

Today I have lived in America almost exactly the same number of years as the average college student. I would not have done so unless I admired, indeed loved, the place. The entire period, however, has recently been labeled that of "the sanctioned lie,"[4] the era, after all, of Nixon's 1952 "Checkers" speech, of an admitted perjurer acting as national hero, of the U-2 flight and the lying connected with it, and of the comment by Schlesinger about the need for a "cover story," already cited. A. J. Liebling observed that Whittaker Chambers "improved his credibility every time he said he had lied." Charles Van Doren was tearfully blessed by the chairman of a congressional committee.

Western society—not only American—operates increasingly on the lie. The selling of products is a form of lie, and to encumber this with a semantic pretending to the reverse (the average American is said to be exposed to 1,600 ads a day) is to impugn communication entirely. After all, the FTC had to enjoin the *Encyclopaedia Britannica*, no less, from sales techniques that were close on cheating—and President Johnson bemoans the fact that so few of our young exercise their right to vote. George Steiner's recent *Language and Silence* is just one of many books seeing the current attack on articulation as one on civilization itself.

Thus, if you had told me two years ago that the CIA had infiltrated (made to lie) the National Student Association,[5] that an ex-movie star of mystagogical persuasions would be Governor of the largest state in the Union, that a sometime presidential adviser would be sentenced to three years in prison (there joining the chairman of a congressional committee), that America was lending napalm to Bolivian dictators to suppress their "rebels," I might well have considered you crazy; but I would, on finding such phenomena the case, not have thought very far out Bob Dylan's remark in *On the Eve of Destruction* that "human respect is disintegrating." It is, indeed, little wonder that the urban Negro

[4]Margaret Halsey, "A College Student's Guide to the Mess We Are In," *Village Voice*, April 6, 1967.
[5]Almost monthly reports of the infiltration of student groups by undercover agents, for the purpose of spying on teachers and pupils alike, can be checked in issues of *The American Teacher*, the official publication of the American Federation of Teachers (AFL-CIO).

has coined the term—"telling it the way it is." Our society seems particularly gifted at the reverse. Meanwhile, every appearance of something called "Communism" is hunted down with the fatal fanaticism of a Captain Ahab ("in tormented chase of that demon phantom. . .").

During the course of this work, then, two types of communication have been considered. These two types to which we have access are best described by Claude Lévi-Strauss, as two paths, "that which arrives at the physical world by the detour of communication, and that which . . . arrives at the world of communication by the detour of the physical." There are, of course, word-worlds beyond those I have considered. As Langer writes, "there is an unexplored possibility of genuine semantic beyond the limits of discursive language."[6] In the beginning was the Word. . . .

For the end of any book on General Semantics must be its beginning. Communication is circular. Word-wisdom is not a matter of diction or logic. It is magic in its uncorrupted sense. It confers meaning on our universe. So what has been studied here has been the social function of verbal utterances, what language does in conjunction with what langauge is—Wimsatt's "affective fallacy," to whose insight I am paradoxically grateful. Without some recognition of this function, intellectual confusion, at best, and moral anarchy, at worst, will be certain to prevail. Such is what Malinowski meant when he said that the sacredness of words is necessary to the existence of any social order. It is, indeed, a functional necessity. The word-world is a *dew*, or distant early warning system. It was a writer, Jonathan Swift, not a scientist, who "predicted" that Mars would be found to have two moons, and another mere user of words, Dr. Johnson, that invisible creatures were the cause of dysentery—before the discovery of microbes. Anatole France suggested a "radium" bomb in 1908. We must acknowledge such, or else, like Cocteau's hero Orphée, we shall be physically destroyed by language. Perhaps this is what the term *overkill* really implies. The final cover story. "Destroy language," the German poet Christian Morgenstern quotes Master Ekkehart as saying, "and, with it, all things and concepts. The rest is silence."

[6]Langer, *Philosophy in a New Key*, p. 81.

344

Teachers like Socrates, and Jesus, and Gotama preached a proper use of words because they respected the sense of harmony symbolism represented. As Aldous Huxley put it, "Words and the meanings of words are not matters merely for the academic amusement of linguists and logisticians, or for the aesthetic delight of poets; they are matters of the profoundest ethical significance to every human being." Such has been a premise of this book. Another has been R. N. Anshen's comment, "For man is that being on earth who does not have language. Man *is* language."

GEORGE ALLEN & UNWIN LTD
London: 40 Museum Street, W.C.1

Auckland: P.O. Box 36013, Northcote Central, N.4
Barbados: P.O. Box 222, Bridgetown
Beirut: Deep Building, Jeanne d'Arc Street
Buenos Aires: Escritorio 454–459, Florida 165
Bombay: 15 Graham Road, Ballard Estate, Bombay 1
Calcutta: 17 Chittaranjan Avenue, Calcutta 13
Cape Town: 68 Shortmarket Street
Hong Kong: 105 Wing On Mansion, 26 Hancow Road, Kowloon
Ibadan: P.O. Box 62
Karachi: Karachi Chambers, McLeod Road
Madras: Mohan Mansions, 38c Mount Road, Madras 6
Mexico: Villalongin 32, Mexico 5, D.F.
Nairobi: P.O. Box 30585
New Delhi: 13–14 Asaf Ali Road, New Delhi 1
Ontario: 81 Curlew Drive, Don Mills
Philippines: P.O. Box 4322, Manila
Rio de Janeiro: Caixa Postal 2537-Zc-00
Singapore: 36c Prinsep Street, Singapore 7
Sydney, N.S.W.: Bradbury House, 55 York Street
Tokyo: P.O. Box 26, Kamata